Microcomputer Interfacing

HAROLD S. STONE
UNIVERSITY OF MASSACHUSETTS, AMHERST

ADDISON-WESLEY PUBLISHING COMPANY

READING, MASSACHUSETTS
MENLO PARK, CALIFORNIA
LONDON
AMSTERDAM
DON MILLS, ONTARIO
SYDNEY

This book is in the **ADDISON-WESLEY SERIES IN ELECTRICAL ENGINEERING**

SPONSORING EDITOR: *Tom Robbins*
PRODUCTION EDITOR: *Marilee Sorotskin*

TEXT DESIGNER: *Herb Caswell*
ILLUSTRATOR: *Jay's Publishers Service Inc.*
COVER DESIGN AND ILLUSTRATOR: *T. A. Philbrook*
ART COORDINATOR: *Joseph Vetere*

PRODUCTION MANAGER: *Sue Zorn*
PRODUCTION COORDINATOR: *Helen Wythe*

The text of this book was composed in Times Roman on a Mergenthaler 202 by Information Sciences Corporation and was printed by R. R. Donnelley and Sons.

Library of Congress Cataloging in Publication Data

Stone, Harold S., 1938–
    Microcomputing interfacing.

    Bibliography: p.
    1. Interface circuits. 2. Microcomputers—Circuits.
I. Title. TK7868.158S76   621.3819′5835   81-17619
ISBN 0-201-07403-6   AACRZ

Reprinted with corrections, February 1983

ISBN 0-201-07403-6
HIJK-DO-89876

TO THE REVOLUTION

"The old order changeth, yielding place to new..."
Alfred, Lord Tennyson

To see a world in a grain of sand
And a heaven in a wild flower,
Hold infinity in the palm of your hand
And eternity in an hour.
William Blake

INSTRUCTOR'S PREFACE

In decades to come historians will look back to the 70s and 80s as the era of the Computer Revolution. Just as the Industrial Revolution marks the period when people learned to harness energy to drive machinery, so the Computer Revolution marks the period when people have learned to harness microelectronics for control and for information processing. Within of a decade of its introduction, the microprocessor made an enormous impact on the way we live and work. Who can recall the annoying difficulty of doing long division by hand, to say nothing of such transcendental calculations as compound interest, square roots, and trigonometry? Today's electronic calculator places all of these calculations at your fingertips at essentially zero cost. But the calculators of the early 70s were only precursors of the innovations to come.

The microprocessor has spawned the personal computer, the small-business computer, the word processor, the data communications network, the automotive computer, and the intelligent telephone branch exchange. Yet this is still only a beginning. The microprocessor has been used in instruments and appliances in place of mechanical or discrete electric components. In such applications it yields lower cost, greater reliability, and greater functionality than former designs. But the microprocessor also makes possible a new technology that heretofore has not existed. In the laboratory, the logic analyzer is a microprocessor-controlled oscilloscope that enables the engineer to capture and analyze electronic waveforms in a manner that had never been possible before. In medicine, the microprocessor has led to the CAT-scanner and the ultrasonic scanner that have dramatically improved the ability to diagnose illnesses. In merchandising, the point-of-sales terminal that reads product labels automatically provides greater control of inventory, as well as faster, more accurate handling of sales. The microprocessor-controlled reading machine that automatically scans printed text and speaks the words it sees aloud has brought new vision to the blind. The main limitation on the innovative applications of microprocessors today is not technological, but rather one of imagination and skill.

To help surmount the human limitation, this textbook is offered as one way to introduce the student to basic principles of microprocessor technology. A primary goal is to increase the pool of innovators. It is oriented to an undergraduate curriculum, and is ideally suited for juniors and seniors in a Computer Engineering, Electrical Engineering, or Computer Science program. A course based on this text will give the student a strong foundation in techniques for connecting computers to peripherals and communications devices, and in the methodology for programming the computer to control external devices in real time.

The well-prepared reader has had instruction in hardware, software, electronics, and mathematics. But the material presented here is modular so that an instructor can skip portions of the text that refer to topics that students at particular institutions will not yet have mastered. A breakdown of the prerequisites is as follows:

1. *All Chapters*: The student should have some exposure to microprocessors and logic design through such textbooks as Blakeslee (1979), Klingman (1977), Kraft and Toy (1979), Krutz (1980), or Peatman (1977). This general type of textbook introduces the student to the logic components, design techniques, and the structure of digital computers. The student should be comfortable with assembly language, but need not have extensive skills in this area. It is desirable for the student to have read such textbooks as Gear (1980) or Wakerly (1981) that cover assembly language for many different machines.

2. *Chapter 2, Transmission Lines*. Prior exposure to transmission-line theory is helpful for Chapter 2, but not absolutely necessary. The chapter is self-contained in that all background required to support the physical concepts is developed within the chapter. In curricula in which the electronic aspects of interfacing have been omitted, the instructor may choose to skip portions of Chapter 2 (grounding, shielding, and transmission lines), Chapter 3 (bus interconnections), and Chapter 7 (magnetic-recording techniques).

3. *Chapter 7, Linear Systems*. Some results and equations in this chapter are cited from other sources rather than derived in the chapter. A student should know Laplace transforms and transfer functions for full appreciation of this material. The exercises require a knowledge of electronics as well. The material may be skipped at institutions that teach microprocessor interfacing earlier than linear systems.

4. *Chapter 9, High-Level Language Programming*. The student should be familiar with some high-level language such as Pascal, ALGOL, Ada, PL-I, FORTRAN, or COBOL. The notation in the chapter is basically Pascal, but should be quite understandable for readers familiar with any of the first four languages cited here. Where the only high-level language in the curriculum is FORTRAN or COBOL, before the students read Chapter 9, the instructor may wish to incorporate a brief tutorial on a block-structured language.

The presentation of material in the text is three-tiered. Each chapter contains

1. Basic principles.
2. Applications of the principles in present technology.
3. Specific examples of the use of the principles.

Principles are stressed by necessity. Principles tend to be the foundation of expertise. They tend to change very slowly, if at all, over long periods of time. Details and specific facts quickly become obsolete. In the microprocessor industry, new generations of memory and microprocessors appear every two to three years. This means that details taught to a sophomore will be obsolete by the time that sophomore graduates. A curriculum must, therefore, rest on the principles that support the technology. The student must master these first, and must learn to apply them. As the industry advances and the specific details change, the student must be able to adapt to these new details without outside instruction. Therefore, a college curriculum should prepare the student for self-education in the future. To do so requires a thorough foundation in basic principles.

The nine chapters in this text are more than sufficient for a semester course in microprocessor interfacing. The instructor can easily select a subset of material to adapt the text to any particular curriculum. Core material that should be in all curricula consists of

Chapter 1, basic microcomputer structure
Chapter 3, bus interconnections
Chapter 5, serial interfacing
Chapter 6, parallel interfacing
Chapter 9, software development

Curricula in which electronic design and logic design is stressed should add

Chapter 2, grounding, shielding, and transmission-line techniques
Chapter 4, memories

Curricula that stress the use of the microcomputer as a control element should incorporate

Chapter 7, magnetic-recording techniques
Chapter 8, CRT-controller design

Now let's turn to methods of instruction for the material. Lectures should be coupled with a computer laboratory in which the student can perform simple interfacing experiments including the development of elementary control software. The experimental laboratory in conjunction with the course should occupy roughly three hours per week and should be followed later in the curriculum by one or more project-design laboratories devoted to microprocessor-based designs. The project-design laboratory gives the student an opportunity to integrate information from many subject areas, such as interfacing techniques, software development, and communications.

The experiments in the text are sufficient for a full semester of laboratory work. The reason for an experimental orientation instead of a design orientation is that the information is passed quickly and efficiently when the student does not have to design and debug the bulk of the experimental apparatus. The student uses existing equipment and commercially available boards to learn the principles of interfacing. The student exercises the equipment through small digital project boards and simple interfacing software. By observing the behavior of the equipment on oscilloscopes and logic analyzers, the student learns about such basic notions as noise reduction, electrical loading, timing, hysteresis, handshaking, skew, etc. The experiments in a laboratory should demonstrate various phenomena and should illustrate preferred approaches for dealing with fundamental problems. After completing the experimental lab, the student should be well prepared for subsequent project-design labs.

It would be rather ironic in this age of high technology to approach microprocessor education in a totally traditional form. This textbook is an example of a technology that is centuries old. Obviously, the printed word is an effective way for presenting information because it would not have survived to this day if it were not. But can we do better? In particular instances, new technology enables one person to do in one day what formerly took four people to do in a week. Can new technology help the academic community educate students more effectively and efficiently? The search for a better way has led this author to develop an instructional system for this course consisting of this text plus a set of color video tapes. Tapes are produced by the Association for Media-Based Education for Engineers (AMCEE) at Georgia Institute of Technology in Atlanta, Georgia. The tapes may be ordered by writing to Addison-Wesley Publishing Company, Reading, MA 01867; Attention: Tom Robbins, Acquisitions Editor, Computer Engineering.

The instructional system is modular in that the text stands on its own and can be used in the traditional ways. The tapes too are self-contained and can be used independently. Together, the tapes and the text make up an instructional system that is far more effective than either medium by itself.

To see how the two work together, consider the material on transmission lines in Chapter 2. The student is told about reflections on transmission lines and how terminations can remove or reduce reflections. The student has to see this to appreciate the ideas fully. Experiments illustrating the ideas are demonstrated on the video tapes. Because the experiments show waveforms changing in time, and show them with their normal spikes and jitter rather than as idealized waveforms, the student gains experience with the real world rather than an artificial one. The key here is that there is information in the dynamics of the video image as it changes in time. That information is lost when the image is photographed or drafted as a figure in a textbook. When specific comparisons are made on the videotape, the images appear in rapid succession so that the student can quickly grasp what similarities and differences exist. The behavior of a phase-locked loop acquiring phase lock appears vividly on video as a sudden change of frequency of a voltage-controlled oscillator. The jitter in the oscillator at the threshold of acquisition is clearly visible. How can this information be displayed in a textbook? For waveforms changing in time, the video image is clearly superior to the printed image.

This author has often prepared classroom or laboratory demonstrations to illustrate basic ideas. The effort involved in setting up a demonstration is considerable and not always successful. Some demonstrations work well on the bench, but fail when the equipment is moved to the classroom. A probe may fall off, or a connection might not be tight, or a noise ''glitch'' may cause the logic to latch in a failure mode. The experiments on the video tape all work correctly. They were carefully set up and video taped in operation so that the course instructor need not repeat the effort in the setup nor take the risk of the experiment failing.

The video medium leads to a better presentation of the waveforms than does the actual physical equipment. The physical size of an oscilloscope or logic-analyzer display is only 10 to 20 cm square, which is too small for a classroom of 30 students. This forces the instructor to set up the experiments in a laboratory and demonstrate them to small groups of students so that each has an opportunity to study the principles being demonstrated. Apart from the inefficiency of this method, it does not resolve the basic difficulty of pointing to specific places on a small display screen. Pointing at the images is not very effective because the instructor's hand tends to block large portions of the display from view. However, the image of the same display on the video tapes is superior to the oscilloscope because the image is enlarged. Moreover, electronic superposition techniques permit the instructor to point to and label the most highly detailed parts of a waveform with no obstruction of view to other parts of the image. The video tapes relate the waveform to a schematic by using zoom and pan to illustrate various regions of the schematic, with those images juxtaposed between images of waveforms that appear at selected points on the schematic. The information is presented at an extraordinarily fast pace compared with classroom discussion, yet is easily comprehensible because of the way the video medium is used to advantage. Should the student wish to review specific waveforms, it is a very simple matter to rewind to the point of interest and play the material again. Consequently, the video tapes are an extremely attractive solution to the laboratory demonstration problem. There is no setup overhead, the equipment is inexpensive, and video is more effective than the laboratory equipment itself for reaching large groups of people. The tapes, like the text, are prepared in a modular fashion so that the instructor can select specific material to support lectures and laboratory work.

Because of rapid changes in microprocessors still to come, we anticipate future editions of the textbook and video tapes to be issued at regular intervals with new chapters incorporated to cover various technological advances and to maintain a blend of basic principles and current technology. To find out what new material or supplementary texts are available, write to Tom Robbins at the address on page viii.

Many people beside the author have made substantial contributions to the textbook and video tapes. The author owes a deep debt of gratitude in particular to John Wakerly for his timely and thoughtful comments throughout the project development. Other manuscript reviewers have added their unique perspectives and have helped to create a better textbook than the author could have done in their absence. Among the many reviewers were Jack Lipovski, Martha Sloan, Jacob Abraham, Ed Bruckert, and Dominique Thiebaut. Through John Fitch's skills in video production and direction, I was able to develop the accompanying video-tape course, but he deserves the bulk of the credit for showing the author the power of the medium and the techniques for tapping its unique capabilities. Tom Robbins, the acquisitions editor for the project, maintained his enthusiasm for the project from our very first phone conversation through the difficult times of final book production. His management activities behind the scenes freed the author from many frivolous problems, and let the author focus his activity on the textbook itself. Marilee Sorotskin's gift for the details of editing and consistency added materially to the quality of the exposition. Finally, the disk operating-system for the word processor on which the book was developed was written by my wife, Jan Stone. Her support both as a spouse and as a live-in systems programmer was extraordinary, and was a critical ingredient in the project development.

Amherst, Massachusetts
May 1982

H. S. S.

READER'S PREFACE

This book is intended for both the undergraduate and the professional reader. Undergraduates should be majors in a computer engineering or enrolled in a computer science program that has exposed them to logic design, assembly-language programming, and a high-level language prior to using this textbook. The professional reader with training in electrical engineering, computer science, or other technical areas is likely to have a sound technical background but needs to brush up on microprocessor technology. This reader will find it useful to browse through the book to learn the major subject areas discussed, and then to concentrate on the unfamiliar material.

Topics are covered three different ways. Each chapter opens with a discussion of basic principles, followed by methods for applying these principles. The chapters close with detailed examples of the principles put to use. The principles are the foundations of microprocessor technology and will continue to be as important in the next decade as they are today. However, the devices available change rapidly as technology advances. The processors, memories, and I/O ports that a student learns about in a sophomore laboratory are obsolete by the time student graduates. Only the principles remain relatively stable within this time frame.

To put this textbook to best use, the reader should learn the principles first, then how to apply them using current technology. The examples in the textbook illustrate practical designs that use real devices available in 1982. Armed with detailed specifications of new devices and with the basic information contained in this textbook, the reader should have no difficulty adapting to the most modern devices.

An essential part of the undergraduate learning experience is the experimental lab associated with the textbook. The experiments clarify the principles. Practice in applying the principles can come in the experimental lab or in a later project-design laboratory.

The professional reader undoubtedly has had some laboratory experience. Although having an experimental lab while reading is useful, it may not be necessary for those readers who have older degrees in Computer Engineering or Computer Science and who wish to use this book to bring themselves up to date. These readers should focus on very specific topics. They will probably be able to absorb the material through reading without conducting the lab experiments. Some readers may have sufficient equipment at their disposal in their companies to be able to conduct selected experiments where the experiments are central to the learning process. Several demonstrations are available on color video tapes and may be accessible to the professional through a company library or short-course. In any case, the professional reader should have the experience and maturity to recognize what topics in the textbook must be mastered and to devise a strategy for mastering them.

There are several reader objectives that this book addresses. Readers who are or who wish to become professional designers will find the material to be quite relevant to their work. These readers need a thorough background in electronics and logic design in addition to the material taught in this text. Additional background in transmission lines (for Chapter 2) and linear systems (for Chapter 7) may also be useful. Another group of readers will be concerned with connecting microcomputers to I/O devices or to other microcomputers, and will probably use existing interfaces instead of designing new ones. This group of readers should focus attention on Chapters 1 (microprocessor structures), 5 (serial interfacing), 6 (parallel interfacing), and 9 (software development). Chapter 2 (shielding, grounding, and transmission lines) may be helpful if the reader must specify the physical connections between systems. Chapter 3 (bus interconnections) covers protocols and timing questions that may also be important issues when configuring complex systems.

Another reader of the textbook may be strong in software and relatively weak in electronics. A typical reader of this type may wish to control I/O through software without becoming expert in logic design. This reader will find Chapter 9 (software development) especially illuminating, and will also find topics of interest in Chapters 1 (microprocessor structures), 4 (memories and DMA), 5 (serial interfacing), 6 (parallel interfacing), 7 (magnetic-recording techniques), and 8 (CRT-controller design).

The color video tapes associated with the textbook are an extremely effective way of observing the principles in action. We particularly recommend the tapes for readers who have limited access to experimental equipment because they provide vivid demonstrations of several of the more important experiments. The professional may find a short-course environment with video tapes to be an effective means of learning the material, not only as a way of observing experiments, but as an opportunity to raise and answer questions through class discussions.

I am most interested in the readers' reactions to this textbook. The intended audience is quite broad with diverse skills and backgrounds. Discussions that are over the head of some readers may be too basic and trivial for others. Comments on the strengths and weaknesses of the material in the context of its use are greatly appreciated and may strongly influence future revisions of the material.

Amherst, Massachusetts   H. S. S.
May 1982

CONTENTS

1 / MICROCOMPUTER STRUCTURES

This chapter reviews the general characteristics of microcomputer systems. We focus here on the functional description of the major components and on the system structure. By understanding these facets of microcomputers, we will be able to select among several alternative approaches to interfacing and to work easily with both software and hardware to put together complex systems. The functional descriptions in this chapter treat data and control flow exclusively, and ignore specific details of timing and electronics. Later chapters carefully delve into these details and should be sufficient to prepare the reader for practical interface design. This chapter, like those that follow, opens with a general description of the major concepts presented and ends with specific examples to illustrate actual implementations of the concepts.

1.1 BASIC MICROCOMPUTER STRUCTURE

A very simple microcomputer system is composed of three types of modules typically connected as shown in Fig. 1.1. The components are

1. a microprocessor, which contains the control logic and arithmetic unit of the system,
2. a memory, which holds programs and data, and
3. an input/output (I/O) system, which contains one or more ports that connect to such external devices as terminals, disks, printers, and communications modems.

Fig. 1.1(a) shows a single bus system through which the memory and I/O system communicate with the processor. In this system the processor is the master controller. It initiates all activity on the bus by issuing commands to the memory and I/O systems. The bus carries only one transaction at a time, so that commands are issued sequentially, one at a time. The memory and I/O systems respond to the commands, but do not issue commands in turn. If we monitor what happens on the bus over a period of time, we see the processor issuing a sequence of commands, with each command directed to a particular port or memory cell. One type of command instructs the destination to accept data from the processor, and the data from the processor accompanies the command. Another type of command tells the destination to return data to the processor, and the destination replies by sending the requested data back to the processor. So the flow of information is from the processor to memory and I/O, with flow in the reverse direction in response to processor commands.

A slightly different arrangement is shown in Fig. 1.1(b). Here the I/O and memory systems have independent paths to the processor rather than a shared path as in Fig.

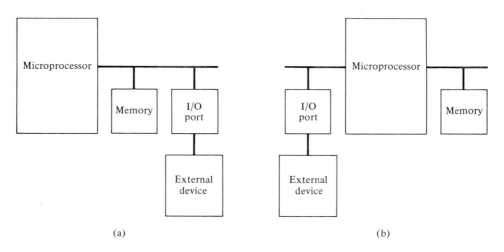

FIGURE 1.1 The basic structure of microcomputer: (a) One-path system; (b) two-path system.

1.1(a). Because the paths are separate and independent, two different transactions can be active at the same time, one on each bus. That is, the processor can issue commands to memory while simultaneously issuing commands to the I/O system. This form of microprocessor has I/O bus control embedded on a chip, together with other conventional microprocessor functions.

The idea of embedding additional functions on chip, such as the ability to control I/O and memory independently, has been carried much further than Fig. 1.1(b) indicates. The I/O ports themselves have been integrated with the processor, so that a microprocessor can be connected directly to external devices and does not need supporting I/O-port chips. In addition, such processors often include a substantial amount of memory integrated with the other functions on one chip. In this form, the microprocessor is truly a single-chip microcomputer, since it contains all of the functions shown in Fig. 1.1(a).

In either of the systems shown in Fig. 1.1, the basic system behavior is the same. The processor interaction with memory is typically a repetition of the sequence below:

1. Fetch an instruction from memory.
2. Execute the instruction, possibly reading data from or writing data to memory.

A special processor register, the *program counter*, controls which instruction to execute next. The execution of each instruction modifies the program counter in a prescribed way, so that when the processor has executed one instruction, the program counter has been updated to indicate a new instruction to execute. The execution of a single instruction, in general, involves one or more additional bus transactions that depend on the instruction executed. For example, the processor may read from or write to memory to exchange data between internal registers and memory. For I/O transactions the processor may obtain status or data from an I/O port or send instructions or data to a port. Even though the processor performs no bus transactions during the execution phase of an instruction, the processor may alter internal registers other than the program counter, which every instruction updates. Figure 1.2 shows an instruction execution graphically, including the relative timing of the memory transactions and the independent activity of the processor.

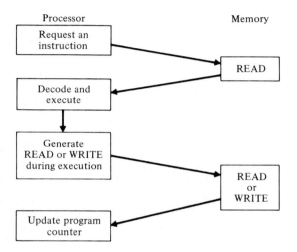

FIGURE 1.2 The time sequencing for processor/memory interactions during the execution of a single instruction.

The I/O interface described thus far appears to behave much like a memory interface. The processor can read data from and write data to memory or to the I/O system using the same type of interface for both memory and I/O. Some computers have a shared common bus for memory and I/O, so for these computer systems the processor-memory interface is essentially the same as the processor-I/O interface. But I/O is somewhat different from memory because of timing and synchronization, in that an I/O interface actually has a superset of the memory-interface functions.

Memory cycles require a fixed maximum time, and memory responds to a processor command within this fixed time. The I/O system, however, has to control or sense events external to the computer whose timing is totally independent of the computer timing. When a processor issues a command to an I/O port to accept a datum from an outside source, that datum can arrive at any time in the future (if it arrives at all), and the state of the processor at the time of arrival is unpredictable. To deal with data moving to and from the external world, the processor needs to be able to synchronize its activities to the external events. Most implementations support two general types of synchronization described in more detail below. These are

1. interrupts, and
2. periodic status checking,

where interrupts are port-initiated and status checks are processor-initiated.

The I/O subsystem synchronizes its activity to the processor when external events occur through a service request transmitted to the computer over the I/O bus. This signal, usually called an *interrupt request*, provides one means for I/O synchronization. The other way to synchronize is for the processor to interrogate the port for status information. Port interrogation is normally an I/O-read transaction on the bus, and the port returns status rather than data. Of course, if the port replies that no event has occurred, the processor has to interrogate again. However, when a port signals an interrupt, the interrupt signal is maintained as an active signal on an input pin of the microprocessor until it is acknowledged by the processor; the processor does not have to issue periodic I/O-bus transactions to read the interrupt signal.

Given this basic information concerning the function of major components in a microcomputer system, consider the structuring of a system to serve particular needs. Figure 1.1 has two different configurations of modules. Which of these is preferred and why? Before trying to answer these questions, consider what kinds of answers are suitable. Design problems have many different solutions. Sometimes there is no best solution, and all solutions are compromises of one sort or another. In most cases, however, the best solution depends on the application, and different approaches must be used for different situations. Technology also plays a significant role in biasing design decisions. What is best in 1980 will not necessarily be the best in 1990. What is rejected as infeasible in 1980 might be standard practice in 1990. The key to being able to make intelligent selections from several alternatives is the ability to understand the options available, the requirements of the application, and the capabilities of current technology.

Returning to Fig. 1.1, we see the chief difference in the systems is whether there are one or two data paths connected to the processor. The system with two data paths could conceivably have simultaneous transactions on both paths and thus could be somewhat faster than the one-path system. More logic is required to run two paths concurrently than for a single path. Hence, the microprocessor in Fig. 1.1(b) may be somewhat more complex than the one in Fig. 1.1(a). Actually, because of the extra logic required to control I/O and memory concurrently on one chip, a microprocessor with two paths typically is less complex in other respects. Technology limits the amount of logic that can be put on a single chip; so that as complexity is added to enhance some particular functions, other functions have to be abandoned. Only advances in technology permit a net increase in chip complexity. Therefore, if we compare two systems configured as shown in Fig. 1.1 and using microprocessors of the same vintage, we would expect the processor with two independent data paths to lack some of the facilities of the processor with only one data path.

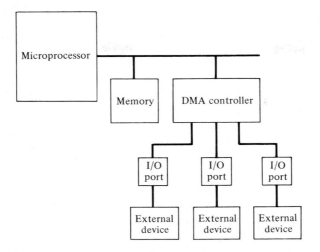

FIGURE 1.3   A microcomputer with a direct memory-access controller.

There is another difference between the systems that is brought out more clearly by Fig. 1.3. Here we see a separate module known as a *direct memory-access* (DMA) *controller* incorporated in the microcomputer system. The DMA controller can issue commands to the memory that behave exactly like the commands issued by the processor. In this sense, the DMA controller is a second processor in the system, but it is dedicated to an I/O function. As shown in the figure, the DMA controller connects one or more I/O ports directly to memory so that data can be transferred between these ports and memory without going through the processor, and with no direct program intervention. Instead, the I/O data stream passes through the DMA controller, but much faster and more efficiently than through the processor because the DMA channel is specialized to the data-transfer task.

The system shown in Fig. 1.3 has but a single path to memory so that no more than one memory transaction can be in progress at a time. Hence, when DMA is active, the processor must be idle; and, conversely, DMA is idle when the processor is active. DMA controllers are normally used for devices that transmit data in bursts, especially high-speed bursts such as blocks of data stored on disks. These bursts are frequently of such high-speed that no microprocessor can control the data transfers on a byte-by-byte basis by executing instructions to process each successive byte.

The sole data path in Fig. 1.1(a) can be used to support DMA transfers simply by making one of the ports into a DMA channel, which in turn is connected to one or more I/O ports. The I/O ports in the two-path system in Fig. 1.1(b), however, are connected to the processor, and not to memory. Any port to be controlled by a DMA controller must be connected to a DMA controller that has access to memory, as does the controller shown in Fig. 1.3. Hence, one way to incorporate DMA into Fig. 1.1(b) is to connect the DMA controller between the memory bus and I/O bus. The controller then provides a direct path from the I/O port to memory that can be used in place of the path through the processor. However, a controller that bridges two buses is more complex and probably more costly than the simpler one-bus controller shown in Fig. 1.3.

Returning to the questions concerning which configuration in Fig. 1.1 is better and why, we conclude, on the one hand, that the one-path structure is less complex than the other, and provides more readily for DMA. On the other hand, for non-DMA applications, the two-path system integrates some I/O functions on the processor chip, and thereby may reduce the need for specific chips related to the I/O-bus interface. Moreover, if the I/O bus can truly run concurrently with the memory bus and if both paths are kept busy simultaneously, the two-bus organization has the higher performance. At the present, microprocessors that have two-path capability tend to be designed for minimal parts count, and are most heavily used in low-end applications. Communications controllers, data-acquisition systems, and disk-controllers are three typical applications that require a low-cost, high I/O performance microprocessor. The processor with on-chip I/O may be more satisfactory for these applications. For applications less sensitive to the cost of a few I/O chips, the one-bus processor may be preferable, especially if the application benefits from any additional computational functions that can be integrated in the processor, thus trading off the enhanced I/O functions inherent in the two-bus processor. Office and small-business applications, as well as limited scientific applications tend to have these characteristics and are candidates for the one-bus microprocessor.

In the future, decisions of this nature will be even more complex as new variations in microprocessor architecture emerge. One current trend is to reduce many chips to one chip. This is best exemplified by the single-chip computer that combines memory, I/O, and processor. Another trend is to provide for greater parallelism and independence of operation — one product of which is the dual-processor chip that combines two independent microprocessors. More changes of this type will come at what may be a bewildering pace. This textbook should provide the reader enough basic principles and detailed information to evaluate and use the evolving technology.

This completes our discussion of the gross details of the interactions among processors, memories, and I/O systems. The next sections expand on these interactions, providing more detail about the exchanged information. When we review real systems at the end of this chapter, we will see various ways the functions and interactions have been implemented. (Timing and other details required for logic design are left to later chapters.)

1.2 THE MEMORY INTERFACE

Conventional main-memory systems are *random-access memories*, often called RAM in computer jargon. In these systems all data are stored in fixed-sized chunks called *words*, and each word in memory has a unique address. Access to data is made by address; that is, for each memory operation the processor supplies the address of the datum, and the address uniquely determines where the access is to be made. Each memory operation takes a fixed length of time, and is usually called a *memory cycle*. The term ''random-access'' in this context means that data can be accessed in arbitrary, random order and that the access-time is, per cycle, a fixed constant independent of the sequence of items accessed. A memory that is not a random-access memory has access times that depend on the sequence of accesses. For example, a magnetic tape can access the next item on the tape in one tape READ operation, but hundreds or thousands of read operations are required to access data on the tape in regions far from the present head location. Memory systems that have the strictly sequential property of magnetic tapes are called *sequential-access* memories.

Magnetic disks with movable heads have some sequential-like and some random-like characteristics. The head can be moved to any track at random, but once the head is at a desired track, data on the track are accessed sequentially. Actually, even the track-to-track movement is not random-access. Track-to-track movement is sequential by track. Remote tracks take longer to reach than nearby tracks. Even though the time required to move to a remote track may be considerable, the head movement of a disk is very much faster than the delays suffered in such a purely sequential memory as a tape on which the processor must access all data between the current head position and the final head position. The moving-head disk is analogous to a phonograph, and head positioning corresponds to moving the phonograph arm to a specific band of music. By moving the arm to the desired band, you do not listen to the music skipped. Hence, moving-head disks are typically viewed as quite different from sequential-access memory tapes. The term *direct-access* memory is often applied to such disks to make this distinction.

Returning to the structure of random-access memory, we find each word is composed of bits, and the number of bits per word is called the *word length* of memory. Accesses between processor and memory exchange one word (or part of a word) at a time, but never more than one word. Each memory transaction reads one word from or writes one word into a given address, but does not operate on words at more than one address. When a processor must access a block of memory, the processor generates a stream of accesses and supplies an address with each access. It is possible to access a part of a word in one transaction, and some memory systems are built to give this added flexibility.

The number of bits per word has been steadily increasing over the years, so that today one can find microprocessors with word sizes of 4, 8, 16, and 32 bits. The first microprocessor, the Intel 4004, has a 4-bit word. Device technology in 1970 precluded anything larger than this. By the mid-70s word size had climbed to 8-bits in the 8008 and 8080 families from Intel and in the 6800 family from Motorola and American Microsystems. The microprocessor industry entered the 80s with the introduction of micros with 16-bit words in the Z8000 family from Zilog and the 8086 (iAPX86) family from Intel. The Motorola MC68000 family of microprocessors was introduced for memories organized in 16-bit words, but is readily upgradable to 32-bit word memories. Intel's iAPX-432 is unquestionably organized for 32-bit words.

Typical word-organized memory is shown in Fig. 1.4, with each word in memory having a unique address, and the addresses are successive integers starting at 0. Figure 1.4, however, does not show the individual bits, and it does not describe the word length of memory. Memory systems are becoming more complex than the system of Fig. 1.4 because of the added flexibility of access to partial words as well as to full words. One way of organizing memory for this purpose is shown in Fig. 1.5(a). In this memory, words are 16-bits long. Since character data are typically eight bits per character, the system is designed to give access as easily to 8-bit data as to 16-bit data. The usual convention is to call an 8-bit datum a *byte* and a 16-bit datum a *word*. (Some microprocessor literature refers to 16-bit data as "halfwords.") To facilitate access to both bytes and words, each byte is given a unique integer address, with the integers running sequentially starting at 0. A word then consists of two adjacent bytes, and a word access is made by supplying the address of one of the bytes in that word with a function signal indicating that the access is to a word, not a byte.

BYTE
ADDRESSES:

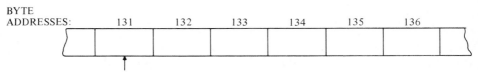

Data cell for word with address 131

FIGURE 1.4 A word-organized memory.

There are several possible ways to organize a memory into both words and bytes, and it is rather unfortunate that the industry has not settled on a standard way to do this. Whereas there are both advantages and disadvantages to each of these schemes, there are severe difficulties in compatibility and data exchange among the computers that use different schemes. A few of these schemes are illustrated in Fig. 1.5.

In Fig. 1.5(a), the addressing scheme requires word data to have an even-numbered address. Each word, then, consists of two bytes, one byte with an even address and the other byte at the next higher odd address. The address of the word is the address of the even byte. Arbitrarily, the byte with the least significant address is stored as the least significant byte of the word. This is the scheme used in the LSI-11 microcomputer. The fact that words must be located on even-address boundaries tends to be constraining. In contrast, Fig. 1.5(b) shows a memory in which words occupy successive integer addresses and the words overlap. This scheme is used in the Intel 8086 (iAPX86) microprocessor. The overlapping of words eliminates completely the problem of structuring data to force full words to lie on even-numbered address boundaries, and thus eliminates one unnecessary level of programming difficulty.

But Fig. 1.5(b) is not necessarily the best solution either. There are two possible ways of building a word from two successive bytes. The first comprises schemes in both Fig. 1.5(a) and (b), both of which treat the byte with the least significant address as the least significant byte of the word. The other choice, as shown in Fig.1.5(c), is to treat the byte with the least address as the most significant byte of the word. This scheme is used in the 6800-family of processors. (This family uses byte-organized memory, and accesses to words require two successive byte accesses.) One of the obvious advantages of the scheme in Fig. 1.5(c) over that in Fig. 1.5(b) is simply an advantage in the human interface. Program listings, memory dumps, and many similar software support tools typically give the contents of memory byte-by-byte in order of ascending address. This inherently places bytes with lower addresses to the left of bytes with higher addresses; in other words, the lower the address, the more significant position. A programmer has to reverse the positions of the bytes mentally in order to interpret their correct meaning. Consider, for example, the fragments of program listings shown in Fig. 1.6(a) for an 8086 and Fig. 1.6(b) for a 6800 microprocessor. Notice that the bytes for the address in the 8086 fragment appear in reverse order in the listing, but they appear in the correct order in the 6800 listing.

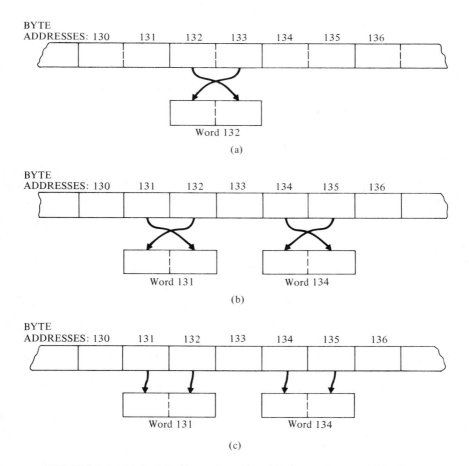

FIGURE 1.5 (a) An LSI-11 memory; (b) an 8086 memory; (c) a 6800 memory.

The human-interface problem illustrated in Fig. 1.6 does not give a complete picture of relative advantages and disadvantages of the several approaches to memory organization. In fact, practice is not standardized because there is no clearly "best" decision. The resulting chaotic state of affairs is felt whenever programs, data, or the programmers themselves move from one kind of memory system to another. See Cohen (1981) for a humorous, but rather revealing exposition of this standardization problem.

```
OPCODE ADDRESS  ...                OPCODE ADDRESS       ...
FE      1300    LDX     1300        A1      0013       MOV AX,1300
7E      1416    JMP     1416        EA      1614 1214  JMP 1416,1412
                ...                                    ...
```

           (a)   (b)

FIGURE 1.6   Fragments of assembly language programs: (a) 6800 program; (b) 8086 program.

From the functional description of memory, we can now see the types of signals that must be exchanged between a memory and a microprocessor. These are shown in Fig. 1.7. Obviously there must be lines that carry address and data information. For READ, the address lines are activated by the microprocessor, and the data accessed are returned on the data lines by the memory. For WRITE, the microprocessor supplies both the address and data. During a cycle in which IDLE is asserted, the memory is inactive. The lines labeled READ, WRITE, and IDLE force the memory into one of three of its possible modes. The actual signal lines or wires used in microprocessor systems may differ from those shown in the figure in the manner in which information is encoded or multiplexed, but every memory system requires at least these three modes.

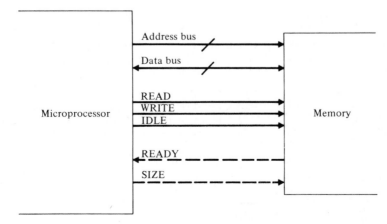

FIGURE 1.7   A processor/memory interface.

Dotted lines shown in the figure represent lines that appear in some, but not necessarily all systems. The line labeled SIZE indicates that an item accessed is a word or part word. If the memory system supports access to both 8-bit bytes and 16-bit bytes, then SIZE determines (encodes) whether the access is to 8 or 16 bits. Typically, SIZE is not used in READ operations because the processor can select from a full word the information needed for the access. But WRITE operations do use the SIZE field. Up to one full word of data can be altered by a WRITE operation. If, for example, the processor needs to update a single byte, it must supply the address of the byte and specify a SIZE of one byte. In this case, the memory system perturbs only that part of the word that is to be rewritten and leaves all other bits in the word unchanged.

The other dotted line is labeled READY and represents a signal from the memory to the processor. When we reach a discussion of timing of memory transactions in Chapter 4, we will discover that slow circuits and long propagation delays can lengthen the response time of a memory to the extent that it cannot respond within the worst-case memory cycle time. The READY line is used to "stretch" the memory cycle time in systems where this is necessary. In effect, the processor initiates a memory transaction, then freezes until the READY indicates that it is safe to continue. A READY line permits the designer to intermix fast and slow memory chips and to design a system that is able to run at the speed of the fast memory for accesses made there. While many popular micros have a READY input, many others do not and thereby force memory accesses to complete within one clock cycle. There is a firm upper bound on the memory access-time of these microprocessors, including delays suffered from propagation along data paths. With a READY signal, arbitrarily slow memories (or peripheral devices that are connected to the processor as memory) can be accommodated.

The signals shown in Fig. 1.7 cover the great bulk of microcomputer memory systems. These are the signals that we assume present in the remainder of this textbook when we consider interfaces between memory and processor.

1.3 THE I/O INTERFACE

At this point we turn our attention to the internal behavior and functional description of the I/O system. The I/O system is basically a very small external memory whose registers are connected to peripheral devices. A typical port in this type of system contains one, possibly two, and more rarely eight to sixteen registers. The registers hold data in transit from computer to peripheral or from peripheral to computer, or they hold control information. The I/O port also contains logic for controlling data transfer between the port and external devices.

I/O Port Structure and I/O Transactions

The first computers did not have separate I/O ports. I/O on these machines was performed solely through the accumulator. In the late 40s and early 50s, the extra cost of a separate I/O system was very high, and the returns were rather risky because the extra logic could well reduce the system reliability to the extent that gains in I/O efficiency were outweighed by the diminished system availability. The disadvantage of this scheme is that when an accumulator is busy with I/O it cannot be used for other purposes. Consequently, programs with extensive I/O had computation speeds severely limited by the I/O data-transfer rates. Very early in the development of computers, buffered I/O was introduced and became commonplace. By *buffered* I/O, we refer to the use of one or more separate registers through which data are transferred between the computer and external devices. If an external device communicates with a special I/O register for data transfer instead of with the accumulator, then the accumulator can be used for other calculations while the I/O is in progress. The buffer has evolved to what, in a microcomputer, we call an *I/O port*. The principal function of an I/O port is to serve as a way station for data in transit between the computer and the external world. A second function of an I/O port is to provide the control logic and signals between the computer and the outside world that is necessary for data transfer.

The structure of a very simple I/O port is shown in Fig. 1.8. Here we see the data register (for data in transit), a control register to hold commands from the processor to the port, and a status register accessible to the processor that tells the computer what is happening or what has recently occurred during the data transfer. By incorporating a status register in the port, the port provides a means for a processor to monitor I/O activity and to be able to exchange data with the port when it is safe to do so.

Interactions with the I/O subsystem fall into two broad classes — program-controlled and interrupt-driven. *Program-controlled* I/O, the type of interaction in which all transac-

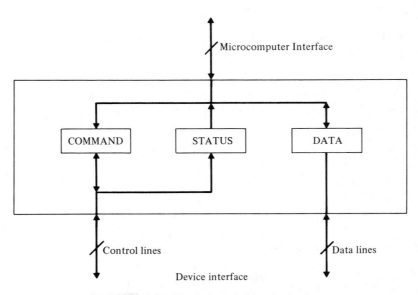

FIGURE 1.8   The structure of a typical I/O port.

tions are initiated by an executing program, is shown for both READ and WRITE transactions below:

I/O READ

1. Test the status register of the port and wait for READY. (A new command cannot be issued if one is already in progress.)
2. Pass a READ command to the control register of the port. After initiating the READ, the microprocessor can make other calculations. When the processor reaches a point at which it must accept the I/O datum, it proceeds to the next step.
3. Test the status register of the port and wait for READY.
4. Read the data register into the processor. Perform Step 2 next, without retesting the status register to see if a new READ can be initiated.

I/O WRITE

1. Test the status register of the port and wait for READY.
2. Transfer the next output datum to the data register of port.
3. Transfer a WRITE command to the control register of the port. The processor passes control to other tasks that can be performed while the I/O operation proceeds concurrently.

Figure 1.9 is the flow-diagram of a program-controlled I/O transaction. During the time a port is busy, the processor can execute instructions related to a different computation or can initiate other I/O activity. This occurs, as shown in Fig. 1.9, after the processor issues a new command and enters a normal execution state. When the processor reaches the point at which one more datum can be transferred through an I/O port, it executes instructions that interrogate the port status again. In Fig. 1.9 this activity appears at the top of the flow chart.

A graphic illustration of the timing for I/O READ and I/O WRITE appears in Fig. 1.10. Observe how I/O and program execution proceed concurrently because of the buffering of I/O through a port. For the READ, the concurrent activity begins immediately after issuing the I/O READ or I/O WRITE command to the port. Timing variations shown in the figure illustrate situations in which the port is idle, waiting for the processor, and in which the processor is idle, waiting for the port.

As a concrete example, consider a port connected to a typical external cathode-ray tube (CRT) terminal. We assume the port transfers 30 characters per second; thus the port is busy for about 33 ms for each character transferred. The processor can spend part or all of the 33 ms on other tasks. If the processor completes the other tasks before the 33 ms is through, the processor loops at the I/O READ or I/O WRITE Step 1 while waiting for the operation to terminate. Should the processor take longer than 33 ms, the I/O port will complete its operation before the processor interrogates the port for status. A buffer for additional tasks for the I/O port might be part of the port itself, which would permit the port to initiate new operations from the collection of tasks waiting to be done. If it is not possible to buffer tasks, or if the task buffer empties, the I/O port will be idle until it is interrogated by the processor and given new tasks to perform.

For a system that contains a single I/O device, the speed improvement from buffering data transfers through an I/O port is at most a factor of 2 over that of a system with no buffering and no concurrency. The reason is simply that an unbuffered system takes a time equal to the *sum* of I/O and computation times, whereas a buffered system takes a time at least equal to the *maximum* of I/O and computation times. But given any two numbers A and B, the sum $A + B$ is never more than twice the largest of the numbers. Hence, overlapping computation with I/O activity can never boost performance by more than a factor of 2.

Then why is there so much concern about I/O efficiency and concurrent I/O? The reason is clear when you look at I/O-intensive systems. More important than overlapping I/O

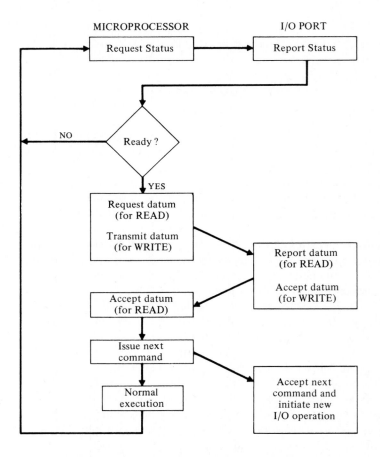

FIGURE 1.9   A typical program-controlled I/O transaction.

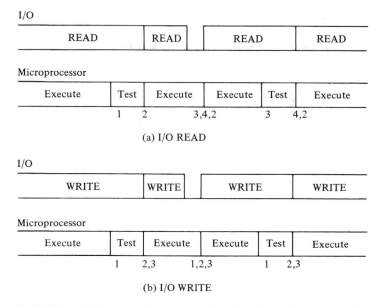

FIGURE 1.10 Timing for I/O operations. (Numbers refer to steps that occur at corresponding times.)

with computation is the need to overlap the I/O for one device with the I/O for another. In fact, if there are N devices in a system, then execution time without buffering is the sum of the N I/O times and computation time, whereas with buffering, execution time can be brought down to the neighborhood of the longest of these times. The improvement in this case is at most a factor of $N + 1$. Although this factor is rarely achieved in general-purpose systems, factors of 3 to 5 are frequently attained. In special cases, such as control of multiple terminals in transaction-processing systems, the factor might be much higher.

The cost of I/O ports has been brought down dramatically through the use of large-scale integration (LSI), so that basic powerful chips now cost only a few dollars. The cost of several I/O ports may increase the system retail price of a computer by a few hundred dollars, but if performance gains are factors of 3 to 5, then the expenditure is well justified.

Interrupts

We indicated in the opening pages of this chapter that there are at least two general strategies for I/O, one initiated by the processor (program-controlled I/O as treated above) and the other initiated by the port (*interrupt-driven I/O*). Like program-controlled I/O, interrupt-driven I/O runs concurrently with processor execution. The difference between the two is the mechanism for detecting when an I/O port has completed an operation. For program-controlled I/O, the processor interrogates the port. For interrupt-driven I/O, the port generates a signal to the processor, called an *interrupt request*, at the completion of an operation. The processor responds to this request, recognizes that the device is no longer busy, and initiates a new transaction. Thus there is no need to interrogate the port to find if the port is ready. The interrupt request conveys the ready information. On the other hand, the interrupt request does not indicate which port is ready, so that part of the interrupt transaction involves port identification as follows:

I/O READ

1. The processor signals the port to enable the port interrupt. In this state, the port asserts a level signal on the INTERRUPT REQUEST signal line when the port detects that an I/O operation has terminated. (If the port interrupt is disabled, then the port will not assert INTERRUPT REQUEST when ready, but will indicate its status continuously in a status register that can be read by the processor.) As part of this transaction the processor also initiates a READ operation, during which the port reads external data. At the conclusion of this step, the processor turns to other computations while the I/O port is busy accepting data from an external device.
2. The I/O port completes the data transfer and asserts an INTERRUPT REQUEST signal.
3. When the INTERRUPT REQUEST is first asserted, the processor may be in an uninterruptible state. At a later time when interrupts are permitted, the processor interrupts its current activity and begins a device-identification transaction. Device identification can be implemented many different ways. Three different ways are
   a) The processor transmits a signal to the I/O system as a whole that it is now acknowledging an interrupt request. The highest-priority port with a pending request responds to the broadcast signal by placing its identifier on the I/O bus. The processor accepts the identifier, and initiates execution at an address that is a function of that identifier. In effect, the port identifier forces the processor to branch to a subroutine for servicing that particular port.
   b) The processor transmits a signal to each port individually, starting with the highest priority port and moving in descending priority to the port with the lowest priority. Each port responds to this interrogation with a reply that indicates whether it has an active interrupt request. When the processor first detects an active request, it discontinues the device-identification process, and branches to a subroutine that processes the port that requested service. If only one device can post an interrupt at any given time, the device-identification transaction can be omitted.
   c) The processor has at least as many distinct interrupt request lines as there are I/O ports, and each port asserts a different line. When the processor responds to an interrupt it branches to a location that is a function of the highest-priority request asserted at the time of the branch. This location contains the first instruction of a subroutine that processes the corresponding I/O port.

4. If, in the process of identifying the highest priority requester, the device-identification step does not acknowledge an interrupt, then the software that processes the specific port issues an acknowledgment to the port that it is responding to the port's interrupt request. If the port receives the acknowledgement during device identification or subsequently, the port responds to the acknowledgment by removing its request.
5. The processor executes a program that accepts the datum read, and issues another READ command at this point if more data are to be transferred. At the conclusion of the I/O transaction, the processor returns to the interrupted program.

I/O WRITE

1. The processor enables the interrupt request of the I/O port, and transmits to the port an output datum and a WRITE command.
2. The processor returns to other activities while the port transfers the datum to an external device. When the data transfer is complete, the port asserts the INTERRUPT REQUEST signal.
3. At a later time, the processor suspends its current processing, and identifies the interrupting port.
4. The processor issues an INTERRUPT ACKNOWLEDGE to the device identified in Step 3. This device (and only this device) removes its interrupt request. (This can be part of the device identification as indicated for the READ transaction.)
5. If the processor has additional data to transfer, it passes another datum and a WRITE command to the port. In any case, the processor returns to the program suspended when the interrupt activity began.

The READ and WRITE transactions are essentially the same, except for minor differences relating to the direction of data flow. Steps 2, 3, and 4 are identical for the two functions.

Figure 1.11 shows the interrupt-driven I/O transaction. Compare this to Fig. 1.9 to see the differences between interrupt-driven I/O and the program-controlled I/O described earlier.

There is some confusion in the use of the term "interrupt." Some writers intend it to mean the request in Step 1, whereas to others it refers to the processor actions in Step 2. These are quite distinct, even though both are invoked during an interrupt transaction. Step 2 conveys an idea that is closer to the dictionary meaning of the word. In Step 2, when the processor first responds to the I/O port, the processor has reached a point at which the program in progress can be suspended temporarily while the processor initiates new I/O operations. When the I/O processing has been completed, the processor returns to the suspended program. The term "interrupt," then, refers to the act of suspending one program, temporarily executing another, and then continuing with the suspended program.

Note that the processor does not, in general, respond immediately to an interrupt request. Hence, an interrupt request must be held continuously until it is acknowledged.

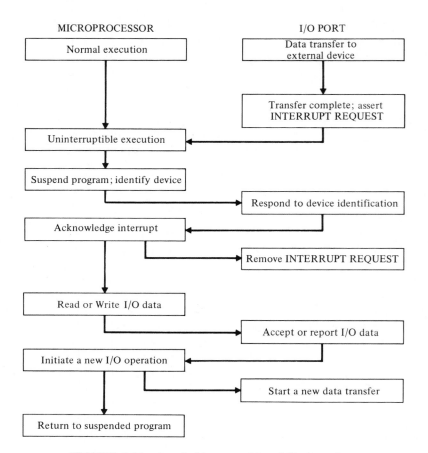

FIGURE 1.11   A typical interrupt-driven I/O transaction.

Note also that when the processor does honor an interrupt request, it honors only one. Hence, if two or more requests are pending when the processor interrupt occurs, the interrupt-acknowledge transaction is recognized by exactly one I/O port, and only that port removes its interrupt request. All other requests remain pending. At a later time each of these will be honored, but one at a time, by a similar interrupt-acknowledge transaction.

The processor must, in general, have some mechanism for temporarily disabling its interrupt response, and for reenabling that response at a later time. Consider, for example, a processor that polls the ports sequentially during the device-identification transaction. The ports hold their requests pending during this transaction, since no port was acknowledged when the processor initiated the poll. If the interrupt system is not disabled at this time, then the pending requests will interrupt the processor continuously during the polling sequence, and the processor will not complete the poll. Therefore, any processor that requires polling for device identification must automatically disable interrupt requests when an interrupt occurs. Many processors have a status bit called an *interrupt mask* for this purpose. When the mask is on, the interrupt system is enabled; otherwise it is disabled. The mask is usually controllable by program, but it also changes state automatically when an interrupt occurs and prevents any further interrupts until the processor has a chance to process the present one and further interrupts can be permitted again.

Some processors offer both maskable and nonmaskable interrupts: The former are controlled by an internal interrupt mask, and the latter are not. When a nonmaskable interrupt request appears, the processor honors that request at the end of execution of the current instruction, and there is no way for the processor to disable the interrupt. To prevent repeated interrupts from a single nonmaskable-interrupt request, the request must be edge-triggered and not level sensitive. Because the processor must sense a transition on the nonmaskable interrupt line, it is somewhat risky to drive this line from more than one source. The problem is that while one request is pending, the signal line is held in a fixed state. If any other request occurs on this line during this period, the active edge of the later request cannot be sensed by the microprocessor.

The Interrupt Interface

A suitable interface for implementing interrupt transactions is shown in Fig. 1.12. In this case, a port ID functions as a memory address. Each port has a unique identifier in much the same way that each word of memory has a unique address. The processor issues a port ID to access a port just as it issues a memory address to access a word of memory. Carrying the comparison with memory somewhat further, we see the three control lines — labeled respectively, PORT READ, PORT WRITE, and PORT IDLE — that control the timing and direction of information transfer between the processor and the port. When PORT WRITE is asserted, the processor transmits information on the data lines to the port. Conversely, when PORT READ is asserted, the processor requests information from the port to be sent on the data lines. When PORT IDLE is asserted, the interface is inactive.

Because a port possibly contains many registers, the port ID is not sufficient in itself to identify the register accessed during any given transaction. Most ports have at least a data register and a command/status register. Writing into the latter register includes instructions to the port to read or write, and enables or disables the interrupt request. The READY/NOT READY status of the port is also usually held in this register, and is accessed by the processor for program-controlled I/O. Figure 1.12 shows a COMMAND/DATA line that qualifies a port transaction to distinguish access to the command/status register from access to the I/O data register. The COMMAND/DATA line actually functions as a secondary ID, and can be implemented in several lines to distinguish among many more functions than just COMMAND and DATA; the figure indicates the secondary ID function of this line in parentheses.

Separate lines are shown for both INTERRUPT REQUEST and INTERRUPT AC-KNOWLEDGE. Actually, only the INTERRUPT REQUEST function must have a separate line. The INTERRUPT ACKNOWLEDGE function can be implemented as one of the functions carried on the secondary ID (COMMAND/DATA) line.

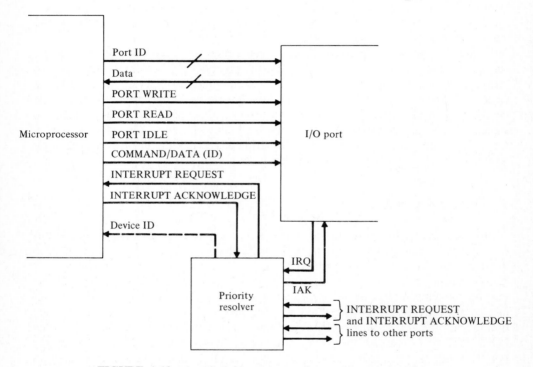

FIGURE 1.12   A typical microprocessor/input-output port interface.

Figure 1.12 also shows as a dotted line the signal necessary to resolve device identification when a processor responds to an interrupt request. Interrupt-request lines from each port converge on a module labeled "priority resolver," whose output is a device ID that is transmitted to the processor. Device identification is implemented in so many different ways that no single figure can do it justice. The dotted line, therefore, at best conveys the intent that the priority resolver is not universal and that actual implementations may differ greatly from that shown. Those implementations without priority resolvers connect the interrupt request lines from all ports in an OR fashion, so that the microprocessor observes a request if any port raises one. In such systems the interrupt-acknowledge signal from the microprocessor is usually returned to the port on the bus-interface lines in the form of a command, since without a priority resolver the only way to direct the acknowledge to a particular port is through the port-address lines on the I/O bus. (We treat this topic in more detail later in this chapter.)

Device Identification

We have hinted that there are several different ways in practice to implement device identification. The two most popular methods are *polling* and *vectored interrupts*.

Polling is a software technique for device identification that is used where no hardware support for device identification exists. Since many 4-bit and 8-bit microprocessors were designed in the early part of the 70s when logic complexity on one chip was quite limited, polling is the usual method for device identification on such processors. The logic supports interrupts only to the extent that when an interrupt is honored, the processor saves its present state and sets its program counter to a fixed address. Once control passes to that address, it is up to the I/O program there to interrogate the ports that may have caused an interrupt, and to process I/O for the first port discovered to have a request pending. If several ports are active simultaneously, the I/O program should interrogate them in the order of priority, running from the most important to the least important. Normally the high-performance devices are queried before the low-performance devices, although there are valid reasons to do the opposite. Whereas a high-performance device with substantial internal buffering can be idle safely for a short period between data transfers, a low-speed device without internal buffering may actually lose data if idle for too long a time. In this case, it is wiser to avoid lost data, and to treat the low-performance device before the high-performance one, at the risk of degrading performance slightly.

When a large group of devices — say, a collection of video terminals — are all of the same priority, the polling sequence should favor no particular device. Here a suitable polling algorithm queries the terminals in a fixed order until it finds one with a request. For the next interrupt, the polling algorithm continues polling terminals in sequence from where it left off on the last interrupt. This round-robin scheme gives equal weighting to all terminals on the average.

We mentioned that hardware required to support polling is minimal. The hardware must do at least the following actions in executing a microprocessor interrupt:

1. Disable additional interrupts long enough to perform the next two steps and to acknowledge the interrupt to the interrupting port,
2. Save enough of the present state of the processor to enable a return to the interrupted routine, and
3. Load a new program counter from a fixed location (or jump to a fixed location in memory).

The state saved must include the program counter plus other machine status that cannot otherwise be saved. Some microprocessors save more than this when executing an interrupt. The other items saved are status bits and general registers that are very likely to be modified by the interrupt program when it takes control. Since any register or status word altered by an interrupt program must be preserved prior to being modified, software instructions will have to save them unless the hardware saves them first. Before the interrupt program returns to the interrupted routine, the altered registers are first restored to their original values. The more information automatically saved by the interrupt hardware, the less that needs saving by the interrupt software. But state saving can be taken too far. Any data saved by interrupt hardware that is not altered by the interrupt program need not have been saved, and the burden of saving and restoring this data lowers performance unnecessarily.

One of the necessities mentioned above is that interrupts must be disabled at least until a new program counter is loaded. The reason for this is that the microprocessor honors an interrupt by initiating a sequence of operations that culminates in setting a new value in the program counter. What happens if an interrupt occurs while executing this sequence? The program counter determines where an interrupted program will be reinitiated. But the interrupt sequence built into the hardware has no accessible program counter associated with it, so that there is no way to store information about where this sequence should be reinitiated. The only restart information that can be preserved is the new program counter, which contains a valid restart point only when the interrupt sequence has terminated.

Let us focus on the other method for device identification—vectored interrupts. Vectored interrupts identify a requesting port through hardware that selects the highest priority requester from among all the ports with interrupts pending. The priority-resolution hardware returns a port ID to the processor, either in response to a query from interrupt software or in response to the INTERRUPT ACKNOWLEDGE signal generated when an interrupt is honored. The processor then uses the port ID as an index into a table, and retrieves an entry point to an I/O subroutine for the corresponding port. The "vectoring" in this case is the transformation of the port ID into a starting address so that control is passed directly to the proper routine without first going through a costly polling operation to find which port needs service. We cannot say much about the process that maps the port ID into a subroutine address because almost every microprocessor uses a scheme unique to that processor. Figure 1.12 shows the priority resolver as a device external to the processor. The resolver can be embedded in the micro itself, distributed through the I/O ports (with each port containing a part of the resolver function), or can be implemented in a separate module as shown in the figure. Chapter 3 provides more details about methods of resolving priority conflicts.

Micros with no internal capability for vectored interrupts can be given this capability through the use of an external priority resolver. Interrupt requests are passed to the resolver, as shown in Fig. 1.12, which in turn requests an interrupt from the processor. The software in the processor interrogates the priority resolver for the ID of the highest-priority requester, and thus avoids the polling sequence. Interrupt acknowledgment is then done by the device service-routine, which removes the interrupt request. A more sophisticated approach has the priority resolver acknowledge the highest-priority port when it reports that port's ID to the processor. This approach is suitable when all I/O ports have an identical means for accepting an INTERRUPT ACKNOWLEDGE signal. However, the I/O port interrupt interface is not standardized today, so that priority resolvers tend to implement one type of INTERRUPT ACKNOWLEDGE function or none at all.

I/O Port Addressing

Because of the great similarity between memory and I/O interfaces, the I/O and memory functions often share address and data lines. Two ways of sharing the memory and I/O port interface are common today. They are shown in Fig. 1.13. The first method, called *isolated I/O* treats ports and memory on the shared lines differently, and uses controls to distinguish between the two. The figure shows a line labeled MEMORY/PORT used for this purpose. When MEMORY is asserted, the address lines carry a memory address, and memory responds to the request. When PORT is asserted, memory is disabled, and the I/O system responds to the request. Thus, the MEMORY/PORT signal isolates the address space of ports from the address space of memory. The figure does not show the interrupt and device identification lines. These lines are rarely shared between memory and I/O, and they simply should be superimposed on the figure.

The second way of combining memory and I/O functions is called *memory-mapped I/O*. In this case, there is no difference whatsoever between memory and I/O accesses. All accesses are treated as memory accesses. Each port is selected by access to some specific address (or range of addresses), and memory does not respond to addresses reserved for I/O. Each distinct port function has a unique memory address. To issue a command, the processor writes to the command-register address. To accept data, the processor reads from the data-buffer address.

Processors that utilize port addresses as distinguished from memory addresses must have special instructions for reading from and writing into ports. Typically the instruction repertoire contains:

```
IN      REG, PORT    Read data from the port whose ID is PORT
                     into register REG.
OUT     REG, PORT    Write data from register REG to the port
                     whose ID is PORT.
```

To differentiate between commands and data, some repertoires have additional I/O instructions such as STATUS or CMD, which are are just like IN and OUT, respectively, except that the processor signals the port that these are control transactions, not data transactions. Another way to achieve the same end is to allocate a secondary port address that specifies a function for that port. Hence, a full port ID can be, say, 10 bits, of which the first five select one of 32 ports, and the second five specify one of 32 functions for each port. This reduces the instruction repertoire required for I/O functions to just IN and OUT.

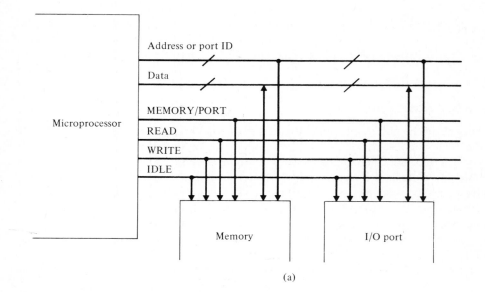

(a)

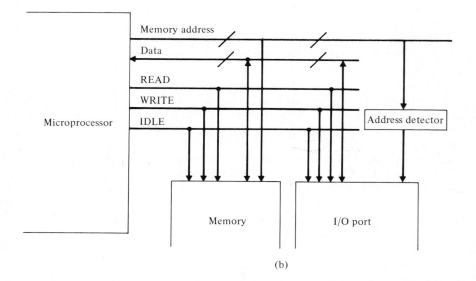

(b)

FIGURE 1.13 (a) The isolated-I/O method for implementing a common interface with I/O ports and memory; the signal line MEMORY/PORT differentiates between memory and I/O operations. (b) Memory-mapped I/O: The address detector selects the I/O port when it reads an address that selects one of the port functions.

Of the two ways to combine I/O and memory functions, neither is clearly better than the other. Memory-mapped I/O reduces the instruction repertoire slightly, while also reducing addressable memory by the amount of address space allocated to I/O. Port addressing takes away no address space, but adds a small complication to the repertoire. When I/O instructions are implemented without the full range of address-modification functions, I/O becomes somewhat awkward to program. In any event, memory-mapped I/O is an option for all implementations, even for microprocessors with I/O instructions and port facilities. It is mandatory only for microprocessors that have no other way to implement I/O.

1.4 THE DMA INTERFACE

DMA adds one more level of complexity to the I/O interface because a DMA controller has independent access to memory. One set of wires can carry at most one transaction at a time. If DMA and a microprocessor share the signal wires to memory, there must be some mechanism to arbitrate which shall have access to memory when both attempt to do so at the same time.

Let us examine the data flow and functional behavior of a DMA transaction.

1. The processor transmits the following information to a DMA controller:
   a) Beginning address in memory.
   b) Block length (number of words to transfer).
   c) Direction (memory-to-device or device-to-memory).
   d) Port ID.
   e) End of block action (interrupt request or no interrupt request).
2. The processor returns to other activities while the DMA controller starts the data transfer.
3. Each time the DMA controller accesses memory, it synchronizes this memory request with an idle period of the processor. To do this synchronization, the DMA controller can either
   a) force an immediate disabling of the processor, or
   b) request a halt of the processor, and await an acknowledgment, or
   c) time the DMA access to a clock interval or status signal of the processor that signals an idle cycle.
4. When the DMA controller accesses an I/O port or memory, it uses the same functional control signals as used by the processor. I/O port activity can be performed on dedicated lines that do not have to be synchronized with the processor.
5. At the completion of the block transfer, the DMA controller raises an interrupt request if the interrupts are armed, and otherwise indicates completion in its status register.
6. The processor recognizes I/O completion (either by an interrupt or by reading the status register); thereafter the activity between the processor and the DMA controller follows the normal post-completion activity of any I/O port.

This description shows that a DMA controller is treated as a standard port before and after a block transfer. During a block transfer, the DMA controller must have the additional capability to synchronize with the processor.

The description also shows just how a DMA controller improves performance. The DMA controller has built into it the program for moving a stream of data between memory and an I/O port. When instructions are built-in, at the very least, the controller does not have to read these instructions from memory and execute them one-by-one. Moreover, the controller can perform several of the elementary actions in parallel, whereas the actions have to be programmed sequentially when implemented with software in the processor. For example, the controller decrements a counter each time it moves a datum. It can overlap the subtraction with memory access, and avoid a time penalty for the arithmetic instructions a program has to execute. Therefore, a DMA controller can achieve a much higher performance for block transfers than can be obtained in software alone. DMA is most frequently used for high-speed I/O, especially tape and disk. Fast disks and tapes move blocks of data at speeds much greater than any program can control, and therefore must be interfaced to computers through DMA controllers.

DMA transfers by their nature, though high in performance, do slow down the processor if the DMA forces the processor to halt temporarily for each I/O data access. The degradation in processing speed is imperceptible if the processor normally has idle cycles that the DMA controller can use to advantage. But if the processor makes heavy use of available memory cycles, performance degradation during DMA block transfers becomes quite noticeable. Of course, degradation would be much worse without DMA if the transfers were done entirely by software.

The DMA interface with the memory, I/O, and microprocessor is shown in Fig. 1.14. In this figure, the I/O ports under DMA control are attached solely to the DMA controller. Signal lines are the same ones that normally interface the ports to the processor. The memory control lines in this figure are the conventional ones we have seen earlier, except that both the processor and the DMA controller exercise the lines in this figure. The new lines are the HALT and HALT ACKNOWLEDGE lines. These are the ones that synchronize the DMA controller to the processor. When the DMA controller needs to access memory, it requests the processor to halt, by asserting the HALT signal. The processor responds with a HALT ACKNOWLEDGE at a later time, at which point the DMA controller takes control of memory. When the DMA controller has completed its activity, it removes its HALT request, and the processor continues from the point of suspension, removing its HALT ACKNOWLEDGE in the meantime.

The dotted line shown indicates an IMMEDIATE HALT type of DMA request. The more usual HALT request may take several clock cycles for the processor to acknowledge. HALT ACKNOWLEDGE signifies that the processor has relinquished memory control indefinitely; the DMA controller is free to make as many accesses to memory as necessary before returning control to the processor. The delay in response to a HALT request comes about because the processor must reach a state in which it can suspend processing. Data held in dynamic registers that are refreshed during normal processing must be moved to static registers, or execution must move to the point where these data are no longer necessary. The purpose of the IMMEDIATE HALT line is to avoid the delay associated with the normal HALT request, but there are severe restrictions placed on the use of IMMEDIATE HALT. Typically, the IMMEDIATE HALT can be used only briefly, for at most one or two accesses, before there is a danger that the processor will not be able to recover its state correctly and return to the suspended activity.

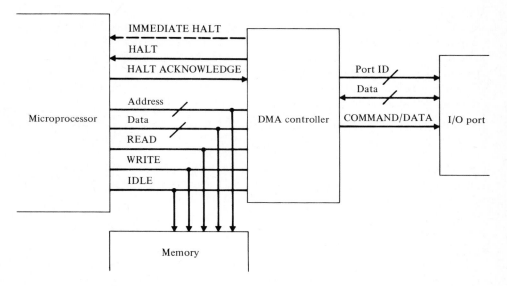

FIGURE 1.14   A typical direct memory-access controller interface.

The IDLE status line can also be used fruitfully by DMA controllers that have the luxury of delaying data transfers until an IDLE point is reached. This makes good sense in systems where IDLE occurs frequently, say on the order of 20 to 30% of the memory cycles. Then there is no need to halt the processor, and DMA is able to achieve high data rates with virtually no impact on processor performance.

Note the inherent efficiency of DMA operations as compared to interrupt-controlled I/O. DMA operations require only one memory cycle to transfer each byte, plus perhaps up to two memory cycles per byte transferred to obtain and relinquish control of the bus. For each byte transferred by an interrupt program, additional processor and memory cycles are required to save status at the time of the interrupt, fetch the instructions for the transfer, and to restore status to return to the interrupted program. The number of memory cycles required to transfer a single byte this way is typically no fewer than 10, and more usually 20 to 30 cycles. Since DMA operations do not require processor assistance, the state of the processor is not disrupted by DMA, and there is no need to store and retrieve state in conjunction with a DMA operation. Also since the DMA controller is internally programmed to transfer data blocks, the controller does not have to fetch from memory individual instructions for a block-transfer operation, and no time is lost to instruction fetches.

1.5 I/O STRATEGY: PROGRAM-CONTROLLED VERSUS INTERRUPT-DRIVEN

Our guided tour of I/O control has been preoccupied with what options are available and how to use them. Now we turn to the question of which method to choose and why. In this section we give criteria for choosing one I/O strategy over another, and offer advice for structuring microcomputer systems for highest performance, while providing for the simplest and most reliable software support possible.

To review the differences between program-controlled I/O and interrupt-driven I/O, we mention that their major differences are the following points:

1. Interrupt-driven I/O must save an interrupted program's state at the start of an interrupt program, and restore that state before returning to the interrupted program. No state saving is required for program-controlled I/O.
2. Interrupt-driven I/O must use software or hardware or both to find which device has posted an interrupt. Program-controlled I/O inherently performs this action when reading device status to determine if a device is ready.
3. Program-controlled I/O must use software testing to determine when a device is ready; interrupt-driven I/O provides this information automatically when an interrupt request is posted.
4. When a program runs several devices concurrently, the program can respond to I/O requests with much shorter latency when the I/O is interrupt-driven than when it is program-controlled.

In Point 1, the overhead burden is greater for interrupt-driven I/O because of state saving. The burden for interrupts in Point 2 is negligible if a system has vectored interrupts. But it can be severe if vectored interrupts are not available and many different devices can be active simultaneously.

For program-controlled I/O the performance degradation problem of Point 3 is strongly related to the latency problem of Point 4. There is a clearly a trade-off between the two. Latency for program-controlled I/O is reduced as the frequency of status checking is increased. But this in turn increases the number of machine cycles lost to status checks.

The normal approach to keeping latency low in program-controlled I/O is to poll the active devices in a cyclic or in a priority order. While polling tends to keep latency low, it does so at the cost of cycles wasted checking status. Therefore the polling should be scheduled frequently enough to meet the latency requirements, but not so frequently as to impair performance. This assumes that there is productive computation that can be performed when the processor is not busy polling. In the special case of a system dedicated to the control of multiple I/O devices, performance degradation from polling may not be a problem because there is no application program that can use available machine cycles.

From Point 1 we conclude that program-controlled I/O in general can yield higher transfer rates than interrupt-driven I/O. The problem, of course, is that program-controlled I/O may also yield higher latency times for responding to I/O devices that require service. The major reason for controlling I/O through interrupts is to reduce latency.

While interrupt-driven I/O is a useful and practical method for achieving low-latency responses to external signals, it is often more costly to develop and debug than software that uses programmed polls to control I/O. Interrupt-driven software is potentially interruptible at any point. The programmer must be aware of this possibility and must plan the program to work correctly regardless of external events that trigger interrupt requests and the sequence in which these events occur. The programmer must make explicit decisions about when to turn on and off interrupts for all or part of the I/O system.

Let's contrast these aspects of interrupt-driven I/O with polling. In the absence of interrupts, subroutines run to completion once they are begun. Hence, the programmer need not deal with the problem of when to disable and enable interrupts for the entire system or for selected devices. Issues relating to such things as nesting of interrupts and reentrant programming are absent or much less critical than in interrupt-driven systems. Polling software, however, generally does have to deal with situations in which the system must respond to a specified external event within a fixed minimum time. When a real-time constraint dictates performance, polling software becomes relatively more difficult to write than it is in absence of such constraints. The cost of creating a reliable, efficient interrupt-driven system may be somewhat higher than that of a polled I/O system, and therefore polled I/O is preferred when it can easily meet the latency requirements. When real-time constraints dictate that interrupts must be used, it may be possible to run a few critical devices under interrupt control and to use polling to run the remaining ones. This may yield somewhat simpler software than software that is entirely interrupt-driven.

Why is interrupt-driven software more complex than polling software? The problem lies in the difficulty in understanding interrupt-driven programs. Between any two instructions an interrupt request may interject a totally different, possibly conflicting, subprogram execution. Every line of code in the handler and in the interruptible code has to be written to satisfy global conventions in order for the interrupts to work correctly. The conventions avoid conflicts by dictating which variables can be accessed, when they can be accessed, and how to communicate information between the interrupt-driven code and the interruptible code. Skilled programmers can master the techniques of writing interrupt programs and can create successful, efficient interrupt systems. Unskilled programmers violate the conventions, or fail to design correct conventions in the first place.

To illustrate the difficulties of interrupt programs, consider the events that occur when an interrupt occurs in a microprocessor. The status of the processor at the time of the interrupt has to be saved, and most implementations save the status on a push-down stack. This presumes that the machine-register stack pointer is pointing at a stack when the interrupt occurs. If a programmer elects to do a "tricky" algorithm, and momentarily in the algorithm the stack pointer is altered to point to the interior of a data structure, then an interrupt will overwrite part of that data structure but only if it occurs just at that time. Hence, as a general rule the stack pointer must never point to anything but a stack. Yet this rule is rarely mentioned in a manufacturer's documentation for microprocessors and seldom appears in textbooks. In fact, early editions of the popular texts by Eckhouse (1975) and Gill (1978) violated this convention in the instruction sequence that initializes the stack pointer, even in examples that demonstrate the interrupt system. Every one of these examples fails in an interrupt environment when an interrupt occurs at a critical point in the program. Although the failures are so infrequent that they are almost unnoticeable, they do indeed occur. Hence, the programmer (or author) can exercise code and believe that it works correctly, and yet the code may not be at all suitable for production use.

If rigid conventions and programming skill are prerequisites for writing interrupt programs, they are insufficient in themselves to surmount the difficulty of debugging faulty interrupt programs. The programmer must have good software tools such as emulators and simulators to aid in diagnosing and correcting bugs in interrupt-driven software. In recent years the microprocessor itself has come to the rescue in such tools as logic analyzers and in-circuit emulators that can store a history of real-time activity for post-malfunction analysis. But for these tools as well as software tools, the tools are useful primarily after a failure occurs. If a failure is truly a rare, time-dependent event, the major obstacle in repairing the problem is to recreate the conditions for the failure. Finding and correcting a bug in interrupt-driven I/O might therefore be a difficult and time-consuming exercise. The basic problem is that interrupt-driven programs are more complex than ordinary programs because of the former's unpredictable changes in the flow of execution.

Given that a useful strategy is to incorporate program-controlled I/O unless interrupt-driven I/O is mandatory, then what conditions force the decision to interrupt-driven I/O? The two following program attributes are key factors in forcing a decision toward the use of interrupts:

1. The program has long periods of computation unbroken by calls to the I/O system.
2. One or more I/O devices has a real-time deadline, with a costly recovery procedure if the deadline is missed.

A reasonable approach to reducing overall programming complexity at the expense of extra hardware is to dedicate a microprocessor to one or more real-time tasks that can be handled by such a dedicated micro in a program-controlled fashion. This microprocessor then interfaces with a second microprocessor for processing data in the absence of real-time deadlines. The dedicated micro plays the role of a high-speed buffer that smooths peak data-transfer requirements, and provides a ''graceful'' transition between the relatively poor latency of the central microprocessor and the tight real-time constraints of the I/O device.

Although programming complexity may be reduced in a two-processor system because of the simplification of some of the real-time I/O programs, running two processors in place of one processor does have additional costs, particularly because the two processors have to be synchronized to each other. The basic problem is that an external device has to be synchronized to the computer. The interrupt system is but one way to implement the synchronization. If the designer chooses to use a dedicated I/O processor, and not use an interrupt-driven approach, then the synchronization activity is moved to the interface between processors. The two-processor software might well be less complex than software for one processor, and part of the reduction in complexity is likely to be attributable to the simplification or elimination of interrupt-driven software. But all solutions, by necessity, must have some means of synchronizing external events to the central processor. If this mechanism does not use the interrupt system, then the software must do something else. Synchronization cannot be absent.

A dedicated microprocessor was once thought to be an intolerably expensive and uneconomical approach to the real-time problem. Today the approach is viable in many applications. In fact, the dual-processor chip has made its appearance because of the issues we have addressed here. The idea in the dual-processor chip is to allocate one of the processors to the control of high-speed I/O while the other processor performs other system functions. Two processors should yield higher performance than one processor, and if our comments are correct, the software for a two-processor system may be somewhat less complex than the equivalent software implemented on a single processor.

1.6 MEMORY AND I/O INTERFACES FOR TYPICAL MICROPROCESSORS

In this section we show the memory and I/O interfaces of several microprocessors to illustrate how they fit the general structure outlined in this chapter.

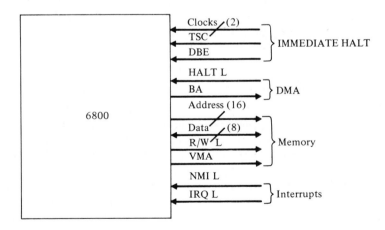

FIGURE 1.15   Interface signals for the 6800 microprocessor.

Figure 1.15 shows a very simple interface for the 6800 family. This microprocessor uses memory mapping for I/O so there are no lines for dealing with I/O ports specifically. However, note the following lines and observe their functions:

1. R/W L and VMA (Read/Write and Valid Memory Address). These lines encode the READ, WRITE and IDLE states as shown in Table 1.1. The suffix "L" denotes a signal that is asserted in the low (logic 0) state. Hence, when the signal line R/W L is in the 1 state, READ is asserted, and when in the 0 state, WRITE is asserted. (See the table. The notation differs from the manufacturer's notation, which denotes a low-asserted signal by an overbar.)

TABLE 1.1   6800 Memory-Interface Signal Encoding

State	R/W L	VMA
READ	1	1
WRITE	0	1
IDLE	X	0

2. HALT L and BA. This is the DMA interface for HALT and HALT AC-KNOWLEDGE, respectively. (BA denotes "bus available".)
3. IRQ L and NMI L. These are two different interrupt request lines. NMI L is a non-maskable interrupt; IRQ L is a standard (maskable) interrupt request. NMI L is edge-triggered because there is no way to disable it within the processor, and a level-sensitive signal would interrupt repeatedly. The 6800 uses interrupt vectoring (two different vector addresses) to distinguish between NMI L and IRQ L, but requires polling or an external priority resolver to identify devices whose request lines are connected together to IRQ L or NMI L.
4. TSC, DBE, and clocks. These lines form an IMMEDIATE HALT type of DMA interface. TSC (tri-state control) disconnects the address lines from the processor, and DBE (data bus enable) disconnects the data lines. With these disconnected, a DMA controller can put its own signals on these buses to initiate a DMA transfer. However, since the microprocessor is immediately disconnected from memory by TSC and DBE control, and in order to guarantee that the program in execution does not fail, it is necessary for the microprocessor to accomplish in the same clock period what it would normally do if DMA did not occur. The DMA controller must "stretch the clock" so that the lengthened cycle is long enough for both the DMA and the processor to access memory. DMA controllers thus have access to the clock generator mechanism to lengthen clock cycles as required and thus permit both a DMA access and a normal processor access to occur in one cycle.

The 6800 has no interrupt acknowledge line, and no hardware on chip to support device identification other than the ability to vector between IRQ L and NMI L requests.

The 6502, representative of the 6500 family produced by Commodore Semiconductor, is illustrated in Fig. 1.16. This particular member of the family is made to be almost pin-for-pin compatible with the 6800, so that the address, data, and read/write signals are identical with those of the 6800. This processor lacks a VMA signal, and thus a memory reference is requested on every cycle. (Some references are simply ignored by the processor, and would become IDLE cycles if a VMA signal were available.) The RDY signal is used by slow memory and peripheral devices to lengthen the cycle time of the processor by an integral number of clock cycles.

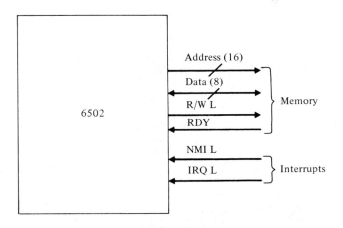

FIGURE 1.16   Interface signals for the 6502.

Like the 6800, the 6502 has two interrupt request lines, one maskable (IRQ L) and one unmaskable (NMI L). Each of these interrupts has its own vector address where the processor finds the address of an interrupt program to run. When many devices are tied to one interrupt request line, the device identification is done by polling or by external priority resolution.

A different type of interface is used in the 8080, 8085, 8086 family of microprocessors. The 8080, which is obsolete, is shown in Fig. 1.17. Memory interface signals follow the convention of this chapter with DBIN signifying READ and WR L signifying WRITE. The absence of either of these signals is an IDLE cycle for memory.

Although we treat the address and data lines as belonging to the memory interface, the 8080 uses these lines for the I/O port interface as well. The 8080 combines the memory and I/O functions by using the address lines to carry either memory addresses or port addresses.

Address and data are on separate lines in this processor. But the processor is packaged as a chip with only 40 pins, so that this leaves too few lines for other functions. Hence, other functions are multiplexed on the data lines. The SYNC signal line signifies whether the data lines contain status information or true data. At the start of each memory cycle the processor reports its status by setting SYNC to 1 and placing the status on the data lines. External latches are supposed to use SYNC as a latch enable, and to capture the status bits for controlling I/O or DMA. The eight status bits show the type of cycle (memory or I/O), and other status as described in Table 1.2. The individual functions of the static bits and their encoding are given in Table 1.2.

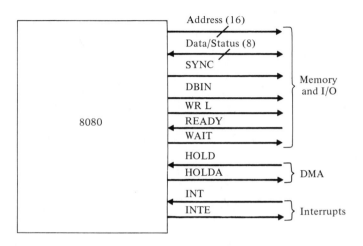

FIGURE 1.17   Interface signals for the 8080.

Note that the signals INP (I/O input) and OUT (I/O output) dictate whether the operation is an I/O operation or a memory operation. If neither is asserted, the operation is a memory operation; otherwise it is an I/O operation and the address bus contains a port ID. MEMR denotes ''memory read,'' which is a READ signal asserted only for memory operations, but WO L is a WRITE signal that is asserted for both memory write and output operations.

Several nonmultiplexed status and control pins are dedicated to the slow memory and DMA functions. Two pins determine the way the processor will respond to slow memory and devices. Cycle lengthening is requested by the external logic on the READY line, and the 8080 acknowledges this request by asserting WAIT. DMA requests are entered through HOLD, which serves the HALT function. Status line HOLDA responds with the HALT ACKNOWLEDGE condition when the 8080 reaches a stopping point. (The 8080 also produces a multiplexed status signal called HALTA, which indicates when the 8080 has executed a HALT instruction. This status does not carry the response to a DMA request.)

Two signals and one status indication define the interrupt interface. INT posts an interrupt request to the 8080. External devices can sense whether or not interrupts are enabled by sampling the INTE pin, which holds the value of the interrupt-enable flip/flop. The INTA state is one of the control states listed in Table 1.2 that is entered whenever the 8080 responds to an interrupt. INTA provides a very clever and simple mechanism for vectoring 8080 interrupts. External logic can sense the INTA state and force onto the data bus an instruction that is essentially a jump instruction with an externally specified starting address. Therefore, an external priority resolver can force a jump to a starting address that is a function of the port ID with the highest priority-pending interrupt. In this way the INTA-status response provides crucial information for determining precisely when to pass a port ID to the processor to initiate a vectored branch to an interrupt program.

TABLE 1.2   8080 State Information Encoding

STATE	INTA D_0	WO L D_1	STACK D_2	HLTA D_3	OUT D_4	M_1 D_5	INP D_6	MEMR D_7
Instruction FETCH	0	1	0	0	0	1	0	1
READ (memory)	0	1	0	0	0	0	0	1
WRITE (memory)	0	0	0	0	0	0	0	0
READ (stack)	0	1	1	0	0	0	0	1
WRITE (stack)	0	0	1	0	0	0	0	0
READ (I/O)	0	1	0	0	0	0	1	0
WRITE (I/O)	0	0	0	0	1	0	0	0
Interrupt Acknowledge	1	1	0	0	0	1	0	0
HALT instruction	0	1	0	1	0	0	0	1
Interrupt acknowledge and HALT instruction	1	1	0	1	0	1	0	0

The 8085 shown in Fig. 1.18 takes a different approach to putting more than 40 different functions onto 40 pins. Here we see address and data on shared signal lines and status signals on dedicated pins. In contrast, the 8080 dedicates pins to address signals, and shares status with data. In the case of the 8085, there are 16 lines total for address and data. Eight of the lines are multiplexed between the low byte of address and the data lines. Signal ALE (address latch enable), when asserted indicates the presence of an address on those lines, and otherwise signifies that they hold data. The DMA lines HOLD and HOLDA are dedicated to specific pins, as are the interrupt lines INTR (interrupt request) and INTA L (interrupt acknowledge). The 8085 has four other lines for interrupt requests that have a variety of characteristics. These are the lines labeled RST 5.5 (RESTART 5.5), RST 6.5, RST 7.5, and TRAP. All interrupts vector to distinct locations in memory, and all except TRAP are maskable. RST denotes a RESTART instruction that is executed when any RST interrupt is honored. This is essentially a subroutine call to a different address for each different type of RST. INTR is compatible with the 8080 INTR signal, and does not force the processor to any specific location when the request is honored. The external device must sense the INTA condition and force a RESTART instruction onto the bus to supply the starting address of an interrupt program. TRAP is simply a nonmaskable interrupt that vectors to a specific location. There is a priority ordering among the interrupts to resolve what to do when two or more different types of interrupt requests are raised.

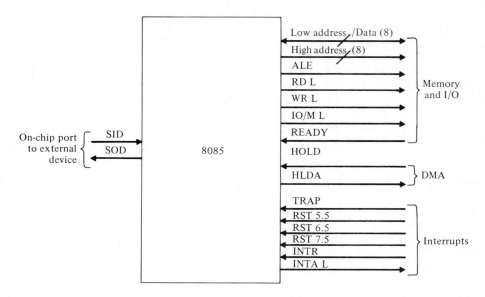

FIGURE 1.18   Interconnections for the 8085.

The sharing of memory and I/O functions is controlled by the lines labeled IO/M L, RD L, WR L, and READY. The IO/M L signal line distinguishes between port functions and memory functions, while RD L and WR L are, respectively, the READ and WRITE signals. (If neither is asserted, the state of the system is IDLE.) READY is a processor input that is used by slow devices and memory, and that forces the processor to use an integral number of extra cycles while waiting for READY to be asserted after initiating an operation. The 8085 differs slightly from the 8080 in the implementation of slow devices in that the 8085 does not produce a WAIT signal when it is delayed by an asserted READY signal.

One final aspect of the 8085 is worth citing here. Note the lines SID and SOD, which respectively carry serial-input data and serial-output data. The 8085 has a built-in I/O port for serial data, and these two lines interface with that port. Hence in this regard the 8085's serial lines fit the structure of the I/O lines with a direct path to the processor as shown in Fig. 1.1(b), except that the port is internal to the processor rather than external to it as shown in the figure.

Another descendent of the 8080, the Zilog Z80, is shown in Fig. 1.19. In some respects the Z80 functional characteristics are like the 6800. Note the separate address and data lines. Note also the INT L and NMI L lines and the absence of a dedicated interrupt acknowledge line. The DMA control lines are BUSRQ L for the HALT function and BUSAK L for the HALT ACKNOWLEDGE function. All of these signals follow the general structure of the 6800 signals. The memory interface, however, follows that of the 8080/8085 family. To distinguish between memory and I/O requests, the lines labeled

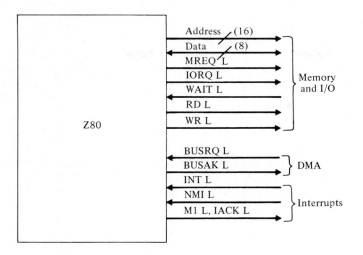

FIGURE 1.19   The Z80 interface signals.

MREQ L (memory request) and IORQ L (I/O request) are asserted by the processor. RD L and WR L indicate READ and WRITE functions, respectively, whereas WAIT L is a signal generated externally by slow devices to lengthen memory cycles by an integral number of clocks.

The interrupt-signal structure of the Z80 is similar to the 8080 family in that the Z80 has a means of acknowledging an interrupt request through signal lines other than those that are part of the memory interface. The Z80 uses a line labeled M1 L/IACK L for two distinct purposes. When this line and IORQ L are asserted low simultaneously, the processor is signaling an interrupt acknowledge. Otherwise, when M1 L is asserted low, the processor is signaling that it is in the first machine cycle (the instruction-fetch) cycle of an instruction. Because the interrupt-acknowledge function does not make use of the memory bus, the Z80 can use this bus for a response back from the port to identify the port and then use the port ID to vector the processor to a particular I/O program. The Z80 has three different modes that have this capability in conjunction with interrupt requests. They are

1. No vectoring. (Invoking an interrupt handler at a specific address.)
2. 8080-compatible. (Accepting a RESTART (RST) instruction from the port in response to IACK to force the processor to one of eight possible addresses.)
3. Expanded vector. (Accepting a 7-bit port code that, when added to a base address of an interrupt-vector table, selects one of 128 possible entry points.)

Moving into the so-called 16-bit processor family reveals the same functions but more severe pin constraints. These processors have 16 bits of data, and normally have a means for generating addresses of 20 to 24 bits. It is very difficult to fit all of these functions into 40 pins, and therefore many advanced processors have 48 to 64 pins. The 8086 shown in Fig. 1.20 squeezes all of its functions into only 40 pins. To do so, it has two modes of operation. A "minimum" mode uses the available pins for single-processor configuration functions. In this mode several control signals are developed on individual pins. In "maximum" mode, the pins are redefined to perform functions useful for multiprocessor configurations. In order to increase the number of control signals, functions that are assigned individual pins in minimum mode are grouped together and produced by a smaller set of pins in an encoded fashion. One input pin, the MN/MX L pin, forces the 8086 into either minimum or maximum mode. Figure 1.20 shows the processor configuration for minimum mode, which corresponds to the discussion in this chapter. (Functions available in maximum mode relate to multiprocessor control functions, and are not treated in this textbook.)

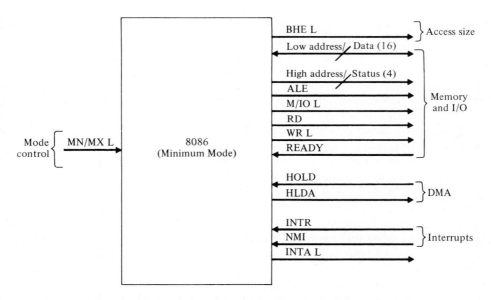

FIGURE 1.20   The interface signals of the 8086 in minimum mode.

Even in minimum mode, the 16 data lines and 20 address lines are too numerous to be assigned separate pins. Hence, the 8086 multiplexes the 16 data bits with the 16 low-address bits. The address-latch enable line (ALE) indicates whether the address/data lines carry an address or a datum.

Interrupt request lines are INTR and NMI, and the INTA L control line indicates an interrupt acknowledge. The NMI interrupt is nonmaskable, whereas INTR is a maskable request line. An NMI request transfers control to a unique specific address and is typically asserted by at most one device. If more than one device is able to make NMI requests, the processor then polls an external resolver to identify the requester. INTR requests are fully vectored. The highest-priority interrupting port returns a single-byte ID in response to the INTA L signal produced by the processor. External logic is required to select the highest-priority port, but the logic is not very complex. The processor then uses the port ID to calculate an offset in an interrupt vector table, and retrieves the starting address of the interrupt program for that port.

Memory interface signals follow the general conventions for the 8080/8085/Z80 family. M/IO L distinguishes between memory and I/O functions on the address/data lines. RD and WR L are the READ and WRITE functions, respectively. READY is an input from slow memory or devices that lengthen the transaction by an integral number of clock cycles. The 8086, like the 8085 and Z80, does not produce a WAIT output on a status line. This particular information has turned out to be superfluous, and is unlikely to show up again in later generations of the 8080 family. The DMA interface is HOLD for a HALT request and HLDA for a HALT ACKNOWLEDGE. Four other lines are multiplexed to hold the four most significant bits of a 20-bit address or 4 additional status bits whose function describes the type of memory access.

Because the 8086 supports both 8-bit and 16-bit accesses, it must distinguish among the two types of access in the memory interface. This is done through the BHE L (high-byte enable) signal. When used in conjunction with the least significant address line, this control bit can facilitate access to 16-bit data that lies either on even-address or odd-address boundaries, as well as access to a single byte instead of a full word. The idea is that memory is organized into two banks of 8-bit bytes, one bank for even byte-addresses and the other for odd byte-addresses. For access to 16-bit words, both banks are active. For access to single bytes, only one of the two banks is active. BHE L plays the role of the select line for the odd-address bank, and A0 L has the same role for the even-address bank. To access a full word on an even-address boundary, both BHE L and A0 L are asserted. Both banks respond. To access a single byte in either bank, the corresponding select signal is asserted. When a full word lies on an odd-boundary, two cycles are required, since the data on the address lines A1 through A19 are different for the two bytes that make up the word. In this case, the 8086 accesses the bytes sequentially, first the byte at the odd-address, then the byte at the next higher even-address. Thus BHE L is used to facilitate both boundary crossing and the SIZE function mentioned earlier in this chapter.

HISTORY AND BACKGROUND READING

Noyce and Hoff (1981) trace the historical development of microprocessors in an interesting discussion of the evolution of the industry. Hoff is recognized as the inventor of the first microprocessor, the Intel 4004, which was first developed in 1969-1970 and marketed in 1971. The idea of putting together a complete processor on a chip had been in many people's heads all through the 1960s as the semiconductor industry produced chips of ever greater complexity. Calculator chips produced in the late 1960s were gradually gaining in capability and led toward the evolution to microprocessors. Hoff's project, in fact, came as a direct result of an effort to build low-cost, high-performance calculators for Busicom, a Japanese firm that has since folded operations. The key idea in Hoff's approach was to use a general-purpose processor with RAM and ROM to implement the calculator functions instead of using the highly specialized functional chips with a shift-register memory that was the more conventional approach. Hoff also pushed chip-design technology by using chips with roughly 2000 transistors, which was about four times the density of more conventional calculator chips. Hoff's design team demonstrated that a general-purpose 4-bit processor was more cost-effective than the conventional design. But even more important was the fact that the 4004 was inherently a general-purpose device that could find use in many applications. These broad applications promised high-production volumes that translated into low unit cost. We know today how correct that reasoning was. The microprocessors and peripheral support chips in high-volume production today typically cost just a few dollars.

The 4004 did not last the decade. It indeed was revolutionary, but once the microprocessor concept was proved to be sound, major development efforts quickly led to the superior processors that supplanted the 4004. In 1972, less than one year after the public introduction of the 4004, Intel produced the 8008, an 8-bit processor that was far more powerful than the 4-bit 4004. At first the public reaction to microprocessors was slow. A new idea has to be significant to overcome the resistance to changing present design and production methods. Within a year or two of the introduction of the 8008 microprocessor, most industries had discovered the power of the microprocessor and were planning new products based on these devices. The 8080's appearance in 1974 had a significant impact on showing what can be done with microprocessor technology. The microprocessor revolution had begun. By 1980, more than 100 different microprocessors had been produced, and sales had reached annual rates of tens of millions of units.

With the technology growing so fast, it becomes an almost impossible job to keep pace with new offerings of processors, memories, and peripherals. The best sources of information are the manufacturers themselves. Major U.S. microprocessor manufacturers (in alphabetical order) include Advanced Micro Devices (AMD), American Microsystems (AMI), Commodore Semiconductor, Fairchild, General Instrument, Harris, Intel, Intersil, Mostek, Motorola, National, RCA, Rockwell, Signetics, Texas Instruments, and Zilog. (This list omits companies such as DEC, HP, and IBM that use their production internally and do not generally market chips to the public.) Osborne and Kane (1978, Vol. 2 and Vol. 3) maintain an extensive and reasonably current collection of material on microprocessors and peripherals chips. These volumes maintain extensive practical information concerning particular chips in addition to the manufacturers' original specification sheets.

Textbooks on microprocessors began to appear *en masse* in the mid-1970s with the growing popularity of the 8080. Microprocessor texts tend to fit into four major areas — logic design, systems design, software, and interfacing. Among the texts that are oriented more strongly to hardware are Doty (1979); Johnson, *et al.* (1979); Fletcher (1980); Givone and Roesser (1980); and Wiatrowski and House (1980). These texts show methods of logic design based on microprocessor technology. A somewhat different approach is taken by the systems-design texts, which generally describe microprocessors in some detail, and show how to use their capabilities in practical systems. These texts tend to put more emphasis on programming and less emphasis on logic design than do the logic-design texts. Among the texts that have appeared in this area are Barna and Porat (1976), Hilburn and Julich (1976), Soucek (1976), Klingman (1977), Peatman (1977), Leventhal (1978), Kraft and Toy (1979), and Krutz (1980). Peatman, Kraft and Toy, and Krutz make particularly good background reading for studying this textbook. Ogdin (1980) and Wakerly (1981) treat programming microprocessors. Wakerly is quite effective in shedding light on the key ideas in programming, while covering an extremely broad spectrum of machines. Interfacing microprocessors has only recently emerged as the principal topic of texts. Two notable texts in this area are Artwick (1980) and Lipovski (1980).

2 / SHIELDING, GROUNDING, AND TRANSMISSION-LINE TECHNIQUES

In the vast majority of microcomputer applications, the microprocessor serves as an ''intelligent'' controller in addition to any other functions it performs. As a controller, the micro senses the activity taking place around it and issues signals periodically to alter the external activity. Micros in automobiles, video terminals, communications links, for example, are almost completely dedicated to a control function. In the automobile, the micro positions mechanical actuators that govern air/fuel mixture and other critical parameters of the internal-combustion engine. In the video terminal, the micro alters no physical or mechanical devices but rather manages a reasonably complex, real-time I/O system that includes at least a keyboard, video display, and serial data link. In communications systems, the control function includes message storing and forwarding, error detection and recovery, and routing-table maintenance. Word processors and small-business systems use the microcomputer for substantially more than the control function, in that the text manipulation and financial record-management computations that characterize these systems are strongly computational rather than control in nature. Nevertheless, the control function is present, and the ability to connect the microcomputer to external peripherals such as printer, disk, and communications link is a critical ingredient in the system's effectiveness.

With the microprocessor almost universally operating as a controller of external devices, there is an inherent need to understand how to interconnect a microcomputer to other system components. This chapter treats the interconnection problem at the electrical level where we see what is necessary for reliable and safe interconnection. Chapter 1 gives a view of the interfaces between the micro and memory and I/O ports in terms of the information that flows across the interfaces. That information has to be converted into a physical form such as voltage, current, or light when it is transported from one module to another. This chapter treats these electrical aspects of the interconnections. The next chapter deals with timing and logical control of the signals on the interconnections.

The electrical issues raised in this chapter are quite real and extremely important. Interfacing is so challenging in its nonelectrical aspects that we would much prefer to ignore the electrical problems if only we could. Ideally we wish to connect points A and B on the microcomputer with points C and D on a peripheral device, knowing that the voltages are compatible, and then to ignore all other electrical aspects of this connection. But the underlying physical laws that dictate what happens over this connection can work against us. When connections that look deceptively simple are made improperly, the connections can introduce excessive noise, lower reliability, and serious hazards. Certain techniques for interconnections have evolved over the years, giving the system designer a wealth of sound ways for implementing interconnections. Standards exist for some important types of interconnections so that at least in these instances, the designer can freely connect components, following the rules of the standard, with relative assurance that the system will function safely and reliably. But even with standard interconnections, unskilled designers can and do make mistakes that negate the value of the standard.

This chapter provides the essential background in the physical principles from which all methods of interconnection evolve. In the latter part of the chapter we look at some basic techniques in current use to illustrate the principles.

2.1 GROUNDING AND SHIELDING

Interconnections are a major of source of noise in a computer system. Typically, interconnections are made through cables or backplanes whose lengths run from roughly 10 cm to 10 m. When cabling is done improperly, electrical noise from motors, electrical storms, or from nearby electronic equipment can easily couple into the cabling where it is then indistinguishable from data and control signals. Electronic transmission on interconnecting cables, especially on long cables, simply does not behave the same as transmission on short interconnections. The basic physical principles are the same for both short and long wires, but many effects are not noticeable on short interconnections, so these connections can be made in the most straightforward possible manner with little risk. The differences in behavior are second-order effects that are essentially indiscernible on short conductors. It is very tempting to ignore these effects for long interconnections as well, but if one does one finds that the effects are quite visible and that they can severely upset the integrity of the interconnections if the interface fails to deal with the effects properly.

As an example of one such situation, consider the interconnection of two chassis, each of which has a separate connection to ground, as shown in Fig. 2.1. The ground point shown in the figure is the electrical ground on the AC distribution system. (This ground is accessible through the large round prong of 3-prong AC connectors required for grounded equipment by the electrical code in the United States.) The signal ground within each of the two chassis is connected to the chassis, and each chassis is connected to the electrical ground of the AC system through the ground prong of the AC connector. If the two chassis are located in the same cabinet or are in close physical proximity, then it is possible to make a safe electrical connection between the chassis ground points on the two chassis. This is shown in Fig. 2.1(a), and is common practice for chassis that are mounted in the same equipment rack. When all of the assumptions on physical proximity are met, the two chassis are at the same potential, so that no current flows through the conductor that interconnects the two chassis ground points. (Actually, the potentials of the chassis could vary a little, and a small current might flow through the conductor equalizing the potentials.)

Fig. 2.1(b) shows a situation in which the chassis are separated by a large physical distance. The ground points in the figure are grounds on different AC connectors. Even when the connectors lie in the same room, if the AC connectors are controlled by different circuit breakers, the ground conductors may be totally separate and distinct conductors whose only point in common is the connection point at the power entrance of the building. If the two chassis lie in two different buildings, the grounds are not connected directly together by a conductor, but rather are each individually connected to an earth connection in their respective buildings, and the earth provides a path for electrical flow between the grounds. In this instance the ground potentials to which the chassis are attached may differ by several volts.

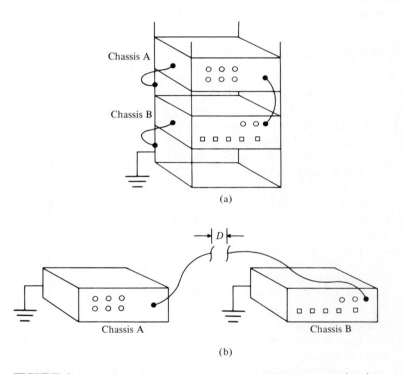

(a)

(b)

FIGURE 2.1   (a) Two chassis grounded together; (b) two remote chassis, separately grounded with large distance D.

Note that a complete loop exists for ground currents with the loop running from the grounding point for Chassis A, through Chassis A to Chassis B, then to B's grounding point, and from there back to the ground point for A. If cables carrying alternating current thread this loop, then the changing field produced by such cables induces a potential across the ends of the loop (between the two grounding points), and a current will flow in the loop. Since the impedance of the loop is rather low, a few volts potential difference can produce several amperes of current, which could do severe damage to electrical components rated for lower currents. Worse yet, electrical storms could momentarily cause very large potential differences while supplying the charged particles that make a massive current flow possible. Under such circumstances the current flow can be sufficiently high to burn cables and destroy electrical interfaces. So although the ground-to-ground connection in Fig. 2.1(a) is safe, the one in Fig. 2.1(b) is not, and violates electrical codes. Even the safe ground-to-ground connection may be inadvisable in cases where the resulting ground loop provides a means for coupling noise onto signal lines.

The ground-to-ground connection in Fig. 2.1(a) creates a ground loop in this system just as the same connection creates a ground loop in Fig. 2.1(b). The difference is that close physical proximity in Fig. 2.1(a) guarantees that the ground loop is not threaded by large numbers of power cables, nor is this loop likely to be threaded by a lightning strike. But it is likely to be threaded by the equipment power cords and signal conductors in the interface cabling, each of which induces a small residual current flow around the ground loop. This flow creates a small voltage difference between the grounds in the two chassis that shows up as a noise voltage, which could be mistaken for signal voltage.

This example makes the point that one should not arbitrarily connect equipment grounds together. Our intuition tells us that all ground points are at the same potential. In reality, ground potentials are not equal because current flow in the ground conductors causes small voltage potentials to develop from one ground point to another. When we confine our design efforts to one printed-circuit board and take precautions to use extra-wide conductors for power distribution, to a certain extent our intuition that all ground conductors are at the same potential is acceptable. Even though the intuition is incorrect, potential differences may be sufficiently small to be ignored.

The situation is drastically different from a system-wide viewpoint. Potential differences in grounds from printed-circuit board to printed-circuit board can instantaneously exceed logic threshold. From chassis to chassis, improper cabling can lead to ground potential differences that have the shape of short signal pulses. They can and do lead to false triggering of logic gates, and in some cases can set up spurious, stable oscillations.

The remainder of this section looks at the problem of grounds and shows basic shielding and grounding techniques for minimizing noise coupled into computers.

Shielding Techniques

Electrical devices, particularly computer devices are sources of electrical radiation. Computers have internal oscillators that run anywhere from less than 1 MHz to over 20 MHz; terminals have horizontal oscillators that operate at about 16 kHz and dot oscillators that operate up to 20 MHz or more. (The function of these oscillators is explained in more detail later in this textbook in the chapter on CRT controllers.) AM radios act as small transmitters at their internal oscillator frequency of 455 kHz, while FM radios transmit at their internal frequency of 10.7 MHz. The office, factory, and home have dozens of devices that potentially pollute the electromagnetic spectrum with noise. (New regulations in effect in the United States severely limit the interference that can be emitted by an electronic device. These regulations apply to items sold after January 1, 1981, but we must still contend with the millions of polluters in place on that date.) Devices sold today that meet the new regulations, nevertheless, generate electrical noise internally. They meet the regulations through shielding and filtering that severely limit escaping radiation. Inside these systems there is still substantial extraneous noise that can disrupt computation.

In any case, computers are susceptible to electronic interference, particularly to interference pickup on interconnecting cables. The interference can originate from low frequency AC power lines, from equipment that fails to meet present radiation statutes, or from noise sources in the interior of equipment that conforms to the radiation statutes. Regardless of the source of the noise, there are basic rules that dictate how to shield, ground, and cable to minimize the noise coupling.

The most common and preferred way to reduce noise is to shield the equipment as shown in Fig. 2.2. If a shield entirely encloses the volume it surrounds, then external noise sources cannot alter the relative potentials of the conductors inside the shield. External noise sources can only raise or lower the potential of the shield and of all elements within the shield. External noise cannot raise one internal point more than another. Since the devices operate on potential *differences*, and external noise produces no such differences within the shield, the noise is effectively decoupled from the shielded electronics. The physical reasoning for this property is rather simple to understand from an intuitive point of view. We use a physical analogy to show the underlying principle.

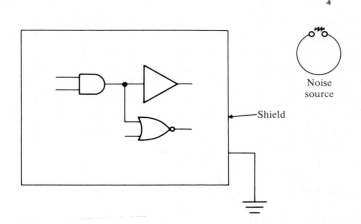

FIGURE 2.2 A shield around a circuit prevents external noise sources from influencing components within the shield.

Suppose for a moment that the shield is charged to a potential of 1 V with respect to some ground point. What is the effect on the conductors inside the shield of this increase in potential? A physical analog for potential is the height of a stretched membrane, where the membrane is firmly fixed on its boundary at heights that correspond to boundary potentials. Figure 2.3 illustrates a stretched membrane that gives the potential everywhere inside a square whose sides are fixed at potentials of 0 V and 1 V. The stretched membrane analogy holds because the shape of the membrane and the voltage potential over the square area both satisfy Poisson's equation,

$$\frac{\partial^2 V}{\partial x^2} + \frac{\partial^2 V}{\partial y^2} = 0,$$

which holds for potential when there is no electrical charge in the interior of the square region. When the region contains electrical charge, the zero on the right-hand side of the equation is replaced by the charge density as a function of x and y. In the equation, the variable V is a function of the coordinates x and y, and the equation constrains the sum of the second partial derivatives with respect to these variables. Since the equation holds for both problems, and the height of the membrane in one problem is analogous to electrical potential in the other, we can visualize the potential by looking at the height of the stretched membrane.

Now consider a shield for a two-dimensional circuit like the one in Fig. 2.2. The stretched membrane analogy indicates that when the shield is raised by 1 V, then the potential everywhere inside the shield is raised by 1 V. (When we stretch a membrane over a frame, all of whose edges lie in a horizontal plane, the membrane will lie entirely in that same plane.) Since Poisson's equation is linear, if we raise the shield by k V, then the influence in the shield is k times the influence of a 1 V shield potential. Circuits within the shield respond to potential differences, but the shield raises all points by the same potential. Therefore external charges create no potential differences within the shield, and the net effect of the shield is to eliminate the influence of outside noise sources.

Although this argument is for two-dimensional shields, the same behavior holds true in three-dimensions. That is, a three-dimensional shield that completely surrounds a volume prevents external charges from influencing the interior of the volume.

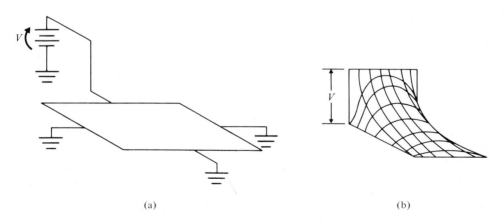

(a)   (b)

FIGURE 2.3   (a) Rigid frame with one edge charge to V volts; (b) stretched membrane with height equal to potential at corresponding points within the frame.

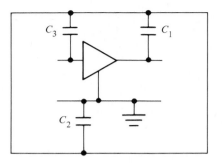

FIGURE 2.4   An amplifier within a shield.

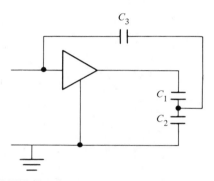

FIGURE 2.5   Equivalent circuit for amplifier inside a shield.

   While the shield has the desirable effect of eliminating contributions due to external noise, it has undesirable effects that we must take into consideration. We briefly review the problems created by the shield, and illustrate how to resolve them. The interested reader should consult the much more detailed and thorough discussion of this topic in Ott (1976) and Morrison (1977).

   Figure 2.4 shows an amplifier within a shield, with the shield capacitance to the input, output, and ground points of the amplifier illustrated symbolically as individual capacitors. These capacitances typically measure a few picofarads up to a few hundred picofarads, depending on the size of the shield and its proximity to the input, output, and ground lines. The equivalent circuit for this amplifier is shown in Fig. 2.5. Note that the capacitors between the output and the shield and between the ground and the shield form a load impedance for the amplifier, with the two impedances in series. The shield is at the midpoint of the series impedance, and thus reaches a voltage of $V_{OUT}Z_2/(Z_1+Z_2)$, where Z_1 and Z_2 are the respective impedances of capacitances C_1 and C_2. This voltage is in turn fed back to the input of the amplifier through capacitance C_3. If the input impedance of the amplifier is very high, we can assume that no current flows through C_3 into the am-

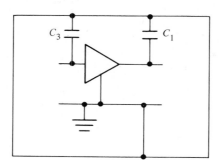

FIGURE 2.6 Proper grounding of the shield eliminates the feedback path through stray capacitance.

plifier, although there may be current flow through C_3 between the output stage of the amplifier and the output stage of the voltage source that feeds the amplifier. The effect of the feedback is to attenuate the gain of the amplifier at high frequencies, which is a highly undesirable side effect of the shielding. To eliminate this side effect, we must break the feedback path. We simply ground the shield as shown in Fig. 2.6, and the feedback is disconnected. This illustrates the first of two fundamental rules on proper grounding and shielding stressed by Morrison (1977):

> *Rule 1:* The shield of an electronic circuit must be connected to the signal ground of that circuit in order to reduce or eliminate the feedback effects induced by the shield.

If all ground points were at the same potential, the first rule would tell us all we need to know. But we realize now that ground is not well-defined. Should we choose a ground point near the amplifier input? Should it be near the amplifier output? Or should the ground point be somewhere else, distant from the amplifier? These questions are settled by Rule 2 below.

To develop the reasoning for Rule 2, note in Fig. 2.7(a) a situation in which a signal generated in Chassis A is passed to an amplifier in Chassis B. The two chassis are connected together electrically through the shield. Within the shield between the two chassis is a cable that carries both the signal wire and the ground reference point. This system has a single point at which the input signal zero-reference point is tied to a ground reference, and also a single point at which the shield is connected to the signal zero-reference point.

Consider what happens when those two connections are made in different chassis as shown in Fig. 2.7(a). In this case the zero-reference point for the signal is tied to ground in Chassis A and to the shield in Chassis B. We have now created a ground loop in that there is an electrical path from the Chassis A earth connection, through the ground-reference wire to Chassis B, and from there to the shield connection. From this point the loop is coupled capacitively to Chassis B earth ground, and from there through the earth to Chassis A. Although the path is not closed with respect to DC current flow, it is closed with respect to AC noise currents. We noted earlier that a closed loop is susceptible to noise pickup due to changing flux from wires that thread the loop. In Fig. 2.7 we show a noise source between the two earth connections that represents the effects of noise from grounds at two different potentials. The ground voltage induces a current flow through the loop, and the current flow on the ground-reference line causes a voltage drop on that line. With current flowing on the ground-reference line, the voltage measured at the amplifier input is not identical to the voltage as measured in Chassis A. The discrepancy is the voltage drop in the ground-reference line due to noise, and the noise is coupled into the amplifier.

To create a faithful replica of the signal current at the amplifier input, we have to eliminate insofar as possible the current flowing in the ground-reference line. The connection shown in Fig. 2.7(b) exhibits one such way of achieving the goal. By attaching the shield to ground at the reference point of the input signal, the ground-reference line between the chassis no longer participates in a ground loop, and thus current cannot flow in this line. Current does flow in the shield, however, but this is not coupled into the amplifier. So the key idea in Fig. 2.7 is to ground the shield in a manner that prevents ground loop currents in ground-reference lines. The reference line cannot be an accurate reference if there is a noise voltage drop on the line. We break the ground loop by choosing the shield grounding point according to Morrison's second rule:

Rule 2: The shield should be connected to earth ground at the zero-voltage reference point for the input signal.

Although Fig. 2.7(b) shows this connection made in Chassis A, it is equally permissible to make both connections in Chassis B. When made in this manner, the zero-signal reference for the input signal is not in the same chassis as the input source, but this is acceptable if no noise current flows in the reference line. In fact, the noise currents flow through the shield between chassis and not through the ground leg of the input circuit.

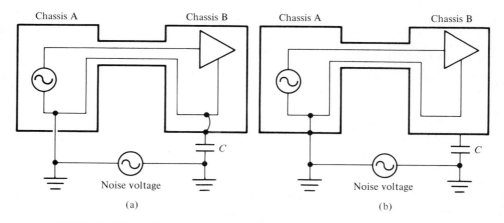

FIGURE 2.7 (a) Improper grounding of shield; (b) proper grounding of shield.

Rules 1 and 2 provide the necessary guidance to show what to do, as a general rule, with shields. There are, however, situations that arise in which one cannot connect all shields to some common reference line because the interconnected devices may be at substantially different potentials. We modify our findings somewhat for such situations as indicated in the next subsection.

Balanced Interconnections

Figure 2.8 shows two chassis connected directly together through the shield on the interconnection cable. Our earlier discussion stated that we cannot arbitrarily ground two chassis together. What if these devices are several hundred meters apart? We are in serious trouble if we use the connection in Figure 2.8 when the chassis are in two different buildings and thus are connected to earth through two separate ground points. Although the noise voltage is effectively coupled out of the amplifier circuit, the current transients on the shield could be enormous, especially during an electrical storm. We may discover that the ground current is large enough to burn or otherwise damage the equipment. How can we avoid the ground loop in the shield in those situations when a direct ground-to-ground connection is hazardous?

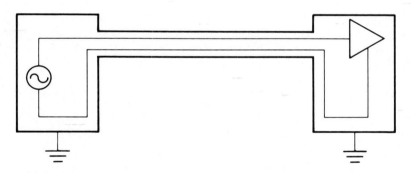

FIGURE 2.8   A signal transmitted from one chassis to another. The distance is so great that the shields cannot be safely connected. The connection shown is improper.

Today's technology provides several possible solutions. Among those possible are

1. Fiber optic link.
2. Optical isolator.
3. Balanced (double-ended) electrical connection.

The two optical methods use different optical technology. Fiber optic links, Method 1, use modulated light transmitted on optical fibers to transmit information. The optical isolator of Method 2 is a single integrated device that contains both a light-emitting diode and a light-sensitive transistor. When this type of device is used for driving interconnection cables, the signals are sent electrically between chassis, and the electrical isolation is achieved by the optical isolator at one or both cable endpoints. The third method is one that uses twisted-pair conductors for electrical signaling, with care taken to make connections such that external noise has minimum influence. For purposes of electrical isolation, the first two methods are superior to the third because the optical coupling eliminates all direct connections between chassis. However, at this writing, fiber optic links are in the early stages of commercial availability, and are rather more expensive than twisted-pair wire connections. (The relative costs could change in the future.) Optical isolators are reasonable in cost, but generally have lower maximum transmission rates than twisted-pair interconnections. So for the immediate future, the twisted pair is the most attractive interconnection for cabling over distances measured in hundreds of meters. When fiber optic connections become less expensive or optical isolators attain higher bandwidths, the electrical interconnection of the twisted pair will be much less attractive.

To make a direct connection between chassis with a twisted pair of conductors, we must use balanced drivers and receivers shown in Fig. 2.9. The balanced driver has two outputs, one of which is high and the other of which is low at any given time. Drivers are constructed so that transitions on the two outputs occur simultaneously, or as nearly simultaneously as technology permits. Transition delays may differ by at most a few nanoseconds in typical devices. The balanced receiver is a comparator whose output is high or low depending on which of the two inputs is at a higher potential. The receiver has a very large input impedance to ground on both of its inputs, and the impedances to ground are equal or nearly equal. We can represent the receiver as shown in Fig. 2.9(c) as an ideal differential amplifier with two load resistors to ground.

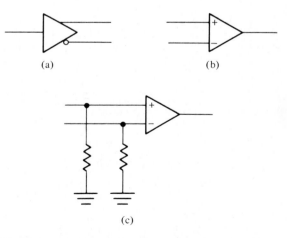

FIGURE 2.9   (a) A balanced driver; (b) a balanced receiver; (c) the balanced receiver with input impedance to ground.

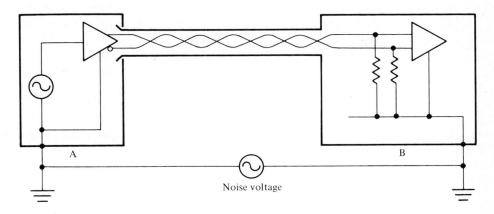

Noise voltage

FIGURE 2.10   Proper interconnection using balanced driver and receiver. The transmission lines should be a twisted pair.

The proper interconnection of the driver to receiver appears in Fig. 2.10. The shields of the two chassis are isolated electrically. When the two earth connections are at the same potential, the current that flows through the interconnecting cable is limited by the high input impedance to ground. Because the driver and receiver are balanced, both legs of the cable have identical source impedances and load impedances. Current flow due to signal potentials should be essentially zero or very low because of the high input impedance. Hence the voltage produced at the output of the driver is equal to the voltage impressed on the input of the receiver, since there is no voltage drop in the cable.

If the earth connections of the two chassis differ in potential, the voltage difference causes a current flow in the loop that connects the two systems together. This is the loop that runs from the earth connection on System A, through to the ground reference point on the driver in A, through the twisted pair interconnection to the receiver, and from there through the load resistors to ground, then to the earth point of B, and from there back to the earth point of A. The important points about this noise voltage are that it raises the voltage in both conductors in the twisted pair equally, and that in the two lines the incremental current flows due to this noise voltage are equal. The current flows are determined by the large load resistors, which are equal in the balanced receiver. Hence, with equal currents flowing in the two conductors, the conductors' voltage drops that are caused by noise will be equal, and the voltages impressed at the receiver input pins will each be reduced by the same amount, namely by the drop in the cables due to the noise voltage. Note that the receiver inputs carry voltages equal to $s(t) - n(t)$ and $-s(t) - n(t)$, respectively. The ideal receiver responds to the difference signal only, which is $2s(t)$, and rejects the noise voltage. Real receivers amplify common-mode voltages as well as differential-mode voltages, but the common-mode gain is many hundreds of times less than the differential-mode gain. In this case the common-mode voltage is the average of the two input signals, which is $-n(t)$. Receivers with very high common-mode rejection

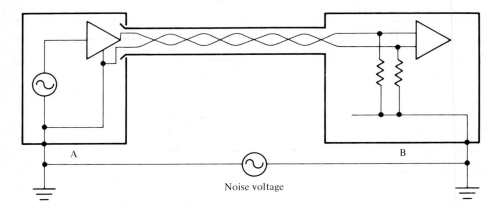

FIGURE 2.11   Proper interconnection using unbalanced driver. The transmission lines should be a twisted pair.

can eliminate the noise voltage completely from digital signals, unless the noise voltage is so large that it lies in an input region for which receiver common-mode rejection is ineffective.

The key idea in the use of balanced interconnections is to accept the noise voltage because it is unavoidable, but to develop noise voltage equally on two different lines while signal voltages are transmitted unequally on these lines. The receiver then uses the noise voltage on one line to nullify the voltage on the other line, effectively subtracting out the noise contribution. In the absence of balanced drivers, it is still possible to adapt this same idea to conventional single-ended drivers as shown in Fig. 2.11. Here the ground point on the driver amplifier is brought across with the single signal line, but the ground is not connected to ground at Chassis B. Rather the ground is used as a reference signal in the differential receiver, as in Fig. 2.10, so that the effects of noise voltages can be subtracted from the signal voltages. In this case the signal lead carries $s(t) - n(t)$ while the ground lead carries $-n(t)$. Hence the differential-mode voltage is $s(t)$ and the common-mode voltage is $[s(t)/2] - n(t)$. The threshold for the receiver should be set halfway between high and low signals, because this is the excursion range of the signal line with respect to ground. In Fig. 2.10, the balanced receiver should have a zero threshold since the difference signals will be positive or negative in value, depending on the data transmitted. The balanced line of Fig. 2.10 is preferred to the unbalanced line because it has higher noise immunity (double the noise-voltage threshold).

2.2 TRANSMISSION-LINE TECHNIQUES

Designers of low-speed electronic circuits normally make the simplifying assumptions that signal propagation over conductors is instantaneous (or nearly instantaneous), and that the received signal is a faithful replica of the transmitted signal. In high-speed circuits, transmission-line effects tend to distort signals on paths that are long compared to the wavelength of the signals propagating on the paths. At 100 MHz, wires only a few centimeters long show nonnegligible transmission-line effects. For 50 to 60 Hz, the effects are unnoticeable in ordinary wiring, but become visible on power transmission lines that run a few hundred kilometers. Transmission-line considerations can generally be ignored in the design of logic circuits that have clock rates from 1 to 10 MHz for paths confined to one printed-circuit board, but there are noticeable transmission-line effects where signals are bused from board to board, and severe effects where signals move from chassis to chassis. Very high-speed equipment that runs with clock rates from 50 MHz to 100 MHz must normally treat even those signal lines confined to one circuit board as transmission lines, except possibly for very short lines. This is particularly true for the high-speed nonsaturating logic families known as ECL (emitter-coupled logic) and CML (current-mode logic). The remainder of this section investigates these effects, and illustrates how to minimize signaling problems due to the effects.

Point-to-Point Transmission

To start this discussion, consider the transmission line shown in Fig. 2.12, in which a voltage is impressed on a line, and transmitted down that line to a load impedance Z_L. From electromagnetic theory, we know that the signal propagates along the transmission line at the speed of light. Both voltage and current propagate together down the line. The transmission line acts as a network of distributed inductance and capacitance as shown in Fig. 2.13 in carrying the propagated signal. When the wave propagation equations are solved, we find that everywhere on the line

$$V_0 = I_0 Z_0,$$

where V_0 is the propagated voltage, I_0 is the propagated current, and Z_0 is the wave impedance of the line, which is a function solely of the inductance L and the conductor-to-conductor capacitance C of the line where both L and C are measured per unit length. Specifically,

$$Z_0 = \sqrt{\frac{L}{C}}.$$

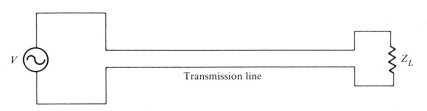

FIGURE 2.12   A transmission line and load impedance.

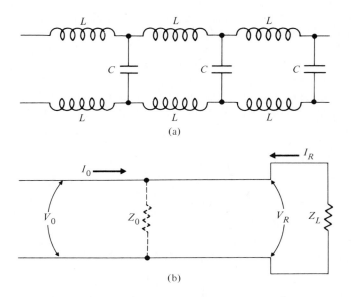

FIGURE 2.13   (a) The equivalent circuit for a transmission line;
(b) direct and reflected voltages and currents in line with
impedance Z_0 and load impedance Z_L.

At the far end of the line, the propagating voltage and current meet the load resistance
Z_L. At this point, as at every other point in the line, Ohm's law must be satisfied, but we
cannot satisfy it with V_0 and I_0 alone because, in general, V_0/I_0 is not equal to Z_L since
this ratio must equal Z_0. Ohm's law requires a reflected wave to appear at the far end of
the line and to propagate toward the source end. The initial voltage and current of the reflected wave are such that the direct and reflected wave together satisfy Ohm's law at the
load resistance. In a sense, the reflected wave is launched by the arrival of the direct
wave, with the mismatch of the load impedance determining the initial state of the reflected wave. The reflected wave, like the direct wave, satisfies the wave equation in the
transmission line. Hence, for the reflected wave we have

$$V_R = I_R Z_0.$$

To develop an equation that describes the state of affairs at the load end, we use the sign
conventions shown in Fig. 2.13 where we see that the reflected voltage and direct voltage
are additive at the load, but the reflected current is in the opposite direction of the direct
current. Consequently, at the load we have

$$V_0 + V_R = Z_L(I_0 - I_R).$$

This gives three equations in the four variables V_0, V_R, I_0, and I_R. Given any one variable, we can solve for the other three. By eliminating I_0 and I_R, we can solve for the ratio

V_R/V_0, which is known as the *reflection coefficient*. With some simple algebraic manipulation we find

$$\frac{V_R}{V_0} = \frac{Z_L - Z_0}{Z_L + Z_0}.$$

The reflection coefficient tells us the magnitude of the reflected wave as a function of the voltage impressed on the line. Note that the reflected wave is not larger than the magnitude of the direct wave, and the reflected wave could have either the same or opposite polarity as the direct wave. For a short circuit load, the reflection coefficient is -1 and for an open circuit the coefficient is $+1$. These two conditions yield the maximum magnitude of the reflection coefficient.

A very interesting and important situation arises when the load impedance Z_L is chosen to be equal to the wave impedance Z_0 of the transmission line. In this case the reflection coefficient is 0, and there is no reflected wave at all. We say in this case that the load resistance is *matched* to the line. Note that if Z_0 is greater than Z_L, the reflection coefficient is negative, so that the reflected wave cancels, in part, the transmitted wave. If Z_0 is less than Z_L the reflection coefficient is positive and the reflected wave reinforces the transmitted wave.

Now we consider several examples to show how various source and load impedances cause different reflections to appear on the line. In Fig. 2.14, the far end is open, and the reflection coefficient is $+1$. Our physical intuition indicates that if we wait long enough the line will charge to the full voltage V_0 impressed on the line. If we have a small source

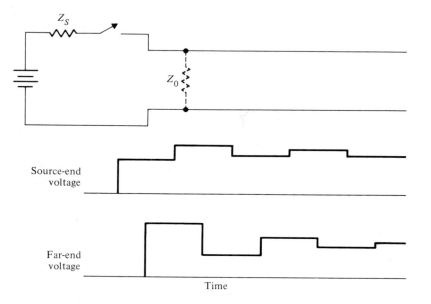

FIGURE 2.14 Voltage waveforms in an unterminated line.

impendance of Z_S, so that the reflection coefficient at the source end is nearly, but not quite -1, then the behavior of the line is as shown in the figure. Initially the voltage V_0 is impressed across the series load of Z_S and Z_0, so that $V_0 Z_0/(Z_S + Z_0)$ is the magnitude of the first direct wave down the line. The wave reflected back has an equal magnitude. When the reflected wave reaches the source, it is reflected back negatively, at almost the same amplitude. The voltage here is the sum of three different waves — the original direct wave, the wave reflected at the far end, and the second direct wave. Since the reflected wave from the far end and the second direct wave are very nearly equal but opposite in polarity, they almost cancel each other. Hence, the voltage at the near end is slightly above the voltage of the first direct wave. The next reflected wave that arrives at the source is negative in polarity and is reflected at almost the same magnitude with positive polarity. The voltage at the source at this time then drops just slightly as the third direct wave is launched down the line. This general behavior repeats for subsequent reflections so that the voltage at the source end of the line oscillates above and below V_0, with the oscillations gradually dying out. At the far end, the maximum excursion from the asymptotic voltage occurs after the first direct wave reaches that end. The voltage at this time is roughly twice V_0. After the second direct wave reaches the load, the voltage swings almost to 0. Subsequent reflections cause voltage swings that alternate above and below V_0, with the amplitude of the swings gradually dying out. The waveforms shown are seldom observed as sharp rectangular waveforms because of the very high frequencies in the transients that are difficult for oscilloscopes to capture. They do appear, however, in the form of smooth transients with overexcursions and subsequent oscillation known as *ringing*.

Figure 2.15 illustrates a slight variation of the previous example. In this case the near end is terminated with Z_0 to match it to the transmission line. The initial direct wave is the voltage impressed on the series connection of Z_0 with the line impedance Z_0, so that $V_0 Z_0/(Z_0 + Z_0) = V_0/2$ travels down the line. At the far end the voltage jumps to V_0, because the reflected wave is equal to the incident wave. This wave travels back to the source where it is absorbed by the matched impedance. When the reflected wave reaches the source, the entire line is charged to V_0. In this case one round-trip propagation charges the entire line.

A line matched at the far end is shown in Fig. 2.16. This line has a load impedance of Z_0. When a wave is impressed on this line it travels to the far end where it is absorbed without reflection. When this termination is used, the source impedance is usually made as small as possible so that nearly all of the output voltage appears at the far end.

A more complex situation appears in Fig. 2.17. In this figure, neither the source nor the load impedances match the transmission line. This line has reflections that travel back and forth on the line until the voltage reaches its asymptotic value. The values of the voltages for the first few reflections are shown in the figure. The asymptotic voltage has to be the voltage across Z_L when it is in series with Z_S alone; that is,

$$V_{\text{ASYMP}} = \frac{V_0 Z_L}{Z_L + Z_S}.$$

The figure shows the voltage approaching this asymptote.

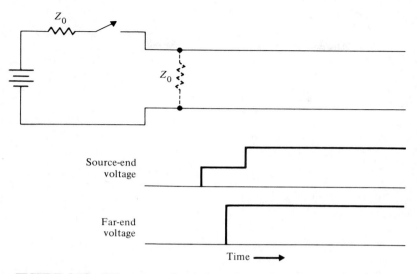

FIGURE 2.15   Voltage waveforms in a line terminated with a matched impedance at the source end.

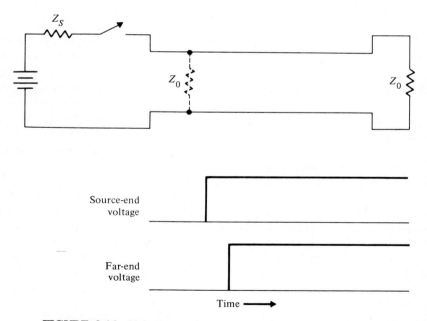

FIGURE 2.16   Voltage waveforms in a line terminated with a far-end matched impedance.

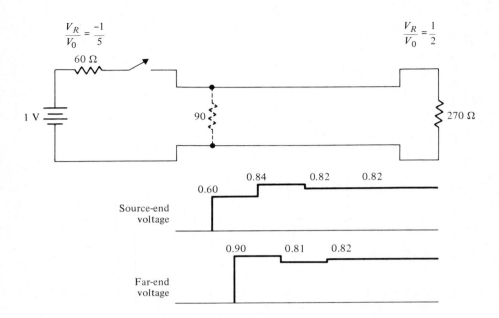

FIGURE 2.17 Voltage waveforms on a line with neither source- nor far-end impedance matching.

The last few examples illustrate a general characteristic of terminations in transmission lines. When a transmission line is terminated by an impedance greater than Z_0, the positive reflection coefficient causes the reflected wave to reinforce the direct wave, and we see the voltage increase after a reflection. If subsequent incident waves all have the same polarity, then the voltage at the load increases monotonically in time. The envelope of the step increments is exponential for a line with a single source and load, and is the superposition of several exponentials for more complex situations. An oscilloscope trace of a charging line shows the steps as smooth transitions, and the line appears to charge to its asymptotic voltage exponentially.

Terminations that are less than Z_0 result in negative reflection coefficients. In these cases, the reflected waves alternate signs, and the observed voltage oscillates above and below the asymptotic value as demonstrated in Fig. 2.14. The resulting ringing has an exponential envelope for simple configurations, and is the sum of exponential decays in more complex configurations. Thus overshoot is a by-product of a termination resistor that is smaller than Z_0, and gradual line charging results from having a load resistor that is larger than Z_0. In a sense, the terminating resistor acts as a damping element. When it is too small, the line voltages overshoot and oscillate. When it is too large, oscillations are completely damped out, but the line voltage is prevented from rising rapidly to its final value.

Applications

Now that we know something about the behavior of transmission lines, how do we use this information when interconnecting systems? For point-to-point lines with a single source and single sink, the problem is relatively simple. Solutions become a good deal more complex for lines with multiple sinks and sources. For the latter, most solutions are at best engineering compromises. First we develop preferred termination techniques for the point-to-point case, and then we deal with the more complex cases.

There are three interconnection methods that are in use for the point-to-point case: The designer should do one of the following:

1. Wait long enough after each signal transition for the reflections on the line to die out, and not attempt to reduce reflections through terminations on the transmission line.
2. Use a matched termination at the far end, thereby producing no reflections on the line.
3. Use a matched termination at the source end, absorbing the wave reflected from the far end.

For low-speed systems, waiting for several round-trip propagations is far easier to do than anything else, and is the best solution. As speeds become more critical we would like to limit waiting to a single one-way transmission time, or at most to a single round-trip time. The second and third solutions are shown in Fig. 2.18. By matching at the load, the reflected wave is eliminated. However, this method results in considerable power dissipated in the load. In this example, the driver gate is an open-collector gate in the 7406 or

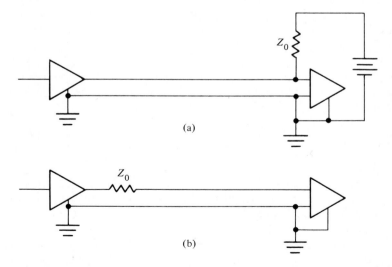

FIGURE 2.18   (a) Far-end matching; (b) source-end matching.

7407 family, and the load resistor is selected to match the cable impedance. Since conductors like flat ribbon cables have a wave impedance on the order of 150 Ω, the driver produces about 30 mA when the voltage excursion is on the order of 4.5 V. The power dissipation in the load resistor is about 60 to 65 mW for pulses that have 50% duty cycle. Multiply this power dissipation by the number of signal lines, typically on the order of 30 to 50 for parallel interfaces, and we discover that two to three watts can be dissipated in the terminating resistors. The power lost is largely wasted because it is expended solely for noise reduction, not for computation or data storage. Other methods of termination can reduce the power lost, but may increase the transient response time.

If the duty cycle is rather low with infrequent active pulses, matched termination at the load becomes more attractive. For example, it is commonly used for floppy disk drives where pulses have about a 5% duty cycle. With this low a duty cycle the power dissipated reduces to about 6 mW, which is much more reasonable.

To avoid power dissipation, many systems use the source-matching method shown in Fig. 2.18(b). This method generates a reflected wave, but the voltage at the far end climbs to full value when the direct wave arrives if the impedance there is infinite. Hence, most applications of this method require special line receivers with very high input impedances. Standard transistor-transistor logic (TTL) gates have input impedances on the order of a few thousand ohms, which disqualify them as line receivers.

In spite of the reflected wave produced by source termination, a source-terminated line can be run at the same speed as a load-terminated line in the point-to-point configuration. In both cases the output of an ideal transmission line is an exact replica of the input. (Second-order effects not treated here tend to alter the rise time of transmitted signals as they pass through a cable.) The source-terminated line, however, dissipates no power in a constant-voltage state, whereas the load-terminated line dissipates considerable power in one of the two logic states, depending on whether the load resistor is returned to ground or to the supply voltage.

The disadvantages of source termination become more apparent when there are multiple taps on the line instead of a single load at the far end. The initial direct-wave voltage on the source-terminated line is only half the final voltage. The direct wave reflects backward at an infinite load impedance with a magnitude equal to the original magnitude. As the reflected wave passes intermediate taps on the line, they attain their full and final voltage (provided that the taps themselves are infinite impedances, and infinitely short). Hence, intermediate taps have to wait for up to one complete round trip before they have the full output voltage available.

The tapped transmission line mentioned here becomes extremely difficult to analyze when the taps are themselves short stubs of transmission lines. Figure 2.19 shows a single driver feeding several receivers on a bus line. The receivers are each located at the end of short stubs of transmission lines, and we assume that all stubs have the wave impedance Z_0 of the main transmission line. In this situation there is no way to prevent multiple reflections from propagating on the line. The reflections all die out eventually, but depending on the locations of the taps and the impedances at the receivers, the reflections can possibly reinforce each other at specific times and places on the transmission line, thereby creating spurious pulses that easily are mistaken for signals.

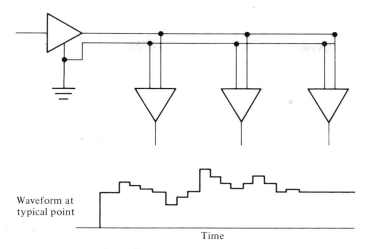

Waveform at
typical point

Time

FIGURE 2.19   A bus driving multiple receivers on a transmission line.

Taps on the transmission line cause reflected waves in two different ways. There are reflections at the receiver ends of the stubs and at the taps themselves. Because the reflections are extremely troublesome, we might be tempted to eliminate the reflections in the stub by matching the receivers to the line. The resulting low impedance rules out this approach. Moreover, no simple scheme can eliminate reflections produced at the taps where the stubs are joined to the line. So we must live with the reflections somehow if we must use the tapped line.

How do the reflected waves produced on the tapped line show up in the received waveforms? As a wave propagates down a transmission line and reaches a stub, part of the wave continues down the main line, part is diverted into the stub, and part is reflected back toward the source. As the direct wave passes by a stub and a load impedance, a short trough appears in the load voltage because of the energy diverted from the direct wave at the stub. Meanwhile, unless the receiver is matched to the stub impedance, the wave diverted into the stub is partially reflected back when it reaches a receiver input. The reflected wave returns down the stub to the tap on the transmission line where it reenters the line, and propagates in both directions. (Part of this wave is also reflected backwards into the stub towards the receiver.) If the stub has an infinite load impedance, all energy diverted into the stub eventually works its way back onto the transmission line, although many reflections in the stub may occur before all the energy is completely returned to the line. If the stub load impedance is not infinite, then it drains energy from the line that reduces the asymptotic voltage at the far end. In any case, the stub gives rise to a series of reflections that propagate down the line just behind the direct wave. Since the stub is presumably short compared to the line length, the several reflected voltages show up at the far end as a collection of peaks and troughs as shown in Fig. 2.19. Note that multiple reflections may reinforce or cancel each other, so that spurious troughs can be large enough to cause a continuous signal to appear as two or more distinct pulses separated by a null signal.

To see how the complex reflections arise, let us examine the tapped transmission in somewhat greater detail. Consider, for example, Fig. 2.20 which illustrates the impedance encountered by a wave propagating down the bus. On a main bus segment the wave impedance is a uniform Z_0. If we assume that the stub also has impedance Z_0, the parallel connection of two line impedances of Z_0 at the tap results in a local impedance of $Z_0/2$. Thus the reflection coefficient at the tap is $-\frac{1}{3}$, and is due simply to the wave impedance of the stub in parallel with the line impedance, and is not due to any real load impedance. Hence, there is a wave reflected back to the source whose magnitude is $\frac{1}{3}$ the direct wave and opposite in polarity. But the direct wave still propagates forward into the stub and down the main line. Now there are three waves on the line—a direct wave propagating toward the load, a direct wave propagating into the stub, and a reflected wave propagating back to the source.

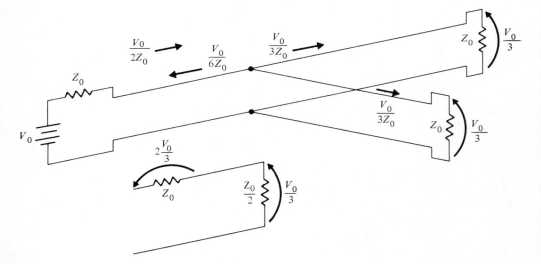

FIGURE 2.20   Voltage and current relations in a tapped transmission line.

Figure 2.20 shows an artificial situation in which all end points are matched to the line impedance, and thus produce no reflections themselves. The asymptotic voltage across the loads in this case is $V_0/3$. This follows because the two loads of Z_0 are in parallel to form an equivalent load impedance of $Z_0/2$. This load is in series with Z_0, forming a voltage divider with Z_0. Hence $V_0/3$ appears across the load impedances, and twice this (or $2V_0/3$) appears across the source impedance of Z_0.

Now we verify that the three propagating waves behave as the asymptotic values predict they should. At the source end, the driver sees a source impedance of Z_0 in series with the transmission line that also has an impedance of Z_0, so that the initial voltage splits equally across the source impedance and the line. Hence the initial direct wave has a value $V_0/2$. When this reaches the tap, a reflected wave of $-(V_0/2)/3 = -V_0/6$ propagates back to the source, where it drops the line input voltage to

$$\frac{V_0}{3} = \frac{V_0}{2} - \frac{V_0}{6}.$$

At the tap, the reflected voltage drops the voltage immediately to $V_0/3$. The current at the tap point is $(V_0/3)/(Z_0/2)$. This current splits evenly in the branches of the tap, since the impedances on the two branches are equal. Consequently, a current with a value of $V_0/3Z_0$ flows in each branch; and since the impedance in each branch is Z_0, the waves propagated in each branch have a voltage of $V_0/3$. Since no reflections occur at any end of this line, the line reaches a steady state at a potential of $V_0/3$ after the direct waves and tap reflection have reached their destinations. Thus, the transmission line calculations agree with the asymptotic calculations.

The circuit in Fig. 2.20 is not a practical circuit, but is shown only for illustrative purposes. While matched termination eliminates end reflections, matched source termination severely reduces voltage available at the load, and matched load termination greatly increases the power that the driver must deliver. Moreover, matched terminations cannot eliminate the reflections caused by taps, so that impedance matching everywhere is neither desirable nor effective.

A more useful way of tapping onto a line is shown in Fig. 2.21. The tap is made with a line whose wave impedance is very high; the stub is kept very short; and the receiver has an infinite input impedance. The high impedance tap prevents the tap from draining significant amounts of energy from the direct wave. The infinite impedance at the receiver reflects all waves that travel into the stub back down the stub to where they reenter the transmission line. The short stub guarantees that waves diverted into the stub will reenter the transmission line with as small a delay as possible.

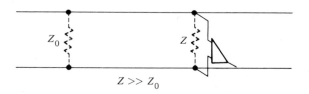

FIGURE 2.21   Ideal ways of tapping a transmission line with a high-impedance short stub and a high-impedance receiver.

The difficult problem in satisfying the demands of Fig. 2.21 is the problem of creating a high impedance stub. Wave impedances on transmission lines depend on line inductance and capacitance, and are difficult to increase over a few hundred ohms. If the line has an impedance of 75 Ω and the stub is an etched line on a circuit board with an impedance of 200 to 300 Ω, some power is still diverted into the stub, but it is only ⅓ to ¼ of the power of the direct wave. When stubs are terminated with an infinite impedance, any wave that enters the stub is reflected back to the bus. At the bus the wave splits, and propagates in both directions on the bus, and reflects back into the stub. We have seen earlier that subsequent reflections in the stub repeat this process until all of the stub energy is returned to the transmission line, half in the source direction and half in the load direction.

As long as reflections are small compared to the direct wave, the peaks and troughs visible in the direct wave arising from stub reflections will be small and will die out as the line charges to the impressed voltage. The depth of the troughs depend on the impedances that terminate the stubs, and the decay time depends on the length of the stubs and the length of the line. In critical applications, the transmission line should be routed to each receiver input, so that stub length is essentially zero, and the wave impedance of the tap should be as high as possible.

Another alternative used in practice is to eliminate all taps from buses. The signal is transmitted using point-to-point driver and receiver pairs. Each receiver has a corresponding driver that forwards the signal to the next point on the bus. This method increases the delay in propagation time because signals pass through many receiver/driver pairs in moving from one end of the bus to the other, but each segment of the line is point to point and can be terminated properly for noise-free operation.

The most complex situation encountered in practice is the one depicted in Fig. 2.22. This figure shows a line with multiple taps in which each tap has both a driver and receiver. In this case, neither sources nor loads can be terminated because all termination impedances are in parallel and will draw excessive power. This type of bus is used commonly in multiboard applications, where each board is a tap on the bus line with a receiver and driver for each bus wire. Systems function satisfactorily without termination in the 1 to 10 MHz range when the bus is contained in a single chassis, and has a length not exceeding 0.2 to 0.3 m. As frequencies or distance or both increase, this busing method breaks down because of the noise on the transmission line caused by all of the reflections. The IEEE-488 bus standard covers a bus for peripheral devices that could be up to 20 m at 500 K-bytes per second, and up to 10 m long to attain 1 M-bytes per second. To achieve this type of performance, the standard recommends that each tap on the bus be that shown in Fig. 2.22(b). Each device has a pull-up and pull-down resistor whose parallel equivalent is about 2 kΩ. The resistors act as a local voltage divider that sets the quiescent voltage at about 3.3 V. Hence, when no active device drives the bus line, the line goes to a logic 1. The termination at each device is too large to match the line impedance, but it does absorb some of the energy that reaches it, and reduces the energy returned in reflected waves. As more devices are added to the bus, the effect of the termination resistors is to create a greater burden on a gate that drives the bus. The IEEE standard states that the bus can achieve a data rate of 500 K-bytes per second for buses up to 20 m in length, with up to one device per 2 m of cable. An even higher data rate is achievable if the maximum length of the cable is limited to 10 m with up to one device per meter of cable. The higher speed requires devices to be placed closer together, but the maximum number of devices on the bus is not increased in spite of the closer proximity of devices. Loading effects caused by additional devices on the bus tend to reduce the maximum speed.

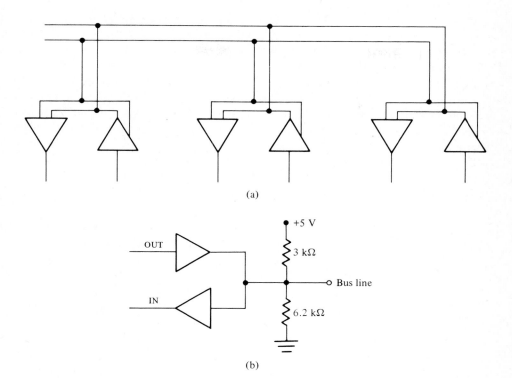

(a)

(b)

FIGURE 2.22   (a) A transmission line with multiple drivers and receivers; (b) IEEE-488 bus-connection conventions.

A quite suitable technique for reducing noise is shown in Fig. 2.23, and is known as active termination. Active termination is simply the termination of all bus lines through matched impedances to a common power supply whose voltage is fixed at the logic threshold, about half way between ON and OFF voltage levels. Although reflections will occur on the line because of the taps on the line, any reflections that propagate to the end of the line will be absorbed at the active terminator. The current supplied by the active terminator need not be very large because the bulk of the current is supplied by the logic power supply. In fact, if half of the lines are high and half are low, then current that flows from high levels into the load resistors at the active terminator flows through the remaining load resistors into the low lines, and the terminator supply delivers no current at all. It only delivers current (or absorbs current) to correct current flow imbalances when the bus lines are not evenly distributed among high and low levels. The active terminator also reduces power dissipation in the termination resistors if the bus lines are about evenly distributed between high and low levels. If there are N bus lines, and the voltage across the termination resistor is $V/2$, the power dissipation is

$$P_{\text{ACTIVE}} = \frac{N(V/2)^2}{Z_0},$$

while the power dissipated into a passive load to V for $N/2$ low bus lines is

$$P_{\text{PASSIVE}} = \frac{(N/2)V^2}{Z_0} = 2\,P_{\text{ACTIVE}}.$$

One last advantage accrues to active termination. The drivers commonly used for bus systems are tri-state drivers that have a low, high, and off (or high-impedance) mode of operation. When all drivers are off, an unterminated bus line is free to float up or down or remain at its last potential, so that when a driver attempts to charge the line it may have to charge the line by as much as V. Bus signaling must take this into account as a charging delay for the line. With active termination, the bus is held at the logic threshold when all drivers are off, so that no line has to be changed in potential by more than $V/2$. This reduces the charging delay for long lines by about half.

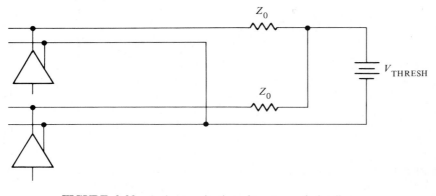

FIGURE 2.23   Active termination of two transmission lines.

Graphical Methods

Transmission line analysis for linear loads as derived in previous sections requires only simple algebra. For nonlinear loads, such as the input stages of gates and receivers or the output stages of source drivers, computation becomes very difficult, but we can fortunately draw upon graphical techniques to show the behavior of the transmission lines. The basic idea is outlined in Fig. 2.24. The figure shows a point-to-point transmission line and a graph of the two curves that shows the voltage-current relationships at the source and load ends of the line. The point of intersection of these curves is the unique point that satisfies both relationships, and is therefore the steady-state operating point of the line. Now suppose that the driver output is initially at 0 V, and changes suddenly to V volts as a pulse is initiated on the line. Because the driver is impressing voltage on a transmission line, the voltage and current must satisfy the source relationship of Fig. 2.24 and the transmission line equation $V = IZ_0$. These two equations are shown in Fig. 2.25, and their point of intersection marks the voltage and current impressed on the line by the

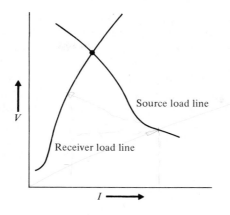

FIGURE 2.24   Voltage versus current at
driver and receiver for a transmission line.

initial signal. This is intersection point 1 in Fig. 2.25. At the load end of the line, the line
must obey the transmission equation $V = IZ_0$ as before, and the load curve shown in the
figure. The V in this case is the sum of the direct and reflected voltage, but the current is
the difference of direct and reflected current. To calculate the reflected voltage and reflected current, we simply draw a straight line from the source operating point with a
slope of $-Z_0$ until it intersects the load curve. This new straight line represents a voltage
that adds to the direct wave voltage, but one whose current subtracts from the direct wave
current. The intersection point, then, shows the operating point at the load when the direct
wave arrives there. This intersection point is point 2 in Fig. 2.25.

By continuing this reasoning, we can determine the voltage at the source when the reflected wave reaches the source by drawing a line with positive slope Z_0 from the load
operating point to its point of intersection with the source operating point. The figure
shows this intersection point as point 3, and it clearly is the sum of three voltages and
three currents due, respectively, to a direct wave, a wave reflected at the load, and a wave
reflected by the source. Note that the process can be continued; and if it is, it eventually
terminates with the intersections falling on the steady-state operating point. The voltages
at intersections 1, 3, 5, etc., when plotted as shown in Fig. 2.25, give the voltage at the
source as a function of time; and, similarly, the even-numbered intersections give the load
voltage.

The graphical method is extremely valuable in analyzing very high-speed circuits
where typically one type of driver and receiver are used through most of a design. The
voltage excursions derived from the graphical method hold regardless of the length of a
transmission line, with the length determining only the time scale of the voltage transitions. So all transmission lines driven by one type of driver/receiver pair can be treated by
one graphical analysis. The analysis should consider the transition not only from low to

high voltages, as shown in Fig. 2.25, but from high to low as well. The voltage/current relations are generally different at high and low driver outputs, so the results obtained by high and low output analyses tend to be quite different. The analyses predict the "ringing" waveform that will be present on the line during a transition, and they are useful in establishing how long a wait is required before the signal becomes stable. If ringing is excessive for unterminated lines, the effects of termination can be calculated by using the voltage/current relations for a terminated line in place of the source-output or load-input curves used in Fig. 2.25.

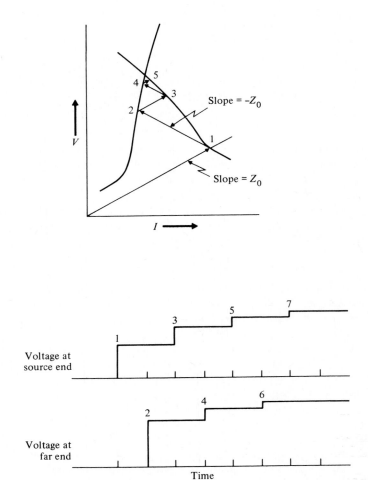

FIGURE 2.25 Graphical solution of voltage waveforms on a transmission line.

2.3 PUTTING THE TECHNIQUES INTO PRACTICE

There is a wealth of information in the prior sections of this chapter that illustrate the principles governing the physical behavior of interconnections. In this section we examine a number of implementation techniques based on those principles. The material is organized such that we start with small geometries and work toward larger ones. We start with problems that appear within the confines of one circuit board, and work our way to backplane connections, board-to-board cabling, and finally chassis-to-chassis connections.

Intra-Board Connections

Circuits that operate under 10 MHz tend to be less sensitive to the problems raised earlier than faster circuits. Nevertheless, long conductor runs that operate at 10 MHz and above feel the transmission-line effects and need to be treated carefully. Otherwise, conservative board layout with large conductors for power distribution and sufficient decoupling of all components should be generally reliable and satisfactory.

Long runs often occur in memory systems, where system timing is also quite critical. If memory cycle time has to be lengthened because of ringing on the bus lines, the performance of the entire system degrades. Consequently, normal practice treats high-speed memory as a source-terminated transmission line, as shown in Fig. 2.26.

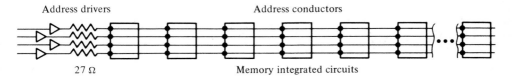

Address drivers   Address conductors

27 Ω   Memory integrated circuits

FIGURE 2.26   Address lines in a memory treated as transmission lines with matched source impedances.

This figure shows memory-address lines routed serially through a bank of chips, which is in essence a tapped transmission line with extremely short stubs of very high impedance. The conductor layout should be parallel straight lines of uniform separation to establish a transmission path of uniform wave impedance. Memory chips should be uniformly spaced on the address conductors, with the pins of the chips directly over the corresponding address conductors. When soldered to the conductors, the pins become the stubs of the taps on the transmission line. Uniform spacing has the effect of distributing input-pin capacitance uniformly on the line, thereby giving the line a uniform wave impedance. For MOS memories, each input pin has a few picofarads of capacitance and a very large resistive impedance. Consequently, if an address line visits say 20 chips, one might expect about 100 pF of capacitance on the line, which is a fairly substantial capacitive load to drive. But since the capacitance is distributed uniformly over the conductor and not lumped at a single pin, the distributed capacitance and distributed line inductance together make the conductor appear as a transmission line with a purely resistive impedance, typically from 20 to 30 Ω.

If the line is not terminated, we have the situation depicted in Fig. 2.14, with noticeable ringing when the address lines are asserted. The address lines must be stable before a memory access can be made, so the effect of the ringing is to increase the delay between address enable and memory access. Standard practice in high-speed memory designs calls for source termination of the address lines with a small series resistor placed at the driven end of each line as shown in Fig. 2.26. The source termination absorbs reflections caused by the taps, so that the line charges after about one round-trip propagation delay.

Another application of transmission-line theory that is prevalent in intra-board designs is the use of an input diode to prevent a gate input from making large negative excursions. When a diode clamp is incorporated into the input circuit of a gate as shown in Fig. 2.27(a), the V versus I characteristic of the gate input becomes that of Fig 2.27(b). The input is clamped to a small negative voltage and will not follow large negative excursions of an external signal. Although individual gates do not normally deliver large negative output voltages, such voltages can and do creep into systems because of reflected voltages on transmission lines with negative reflection coefficients. Large negative excursions show up as ringing, and greatly increase the settling time of gate inputs responding to step changes of voltage. The diode clamp limits the negative excursion, bringing the gate more quickly to its quiescent state. The diode clamps are integrated into virtually all TTL gates at present, so that logic designers need not take special precautions regarding the negative transients.

Backplane Connections

Board-to-board connections made with printed-circuit backplanes seldom exceed 0.2 to 0.3 m in length. At typical microprocessor speeds it is not necessary to use balanced drivers and receivers for noise reduction for this type of connection, but some care in grounding and signaling is still required. Backplanes normally take a ''bus'' approach in which all major signal lines are continuous across the backplane, and individual circuit cards plug into the backplane to contact the lines as taps on a transmission line.

Active termination, as shown in Fig. 2.23, is the major technique for noise reduction on the bus in use today, although many systems use no termination at all. Noise on backplanes is unavoidable, however, as reflections from the several stubs on the bus inevitably corrupt the signals. Active termination at best reduces settling time; it does not eliminate the sources of the reflections at the taps where each circuit card attaches to the backplane. In the face of the inherent noise on a bus, the bus must be sufficiently short to permit reflected waves to decay during the setup time of bus signals. Printed-circuit layout is very critical in contributing to fast decay time. Drivers and receivers on the printed-circuit card must be located as close to the bus connector as possible in order to keep the stub of each tap as short as possible. High input-impedance on the receivers is essential as well in order to reflect most of the power that enters each stub back onto the bus. A sound, conservative policy limits each board to one driver and receiver per bus signal, thus eliminating reflections from multiple sources and sinks, and limiting the length of the stubs on the boards.

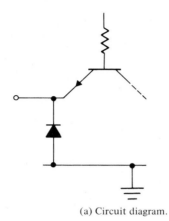

(a) Circuit diagram.

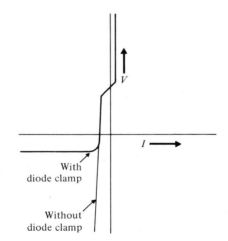

(b) Input voltage versus input current.

FIGURE 2.27   A diode clamp on a gate input to prevent large negative excursions of voltage.

Special drivers and receivers are especially useful for backplane connections. Table 2.1 and Fig. 2.28 illustrate some of the more popular bus drivers and receivers. The 7424X family is particularly advantageous for use as drivers, receivers, or transceivers. Each member of this family is a 20-pin dual-inline package (DIP) with eight signal lines. All devices have tri-state drivers with high-current output capability suitable for driving several taps on a transmission line. The level of integration is high with respect to typical levels for drivers and receivers, so that these devices make good use of board area. Table 2.1 gives the electrical characteristics for these packages for both the Schottky (S) and low-power Schottky (LS) versions of the devices. The differences between the devices are in delay, power consumption, and drive capability. The LS devices have roughly twice

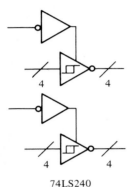

74LS240
74S240

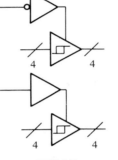

74SL241
74S241

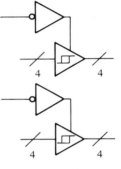

74LS244
74S244

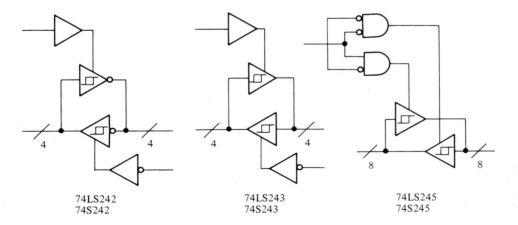

74LS242
74S242

74LS243
74S243

74LS245
74S245

FIGURE 2.28   Drivers and receivers (continued on next page).

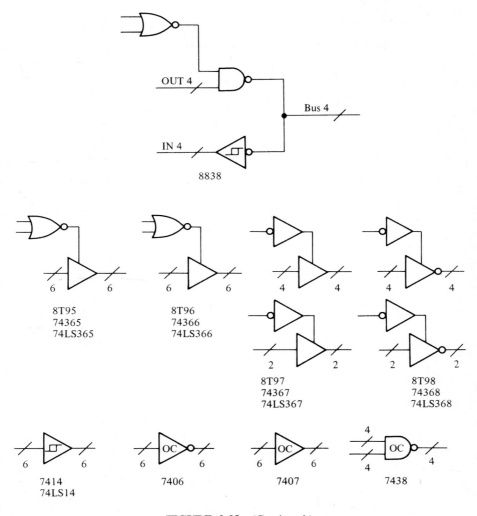

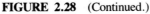

FIGURE 2.28   (Continued.)

the delay as the S devices, but they are still very fast. The net increase in delay through a driver and receiver for LS over S-type devices is at most only about 18 ns, which is tolerable for most systems in the 1 to 5 MHz range. LS logic dissipates much less power and has half the input loading of S logic. For this reason the LS devices should be used wherever possible. The major exceptions to this rule are high-speed microprocessor systems (8 to 10 MHz clock speed), and situations where the 24 mA drive capability of LS logic is pressed almost to the limit. In the latter case, it is possible to compromise and use S logic for drivers (to attain the necessary drive capability), while using LS logic for receivers (to reduce the loading as much as possible).

TABLE 2.1   Popular Drivers and Receivers

Device	Type	Max Delay	Output Drive	Input Load	Packaging
74S24X	DRVR/RCVR	9 ns	48 mA	0.4 mA	20-pin DIP (240,241,244,245) 14-pin DIP (242,243)
74LS24X	DRVR/RCVR	18 ns	24 mA	0.2 mA	20-pin DIP (240,241,244,245) 14-pin DIP (242,243)
8T9X	DRVR/RCVR	13 ns	48 mA	0.4 mA	16-pin DIP
7436X	DRVR/RCVR	22 ns	32 mA	1.6 mA	16-pin DIP
74LS36X	DRVR/RCVR	22 ns	24 mA	0.4 mA	16-pin DIP
8838	DRVR/RCVR	27 ns	50 mA	0.1 mA	16-pin DIP
7414	RCVR	22 ns	16 mA	0.8 mA	14-pin DIP
74LS14	RCVR	22 ns	8 mA	0.4 mA	14-pin DIP
7406	DRVR	23 ns	40 mA	1.6 mA	14-pin DIP
7407	DRVR	30 ns	40 mA	1.6 mA	14-pin DIP
7438	DRVR	22 ns	48 mA	1.6 mA	14-pin DIP

All of the devices in the 7424X family have a small amount of noise immunity when used as receivers because of hysteresis in the input circuits. The input-voltage threshold for changing a logic 0 to a logic 1 is about 0.4 V higher than the threshold for changing a logic 1 to a logic 0. Hence, a low signal has to move across a threshold, say 1.6 V to be recognized as a logic 1. After crossing the threshold, the signal has to drop at least 0.4 V lower to 1.2 V to be treated as a logic 0. Thus the gate can sustain roughly 0.4 V of noise on the input while crossing the threshold without changing state.

Other popular driver/receiver chips in wide use are in the 8T9X (7436X) family. This family has six driver/receivers per chip instead of eight as in the 7424X family, and has no hysteresis for noise protection. Consequently the 7424X family is recommended over the 8T9X family for new designs. Another popular family of driver/receivers is the 8838 family, also called DS8838, MC3438, and 8T38. These transceivers are intended for buses with a characteristic impedance of 120 Ω. Noise immunity for this family is very good because the parts have about 0.8 to 0.9 V of hysteresis. The packaging density is a little lower than the 8-bit 74S245 and 74LS245 transceivers, but is greater than the other 74S24X and 74LS24X parts.

As manufacturers improve their products, advanced devices to replace the ones mentioned here will appear. TI, for example, has a new family of high-speed, low-power parts with numbers 7464X that are pin-for-pin replacements for some of the 7424X parts. Similarly, several manufacturers produce 81LS9X parts that are low-power Schottky replacements for the 8T9X parts. The designer must stay abreast of new developments to be sure to make the most intelligent selection of parts at any given time.

Open-collector drivers are used in bus-type systems where two or more gates drive a signal line simultaneously. The most popular choices for this purpose are the 7406, 7407, and 7438 drivers also shown in Fig. 2.28 and Table 2.1. These devices can be operated more successfully in a matched-termination mode than can the tri-state drivers discussed earlier. The key to this success is that the drive capability of these chips is compatible with the termination resistance needed to match a transmission line. Assuming that a bus on a backplane has a wave impedance of 150–200 Ω, the matching pull-up resistor draws about 25 to 35 mA when the collector is in a low (logic 0) state. The 7438 device can easily drive this and several receiver inputs simultaneously. A 7406 or 7407 can deliver up to 30 mA, which is sufficient to drive a single load resistor of 150 Ω or more, provided no other gate inputs load the bus. Thus all of these open-collector devices are typically used in a configuration with matched termination at the load where the required load resistor is returned to 5 V. The 7406 and 7407 are used in point-to-point systems, and the 7438 in bus systems with multiple drivers. Where termination is not critical, the 7406 and 7407 are used in bus-type systems, but with a higher pull-up resistance to decrease the drive requirements at the risk of introducing transmission-line mismatch.

The last type of device worth mentioning is the 7414 family of Schmitt triggers. These are frequently used as bus receivers, and have the advantage of larger noise immunity than the 7424X family of drivers/receivers. With six receivers per device, the board area consumed per device is roughly double that of the 8T9X family (which has both drivers and receivers in one device) and more than double that of the 7424X family.

In these bus-type systems, improper grounding is a major source of difficulty. The problem is that over the length of a ground bus, large current transients can move various points on the ground conductor away from 0 signal potential. Consider, for example, the situation shown in Fig. 2.29. In this case a signal on the bus goes through a bus receiver, and from there it enables a tri-state driver onto the bus. When the driver comes on, suddenly eight signal lines on this board sink current, say 15 mA per line. The current transient from these drivers is then roughly 0.1 A. Assume the ground line shown in the figure carries the current transient, then moves suddenly above the ground-reference point for the tri-state control signal. The tri-state control signal then drops below threshold relative to the receiver ground point; and when it drops, the eight tri-state drivers shut down. The sudden reduction in current flow through the ground lead returns the receiver ground reference back to its original state where the tri-state control signal is again recognized as a 1. The system then oscillates in this condition until the tri-state control signal is removed.

Whereas a current transient of 0.1 A appears to be too small to cause a problem of this sort, in reality this type of problem appears all too often. Current transients can well exceed the 0.1 A mentioned in the example because of two factors other than the actual drive requirements of the bus. One factor is the current transient in TTL gates that occurs when the gate switches between logic 0 and logic 1 on the output. The other factor is the fact that the receivers of the driven signals will also experience current transients as they change state in response to the data sensed on their inputs. If the instantaneous current transient produces a noise voltage high-enough to shut down the tri-state drivers, the bus will oscillate. The best way to avoid this type of problem is to provide high-capacity power distribution conductors on the system backplane and on every circuit board.

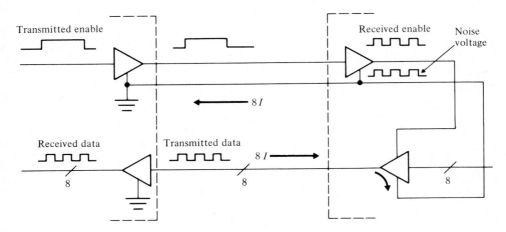

FIGURE 2.29   A stable oscillation of noise voltage on a ground wire.

Board-to-Board Connections

Connections between boards follow the rules of backplane connections when cables are very short, say 0.2 to 0.3 m in length. As cables increase in length, the interconnection schemes must take into account such sources of noise as transmission line reflections, cross-talk, and inadequate grounding. Our earlier discussion suggests that twisted-pair conductors and differential drivers and receivers are the safest and most reliable interconnection scheme. Cables composed of many twisted pairs of wires are widely available to provide the basic interconnection technology. A sample of useful differential drivers and receivers appears in Table 2.2. Configurations for matched terminations appear in Fig. 2.30. Figure 2.30(a) shows a matched load resistance returned to the power supply voltage. Since it is crucial to have an equal noise voltage drop on each arm of the twisted pair,

TABLE 2.2   Balanced Drivers and Receivers

Device	Type	Max Delay	Output Drive	Input Load	Packaging
26LS31	DRVR	20 ns	20 mA	0.4 mA	16-pin DIP
26LS32	RCVR	25 ns	8 mA	2.8 mA	16-pin DIP
MC3487	DRVR	20 ns	48 mA	0.4 mA	16-pin DIP
MC3486	RCVR	30 ns	8 mA	0.1 mA	16-pin DIP

the termination resistance is split with half on each arm. The matched load resistors are returned to ground in Fig. 2.30(b). Because none of the drivers discussed in the text can
drive a terminating resistor returned to ground, the load resistors for all of these drivers
should be returned to the power supply voltages shown in Fig. 2.30(a) rather than to those
shown in Fig. 2.30(b). Figure 2.30(c) shows the matched load resistance bridged across
the two outputs. This interconnection method has the same problem as Fig. 2.30(b) for
drivers that cannot drive a small resistance returned to a low voltage. The method is not
suitable for the drivers described in this chapter. The last method, source termination, is
shown in Fig. 2.30(d). Source termination is preferred to the load termination of Fig.
2.30(a) because of the former's low power consumption. However, source termination
does produce a reflection on the line that is absent when load termination is used, and the
reflection may cause a problem if several receivers are connected to the line at intermediate points. These receivers must wait longer to receive the full line voltage when source
termination is used than when load termination is used.

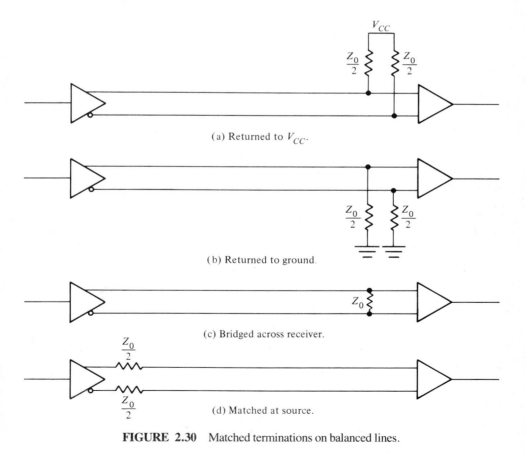

(a) Returned to V_{CC}.

(b) Returned to ground.

(c) Bridged across receiver.

(d) Matched at source.

FIGURE 2.30   Matched terminations on balanced lines.

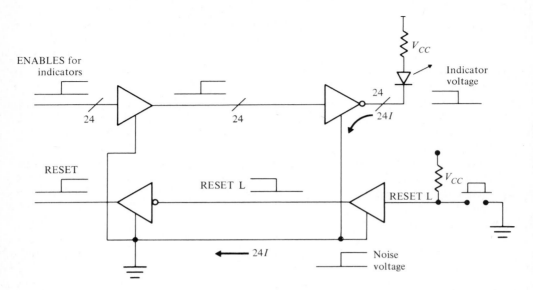

FIGURE 2.31   A problem due to inadequate grounding (often mistaken for a cross-talk problem).

One of the sources of noise that arise in board-to-board connections is that of cross talk. Cross talk refers to noise induced on a signal line by adjacent signals. Signals in adjacent lines couple to each other through both inductive and capacitive effects, and the coupling tends to increase as the length of adjacent lines increases and as the spacing between the lines decreases. Because shielding and grounding techniques that eliminate other noise sources also reduce cross talk, we do not give special consideration to cross talk in this textbook.

Flat-cable interconnections for board-to-board connections are widely used today because of the variety of connectors available and the convenience of attaching connectors to the cables and boards. They are somewhat more noise sensitive than twisted-pair conductors, but are quite usable in many systems, provided that the cabling system follows basic rules to deal with the problems of transmission-line mismatch, cross talk, and improper ground reference. The techniques for terminating double-ended lines and single-ended open-collector lines deal adequately with the transmission line problems. Many systems that use flat cable rely on matched-load termination of single-ended signals using 7438 drivers.

Ground problems and cross talk problems are resolved by similar techniques so we treat them together. (Signals coupled into nearby lines because of poor grounding are often mistaken for cross talk.) A mistake often made in cabling systems is the lack of an adequate ground return. Cable conductors have much less current capacity than do backplane conductors, and they carry current over larger distances, so that changes in ground reference levels are quite evident. The best policy is to use double-ended signals on ca-

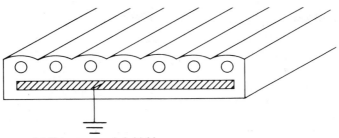

(a) Using a grounded shield.

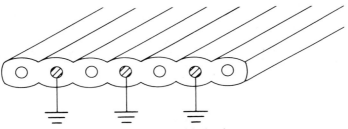

(b) Alternating ground conductors with signals.

FIGURE 2.32   Two methods for improving grounding and reducing cross talk in flat cable.

bles even though the conductors are not twisted together. The next best policy is to use single-ended signals, but with one ground wire for every signal wire that carries a nonnegligible current. Too many systems have failed because the designer expects three or four conductors to return the ground current produced by 20 to 30 drivers. The voltage drop on so few conductors inevitably is large enough to alter the reference levels on receivers so that they trigger improperly when many signals change simultaneously. One disastrous example of this mechanism is shown in Fig. 2.31. This shows a cable between a microcomputer and a control panel. The cable drives the control panel with indicator lights, and receives from the control panel switch-position information. Suppose that the program runs with all lights out until it reaches some specific point where it lights 24 indicators. When the 24 lines in the cable switch, the return current in the single ground lead causes it to rise in potential. The RESET line from the front panel, which is high when unasserted, appears to drop relative to ground at the computer. If the voltage developed in the ground wire is on the order of an instantaneous 1.5 V to 2.0 V, the computer may reset. Many designers know the maxim, "When all but one wire in a cable change state simultaneously, that one will change too." Inadequate grounding is one reason for the truth of this maxim.

Two ways of providing adequate grounding in flat cable are shown in Fig. 2.32. One way is to provide a ground plane in the cable. This is usually a woven ground with high-

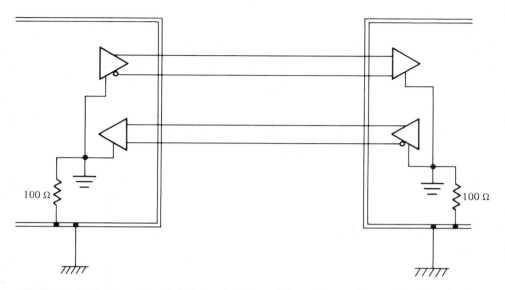

FIGURE 2.33 Ground/earth isolation in balanced lines. The earth ground on the chassis is isolated from the logic ground (signal ground) by a resistor to prevent low-impedance ground loops.

current capacity. The other way is to provide a ground-wire between every pair of signal conductors. Both techniques reduce capacitive and inductive coupling between signal wires, so they both serve to reduce cross talk. The high-current capacity reduces voltage differentials on ground references. Thus good grounding solves both cross-talk and ground-potential problems. In proposing either of these solutions, the designer must be absolutely certain that the ground points at either end of the cable can be safely connected together. This limits safe use of this technique to 10 to 20 m. For longer distances it is absolutely essential to use double-ended signaling, which does not require remote devices to be at identical ground potentials.

Chassis-to-Chassis Connections

If the chassis are close enough to have their grounds connected, the single-ended solutions will be satisfactory. If not, double-ended signaling is required. A safe implementation is shown in Fig. 2.33 where we see the logic-ground reference isolated from earth ground by a small resistor protecting against low-impedance ground loops.

OTHER SOURCE MATERIAL

Perhaps the most authoritative treatment of correct techniques for grounding and shielding is the five volume series by White (1971). The first volume of the series addresses models and sources of electrical noise. Volume 2 treats test methods and procedures. The most pertinent material for our purposes is in Volume 3, which is directed towards methods for controlling and reducing interference. Volumes 4 and 5, respectively, treat test instrumentation and interference-prediction techniques. The book by Morrison (1977) cited in this chapter is quite readable and useful, although it is primarily directed toward nondigital applications and does not treat problems specific to interfacing computers. Ott (1976) covers general problems in grounding and shielding and their solutions. This textbook is easily adapted to the particular requirements of computer systems. Blakeslee (1979) has produced a very good text on modern logic-design with two chapters covering problems related to grounding, shielding, and transmission theory. Although the discussion is necessarily less thorough than White, Morrison, and Ott, the textbook shows very clearly how the noise problems surface in interfacing and digital design, and what techniques are available to solve the problems.

The material on transmission lines and reflections is available in most undergraduate textbooks on electricity and magnetism. Graphical methods for analyzing nonlinear drivers and receivers are described in Blakeslee (1979). Recommended methods for making electrical connections to computer buses appear in several published standards. Of most interest are the IEEE-488 bus (IEEE, 1975), the IEEE-796 bus (IEEE-796 Bus Working Group, 1980), and the IEEE standard version of S-100 bus (IEEE Task 696.1/D2, 1979).

EXPERIMENTS

2.1 *Effects of shield capacitance*. Construct a unity-gain amplifier as shown in Fig. E –2.1. The three 100 pF capacitors model the capacitance of a shield, respectively, to the input, ground, and outputs of an amplifier circuit. Observe the output of the amplifier in response to a square wave input with the 100 pF capacitor to ground in the circuit, and observe the output again with this capacitor shorted. Vary the frequency of the square wave input to find frequencies at which the differences are most dramatic.

When the capacitor is shorted, the feedback path from output to input is broken. When the capacitor is in the circuit, the feedback path is active, and the output wave form is distorted. What is the major effect of the feedback path? Construct a mathematical model of the amplifier circuit, and calculate the behavior with and without the shunt across the 100 pF capacitor to ground. Compare your calculations to your observations.

2.2 *Transmission line reflections*. Obtain a 10-m length of 75 Ω coaxial cable, or any other readily available coaxial cable with an impedance in the $50-150\ \Omega$-range. Construct a circuit that drives this transmission line with an open-collector 7407 driver as shown in Fig. E –2.2. The source resistor should be as close to the driver as possible, and the wiring from the source resistor to the cable should be as short as

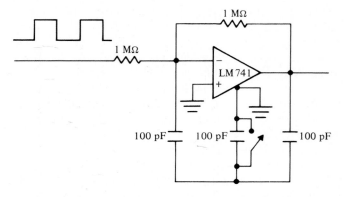

FIGURE E–2.1 Experimental setup for studying the effect of shield capacitance.

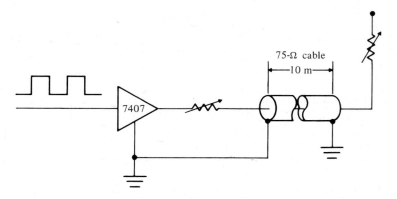

FIGURE E–2.2 Experimental setup for observing reflections on a transmission line.

possible. Observe the waveforms at the cable input and output as a function of the source and termination resistance.

With the source resistance initially 0, set the load resistance to ⅓, ½, 1, 2, and 3 times the cable impedance. With the load impedance set equal to the cable impedance, set the source resistance to ⅓, ½, 1, 2, and 3 times the cable impedance. For each of these cases, calculate the waveforms at the cable input and output as a function of time, and compare the calculated answers to your observations.

2.3 *Balanced versus unbalanced interconnections.* Construct two different driver/receiver circuits as indicated in Fig. E–2.3. Circuit (a) is single-ended and uses an open-collector driver connected to one input of an LM741. The other input is connected to a fixed voltage at the logic threshold of about 1.4 V. Circuit (b) is

double-ended. The two drivers place complementary signals at the inputs of an
LM741. Generate a square wave of 10 kHz to both circuits, and observe the LM741
outputs. The outputs should be square waves with sloping leading and falling edges.
Generate a square wave 15 kHz from an independent generator, and couple the signal to the circuits through 0.1 μF capacitors as shown in the figure. Observe the output of both the single-ended and double-ended receivers. Vary the noise source frequency and amplitude. The noise should be quite visible on the output of the single-
ended receiver and virtually undetectable on the output of the double-ended receiver.
Repeat the experiment with the coupling capacitors replaced by 10 kΩ resistors. The
noise on the output of the single-ended circuit should be much more in evidence because of the direct coupling of the noise into the receiver circuit. Noise may be more
visible on the output of the double-ended circuit, but should still be significantly less
than the noise on the output of the singled-ended circuit.

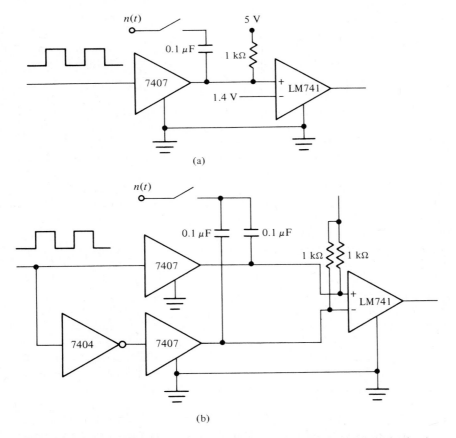

(a)

(b)

FIGURE E−2.3 Experimental setup for observing common-mode noise rejection in a
balanced line: (a) Single-ended transmission; (b) double-ended transmission.

PROBLEMS

2.1. Assume that a very long transmission line has a short stub, and that the stub is terminated with an infinite impedance. Intuitively speaking, all energy that enters the stub should be reflected back onto the line. The stub has no effect on the asymptotic behavior of the voltage and current on the transmission line. Calculate the voltage at the tap where the stub leaves the line, and at the open end of the stub in response to a step voltage impressed at one end of the line. Show that the stub charges asymptotically to the full voltage on the line.

2.2. Assume that a transmission line has a length that requires $5T$ time units for a signal to traverse. Assume also that there is a tap of length T located $2T$ from the source end. If the impedance of the line is Z_0, the source-end and far-end impedances are each $2Z_0$, and the tap has an infinite termination impedance, what are the expected waveforms for the source end of the line, the far end of the line, and the point of the tap for the first $5T$ time units after impressing a unit step voltage on the line. Plot the waveforms and show the asymptotic voltage on the line.

2.3. TTL logic has the following characteristics:
   a) When an output is high, it has a voltage of 3.6 V with no load. The voltage drops as current is drawn, and the apparent internal impedance is approximately 120 Ω. (Assume that this characteristic is linear.)
   b) When the output is low, the voltage is 0.3 V. The voltage rises as current into the output increases. Current flow is from the inputs driven by the gate into the gate output. (The gate is acting as a current sink.) A typical gate can sink 16 mA with the voltage rising to about 0.8 V. (Assume that this is a linear rise).
   c) A high gate input is at 2.0 V or more, and draws about 50 μA for all voltages above 2.0 V.
   d) A low gate input is below 0.8 V, and sources 1.6 mA at 0.3 V. In the region between 0.0 V and 0.8 V, the impedance of the gate is approximately 50 kΩ. (Assume this is linear.) The gate input is clamped by a diode, so the diode cannot go more negative than 0.6 V.

   Use this description of TTL logic to draw curves for V versus I for high and low outputs and for high and low inputs. Fill in the unspecified parts of the curve with your best guess (or intuitive interpolation).

   Use the curves you have drawn to compute graphically the transmission line behavior of a TTL gate driving a TTL gate over a transmission line of 150-Ω impedance. Compute and plot the response for a gate output going from high to low and low to high.

2.4. Repeat the graphical solution of Problem 2.3 for a logic family whose output impedance is 2 k Ω instead of 120 Ω. Show the response going from high to low and from low to high. Comment on the advantages or disadvantages of the large output impedance.

2.5. Repeat the graphical solution of Problem 2.3 for a gate that does not have an input diode clamp to hold the input from going low. Assume that the V versus I curve for this problem is obtained by simply extrapolating the curve from the nearest region in which the *V* versus *I* curve is defined. Comment on the advantages of the clamping diode in TTL logic.

2.6. You are given a pair of devices with a transmission line running between them, and you are to determine the *maximum* rate of transmission of signals between the devices under various termination conditions. The transmission line receiver must have a signal present for at least 10 ns at a voltage less than 0.8 V for a logic 0 or greater than 2.0 V for a logic 1 in order for the device to produce this same signal on its output. For voltage fluctuations above 2.0 V or below 0.8 V, with a duration less than 10 ns, the receiver output is not predictable. The source voltage is 3.3 V and 0.3 V for logic 1 and logic 0, respectively. For this problem assume the idealized voltage source is a battery connected to 3.3 V (for logic 1) or 0.3 V (for logic 0), even though this model is not necessarily correct in actual practice.

Assume that signal propagation down the length of the line takes 10 ns. Calculate the maximum signaling rate on the line for the following terminations.

a) Zero source impedance, Z_0 (matched) load impedance.
b) Z_0 (matched) source impedance, infinite load impedance.
c) $3Z_0$ source impedance, $9Z_0$ load impedance.
d) $9Z_0$ source impedance, $3Z_0$ load impedance.
e) Assume that the line can be tapped at arbitrary points with stubs of zero length and infinite impedance. What is the maximum signaling rate when the terminations of part a are used? What is the maximum rate when the terminations of part b are used?
f) Assume that a second receiver is tapped from the line so that the stubs to the two receivers are both of equal length and the point of the tap is a 9-ns delay from the transmitting end. Find a good way to terminate this line, and estimate the maximum signaling rate. Give a convincing argument that this termination method is good.

3 / BUS INTERCONNECTIONS

Now that we have covered both the high-level functional description of microcomputers and have looked as well at the lowest-level of implementation details, we will work our way quickly into practical interfacing techniques. This chapter treats the data paths that tie together the processor, memory, and I/O modules of a microcomputer. The strategy followed for these interconnections is similar across all microcomputers; they make use of a general structure that we call a *bus*. A bus is a collection of signal lines that carry module-to-module communications in a microcomputer. In almost all cases bus lines are unbroken, and modules simply tap onto a bus by connecting their respective inputs and outputs directly to corresponding bus signal lines. (The only exception to this rule is for signal lines used for priority resolution, as described later in this chapter.)

For high-performance applications, buses must be restricted in length, thus limiting their use to the short module-to-module connections within a computer chassis. Although these buses can be extended from one chassis to another, performance and reliability suffer as bus length increases. For the longer and lower-performance interconnections, most microcomputer systems rely on special buses, quite separate from their high-speed internal buses, or on other point-to-point connections in order to isolate the high-speed buses from the long physical buses, thereby reducing the degradation caused by excessive bus length. Exceptions to this practice occur in low-speed applications where the internal bus runs slow enough to be extended to a second chassis with little or no performance penalty. With just one type of bus, the system avoids an additional burden of integrating two distinct bus systems and protocols.

3.1 BUS FUNCTIONS

The signal lines that collectively form a bus break naturally into three groups as shown in Fig. 3.1. One group of signals carries the basic information to be communicated on the bus; the other two signal groups guarantee that the information is delivered during a bus transaction. From the earlier discussion of the functional behavior of a microprocessor, we know that the first group of signals carries such information as

1. memory address (or port ID),
2. data, and
3. command type (READ, WRITE, DATA, STATUS).

Since there are a vast number of different buses in use, there is a wide variation in just what information is carried on the first group of lines. Generally speaking, this group carries information that one module needs to convey to another in order to invoke a remote

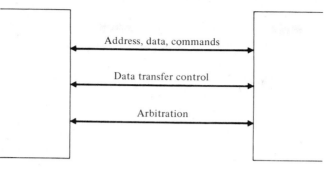

FIGURE 3.1   Bus signal and control lines.

function, response, or change of state in the remote module. In order to pass the information, the bus itself has to be controlled and operated correctly. The other two groups are dedicated to different aspects of the latter function.

The second group of signal lines controls the timing of the data transfer. This group is often called the *data handshake lines*, and contains the signals that dictate when each individual data transfer begins and ends. The handshake lines have a role analogous to traffic lights on a roadway. The handshakes start and stop transactions, and they exert the same functional control on all transactions regardless of transaction type.

The type of transaction comes into play on the third group of lines, the arbitration lines, which give critical transactions priority over less critical ones when deciding what transactions shall access the bus. This third group of lines arbitrates which module gains access to the bus. The necessity for arbitration is due to the inherent problem that occurs when two or more modules attempt to transmit information simultaneously. If module A spews forth a logic 0 while module B attempts to transmit a logic 1 at the same instant of time, we say that there is a *bus conflict*. The signal actually delivered depends on the logic family that drives the bus. A line driven by open-collector drivers moves to the 0 state during any conflict, so that in the given example, the logic 1 output by module B is lost. Then one or both modules lose data at the point of conflict, and what data are lost is unpredictable. Hence, conflicts almost certainly result in a communications failure on the bus. To ensure reliable communication, as a general rule only one module at a time can transmit on the bus, although potentially all other modules can accept the transmission and change state in response to it.

A bus conflict can be more disastrous than portrayed here. For example, what happens when tri-state drivers engage in a bus conflict? In this case, there is a possibility of damaging the bus drivers because the conflict creates a low impedance path from V_{CC} to ground through the output stages of the conflicting gates. The high current through this path can burn out both driving gates. If either gate fails in a shorted condition, the failure could be in conflict with other driving gates on the same signal line, and burn them out as well. If bus conflicts occur during an instruction-fetch cycle, the instruction received by the processor is a corrupted version of its original form, and the incorrect version almost inevitably wreaks havoc in the program.

The role of the arbitration lines is then very clearly defined. They guarantee that, at most, one module at a time transmits on the bus. The first two groups of signals, the information and handshake groups, are thus protected from conflict by the arbitration group. The arbitration group has inherent conflicts because all potential transmitting devices use these lines concurrently as part of the arbitration process. Therefore, in many buses the arbitration lines are driven with open-collector devices, and the arbitration protocol depends on the OR-function logic of the open-collector gate.

Later sections of this chapter treat various methods for implementing both the handshake and arbitration protocols. Even though the context of the discussion is buses, the protocols have a use that extends into other areas of microcomputers as well. For example, an arbitration protocol for selecting one of several potential bus transmitters is also suitable for selecting one of several I/O ports in an interrupt-priority resolver.

3.2 THE BUS HANDSHAKE

Handshake protocols fall generally into three broad classes:

1. synchronous (clocked transfer, one clock period per transfer),
2. asynchronous (unclocked), and
3. semisynchronous (clocked transfer, one or more clock periods per transfer).

Since the specific function of the handshake lines is to indicate the beginning and end of a data transfer, the handshake lines must somehow mark these points through voltage changes in the handshake signals. Some buses have very complex, sequential timing for each data transfer, perhaps requiring a number of different data to pass along the bus during a single transaction. For these buses, the handshake lines signal the beginning and end of each subcycle within the full cycle, as well as identifying the start and end of the full cycle.

The three generic handshake techniques span a spectrum of different approaches from complete control by a clock to no clock control whatsoever. Synchronous protocols are among the easiest to implement because the only control signal is a clock oscillator. The rising and falling edges of the clock signify, respectively, the beginning and end of a bus cycle. All memories, peripherals, and processors on the bus are controlled by the same clock oscillator so that modules operate in "lock-step," advancing cycle by cycle as the clock line ticks away. Not only are synchronous protocols the least complex of the three protocols, but they also, in general, lead to the fastest transactions (provided that the responding devices are fast enough to operate at the bus-clock speed).

Synchronous Buses

The timing of a typical synchronous protocol is illustrated in Fig. 3.2. The top waveform is the bus clock, which synchronizes all modules to a common time base. (It is shown here with a 50% duty cycle, but the actual duty cycle differs for various synchronous buses.) Address and data lines are shown on the next two waveforms. The addresses and data reach their stable values at the beginning of the shaded area, retain their values through the high half-cycle of the clock, and fall at the end of the trailing shaded area. Although the address and data lines are shown in the high-state during the active portion of the clock, they actually can be in either a high or a low state, depending on the information they convey. The figure actually shows the period during which the address and data lines are *stable*, and does not show their logic values.

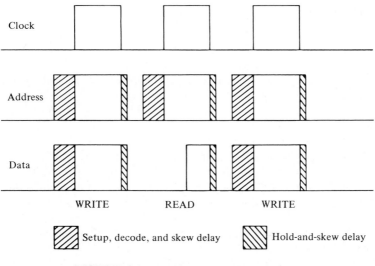

FIGURE 3.2   Timing for a synchronous bus.

There are several different reasons for the shaded area of the waveforms. Fig. 3.3 shows one source of logic delay in the address decoder of a receiving module on the bus. The figure shows a bus transmitter, hereafter called a *bus master*, transmitting to a receiver labeled *bus slave*. There are potentially many slaves on the bus, and the purpose of the address lines is to select a single slave to respond to the bus transaction. Therefore, the figure shows the address lines entering a decoder that detects the slave's address, which then selects this specific slave by producing a signal that forces the slave to load data from the bus when the clock reaches the active phase of its cycle. The decoder has to produce its signal in advance of the rising of the edge of the clock, so that the address lines must be stable for at least the duration of the logic delay through the decoder.

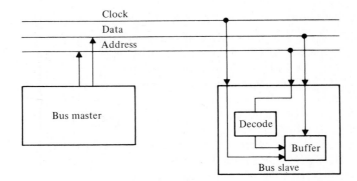

FIGURE 3.3   Typical slave internal structure.

Another related effect that cannot be ignored is the setup time and hold time of logic in the buffer. *Setup time* is the minimum amount of time that a control signal has to be present on an input of a memory device before the clock triggers a transfer into the device. *Hold time* is the minimum time that data has to be held stable on the inputs of a memory device after a clock change triggers a transfer into that device. The setup time for the diagram in Fig. 3.3 for a WRITE into the slave is the time required for the address lines to be stable after they reach the buffer, but before applying a clock to the buffer. The hold time in Fig. 3.2 depends on whether the bus operation is READ or WRITE. For a WRITE, the hold time is the hold time of the buffer in the slave. For a READ, the hold time is the hold time of the equivalent buffer in the master. In both cases, the addresses and data must be stable for at least the duration of the hold time after the clock changes state. Address and data lines need to have identical setup and hold times. If they are not identical, the bus protocol must incorporate setup and hold times that are long enough to satisfy the maximum of the address and data requirements.

In the light of the information on setup and hold times, let us return to Fig. 3.2 to consider how these times are represented in the figure. For a WRITE operation, the master transmits both addresses and data in advance of the rising edge of the clock. During this time the slave decodes the address, and the data lines stabilize at the buffer. When the clock rises, the selected slave initiates an internal WRITE operation, during which it copies the data on its data lines into an address or register identified by the address lines. If the slave is a memory chip, the subsequent delay accounts for the write-access time to memory, usually on the order of 100 to 200 ns for moderate-speed metal-oxide silicon (MOS) devices. Other devices can be bus slaves as well, including I/O ports and discrete registers. Some devices respond faster than the moderate-speed memory, but the fixed-cycle time of the synchronous bus cannot take advantage of the faster response. The falling edge of the clock signifies the end of the bus cycle. At this time, the WRITE operation is complete, and the slave can disconnect logically from the data lines.

The READ operation is similar to WRITE for the address lines, but data lines behave differently. In this case the rising edge of the clock initiates a memory READ in the slave. Some time after the clock rises, the data reaches the output buffer of the slave, which in turn places the data on the bus. The data has to be on the bus at least one setup time before the falling edge of the clock, where the setup time in question is the setup time of the master's data buffer. The slave holds the data on the bus at least one hold time after the falling edge of the clock in order to satisfy the hold-time requirements of the master.

Reexamination of Fig. 3.2 shows we have accounted for the general form of the shaded area, although we have not accounted for exact lengths of time. Note that the setup time is shown much longer than the hold time because the setup time includes the decoding delay in the slave, as well as other factors we now examine.

Among the other sources of timing delay accounted in the shaded area is *signal skew*, which is explained more fully in Fig. 3.4. The top two waveforms show the signals on two address lines as they appear at the bus master. Both signals are assumed to change at exactly the same instant for the purposes of this discussion although, in reality, the master itself may produce these signals displaced slightly with respect to each other. The master transmits the signals over the bus to the slave, which sees the signals as shown in the lower two waveforms of the figure. Note that the signals no longer change at the same instant of time, but now one changes D time units later than the other. This change in relative timing produced somewhere in the bus system is what we mean by *skew*.

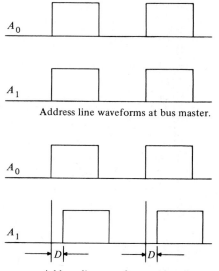

Address line waveforms at bus master.

Address line waveforms at bus slave.

FIGURE 3.4 Skew in signal transmission. The delay D is the skew in the signals.

Several different sources of skew account for the delay. One source is a difference in the propagation delays of the two signals because the signals follow slightly different paths in going from master to slave. Propagation delays usually influence skew less than the varying logic delays through gates on the path from master to slave. Gate delays may vary from chip to chip by 10 to 20 ns, depending on the chip family. Since each of the bus signals travels through a different set of gates, the end-to-end propagation time is rarely the same for all bus signals. The rise time and fall time of a signal also affect skewing delays. A gate recognizes a change in a signal when the signal voltage passes the gate threshold. If capacitive effects stretch out the rise or fall time, there is an apparent increase in the delay between the start of a signal transition and the time when the transition is recognized. Since this time also depends on the gate threshold, differences in gate thresholds contribute to differences in skew in much the same way that rise and fall times impact skew.

To compensate for skew, addresses must stabilize at least one maximum skew time earlier than in the absence of skew, just in case some address line is delayed by skew relative to the rising edge of the clock. Hence the shaded area said to be setup time in Fig. 3.2 includes this skew time plus the decoding time and address setup time. Note also that the hold time for data written includes skew to protect against problems caused by clock skew. If the clock were delayed relative to the data during the propagation of the signals from master to slave, then the apparent hold time of data at the slave is diminished by the amount of the skew. Hence, for a WRITE cycle the master has to assert data for at least one hold time plus one skew time after the clock edge falls.

It is interesting to consider the effects of propagation delays on hold time. For the READ operation, propagation delays actually reduce the hold time somewhat, whereas for WRITE operations they have no effect unless increases in propagation delay tend to increase clock skew also. Consider the READ in Fig. 3.2, for example, and observe what happens if there are significant propagation delays between master and slave. When the master drops the clock signal at the end of the cycle, the output data at the slave remains stable at the master's input buffer for at least one round-trip propagation time between master and slave. This is true because the clock edge change has to propagate from master to slave, and the resulting changes on the data lines then propagate back to the master. Technically speaking, a slave can reduce hold time by the amount of a propagation delay, but in practice it is very difficult to do so. The propagation time delay depends on the relative positions of the master and slave on the bus, and this varies from configuration to configuration. Yet the slave module has to be engineered to work in every configuration, so that at best the slave can take advantage of the shortest propagation delay that can occur in any configuration. This delay is so unpredictable, and likely to be very small in any event, that it is rarely worthwhile to consider.

This brings us to the end of our discussion of the details of Fig. 3.2. To summarize the effects that limit the bus bandwidth, we have

1. setup time of data and control signals before clocking data into a buffer,
2. address decode delay,

3. skew time of address and data signals relative to a rising and to a falling clock edge,
4. hold time of data at a buffer input, after clocking data into the buffer, and
5. one round-trip propagation delay (for the READ operation).

The bus cycle time cannot be smaller than

$$T_{\text{SETUP}} + T_{\text{DECODE}} + 2T_{\text{SKEW}} + \text{MAX}(T_{\text{HOLD}}, \; T_{\text{RT-PROP}}),$$

where the MAX operation recognizes that propagation delay can be overlapped with hold time. If the cycle time of a bus is shorter than the time given here, the signaling rate fails to meet the signal specifications for modules that connect to that bus, so that incorrect or unreliable computations may result. Even this upper limit on bandwidth is overly optimistic. In practical situations, the master itself has an internal delay between transactions, and the slave has a nonzero access time, both of which increase the minimum cycle time and decrease realizable bandwidth.

The primary advantage of the synchronous system is simplicity. Data transfers are controlled through a single signal, and the data transfers run with minimal overhead in terms of skew, setup, hold, and propagation delays. However, the synchronous bus has a serious problem in dealing with slow slaves connected to the bus. The synchronous bus described thus far cannot accommodate devices whose access time is greater than the time available during a clock period. With the given bus protocol, the clock rate has to be set slow enough to satisfy the slowest device on the bus where the device's response time includes the effect of propagation delays due to physical separation. But this reduces the bandwidth for all transactions, and the slow device has thereby decreased the potential system performance even though the slow device is rarely accessed.

Asynchronous Buses

For the computer that drives a mix of devices with widely varying access times, the synchronous protocol may be inappropriate because the bus runs at the speed of the slowest device. Intuitively speaking, it is advantageous to have fast transactions for fast devices and slow transactions for slow or distant devices, so that transaction time varies with the device rather than being fixed for all time by a system clock. The timing and control signals for a typical asynchronous bus that has these characteristics appear in Fig. 3.5.

This bus is said to be a *fully interlocked asynchronous bus*, and is by far the most popular asynchronous protocol in use today. The DEC Unibus for the PDP-11 family is one notable implementation of this protocol (Digital Equipment, 1979). The term *fully interlocked* stems from the way the two control signals work together during a bus transaction. The control signals in the figure are called MASTER and SLAVE, and take the name of the module that produces their respective signals. The interlocked protocol requires changes to alternate between the control signals and to occur sequentially, with a change in one signal arming the other for its subsequent change. By interlocking in this manner, the information on address and data lines is guaranteed to be transmitted without conflict and without loss or duplication by the bus.

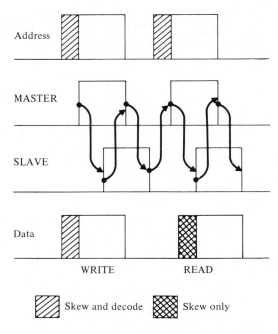

Address

MASTER

SLAVE

Data

WRITE   READ

▨ Skew and decode   ▧ Skew only

FIGURE 3.5   Timing for a fully interlocked asynchronous bus.

For the WRITE transaction, the bus master places address and data on the bus. After a delay to allow for skew, decoding, and setup time, the bus master raises MASTER, which signifies to the slave that the data can be accepted. Raising MASTER thus triggers a slave memory to initiate a WRITE cycle, and latches data into a slave buffer register. In any case, action at the slave takes place only after MASTER is asserted.

While the slave is busy copying data in response to MASTER, the SLAVE signal remains low. When copying is completed, the slave module raises SLAVE to signify, "I've got it." The handshake continues with MASTER going low ("I see you've got it"), and SLAVE going low ("I see you see I've got it"). The last two transitions are part of a sequence to guarantee that neither MASTER nor SLAVE changes too quickly. SLAVE stays high as shown in the figure until the MASTER signal goes low, thus ensuring that the high SLAVE signal has been observed and acted upon. Only then does SLAVE go low. Similarly, a new transaction cannot be initiated until SLAVE goes low signifying the end of the present transaction. Hence the rising edge of MASTER (and the transitions on the address and data lines) are interlocked to the fall of SLAVE.

A READ transaction is very similar to a WRITE, with the high value of MASTER initiating the operation at the slave after the bus master places an address on the bus. SLAVE goes high after the slave module accesses the datum requested and places it on the bus. In this context, a high value on SLAVE signifies, "The READ is complete."

This triggers the master to load its buffer from the bus. During this period SLAVE must remain high, and the data lines must be stable. If the slave were to change these signals prematurely, the master could read incorrect information. When the master has completed its acceptance of data, it drops MASTER (''I've got it''), and then SLAVE drops (''I see you've got it'').

The reasons for the interlocking become clear when we consider how a partially inter-locked protocol can fail. Consider the two situations shown in Fig. 3.6. In Fig. 3.6(a), we permit SLAVE to drop a fixed time after it rises, without waiting for MASTER to drop. Likewise, we also remove the interlock between the falling edge of SLAVE and the lead-ing edge of MASTER. Also in Fig 3.6(a), SLAVE goes down well before MASTER does, and we see that the transfer is done safely. The dotted lines show SLAVE delayed somewhat with respect to MASTER, possibly because of long propagation delays or sig-nal skew. In this case, if MASTER drops and rises again while SLAVE is high, it may mistake the high value of SLAVE for a response to the next transfer. This situation is shown in Fig. 3.6(b). Now the master may remove data and addresses too quickly from the bus for the slave to accept the new data. As a result, one transaction is lost.

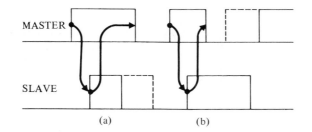

FIGURE 3.6   Examples of signaling with a partially interlocked asynchronous protocol.

Although partial interlocking as shown in Fig. 3.6 lacks the safety of full interlock-ing, it can be made safe provided that master and slaves adhere to a strict set of timing constraints on the noninterlocked transitions. The advantage of eliminating part of the in-terlocking is that the bus transaction can be made a little faster so that the bus bandwidth can be greater than it would be in a fully interlocked protocol. But tight constraints usu-ally result in higher manufacturing cost, making the partially interlocked protocols less desirable in general, although useful in specific applications where the extra expense is justified.

Returning to Fig. 3.5, we note in this protocol shaded areas that represent roles simi-lar to those represented by the shaded areas of the synchronous protocol. Addresses have to be raised before MASTER at least early enough to permit address decoding and buffer setup, and to protect against skew on the address lines relative to MASTER. Hold times are not shown specifically, but exist nevertheless. Hold time is usually incorporated into the slave by delaying the SLAVE signal one hold time after a WRITE is completed, or after presenting data on the bus for a READ. Obviously, the hold time can equally well be incorporated into the master, with the SLAVE signal being presented concurrently with an event while the master delays its actions one hold time after receiving a transition on SLAVE. Whichever of these techniques is used in a protocol, that technique has to be used consistently for all slave and master modules, for otherwise the protocol will not work correctly. Deskewing data and address signals relative to MASTER and SLAVE can normally be combined with hold time, since skew effects are treated by inserting delays in the protocol, in much the way that delays for hold time are inserted into a protocol.

The wide acceptance of the fully interlocked asynchronous protocol is largely due to its reliability and its general efficiency in dealing with devices that have a broad range of response times over long buses. But the protocol is inherently slower than the synchronous protocol because of extra propagation delays. The minimum cycle time for a READ operation must account for

1. deskew (and setup time) of addresses to slave,
2. address decode at slave,
3. deskew (and hold time) of data returned by slave, and
4. two round-trip propagation delays of MASTER and SLAVE signals.

The first three items in this list are comparable to those for synchronous buses, but the propagation delay for the fully interlocked handshake is double that of a clocked bus. Information is passed up and down the bus twice per transaction for asynchronous buses, but only once for synchronous buses. The second round trip is omitted for synchronous protocols because the devices are known in advance to respond within a fixed maximum time. The purpose of the second round trip for an asynchronous bus is to convey completion information that is not bounded in advance.

Semisynchronous Buses

Because the propagation delays of the asynchronous bus severely limit maximum bandwidth, many bus designers have turned to "hybrid" buses that combine the advantages of synchronous and asynchronous buses. One such bus is the *semisynchronous bus* that appears in Fig. 3.7. This bus has two control signals, CLOCK (from the master) and WAIT (from the slave). In some sense the signals play the role of MASTER and SLAVE for the asynchronous bus, but the propagation delays are half those of the asynchronous bus because a single round trip is all that is necessary for a successful handshake. For fast devices, the bus is essentially a synchronous bus controlled by the clock alone. If a slave is fast enough to respond in one clock cycle, it does not raise WAIT, and the semisynchronous bus behaves like a synchronous bus. If the slave cannot respond in one cycle, it raises the WAIT signal, and the master halts. Subsequent clock cycles find the master idle as long as WAIT is asserted. When the slave can respond, it drops WAIT, and the master accepts the slave response using the timing of the standard synchronous protocol. The semisynchronous bus thus has the speed of the synchronous bus and versatility of the

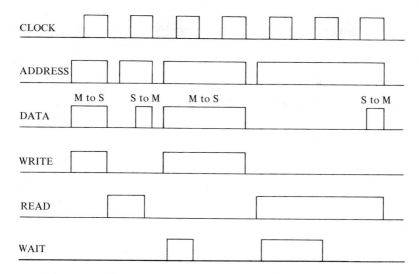

FIGURE 3.7 A semisynchronous bus with cycle times increased by a WAIT signal.

asynchronous bus. However, the length of the semisynchronous bus is limited by the requirement that WAIT must be asserted within a fixed period of time. So these buses cannot have an indefinitely long length, but there is no equivalent timing constraint for asynchronous buses.

Another way to retain the advantage of the fast synchronous protocol while accom-
modating slow devices is with the use of a "split-cycle" protocol as shown in Fig. 3.8. In
this case a READ is split into two separate transactions. During the first transaction, the
bus master transmits an address to a slave, and then disconnects from the bus. Other masters then use the bus until the slave is able to return the requested data. At this point, the
slave initiates the second part of the split cycle by accessing the bus *as a master* and
transmitting the data to the requesting module, which responds *as a slave*. The split cycle
places a greater burden on the master and slave modules because each type of module
must have the logic to assume both master and slave roles. Moreover, the bus protocol assumes that many different bus masters access the bus at different times, so that every
module must also contain the logic for bus arbitration protocol in order to gain access to
the bus as a master.

The split-cycle protocol differs slightly in the information passed on the bus from the
protocols studied above. For a READ transaction the master supplies a unique identifier
for itself together with the address of the requested data so that the slave can return the requested data to the master. In fact, the master identifier is the address used during the
second part of the split cycle, and both halves of a READ follow the protocol of a WRITE
cycle.

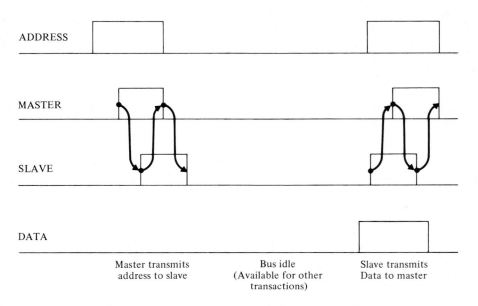

ADDRESS

MASTER

SLAVE

DATA

Master transmits   Bus idle   Slave transmits
address to slave   (Available for other   Data to master
                            transactions)

FIGURE 3.8   A split-cycle protocol READ transaction.

Clearly the performance of a split-cycle protocol depends on being able to use the bus time between the cycle halves for other transactions. Thus the protocol is most suitable for systems with multiple processors or multiple DMA devices on the bus; it makes little sense for low-performance systems. This type of protocol is used in high-performance minicomputers such as DEC's VAX-11/780, but has rarely been used in microcomputers until the introduction of the Intel iAPX-432 in 1981.

3.3 ARBITRATION PROTOCOLS

The purpose of arbitration has been discussed earlier, namely to guarantee conflict-free access to a bus. Bus arbitration is absolutely essential in systems that have two or more bus masters, and is not necessary for systems that have but a single master. But even in the latter case, the lines and logic required for arbitration are normally included in general-purpose modules so that these modules can be used in both contexts. Also, a system initially configured without DMA can be upgraded to a system with DMA, with the required arbitration facilities already in place.

One of the simplest possible arbitration techniques is called a *daisy chain*, and is shown in Fig. 3.9. The idea is that a single arbiter (the microprocessor itself in a single-processor system with DMA) has exclusive access to the bus until a request for access comes from a DMA device or other processor (identified as the small modules in the figure.) In response to a REQUEST signal, the arbiter issues a GRANT. This signal passes

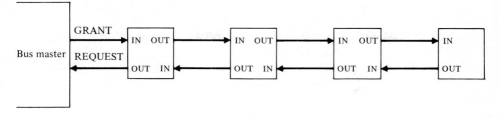

FIGURE 3.9   Daisy-chained bus arbitration (2 wires).

sequentially through the other potential bus masters. The first requesting module that receives GRANT takes control of the bus for one transaction. While that module has control
of the bus, it does not pass the GRANT to the next module on the bus. Consequently, no
other module has access to the bus.

Typical timing of this protocol appears in Fig. 3.10. The first transaction shows a particular module generating a REQUEST, and eventually receiving a GRANT. For this
transaction, there is no REQUEST into the module, and no GRANT is passed on by the
module. For the next transaction the module is inactive. It receives a REQUEST, which it
repeats. When a GRANT appears later, it passes this on to the lower-priority modules. For
the last transaction the module both generates a REQUEST and receives a REQUEST.
The module maintains an active output on REQUEST through its bus transaction and
through that of the lower priority device. When the GRANT reaches the module in
response to the REQUEST, the module takes control of the bus and maintains an inactive
output on GRANT. At the conclusion of its transaction, it passes GRANT down the daisy
chain because the REQUEST input is still active.

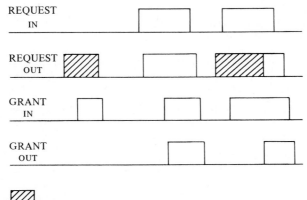

FIGURE 3.10   Daisy-chain timing.

The sequential flow of GRANT is crucial in this case. The protocol attempts to grant high-priority requests before low-priority requests, so that GRANT is routed to the modules in the order of priority. In essence, each module in succession is offered access to the bus; and the first that has a pending request accepts access.

Although the protocol appears to have all the desired characteristics, it has timing hazards that can lead to bus failures unless special precautions are taken to eliminate the hazards. Let us first investigate what problems exist, then show a popular 3-wire protocol that is hazard-free.

The arbitration protocol we have described appears to work correctly, because one module at a time receives the opportunity to take control, and therefore only one module can be granted bus control for any specific cycle. Once a module begins a cycle, that cycle must run to completion. If a higher-priority module wrests control of the bus away from a lower-priority module in the midst of a cycle, the aborted cycle may appear to be correct to the bus master or bus slave and will result in a communication failure. Therefore, a high-priority module must recognize that the lower-priority modules can be in one of three states, namely,

1. idle,
2. holding a pending request, or
3. actively controlling the bus.

The high-priority module can take control only if no lower-priority module is in the third state. The REQUEST/GRANT protocol, however, passes only one bit of information from the lower-priority modules. This bit by itself cannot distinguish among three different states. The critical distinction is between a pending request and active control of the bus. Therefore, to make the protocol safe each module uses the GRANT as well as the REQUEST signal to determine the state of the lower-priority part of the bus. Specifically,

1. if GRANT is low and REQUEST is high, there is at least one pending request, but no lower-priority module has active control of the bus, and
2. if GRANT is high and REQUEST is high, then a requesting module has been granted bus control and is currently conducting a transaction.

If a high-priority module generates a bus request while GRANT is high, it cannot take control of the bus. Safe arbitration requires that the module must see GRANT change from low to high *after* REQUEST is raised, and thus the leading edge of GRANT triggers the bus-control decision as the GRANT signal passes down the arbitration lines.

Edge-triggering on GRANT is necessary, but in itself does not provide complete protection from timing hazards. The protocol must ensure that the decision to take control of the bus is made sequentially, one module after another, and propagates in one direction on the bus. To see what happens when this rule is broken, consider what happens when the protocol in Fig. 3.10 is changed ever so slightly to violate the rule. Assume that when a module in control of the bus completes its transaction, that module passes GRANT on to the next lower-priority module, whether or not there is a REQUEST pending from that part of the bus. This protocol appears to be reasonable because a REQUEST from a lower-priority module may be propagating up the bus at this very instant of time, and the requesting module may be able to take control when the GRANT arrives without having to wait until the next arbitration cycle. The timing hazard in this protocol appears in Fig. 3.11. Assume that the controllers are numbered 1, 2, and 3 in descending order of priority, and that we observe the bus with Controller 2 performing a transaction. Let us also assume that while Controller 2 is active, Controllers 1 and 3 are both inactive, and that both generate REQUEST signals shortly after Controller 2 terminates. Signals propagate in both directions from Controller 2. GRANT continues down the bus to the lower-priority modules, while REQUEST drops low and propagates towards the bus arbiter. As GRANT propagates to Controller 3, if this controller generates a request before the leading edge arrives, it will take control of the bus when it sees GRANT go high. Meanwhile, Controller 1 sees a high GRANT from the arbiter and a low REQUEST from the lower-priority modules on the bus. In this condition Controller 1 can assume that it is safe to take control of the bus; or, to be sure that it sees the leading edge of GRANT, the controller can output a low on REQUEST (repeating the input condition), then raise REQUEST (reporting its local bus request). The latter situation results in GRANT dropping in response to the low REQUEST and rising again in response to the high REQUEST. In either situation, Controller 1 has taken control of the bus while Controller 3 has control. A bus failure occurs.

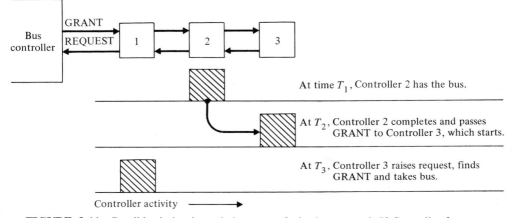

At time T_1, Controller 2 has the bus.

At T_2, Controller 2 completes and passes GRANT to Controller 3, which starts.

At T_3, Controller 3 raises request, finds GRANT and takes bus.

Controller activity ⟶

FIGURE 3.11   Possible timing hazards in an unsafe 2-wire protocol: If Controller 2 passes an inactive signal on REQUEST to Controller 1, Controller 1 can take the bus away from Controller 3.

    The reason for the failure is that in this protocol Controller 2 issues bus grant signals in both directions on the bus when it completes its transaction. With bus grants going in both directions, the protocol violates the basic rule that control decisions have to be made one module at a time, progressing from module to module down the bus.

    The protocol whose timing is illustrated in Fig. 3.10 is safe from this timing hazard because a controller does not pass GRANT to lower-priority modules unless that controller sees an active REQUEST from these modules. Therefore one of two mutually exclusive conditions holds when Controller 2 completes its bus transaction in Fig. 3.11. Either Controller 3 has a REQUEST raised or it does not. The two different responses to these conditions are

1. When REQUEST is high from Controller 3, Controller 2 asserts GRANT to Controller 3 while also asserting REQUEST high to Controller 1.
2. When REQUEST is low from Controller 3, Controller 2 deasserts GRANT to Controller 3, and also deasserts REQUEST to Controller 1.

Since these two events are mutually exclusive, the protocol is safe. Nevertheless, poor logic design can cause short glitches on the REQUEST line output to Controller 1 if Controller 3 has its REQUEST high when Controller 2 completes its transaction. The REQUEST from Controller 2 in this case was formerly generated by Controller 2's local REQUEST for the bus. When Controller 2 has completed its activity, the output value of REQUEST changes over to the condition of being generated by the REQUEST from Controller 3. As this state change occurs, a short glitch on the REQUEST line output to Controller 1 proves disastrous. (Additional timing problems caused by Controller 3's changing its REQUEST OUT state almost concurrently with the completion of Controller 2's transaction exacerbate the hazard.) The glitch propagates toward Controller 1, which will take control of the bus when the glitch arrives. Meanwhile, the GRANT propagates from Controller 2 to Controller 3, which takes the bus when it receives GRANT. Should both controllers elect to take the bus, a conflict and bus failure is inevitable. While the conditions mentioned here appear to be somewhat contrived, they are quite realistic and demonstrate the pitfalls of careless logic design and failure-prone arbitration protocol.

One of the most popular methods for arbitration is a 3-wire method shown in Fig. 3.12. This scheme is similar to the arbitration scheme of the DEC PDP-11 Unibus (Digital Equipment, 1979). Two of the three lines are continuous bus lines, with modules having the ability to inject signals onto the lines or to read signals from the lines. One line is the GRANT line, which threads the modules sequentially, and is not a continuous bus line. The REQUEST line of the 2-wire daisy chain becomes a REQUEST and a BUSY line on the 3-wire daisy chain. With the two lines REQUEST and BUSY, we are able to distinguish among the three states mentioned earlier—idle, request pending, and active control.

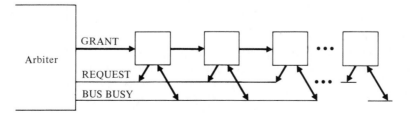

FIGURE 3.12   Safe daisy-chain arbitration protocol (3 wires).

The operation of this protocol is as follows:

1. When a controller has active control of a bus, it asserts BUS BUSY.
2. When a controller requires a bus cycle, it asserts REQUEST.
3. The arbiter transmits a GRANT signal when it detects a pending REQUEST and an inactive state on BUS BUSY. (If the arbiter is itself a bus master, such as a microprocessor, the arbiter can take one or more bus cycles when BUS BUSY falls before responding with a GRANT signal.)
4. A controller passes GRANT to the next controller if GRANT is received when the controller has no REQUEST pending.
5. A controller takes over the bus when
    i)   it has a local request pending,
    ii) BUS BUSY is inactive, and
    iii) it detects the rising edge of GRANT.

For both BUS BUSY and REQUEST, we assume that the bus forms the logical OR of the outputs from the controllers. Most implementations use open-collector drivers for driving the bus, so that the low state must be the active state because this is the state that produces an OR function.

Typical bus timing appears in Fig. 3.13. We see here the interplay of the requests from two controllers, with Controller 1 having priority over Controller 2. In the first transaction, the bus is not busy when Controller 1 makes a request. At a subsequent point in time Controller 1 receives a GRANT, and then takes control of the bus without passing GRANT to the next controller in line. When taking over the bus, Controller 1 raises BUS BUSY to signify that it has the bus. At that point the arbiter removes GRANT. Now the bus is in use, and neither REQUEST nor GRANT is high.

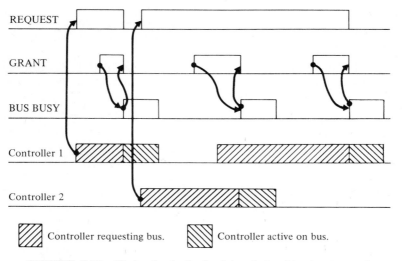

FIGURE 3.13   Timing for the 3-wire daisy-chain arbitration protocol.

Subsequently Controller 2 requires access to the bus and raises REQUEST, which propagates to the arbiter. The arbiter cannot grant access to the bus immediately because BUS BUSY is high. After BUS BUSY falls, the arbiter transmits GRANT to the controllers along the bus. Controller 1 passes this GRANT to Controller 2 because Controller 1 has no REQUEST pending. When Controller 2 receives the GRANT signal, the GRANT goes no further. Controller 2 raises BUS BUSY, lowers REQUEST, and takes over the bus. Meanwhile the arbiter removes GRANT and the arbitration cycle repeats.

Note what happens when Controller 1 requests the bus after passing GRANT to Controller 2. Because Controller 1 raises REQUEST *after* passing GRANT to the next controller in line, it does not remove GRANT when it raises REQUEST; moreover, Controller 1 does not take over the bus even though it sees GRANT high. The protocol prevents Controller 1 from taking the bus because the controller has missed the leading edge of GRANT. If Controller 1 responds to a level signal on GRANT instead of the leading edge, then Controller 1 could wrest control of the bus away from Controller 2 after Controller 2 initiates a transaction. This is an unsafe condition. Hence, the edge-sensitivity to the GRANT signal is essential for the protocol to be safe. Controller 1 eventually receives control of the bus, but this happens on the next arbitration cycle. When Controller 1 eventually takes control, the BUS BUSY signal first drops (Controller 2 completes its transaction), and then the arbiter issues a new GRANT that is accepted by Controller 1.

This protocol is safer than the 2-wire protocol for a number of reasons, although it can fail (as can any protocol) if events on the bus occur too closely in time. We take up this particular type of failure later in this chapter, but for the present we focus on the safety of the 3-wire arbitration protocol. To show the higher reliability of the 3-wire protocol, consider the failure of the 2-wire protocol. Recall that even though the 2-wire protocol is safe when glitch-free, with glitches present it becomes unsafe because Controller 2 can pass contrary information in opposite directions on the bus, and this information can enable modules on either side of Controller 2 to take control of the bus. For the 3-wire protocol, in order for both Controller 1 and Controller 3 to take control of the bus, they both have to see a low on BUS BUSY and a rising edge on GRANT. But GRANT is produced only after the low on BUS BUSY propagates forward to the arbiter. GRANT is not passed directly to Controller 3 from Controller 2. In the 3-wire protocol, the GRANT passes through all of the modules sequentially until the arbitration winner stops the propagation of GRANT. Hence, Controller 3 cannot elect to take control of the bus unless Controller 1 has first had the opportunity to do so.

The 3-wire protocol is insensitive to glitches in many instances. Suppose, for example, that Controller 1 raises its REQUEST just soon enough before GRANT passes through the controller to see the leading edge of GRANT, but the timing is so critical that a momentary pulse on GRANT propagates down the bus to the lower-priority modules. Note that GRANT passes through logic gates as it propagates down the bus, while BUS BUSY propagates in the same direction along a bus wire. In all likelihood BUS BUSY reaches the lower-priority modules before GRANT does. Hence, a requesting module that sees the brief GRANT pulse is likely to do so when BUS BUSY is high, which is an illegal condition. Good logic design dictates that this condition be checked, and that a module that observes this condition be prevented from taking the bus.

The reliability of the 3-wire protocol is the reason behind its general acceptance in the industry. Almost all bus arbitration protocols for high-speed bus systems use the 3-wire system or a variation of it.

3.4 ASYNCHRONOUS TIMING DIFFICULTIES

In our discussion of arbitration we hinted at inherent difficulties in resolving asynchronous signals. The arbitration protocol relies on being able to tell if GRANT occurs before or after REQUEST. Is it always possible to make this decision correctly? If not, what is the failure mode?

The basic problem in resolving timing differences in two signals reduces to that of latching a single datum into a flip-flop. If the datum is present before the clock, the datum is latched successfully. If the datum is not present, the flip-flop latches a quiescent value (presumably a 0), and misses the datum. Every flip-flop and, in fact, every memory element must observe a datum on its input for at least a minimum time in order to copy that datum into memory in response to a clock pulse. This is equivalent to saying that the input signal must contain a minimum amount of energy in order to raise some input buffer above a threshold. The minimum time is usually expressed as a setup and hold time.

It is clear enough that a signal that satisfies setup and hold time constraints can be recognized successfully, but what happens if the constraints are violated? The results are unpredictable and disastrous. Chaney and Molnar (1973) show photos of oscilloscope traces of real devices whose input signals violate setup and hold times. Among the interesting results shown are as follows:

1. Flip-flops enter a ''metastable'' state in which the output lies about midway between a logic 0 and logic 1. The output stays in this condition for a variable and unpredictable amount of time, then relaxes unpredictably to either a logic 0 or logic 1.
2. Flip-flop outputs oscillate in phase with each other (violating the rule that the outputs are complementary) until they relax at complementary logic values an unpredictable time later.
3. Flip-flops stay in a stable state for a time longer than the worst-case transition time, then switch to their final state.
4. Flip-flops output a spurious brief pulse of unpredictable duration before assuming a steady state.

A typical failure mode is shown in Fig. 3.14. Mead and Conway (1980) address the same type of problem in the context of VLSI. Synchronization is a fundamental problem no matter how small or how fast the gate.

The implication of all of these problems is that we cannot depend on the flip-flop falling to a correct and consistent state, nor can we depend on the settling time to be within a maximum period of time. How then is it possible to design a safe, asynchronous system?

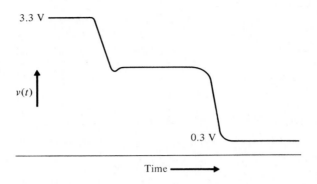

FIGURE 3.14   Output voltage as a function of time for a
flip-flop in the metastable state.

The only way to be sure that a system is free from the clocking difficulties we have
discussed is to use a single master clock from which all other timing is derived. At each
flip-flop we can enforce the setup and hold-time constraints to be met by permitting signals to change only within certain safe periods of time. These safe periods are derived
from the master clock so that each module that produces changes on its signals derives the
safe period for those changes from the same time base as every other module. Because of
propagation delays and skew, there are uncertainties in the edges of the master clock, but
these can be taken into account when producing the windows that gate signals during safe
periods. One way of gating signals safely is shown in Fig. 3.15. In this case, signal X
changes within the setup and hold-time constraints for the Phase 2 clock but is known to
be stable during the change of an earlier clock (Phase 1). So X drives a flip-flop gated
from Phase 1. This guarantees that X is stable when the first flip-flop latches X, and the
first flip-flop is stable when the second latches its value. As long as all signal changes can
be gated from a single master clock, in principle every flip-flop change can be made safe
from asynchronous timing hazards. But if signals can change in truly asynchronous
fashion, as is the case at interfaces between two separate, individually clocked systems,
then timing hazards are inherent. In this case, the designer can at best reduce the problem,
but not eliminate it.

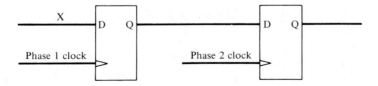

FIGURE 3.15   A safe procedure for gating a signal that is unstable
during the Phase 2 clock setup period.

The method of Fig. 3.15 for guaranteeing that X is read only while X is stable is also used to synchronize X to the system when X can change at any time whatsoever. No problems occur if X is stable for the flip-flop setup and hold times of Phase 1. If X should change within the constraint times, the output of the flip-flop is unpredictable, and the flip-flop may enter the metastable state for an indefinite period of time. The idea is to have the edges of the Phase 1 and Phase 2 clocks far enough apart that the Phase 1 flip-flop is almost certainly in a stable state when Phase 2 triggers the second flip-flop. Whereas there is no guarantee that the first flip-flop will be stable at this time, the longer the period of time between Phase 1 and Phase 2, the more likely it will be that the first flip-flop will stabilize before Phase 2 occurs. For example, if the flip-flop is a 74S74, the stabilizing time should be at least 250 ns. For the bus systems we describe, the raising of REQUEST can occur at any time relative to GRANT. To avoid timing difficulties, both GRANT and REQUEST should be clocked relative to a master clock to guarantee that they cannot change within a critical time of each other.

3.5 INTERRUPT-REQUEST ARBITRATION

The arbitration schemes used to control access to a bus may be used for other purposes as well. Earlier in this textbook we described the functional details of interrupt-device identification, and we mentioned that some microcomputer systems incorporate a priority mechanism to resolve conflicts among interrupting devices. That priority mechanism is often implemented as a 2-wire or 3-wire daisy chain, using the essentially similar bus protocols, which we described, for gaining access to a bus.

The simplest form of device identification is shown in Fig. 3.16. This is a party-line system in which the interrupt request (IRQ) is the logical OR of the request signals generated by the devices. In responding to the IRQ request, the processor must first query

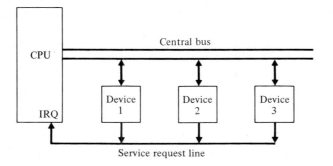

FIGURE 3.16   A party-line interrupt facility.

each device with a polling program to determine which is ready for service. Devices are normally polled in order of their priority, from the highest-priority device to the lowest. Because device polling is so time consuming, the vectored interrupt method has gained in popularity and acceptance. This scheme appears in Fig. 3.17. The scheme shown is essentially the 2-wire system, but it could as easily be the 3-wire system. The REQUEST line is the interrupt request line, and the GRANT line is the status line that indicates when the interrupt is honored by the processor. When the GRANT signal goes high, the device winning of the arbitration cycle places its device code (or some uniquely identifying integer) on the bus. The processor accepts the device code, and computes a starting address for the device-handler software from its device code. Thus, within a few machine cycles of honoring the interrupt, the processor can transfer control to software dealing specifically with that interrupting device. Polling takes a good deal of time, and severely degrades the performance of systems with many devices.

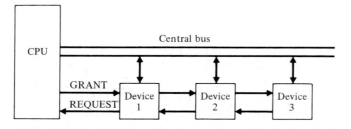

FIGURE 3.17   A daisy-chain priority scheme for a vectored-interrupt system.

3.6 EXAMPLES OF EXISTING BUS PROTOCOLS

In this section we examine implementations of the handshaking and arbitration protocols. The example of a synchronous protocol is drawn from the 6800 family of microprocessors. The PDP-11 and LSI-11 families use asynchronous protocols, with differences between the two families to account for differences in the number of wires in their buses. The 8085/8086 family of microprocessors provides examples of semisynchronous bus protocols.

The 6800 family of processors uses the synchronous protocol illustrated in Fig. 3.18. The example in the figure assumes a 1 MHz clock rate, but within the 6800 family are processors that operate up to 2 MHz, with corresponding reductions in the times shown. The 1 MHz clock has roughly a 50% duty cycle, with the clock's leading and trailing edges providing the timing points for latching or reading all bus signals. Note that the bus master places address and data on the bus at least 200 ns before the rising clock edge, and holds them for a least 40 ns after the falling clock edge. The setup time for READ and WRITE transactions requires that data be valid at least 100 ns before the falling edge of the clock. Among the signals that have the timing of address lines is the signal R/W L,

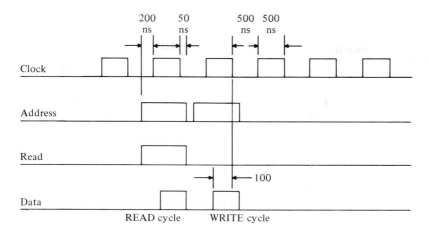

FIGURE 3.18   The 6800 bus timing: A synchronous bus.

which determines if the bus transaction is a READ or WRITE. Hence, at least 200 ns before the rising edge of the clock, the type of transaction is broadcast to all memories and ports on the bus. As we see later for the 8085 microprocessors and its descendents, the 8085 family follows a different procedure and uses separate READ or WRITE signals both to determine the direction of a transaction and to trigger it.

The PDP-11 Unibus provides an example of a purely asynchronous protocol. Figure 3.19 shows the timing for this bus, and gives minimum times for deskewing and decoding. Addresses must be placed on the bus at least 150 ns before raising MASTER, to allow for 75 ns decoding and 75 ns deskewing delays. The slave responds by raising SLAVE as soon as the data lines hold valid information (for READ) or have been latched (for

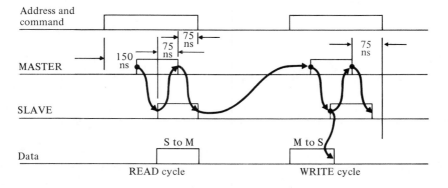

FIGURE 3.19   PDP-11 unibus timing; An asynchronous bus.

WRITE). Thereafter most transitions are spaced at least 75 ns apart to allow for deskewing. For a READ, the master waits 75 ns after seeing SLAVE high before latching data, and waits 75 ns after dropping MASTER before removing the addresses from the bus. For a WRITE, the master drops MASTER without a deskewing delay when it sees SLAVE high, but holds address and data valid on the bus for 75 ns after dropping MASTER.

The general principles of asynchronous handshakes are easily extended for more complex situations. Figure 3.20 illustrates how to multiplex addresses and data on one set of wires using an asynchronous handshake with one extra control wire. This is the technique used in the DEC LSI-11 Q-bus. Each bus transaction consists of two cycles, one in which an address is transmitted from master to slave, and the second in which data are transferred, either from master to slave or from slave to master for, respectively, WRITE and READ transactions. The beginning of a cycle occurs when addresses are placed on the bus, followed by one deskew and decode time later (150 ns) with the raising of the MASTER signal. This signal stays high through both cycles of the transaction. The bus master leaves the address on the bus for at least 100 ns to permit the selected slave to prepare for the subsequent data cycle. There is no handshake on this part of the cycle, so all slaves must respond to address broadcasts within a fixed minimum time, much the way that slaves on synchronous buses have to respond within one clock cycle. The asynchronous portion of the cycle depends on whether the cycle is a READ or WRITE. For a READ the master raises the READ HANDSHAKE signal, and thereafter the SLAVE HANDSHAKE and READ HANDSHAKE perform a fully interlocked handshake. The falling edge of SLAVE HANDSHAKE drops the MASTER signal, and the cycle ends. (Names of signals used here do not follow the naming conventions of the manufacturers, but the reader can easily identify similar names and functions.)

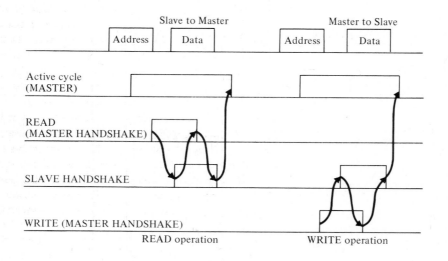

A WRITE cycle is similar to the READ cycle, with the exception that the master places the data on the bus first, and then raises WRITE HANDSHAKE. All subsequent transitions are fully interlocked, and the transaction closes by dropping MASTER in response to the fall of SLAVE HANDSHAKE. The figure does not show the delays inserted in the protocol for deskewing. These are all typically between 75 and 200 ns, depending on the transition. The exact details are unimportant for this discussion, but are given in detail in the *PDP-11 Bus Handbook* (1979).

The 8085 timing shown in Fig. 3.21 is an example of a semisynchronous bus that exhibits bus multiplexing similar to that of the LSI-11 Q-bus. The timing of the bus is somewhat unusual in that the clocking information is contained on the control lines. All bus timing is relative to the rising and falling edges of the control signals, so that the clock itself does not necessarily have to be transmitted on the bus. It is available, however, and can be used or ignored as the designer chooses.

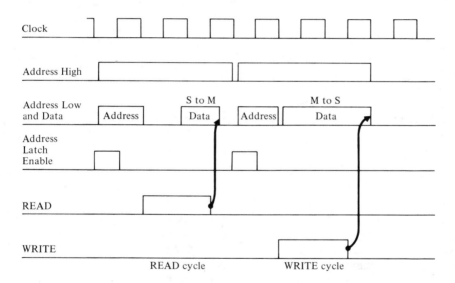

FIGURE 3.21   The 8085 bus timing: A semi-synchronous multiplexed bus.

For this bus, a cycle begins on a falling clock edge with the master raising the signal ALE (Address Latch Enable) while outputting the addresses onto the bus. ALE falls with the rising edge of the bus clock, and triggers external circuitry to latch the address currently present on the bus. The address lines remain stable until the next falling edge of the clock, providing the necessary hold time. The low byte of the address is removed from the multiplexed bus lines when the clock falls to complete its first cycle. This brings us to one clock cycle after the beginning of the transaction. The activity for the next clock depends on whether the transaction is a READ or WRITE.

For a READ, the master asserts the READ signal, holds this signal steady for $1\frac{1}{2}$ clock cycles, then latches data from the slave with the falling edge of READ (approximately concurrent with the rising edge of the clock during the third clock cycle). Hence the slave has $1\frac{1}{2}$ clock cycles to respond to the bus command, and the specific operation is triggered by the active edge of READ. Data should be stable on the bus for one hold time after the fall of READ, which falls in the last $\frac{1}{2}$ cycle of the third clock period. A new memory operation then begins with the falling edge of the clock at the close of the third cycle. Note that only the low address is multiplexed with data. The high address is stable during the entire memory operation. Note also how the clock transitions encoded on the control lines provide separate and distinct times for each bus activity. This guarantees that there is a brief period between the disabling of one set of bus drivers and the enabling of another set.

The WRITE transaction differs from READ at the beginning of the second clock cycle. Here the bus master removes the low address and replaces it with data while asserting the WRITE signal. The leading edge of WRITE triggers a bus transaction that lasts $1\frac{1}{2}$ clock cycles. WRITE drops approximately at the rising edge of the third clock, which notifies the slave that the master has completed its portion of the cycle. The memory operation ends with the falling edge of the third clock. Data and addresses remain on the bus for at least one hold time after the fall of WRITE.

As shown in the figure, both READ and WRITE take three clock cycles to complete. However, these are minimum times. Operations are extended an integral number of cycles depending on the state of the slave signal READY. The bus master reads the READY signal (not shown in the figure) $\frac{1}{2}$ cycle after asserting READ or WRITE, which is $\frac{1}{2}$ cycle before the last full clock period of the transaction. If the READY signal is asserted, then the next cycle is the last. If READY is low, then the master extends the cycle by one WAIT cycle, and reads READY again one cycle later. Because of setup time delays, the slave has to raise or lower READY early enough to reach the master about 100 ns before the clock edge rises in the second clock period. To lengthen a transaction, the slave can hold READY low just long enough to give time for the slave to respond to the command. If READY is used, a separate clock line on the bus simplifies the interface between the slave and the bus because it provides a recurrent edge from which READY timing can be derived.

The difference in philosophy between the 6800 and 8085 families is rather interesting and disconcerting when building ''hybrid'' systems containing chips from both families. Peripherals in the 6800 family need to have READ/WRITE information stable before the rising clock edge triggers a transaction. These peripherals will not operate correctly with 8085-type processors unless WAIT cycles are inserted. When an 8085 issues READ or WRITE, the signal itself is intended to trigger a transaction. But the 6800 peripheral has to use this signal to set up the direction of the transaction, and uses a delayed version of the signal to trigger the transaction. The delay forces a WAIT cycle.

But the situation depicted here is not symmetric. An 8085 peripheral can easily be connected to a 6800-type system. The READ or WRITE produced by the 6800 is ANDed with the clock to provide the trigger required by the peripheral. The unexpected difficulty in interfacing one type of peripheral to another type of microprocessor stems from using READ and WRITE to perform two functions in the 8085 family, but only one in the 6800 family. The polarity of the signal provides the direction of the transaction in both families, but the timing of the signal triggers a transaction only in the 8085 family.

The problem described here has been pointed out by Wakerly (1979) and Borrill (1981). It is possible to design around the problem, as Wakerly points out, by using an address bit to distinguish a READ from a WRITE, since the address becomes stable well in advance of the READ/WRITE control-line activation. Thus a peripheral-chip register can have two addresses, one even and one odd. The even address results in a READ of the register, and the odd address results in a WRITE to the register. Since the address bit replaces the READ/WRITE control line at the peripheral chip, it is entirely possible to issue such nonsensical commands as LOAD from the WRITE address and STORE to the READ address. The latter case is particularly troublesome because the microprocessor and the peripheral will both attempt to put data on the bus concurrently, and the bus interface logic may be damaged by this action.

Not only has the industry not settled on one timing method or the other as a standard, but Intel and Zilog use both. Intel uses both methods in the 8048 family. Zilog's Z80 follows the 8085 method, but the later Z8000 follows the 6800. It is unlikely that this switch is indicative of a move to standardize across the industry, and we expect to see differences in READ and WRITE methodology throughout the 1980s.

3.7 EXAMPLES OF BUS ARBITRATION

Bus arbitration for the synchronous 6800 bus is undoubtedly the simplest arbitration to implement. Timing considerations are shown in Fig. 3.22. A DMA request results in the processor entering the HALT state and issuing a GRANT. The GRANT remains high until the halt request is removed. Since the halt request is sampled by the processor just be-

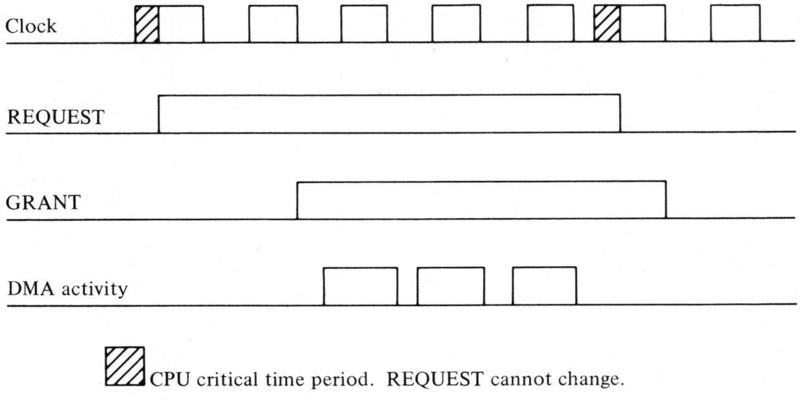

CPU critical time period. REQUEST cannot change.

FIGURE 3.22   The 6800 arbitration timing: A 2-wire daisy-chain protocol.

fore the clock edge rises, the REQUEST signal must be stable during this period. The figure shows that period as a forbidden transition region, with REQUEST changing immediately after the clock rises. The processor honors the REQUEST at the conclusion of a clock cycle, but not necessarily the one following the REQUEST. The processor completes whatever instruction is in progress when it discovers REQUEST high, and raises GRANT at the end of the last clock cycle of that in-progress instruction. The figure shows three cycles dedicated to DMA activity with REQUEST dropping in the fourth cycle. After the fourth cycle, GRANT drops and the processor resumes control.

Several methods are available to implement an arbitration scheme for this processor. The processor requires only two wires, but a 3-wire protocol is compatible with these two control lines. Obviously, REQUEST should be the OR of the individual master requests. To facilitate this capability, REQUEST is actually active in the low state for the 6800, so that it can easily be produced with open-collector drivers. GRANT is intended to thread the masters in order of priority. For the 3-wire protocol, a third signal for BUS BUSY visits all masters, but is not used by the 6800 itself. BUS BUSY protects the processor from being in the HALT state indefinitely. A timer or one-shot connected to BUS BUSY can remove the REQUEST signal if BUS BUSY is inactive for a sufficiently long period. Otherwise BUS BUSY serves the functions described earlier in this chapter.

The DEC PDP-11 Unibus improves upon the arbitration protocol described in this textbook by adding a fourth wire that enables arbitration for the next cycle to be overlapped with the bus transaction for the present cycle. The idea behind this form of arbitration is illustrated in Fig. 3.23. Arbitration times appear on the upper line; data transfer times appear on the lower line. Note that while the data transfer for the first transaction is active, the arbitration for the second transfer takes place. Similarly, the third arbitration is completed during the second transfer. But the 3-wire daisy-chain timing that we described earlier does not permit this overlap, because GRANT does not rise unless the bus is free. The Unibus protocol eliminates this difficulty by splitting the BUS BUSY function into two lines. One signal line in this protocol, also called BUS BUSY, indicates whether a transaction is active on the bus, and serves only this purpose. The second line, ACKNOWLEDGE, is used to respond to the GRANT signal. Both of these functions are served by the one line BUS BUSY in the 3-wire protocol because the response to a GRANT is an active BUS BUSY in that protocol. Dividing the two functions into two separate lines permits the overlapping arbitration and transfer activities.

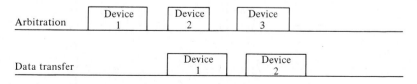

FIGURE 3.23   Overlapping of arbitration and data transfer.

Details of the Unibus arbitration methodology are shown in Fig. 3.24. Note that RE-QUEST starts an arbitration cycle, and that the REQUEST for the second cycle can begin during the first transaction. A GRANT appears at later time, and propagates down the bus. The winner of the arbitration responds with ACKNOWLEDGE, and removes its RE-QUEST (although other REQUESTs may still be present). This winner cannot take control of the bus immediately, but must wait until BUS BUSY goes low. To prevent another arbitration from beginning at this point, ACKNOWLEDGE remains high until the master is able to take control of the bus. When BUS BUSY falls, the master for the second transaction drops ACKNOWLEDGE and raises BUS BUSY as the master initiates the second transaction. The fall of ACKNOWLEDGE triggers a new arbitration cycle. A GRANT is issued by the arbiter if any REQUEST is observed on the bus, and the cycle repeats. Note that in Fig. 3.24 three different masters assert signals on REQUEST, ACKNOWLEDGE, and BUS BUSY lines, with each signal identifying the master that asserted it.

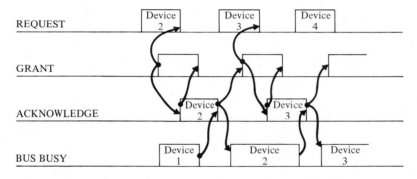

FIGURE 3.24   PDP-11 Unibus arbitration timing: A 4-wire daisy chain.

The arbitration protocols for most microprocessors are designed to be used with tri-state drivers on the address and data lines. To protect these drivers from "bus-fights," when two or more drivers in opposite polarity drive a single line, it is necessary to provide a "guard" time after one set of drivers turns off and another set turns on. The guard time is incorporated in the handshakes for the various microprocessors by providing a brief period between READ and WRITE transactions, and between a master's use of a bus and a slave's access to a bus for a READ transaction. For example, the timing for the 6800 microprocessor raises addresses and data about ¼ cycle after the beginning of a clock period. This provides about ¼ cycle after the last clock period for the transition between sets of drivers on the bus. Similarly, the 8085 protocol provides about ½ clock period between a slave's access to the bus and the master's access on either side of the slave.

Arbitration protocols must account for tri-state drivers as well as for controlling the access to a bus. The IEEE-796 bus (Intel Multibus) arbitration protocol is an interesting

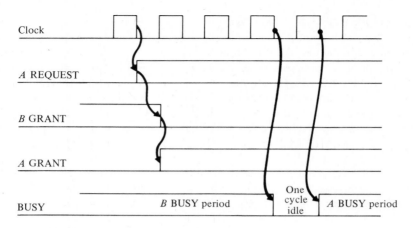

FIGURE 3.25 An IEEE-796 bus arbitration cycle. The idle cycle protects the tri-state drivers.

example of how this can be done. Figure 3.25 shows the protocol with two masters on the bus, Master *B* (which currently is active on the bus) and Master *A* (which currently requests the bus). We assume that *B* has lower priority than *A* and holds the bus, because GRANT is high in the daisy-chain connection to *B*. When *A* raises its REQUEST (which appears on the bus at the same time as the clock signal falls), the GRANT signals on the bus change so that GRANT propagates only up to the highest priority requester. In this case *A* is that requester, so it receives the GRANT signal, and *B*'s GRANT goes low. Then *B* has to relinquish control of the bus at the earliest opportunity. If *B* is a processor, it may complete the several clock cycles of a memory-cycle transaction. Other types of masters may need to complete several memory cycles before reaching a stopping point. At the trailing edge of the last clock in its activity cycle, *B* removes BUSY, and BUSY becomes inactive for one full cycle. Then *A* takes control of the bus, asserts BUSY, and arbitration has been completed. The full clock cycle of inactivity provides the dead time required between sets of bus drivers.

In this protocol, GRANT may be changed several times before a bus is relinquished. As each new REQUEST is posted, the chain of bus masters update their GRANT outputs on the daisy chain. The update has to take place within one cycle, and the master with GRANT asserted when BUSY drops to 0 is the master that takes control of the bus.

In closing, we present one final interesting method for arbitration and device identification. This arbitration method not only selects the highest priority requester when multiple requests are present, but it returns the ID of that requester on the bus back to the arbiter (usually the processor). Hence this method of arbitration is quite suitable for device-identification after a processor interrupt. An additional property of this arbitration method is that all arbitration signals are open-collector, and control lines are continuous conductors to which the bus slaves attach. This is in sharp contrast to the daisy-chain arbitration scheme that requires the bus grant to be discontinuous at each slave so that each slave makes an independent decision about whether to pass the grant to the next in line or to hold the grant for its own bus transaction. The IEEE Standard version of the S-100 bus (IEEE-696.1/D2, 1979) uses this technique for the arbitration of DMA transfer requests.

The bus interface for this application is shown in Fig. 3.26, and is adapted from the IEEE-696 Standard and Borrill (1981). (The notation OC indicates an open-collector gate.) The idea of the interface is to assert HOLD L to request access to the bus, and to await a response on pHLDA, which is the acknowledge signal returned by the processor or bus arbiter. The interface asserts a request by setting the HOLD flip-flop when three conditions occur simultaneously:

1. The device needs access to the bus (BREQ is high).
2. The bus grant has not propagated past this device (pHLDA is low).
3. No other request is active on the bus (the control line HOLD L is passive high).

The three-input NAND that drives the S input of the HOLD flip-flop generates an active low signal when all three conditions hold. If a high-priority request comes *after* a low-priority request, the high-priority request must wait for the low-priority request to be removed before it has access to the HOLD L control line. This guarantees that new requests cannot come at arbitrary times. (Arbitrary changes can produce brief glitches and metastable states.) At the beginning of a new arbitration cycle there are, in general, several outstanding requests, all of which may gain access to HOLD L. The priority-arbitration logic we now describe selects the highest-priority request of those that actively assert HOLD L.

When a device gains access to HOLD L by setting the HOLD flip-flop, it simultaneously sets the ASSERT ID flip-flop. This flip-flop energizes the four ID lines. These lines are compared to the open-collector priority lines to determine whether there is a higher-priority requester. The logic is essentially that of a borrow look-ahead circuit of a binary subtracter. Each ID is a 4-bit binary ID, and high numbers have priority over low numbers. The four lines DMA0 L through DMA3 L carry the complement of the winning ID. Each interface generates four active-low borrows, B0 L through B3 L, by subtracting its ID from the ID currently on the bus. The 4-input NAND that generates HIGH PRIORITY L requires that all borrow signals be inactive high, which is satisfied only by the requesting interface with the highest ID. HIGH PRIORITY L is gated together with HOLD L and pHLDA L at a 3-input NOR to be sure that the request and the bus grant are still active before signaling TAKE BUS to the device.

Losing requesters generate a 0 on the D-input of the HOLD flip-flop. This value is gated into HOLD when the rising edge of pHLDA reaches the interface. Hence, only the winner continues to assert HOLD L after the grant propagates the length of the bus. After the winner completes its bus activity, it removes BREQ, which resets the HOLD flip-flop. Since this is the only HOLD outstanding, HOLD L becomes inactive, and the processor regains control of the bus. Immediately after pHLDA is deasserted, the losing requests and any new requests bid for the bus through another arbitration cycle.

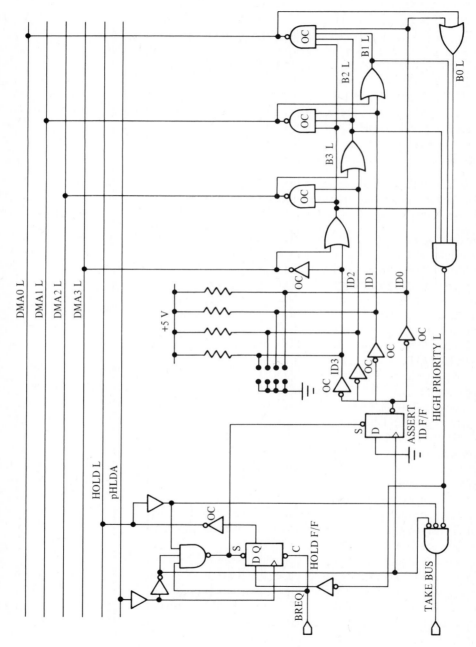

FIGURE 3.26 Priority arbitration logic for the IEEE-696 (S-100) bus.

OTHER READING

A truly comprehensive study of busing that greatly influenced this chapter is the work by Thurber *et al.*, (1972). This treatment covers a very large variety of bus implementations, including many handshake and arbitration protocols not covered in this chapter. Readers will find this to be an excellent source of background information.

The importance of buses and bus standards has only gradually been felt by the computer industry. In the infancy of computers the majority of manufacturers supplied all of the devices that attached directly to the processor/memory bus. Thus this interface was usually proprietary to the manufacturer, and it was not possible to connect "foreign" devices to the bus. Foreign devices, if attached at all, were mostly connected to DMA channels.

Digital Equipment Corporation played a dominant role in fostering the user's ability to interface user-owned devices to its computers. The DEC PDP-1, and later the PDP-8, were its early offerings that supported user interfacing. The introduction of the PDP-11 and the Unibus with memory-mapped I/O had a very a large impact on the idea of using a well-defined bus as a standard digital interface. Eventually the microprocessor industry moved toward the bus as a common interface for microprocessors, memories, and peripheral chips.

The S-100 bus was introduced by Altair Corporation in one of the first personal microcomputers. This bus provided a means for interconnecting processor, memory, and I/O boards in a very general and flexible manner. Almost immediately after Altair's computer was introduced in the mid-70s, dozens of manufacturers marketed what were intended to be "compatible" board-level products that connected directly to the S-100 bus. But the bus had not been standardized, and many products from different manufacturers simply did not work with each other. As part of the IEEE Computer Society standardization effort, a group of volunteers took on the difficult problem of standardizing the S-100 bus. The culmination of this work is the draft standard IEEE Task 696.1/D2 (1979) that incorporates extensions of the bus to 16-bit processors and includes the interesting arbitration protocol described in this chapter.

The need for bus standards is now well-recognized, and the bus literature abounds with information. The Unibus and LSI-11 bus (Q-bus) are thoroughly described in the PDP-11 Bus Handbook (Digital Equipment, 1979). Levy's chapter on busing (1978) brings the discussion up to date with respect to buses on the VAX computer. The references about the DEC bus standards are an excellent source of information on practical implementations of buses that complement the general treatment of this chapter. Borrill (1981) analyzes several concurrent efforts concerning bus definitions and standards.

In dealing with the problem of synchronization, we cited the article by Chaney and Molnar (1973). Until that article appeared, very little concrete evidence existed about the metastable state. It is very difficult to observe the metastable state in a repeatable way, so that when synchronization failures occur it is often difficult to analyze what happened. Fortunately, the problem is much better understood today. Mead and Conway (1980) review the problem for VLSI designers, and show ways of designing safe VLSI chips.

TABLE E–3.1 **Test Programs for Bus Analysis**

			68XX Family
	LDX	#$1000	SET THE X-REGISTER TO POINT TO MEMORY.
	CLR A		CLEAR THE ACCUMULATOR.
LOOP	COM A		COMPLEMENT THE ACCUMULATOR.
	STA A	0,X	STORE THE ACCUMULATOR.
	LDA A	0,X	RELOAD THE ACCUMULATOR.
	BRA	LOOP	

			8080 and 8085
	LXI	H,1000H	SET THE H-L REGISTER TO POINT TO MEMORY.
	XRA	A	CLEAR THE ACCUMULATOR (A := A EXCLUSIVE OR A).
LOOP:	CMA		COMPLEMENT THE ACCUMULATOR.
	MOV	M,A	STORE THE ACCUMULATOR.
	MOV	A,M	RELOAD THE ACCUMULATOR.
	JMP	LOOP	

			8086 and 8088
	MOV	BX,1000H	SET THE B REGISTER TO POINT TO MEMORY.
	MOV	AL,00H	CLEAR THE ACCUMULATOR
LOOP:	NOT	AL	COMPLEMENT THE ACCUMULATOR.
	MOV	BX,AL	STORE THE ACCUMULATOR.
	MOV	AL,BX	RELOAD THE ACCUMULATOR.
	JMP	LOOP	

			65XX Family
	LDA	$00	CLEAR THE ACCUMULATOR.
LOOP	EOR	$FF	COMPLEMENT THE ACCUMULATOR.
	STA	$1000	STORE THE ACCUMULATOR.
	LDA	$1000	RELOAD THE ACCUMULATOR.
	JMP	LOOP	

			Z80
	LD	HL,1000H	SET H-L TO POINT TO MEMORY.
	XOR	A	CLEAR THE ACCUMULATOR.
LOOP:	CPL		COMPLEMENT THE ACCUMULATOR.
	LD	(HL),A	STORE THE ACCUMULATOR.
	LD	A,(HL)	RELOAD THE ACCUMULATOR.
	JP	LOOP	

EXPERIMENTS

3.1 Table E–3.1 gives a very brief program for many different microprocessors. After initialization this program loops through a sequence of instructions that write to and read from a selected memory location. Data written alternate between 0s and 1s on successive passes through the loop.

 a) Select a microprocessor with a synchronous or semisynchronous bus. (A microprocessor from the 68XX, 808X, Z80, or 65XX families is satisfactory.)

 b) Describe the bus activity on a clock-cycle–by–clock-cycle basis as shown for the MC6800 in Table E–3.2. The table gives the value of each memory bus signal as a function of time, and indicates in the comments what happens at each cycle. The analysis should be made on the four instructions within the loop only, and should not include loop-initialization instructions. Use the manufacturer's reference material to determine what happens during each cycle of the execution of each instruction; or, based on your understanding of the microprocessor, estimate what the bus activity is. In Table E–3.1, the first instruction of the loop starts at address 2004_{16}.

TABLE E–3.2   Bus Transaction Timing

CYCLE	ADDRESS	DATA	R/W	VMA	COMMENTS
1	2004	43	1	1	Read opcode for COM A.
2	2005	A7	1	1	Read next instruction.
3	2005	A7	1	1	First cycle of STA 0,X, read opcode.
4	2006	00	1	1	Read offset.
5	1000	XX	1	0	No memory cycle; no data on bus.
6	1000	XX	1	0	No memory cycle; no data on bus.
7	1000	XX	1	0	No memory cycle; no data on bus.
8	1000	DD	0	1	Store data, changing every other cycle.
9	2007	B6	1	1	Start of LDA 0,X; read opcode.
10	2008	00	1	1	Read the offset.
11	1000	XX	1	0	No memory cycle; no data on bus.
12	1000	XX	1	0	No memory cycle; no data on bus.
13	1000	DD	1	1	Read data.
14	2009	20	1	1	First cycle of BRA LOOP; read opcode.
15	200A	F9	1	1	Read offset.
16	200B	XX	1	0	No memory cycle; no data on bus.
17	2004	XX	1	0	No memory cycle; no data on bus.

 c) Connect a dual-channel oscilloscope to the microprocessor. The external sync signal should be connected to the microprocessor control line that asserts WRITE. This signal is asserted once per loop. One channel of the oscilloscope should be connected to the bus clock that is to be used as a timing reference. The second channel is left disconnected, and will be used to probe various bus signals.

d) Load the program in the microprocessor and initiate execution. Set the time scale to display two to three full executions of the loop. If the oscilloscope has a continuously variable time scale, you can expand the display so that one full execution of the loop just fits the display area. Probe each bus control line and one address and one data line. As each line is probed, identify the beginning of the program loop, and verify that the bus signal follows your calculations. Explain any discrepancy.

e) Expand the timing of the display so that one memory cycle just fills the screen. Select a READ cycle, and then select a WRITE cycle. For each of these cycles find the address setup time and the address and data hold times. Compare these times with the specifications for the microprocessor bus.

3.2 Repeat Experiment 3.1 for a microprocessor or minicomputer with a fully interlocked asynchronous bus. Suitable candidates are the PDP-11, LSI-11, or MC68000.

PROBLEMS

3.1 Analyze the Unibus arbitration protocol under the following conditions: The bus has three devices on the line and Device 2 (the second on the line) is currently active on the bus. Assume that sometime between this point in time and the conclusion of the next arbitration cycle, both Devices 1 and 3 raise requests. An arbitration error will occur if Device 3 is granted the bus and initiates a transaction, and subsequently the request is aborted by Device 1 when it takes over the bus. If Device 3 requests sufficiently earlier than Device 1, it should obtain the bus. If Device 3 requests sufficiently late with respect to Device 1, Device 1 should obtain the bus. In between, the protocol must grant the bus either to Device 3 or Device 1, but it must be a safe protocol so that no matter which device gets the bus, that device is assured that it will hold the bus to the completion of its request.

a) Give a timing analysis that shows the bus arbitration is safe if the devices must observe the change in bus grant signal from NO GRANT to GRANT in order to gain access to the bus.

b) Give a timing analysis that shows the arbitration to be unsafe if the devices can gain access to the bus simply by observing GRANT without necessarily observing the change from NO GRANT to GRANT.

3.2 There are slightly different timing requirements for a tri-state bus than for an open-collector bus: A tri-state bus cannot have two or more tri-state drivers active simultaneously, whereas there is no corresponding problem for the open-collector bus. Consider a generic, fully interlocked asynchronous bus, and observe what happens for sequences of operations such as READ/READ, READ/WRITE, etc. For what sequences is it necessary to separate the operations with some idle time on a tri-state bus, when no such time is required for an open-collector bus?

3.3 The Unibus has separate arbitration lines for DMA requests and interrupt requests. There is a single daisy-chain priority for DMA, but there are four distinct daisy-chain priority lines for interrupts. The four lines are prioritized so that if interrupt requests occur on two or more chains, a request on the chain with the highest priority is the one that is recognized. On any daisy chain, the requests are prioritized by the electrical connection because the interrupt acknowledge signal is passed from device to device. All four interrupt daisy chains and the DMA daisy chain pass through each unibus interface.

   a) Give a concrete example in which the four daisy-chain system of interrupt priority is more versatile or powerful than a single daisy-chain interrupt system. Note that at any given time the pending requests on the four daisy chains are totally ordered, so that those requests can be acknowledged in precisely the same order if the four daisy chains are connected to form a single daisy chain by linking them end-to-end from highest to lowest. (*Hint*: all four interrupt chains visit each interface. Would this be the case if there were only one interrupt chain? How might an interface make use of the multiple chains?)

   b) Consider a typical application for a small computer that has two DMA controllers that operate at 300 K-bytes per second, and six low-speed devices that operate under interrupt control. A low-speed device operates at a maximum speed of 1 K-byte per second. The DMA channels transfer data in 4 K-byte bursts, and a bus arbitration is required for each byte transferred. The channels post interrupt requests at the end of each burst. When the computer is operating at maximum I/O capacity, how many bus arbitrations and interrupt arbitrations occur per second? Are these rates consistent with the fact that the interrupt-request daisy chains together have about the four times the bandwidth of the one DMA daisy chain?

   c) Sketch the layout of an alternative approach to the four daisy-chain system that interposes an intelligent interrupt-request arbiter between the computer and the I/O interfaces. This arbiter interfaces the processor with four daisy-chain interrupt-request lines, as required by the Unibus. However, only a single daisy chain that visits all devices extends from this arbiter. The idea is that the devices post interrupt requests on the single daisy chain, and the arbiter somehow converts the requests to four different levels of request. Describe how to construct an arbiter that mimics the functions and timing of the four daisy-chain system so well that the processor cannot easily tell that the devices are connected to a single daisy chain.

4 / MEMORIES

The block diagrams of microcomputer systems in Chapter 1 show that they consist of three major subsystems, namely—the processor, the memory system, and the I/O system. In this chapter we examine the design of memory systems and techniques for interfacing processors to memory. Sections 4.1 and 4.2, respectively, describe the different types of memory and typical memory systems. In Section 4.3, we move to the problem of sharing memory between a processor and a DMA controller and take a detailed look at DMA controller chips.

4.1 TYPES OF MEMORY

Semiconductor memories are the universal memory components in microprocessor systems, but their being so is a relatively recent phenomenon in the computer industry. Through the end of the 1960s and early into the 1970s magnetic memories were the dominant technology. The semiconductor memory industry began in earnest at the start of the 70s with the introduction of a 256-bit memory chip, which is a minuscule capacity by today's standards. The chip barely made a dent in the sales of magnetic memories, but the advantages of semiconductor memory over magnetic memory because of high-speed and the simplicity of interfacing were clearly evident even then. Only the relatively high cost of semiconductor memory at that time precluded its immediate acceptance. By the start of the 80s, one decade later, the 64 K-bit chip was in full production, and the 256 K-bit was on the drawing boards. What happened in the intervening years is that approximately every two to three years, the memory capacity per chip quadrupled. So the 256-bit chip gave way to the 1 K-bit, 4 K-bit, and 16 K-bit chips—and more recently, the 64 K-bit and 256 K-bit chips. Each new generation took no more power per chip than the last, and the difference in cost per chip was inconsequential compared to fixed costs of other system components. The improvement in chip technology in little more than a decade has literally been a thousandfold. The highly developed magnetic-core memory technology quickly dropped from view in the onslaught of the semiconductors. Today semiconductor memory systems for microprocessors almost universally are of three principal types:

1. Dynamic random-access memory (RAM), which stores data passively and requires periodic refresh to maintain data.
2. Static RAM, which maintains data without periodic refresh.
3. Read-only memory (ROM), which maintains data in the absence of power, but which cannot be rewritten in the normal memory-cycle time.

In the following discussion we will describe how to design a generic memory system, and will include those details that are common to all three types of memory. Then we will look at the peculiarities and differences of the three in order to show how the memory interface has to be adapted to these individual characteristics.

General Characteristics of Semiconductor Memory

Figure 4.1 shows the generic memory chip that is the running example of this discussion. The memory has 4 K-bits, organized as a 4 K × 1 array. That is, the memory responds to 4 K different addresses, and each address contains 1 bit. Eight chips can be combined in one memory system to create a memory with 4 K-bytes, and multiples of eight can be used to make larger byte-wide memories. The chip has separate pins for data input and output. Thus the chip has two data pins and twelve address pins (4 K = 2^{12}, so twelve address pins give 4 K unique addresses). There are just two other control pins shown on this chip. A pin labeled CHIP SELECT enables or disables the chip. Hence, if the chip is to respond to a memory request, CHIP SELECT must be asserted; otherwise the chip remains inactive. The second pin is labeled READ/WRITE L, which dictates whether the chip will accept a read request and retrieve stored data, or whether it will accept a write request and transfer the data from the input pin to memory. When the signal is a logic 1, READ is asserted; when it is a logic 0, WRITE L is asserted. For our generic chip, these are all the interface signals other than power connections. This particular chip is intended to be similar to a 2147 static RAM.

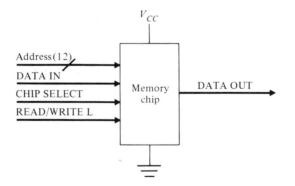

FIGURE 4.1   A generic memory chip, organized as a 4 K × 1 memory.

Now let's look at the timing relationships of the signals shown in Fig. 4.2. Compare this timing with typical bus timing, and you can see that the two are quite compatible, as they must be. The idea is that for both READ and WRITE operations, addresses stabilize before an access is completed. Although Fig. 4.2 shows the address-setup delay before CHIP SELECT, some devices have on-chip delays for CHIP SELECT and

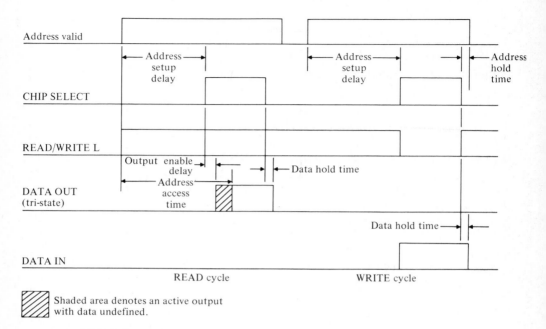

FIGURE 4.2   Timing relationships for signals for the generic memory chip.

READ/WRITE L. For these chips, the addresses may change until or for a short period after CHIP SELECT is asserted at an input pin. In any case, there is a period of time in the memory cycle during which the addresses must be stable. If the address lines happen to change during this critical time, the data retrieved may come from the wrong location or may be a composite of data from several locations. Worse yet, data can be written in the wrong location or in several locations.

The READ operation begins immediately after the chip is selected. Sometime later, the data become valid on the chip outputs. Most memory chips actually respond internally in a continuous fashion to addresses on their inputs. As addresses change, internal decoding logic changes state in a corresponding fashion; but the output drivers remain disabled, and the data in memory is not disturbed in any way. Although neither the READ nor WRITE can take place until the chip is selected, at least part of the logic will already have reached a stable state when the chip select appears. Timing for the WRITE operation is only a slight variation of the READ timing.

A simplified logic diagram for an interface with this memory chip appears in Fig. 4.3. We show 16 addresses coming from the microprocessor, but only 12 are connected to the chip. The remaining four pass through a decoder that produces several different chip selects, which in turn select different chips for different regions of the address space. All

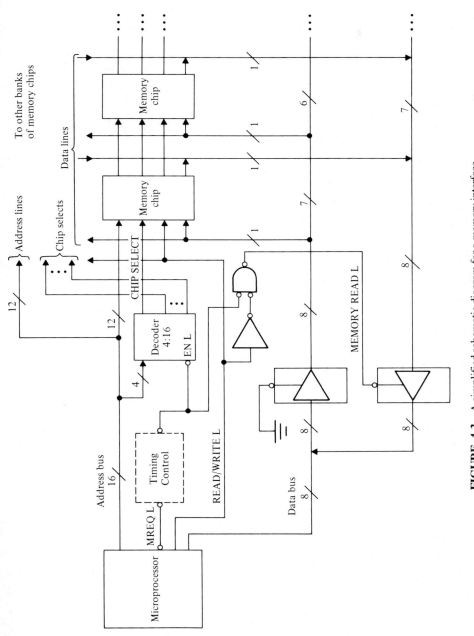

FIGURE 4.3   A simplified schematic diagram for a memory interface.

control signals are passed parallel to a bank of eight chips whose inputs and outputs are connected to the eight data lines on the data bus. This creates a memory with an 8-bit word length. The memory can easily be extended to a 16-bit or 32-bit word length by replicating the memory chips.

Let's compare the timing of the signals for this design with chip requirements. Figure 4.4 is the timing diagram for our design. We show CHIP SELECT delayed with respect to MREQ in order to satisfy the address setup time. A logic element for this purpose and labeled TIMING CONTROL is shown in dotted lines. This element is triggered by the memory request that starts the access cycle. For static-memory designs the control signals produced by a microprocessor usually satisfy the timing constraints of the memory devices, and therefore the TIMING CONTROL logic is unnecessary and can be omitted.

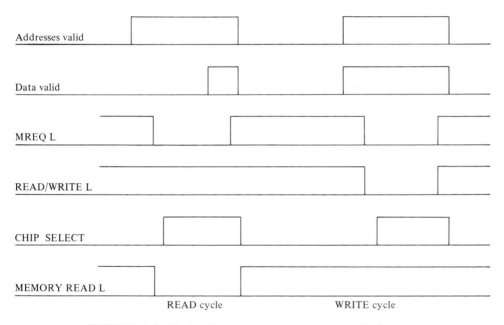

FIGURE 4.4 Timing diagram for the memory schematic diagram.

To create large memory systems from sets of memory chips, we rely on more extensive decoding and the CHIP SELECT signals on the memory chips. A block diagram of a 64 K-byte memory composed of 4 K × 1 chips is shown in Fig. 4.5. In this case the memory has 16 rows of chips, with each row containing eight chips. The high-order address bits are decoded by a 4-to-16 decoder, and each of the decoder outputs enables one row of the memory array. Each column of the array delivers one bit of an 8-bit byte. With 16-K static RAM chips, the array reduces to 4 rows of eight chips. For this case, only the

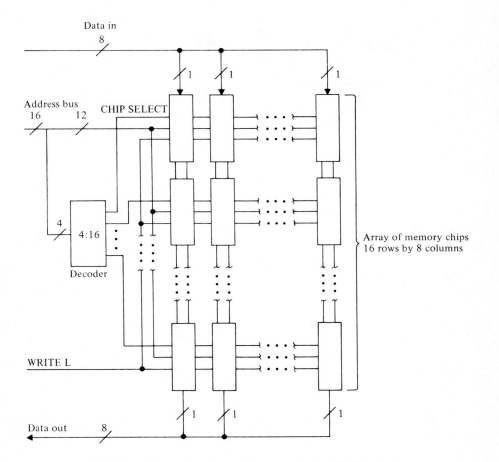

FIGURE 4.5   A 64 K-byte memory constructed with 4 K × 1 chips.

two highest addresses are decoded, and they select one of four rows. The remaining 14 ad-dresses are transmitted to each chip. (Chapter 2 described techniques for designing the address-distribution network in memory systems.)

The memory operation of the tri-state output drivers on the chip require a tad more explanation. When CHIP SELECT is asserted, the memory chip responds, either by going into a WRITE mode or a READ mode, depending on the polarity of READ/WRITE L. If WRITE L reaches the memory chip after CHIP SELECT, then the chip first goes into the READ mode before returning to the WRITE mode. In so doing, the output drivers are momentarily enabled and are no longer in their quiescent high-impedance mode. The out-put drivers remain active for a short period after WRITE L appears on the control pin. The

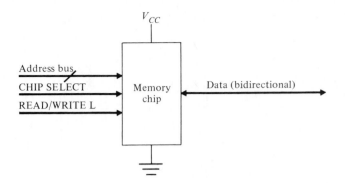

FIGURE 4.6   A memory chip with bidirectional data pins.

designer must take this timing into account in order to prevent the external tri-state drivers and chip-output drivers from clashing with each other.

In the design shown in Fig. 4.3, the output and input data are connected to distinct pins on the memory chip. Consequently, the design is safe from tri-state problems because the internal drivers on the memory chips and the external tri-state drivers do not drive the same lines unless they are connected externally.

Figure 4.6 shows a slight variation of our generic memory chip of Figure 4.1. This variation introduces complications resulting from the tri-state drivers. In this case there is but a single data pin that carries both input and output data. Consequently, a memory design based on this chip requires slightly more care, as we show in Fig. 4.7. The problem is to be sure that the tri-state driver for WRITE, as shown in the figure, does not clash with on-chip tri-state drivers. To eliminate this problem, we show the external tri-state drivers controlled by noncomplementary signals. This allows for all tri-state drivers (including those on the memory chips) to settle to a high-impedance mode after one set of drivers turns off and before a new set of drivers turns on. Designers are often tempted to use complementary control signals for the READ and WRITE tri-state drivers, but find there is no dead time between a READ and a WRITE. Because of varying turn-on and turn-off delays, such designs can suffer from momentary tri-state clashes that produce transients on the bus lines. Occasional bus failures can result when the noise is severe.

In recent years, designers of high-speed systems have used staggered timing of tri-state control signals in order to reduce bus noise. For microprocessors with 8-bit data buses and 16-bit addresses, up to 24 lines can change at the same time. The current generation of microprocessors has increased the number of data lines on the bus to 16 or 32, and the number of address lines to 24 or 32. Hence 40 or more lines can change simultaneously. Our discussion in Chapter 2 suggests that such simultaneous changes can produce noise pulses on the bus. The problem is compounded when brief tri-state clashes momentarily cause high-current flows. Some conservative memory designs stagger the enabling of tri-state drivers so that groups of lines change at intervals (of, say, of 10 ns), avoiding

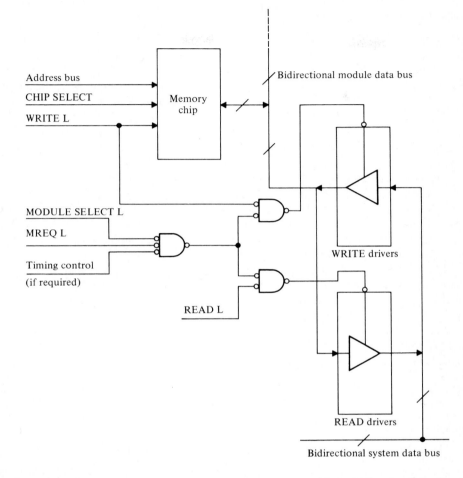

FIGURE 4.7   Tri-state driver control for interfacing memory chips to bidirectional data lines.

the simultaneous change of all lines. A 32-bit data bus can be gated in four 10-ns intervals, with a different 8-bit tri-state driver being gated on during each successive interval. Although the designer need not, in general, stagger the tri-state control signals to reduce bus noise, the designer must always provide some dead time when switching tri-state drivers.

In summary, a typical memory chip needs only two control pins, one for chip selection and the other to select between READ and WRITE access. Chip timing requirements force the designer to consider where and how to place delays in a memory system in order to satisfy chip timing constraints and to guard against tri-state problems.

Static Random-Access Memory (RAM)

The example in the preceding section is a static RAM chip. This is evident because data can be both read and written (so the chip is not a read-only memory) and because the designs that use this memory have no provision for memory refresh. A static RAM maintains information in memory through active circuits. This requires power to maintain, even when the chip is inactive and in a standby (low-power) mode. Therefore static memories require heftier power supplies and greater cooling than do the dynamic memories we will discuss later. Moreover, each static memory cell is about four times larger in area than an equivalent dynamic cell. This is because active data retention in static memories requires several transistors for each storage cell. Each dynamic cell retains data on a tiny capacitor whose geometry is much smaller in area than the equivalent storage mechanism in a static cell. Because of this smaller cell size, a dynamic memory chip typically has about four times as many bits per chip as a static memory chip that uses comparable semiconductor process technology. If we assume that the cost per chip is equal, this difference in memory size translates into a cost per bit that is about four times less for dynamic memories than for static ones.

The primary advantage of static memory is that it is very simple to interface to processors, as we have seen in Figs. 4.3 and 4.7. There is very little hardware overhead required for a static memory, and in small memories it is possible to dispense with the tristate memory drivers included in the designs shown in this chapter.

Memory interfacing is particularly easy with chips whose formats are somewhat different from the 4 K × 1 format in our example. If the 4 K-bits are arranged as a 512 × 8 bit memory, then a single memory chip is sufficient to create a small memory for a simple microprocessor. The 4 K × 1 format of the example requires at least 8 chips for a byte-organized system and 16 chips for a word-organized system.

Read-Only Memory (ROM)

Since ROM does only part of what RAM does, it is obviously less complex and therefore simpler to interface to processors. Programmable ROM (called PROM) is a popular form of ROM found in most low-volume systems. When only one or two copies of a system are to be constructed, PROMs are ideal system components. They are easily programmed by the user, and erasable implementations of PROMs can even be reprogrammed and corrected. As the number of copies of a system grows, the effort involved in programming becomes a chore. In addition, mask-programmed ROMs have a lower unit cost than do PROMs once the initial cost of the ROM has been amortized. Hence, ROMs are more attractive for high-production. Consequently, most PROMs are pin-for-pin compatible with corresponding ROMs, and offer the system manufacturer a choice of components that will satisfy the needs of both low-and high-volume production lines.

The electrical connections to ROM chips are almost identical to those of RAM chips, with the exception, of course, that ROMs do not have a READ/WRITE L pin. They are always in a READ mode. Therefore, the only control that is necessary for a ROM is an OUTPUT ENABLE pin that turns on the internal tri-state drivers. However, many ROMS have a second control pin, CHIP SELECT, as shown in Fig. 4.8. The CHIP SELECT function for ROM places the chip in a low-power standby mode. Because a ROM retains memory in the absence of power, it need not draw power when it is not accessed. Standby mode—which may draw as little as 25% of normal power—disconnects most of the circuits from the power supply, leaving the relatively critical circuits on, so that the ROM can respond quickly to access requests. It is perfectly permissible technically to tie CHIP SELECT to logic 1, and to use the OUTPUT ENABLE control pin much the way that CHIP SELECT is used for RAM; but excess power consumption means excess heat generation, higher operating cost, and perhaps the addition of a fan and air filter. So if a standby mode is available in a chip, the designer should make an effort to use it.

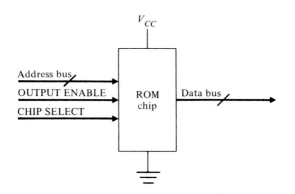

FIGURE 4.8   A typical read-only memory chip.

For microprocessor systems the most popular ROMs in use today have byte-wide formats. For example, a 16 K ROM is organized as a 2 K $\times$ 8 memory. When this format is used, a single ROM contains a contiguous region of byte-organized memory. Hence, a program that fits within that region can be stored in a single ROM chip. Other formats that have fewer bits per address require more than one chip in their minimum configuration and, therefore, are more costly.

Among the most popular read-only memories for microprocessors are byte-wide PROMs of the 25XX and 27XX families. These include the 2704 (4 K-bits), 2708 (8 K-bits), 2716 (16 K-bits), 2532 and 2732 (32 K-bits), and 2564 and 2764 (64 K-bits). The 2704 and 2708 are obsolete and should not be used in new designs. Even larger chips with 128 K-bits and 256 K-bits are becoming available. As the industry continues to advance we can expect further technological advances. High-production systems incorporate pin-for-pin compatible ROMs to reduce system cost. These ROMs are in the 23XX family and include the 2316 (16 K-bits), 2332 (32 K-bits) and 2364 (64 K-bits).

Dynamic RAM

The advances in dynamic RAM have been felt throughout the microprocessor industry. The microcomputers with memories of 32 K- or 64 K-bytes so common today are manufacturable at low cost because of the 16-K dynamic-RAM chip. With the introduction of 64-K RAM and 256-K RAM, the memory-system sizes of typical microcomputers have increased proportionately. The desk-top computer with a megabyte of memory is no longer a dream of the future.

Dynamic memory, unlike static memory, cannot retain data indefinitely without external support logic. The problem is that information is stored as electrical charge in small capacitors, and the charge tends to dissipate over a period of time. Hence it is necessary to refresh memory periodically in order to preserve data. The nature of this problem and the role of refresh is illustrated in Fig. 4.9.

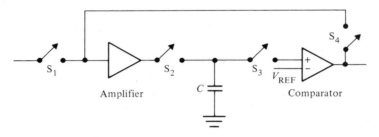

FIGURE 4.9 A symbolic diagram of the structure of a dynamic memory cell: The switch states for WRITE are S_1 and S_2 closed; for READ, switches S_2, S_3, and S_4 are closed; and otherwise the switches are open.

Capacitor C in the figure is the memory element. Switches on either side of the capacitor are actually field-effect transistors that are controlled by the address decoding circuitry, but in this simplified illustration we show them as toggle switches. To write data in the memory, we close switches S_1 and S_2. This connects C to the input data through the amplifier. A logic 1 charges C, and a logic 0 discharges C. Then we open the switches, and C is isolated from the rest of the chip. The information is now captured as the charge on C and, in an ideal situation, the information will remain in the cell indefinitely.

The READ operation is much the same as the WRITE. The output switch connects C to a comparator, which decides if the stored voltage is less than or greater than a reference voltage. The output of the comparator is a logic 0 or logic 1 depending on the outcome of this decision. Reading the cell may disturb the charge in the cell so that the READ operation has to be followed by a recharging of the capacitor. In this case, the comparator output (or a flip-flop that latches the comparator output) is switched to the amplifier input, and switch S_2 closes. Then the datum in the cell is restored to its original value by recharging or discharging C.

The problem with this type of memory is that the storage medium is not ideal. This type of memory "forgets" information over a period of time. The leakage resistance across the capacitor provides a discharge path, and the stored charge dissipates slowly. Eventually the voltage drops below the reference threshold and the stored datum is unrecoverable. Note that a READ operation refreshes the cell so that information can be maintained by reading each cell in the memory periodically.

Dynamic memories available today have minimum refresh rates on the order of one refresh every 1 to 2 ms. The refresh burden would be intolerable if each cell on a chip had to be read individually within the refresh period. This works out to one access about every 15 to 60 ns for chips in the 16-K and 64-K size. Chip manufacturers greatly simplify the problem by arranging the chips in two-dimensional arrays of bits, usually square in shape, so that all bits in a row are refreshed when any one bit in that row is read. Hence, refreshing requires only that each row of bits be read once every 1 or 2 ms. For 16-K chips arranged in arrays of 128×128, refresh must be done at the rate of 128 READS per refresh period, or about 1 READ every 8 to 16 μs. Since memory cycle times are on the order of 250 to 500 ns, refresh occupies only 2–3% of the available memory bandwidth.

Dynamic memory, therefore, imposes an overhead burden that neither static RAM nor ROM has. It has to have refresh logic to preserve information. A controller for a "worst possible" case is shown in Fig. 4.10. This design contains all of the elements that might be required, whereas in special cases we can greatly simplify it.

The idea in this design is to generate the sequence of addresses for refresh cycles in the counter. With each tick of the refresh clock, the counter advances, and the controller generates a memory request at the new address. The controller contains an arbiter, whose function is to handle situations in which the refresh request conflicts with a memory request from the processor. One or the other must be delayed because memory cannot do both simultaneously. To be sure that a minimum rate of refresh is maintained, we presume that the arbiter delays the processor request by generating a WAIT signal.

Although the controller is not very complicated, it is unnecessarily complex for small memories, where a few static RAM chips suffice for the entire application. Therefore dynamic memory tends to be used where applications require larger amounts of memory, and small memory systems tend to use static RAM.

Refresh controllers need not be as complicated as that shown in the figure. Many different approaches have led to simplifications of the basic idea. Here are some of the more useful.

1. Special chips have been designed that implement most of the functions of the controller in a single chip. These include the Intel 3242 and Motorola MC3480. These chips reduce the size and cost of the controller, but the functions are the same as those shown in the figure.
2. The arbiter function can be eliminated if it is possible to refresh memory during cycles left idle by the microprocessor. These idle periods must be at least as frequent as the refresh rate. For the 6500 and 6800 families, the system clock has a 50% duty cycle, and all READs take place in the latter half of the duty cycle. Then refresh can be

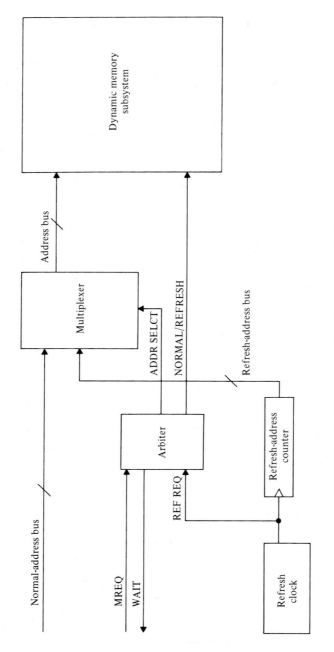

FIGURE 4.10   The structure of a refresh controller for dynamic memory.

done in the first half of the cycle without slowing down the processor if the memory cycle time is half of the processor cycle time. (This technique can be used with many other processor families besides the 65XX and 68XX families.)

3. The entire controller can be implemented in software. The idea is to have an interrupt subroutine that refreshes memory by reading a block of addresses. The interrupt routine is awakened every 1 to 2 ms by a clock interrupt. This solution is very inexpensive but places a higher burden on the processor and is not useful if the refresh subroutine increases latency to other interrupts beyond a critical threshold. If the microprocessor has a BLOCK MOVE instruction, the software burden is significantly decreased because one instruction can refresh memory during an interrupt.

4. The microprocessor can control the refresh through special-purpose internal logic. The Z80 processor, for example, produces a refresh address and a REFRESH control signal during a cycle when the bus would otherwise be inactive.

5. The dynamic RAM chip, itself, can implement the refresh controller. If all controller functions are on the RAM chip, then the RAM refreshes its own data, and functions as a static RAM chip except possibly when an external access conflicts with a refresh access. Some RAM chips contain an address counter for refresh and rely on an external signal to indicate when to refresh.

In short, new technology has reduced the burden of refresh to the point where its cost may be quite small.

Interfacing to dynamic RAM chips themselves is more complicated than for static RAM chips because the dynamic chips use address multiplexing, for which timing is critical. The problem is that we need 14 address pins for 16 K-bit chips and 16 pins for 64 K-bit chips, but the packages have to be as small as possible to keep the memory systems dense and the speeds high. Hence the 14 addresses of a 16 K $\times$ 1 chip are multiplexed on seven pins, and similarly the 16 addresses of 64 K $\times$ 1 chips use eight pins. Typical 16-K and 64-K chips are shown in Fig. 4.11. The 16-K chip is the MK4116 (also known as the Intel 2117, and by other part numbers from other manufacturers). This chip has 16 pins in all, with four used for power, seven for addresses, two for data, and three for control. The 64-K chip, Motorola's MCM6664, is almost a pin-for-pin replacement of the MK4116. By reducing the power-supply pins on the MCM6664 to two from four, we have two pins available for other functions. One is used for the addressing, and the other for refresh.

The multiplexing of addresses requires one more pin for control than on static RAM chips. The figure shows three control pins labeled ROW SELECT L, COLUMN SELECT L, and WRITE L. The chip select of a static chip has been replaced by row and column selects. These selects indicate which address is on the address lines when the chip is selected. Timing for the control signals are shown in Fig. 4.12. The timing is quite critical since the row addresses have to be held long enough to satisfy setup and hold-time constraints; then they have to be removed quickly enough to let the column addresses set up. The designer needs to keep the row address timing short to meet the memory cycle time requirements, yet also needs to keep it long enough to meet the setup timing requirements. Refresh cycles do not require a column address, since all bits in the same row are

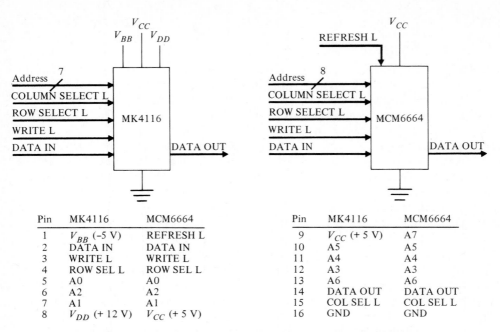

Pin	MK4116	MCM6664
1	V_{BB} (−5 V)	REFRESH L
2	DATA IN	DATA IN
3	WRITE L	WRITE L
4	ROW SEL L	ROW SEL L
5	A0	A0
6	A2	A2
7	A1	A1
8	V_{DD} (+ 12 V)	V_{CC} (+ 5 V)

Pin	MK4116	MCM6664
9	V_{CC} (+ 5 V)	A7
10	A5	A5
11	A4	A4
12	A3	A3
13	A6	A6
14	DATA OUT	DATA OUT
15	COL SEL L	COL SEL L
16	GND	GND

FIGURE 4.11   A comparison of a 16-K and a 64-K dynamic RAM chip.

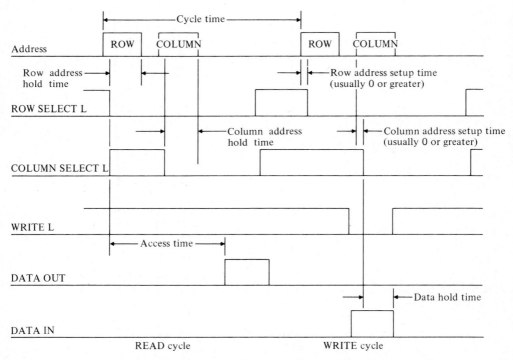

FIGURE 4.12   Timing relationships for the signals of a dynamic memory chip.

refreshed simultaneously. The MCM6664 refreshes automatically each time the RE-
FRESH L control is asserted. Both chips are compatible in refresh requirements as well as
in pinouts. The refresh cycle is 2 ms, and each of 128 addresses must be read during this
period. Hence, it is very simple to modify existing memory-system designs to change
from 16 K-bit chips to 64 K-bit chips.

Upgrading a memory system from 64 K-bytes to 256 K-bytes is nontrivial for microcomputers with only 16 address lines because the upgrade must incorporate a means for
accessing the expanded memory. The microprocessors that can best use the 64 K-bit and
256 K-bit chips have extended addressing, with address sizes of 20 bits or more. These
processors include the 8086, MC68000, and Z8000.

A simplified schematic for a dynamic memory is shown in Fig. 4.13. This controller
does not have an arbiter because it refreshes during the first phase of a two-phase clock.
All processor accesses are made during the second phase, and therefore the refresh cycle
cannot conflict with processor requests. In this design the system clock rate is 1 MHz, and
refresh requests are generated every 8 clocks. The rate is a little less than twice the
minimal rate for refresh. High-speed logic multiplexes the 7-address lines from one of
three sources: The high-address bits, the low-address bits, or the refresh counter. Delays
are generated from a tapped delay line and are designed to satisfy the setup times for row
and column addresses, as well as to terminate the cycle. Both refresh and normal requests
are changed from level signals into pulses by individual 225-ns delays. This makes the
remainder of the memory timing insensitive to the pulse width of the request levels. Two
delays are triggered by either request pulse. One delay is 300 ns, and generates the ROW
SELECT L signal to the memory array. The second delay is 75 ns, which delays
COLUMN SELECT L until the row addresses have been accepted by the memory. While
the ROW SELECT is active and COLUMN SELECT is inactive, the row address (low-
order address) is multiplexed onto the address bus. Then the 75-ns delay terminates and
COLUMN SELECT L is asserted. At this time the column address (high-order address) is
multiplexed onto the address bus. For READ cycles, the falling edge of the 300-ns delay
triggers a latch to accept memory data at the end of the access period. This gives the
memory about 200 ns before the next access. Chip specifications require this quiescent
time for precharge of internal circuits. The tri-state latch output drives the external data
bus and meets the timing requirements of the bus system, and thereby isolates the memory
timing from the bus timing.

The relative arrival of COLUMN SELECT L and the column address is very critical.
Typical chip specifications permit the column addresses to change concurrently with
COLUMN SELECT L, but the addresses should be stable from this time on. Address
lines must be treated as transmission lines and properly terminated. Otherwise reflections
on the address lines may lead to unstable signals at the chips. The figure shows source
termination on the address lines for this purpose. Another alternative is to delay
COLUMN SELECT L relative to the multiplexing of the column address to be sure that
the column address is stable when COLUMN SELECT reaches the memories. Multiplexing, refresh circuitry, and tight tolerances on timing make this design more complicated
and more difficult than a static memory.

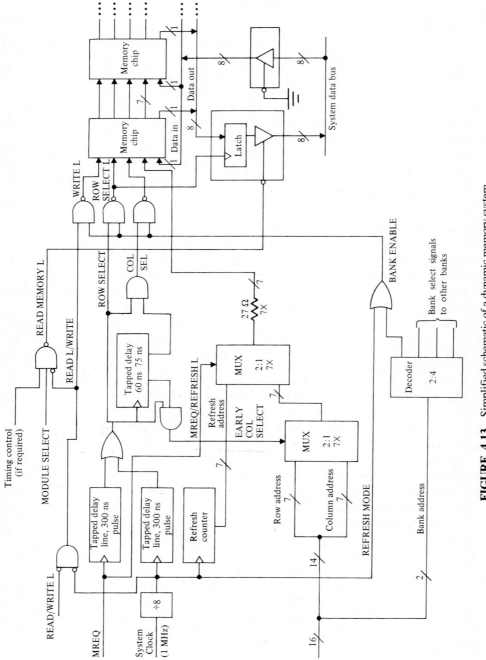

FIGURE 4.13 Simplified schematic of a dynamic memory system.

We have not described the power distribution, grounding, and power decoupling required for a good memory design. A perfectly good memory design can fail solely because of poor power distribution. Dynamic RAM is particularly sensitive to power distribution because of the high-speed switching of the address-multiplexing control signals. Designers must follow manufacturers' recommendations on these points and should review the principles discussed in Chapter 2.

4.2 MEMORY SYSTEMS

The microprocessor revolution has changed the way that computer systems are organized. Where early trends concentrated the activity into a single processor with supporting DMA channels, the modern trend is to incorporate a microprocessor for each important function. We often see two processors in systems, one for computation and one for disk control. If a system also has a graphics display, a third processor performs this task. The number of processors reaches five in some systems, and there is no particular reason why it should stop there.

In multiprocessor systems, a critical aspect of memory design concerns the sharing of memory between two (or more) processors. The same type of designs apply to sharing of memory between a processor and a DMA channel. This section treats basic techniques for facilitating the sharing. We focus exclusively on memory systems that are so-called "one-ported," that is, can honor one request at a time. It is possible to create a fully "dual-ported" memory, which can actually respond to two requests simultaneously; but this requires very sophisticated design and is usually limited to tiny memories, say of 256 bytes in size. Such a memory has two independent access paths to each of its cells, and a provision for detecting when a READ and a WRITE occur at the same cell simultaneously. The latter condition should result in the READ operation receiving the data from the WRITE operation, rather than its receiving the prior contents of memory. Conflicts caused by two simultaneous WRITEs to the same cell have to be resolved by forcing one to occur before the other. The standard memory chips described in the previous section are generally not suitable for this purpose.

The one-ported memory systems that we describe here accept requests from two or more sources. If the memory system has a cycle time much shorter than the cycle time of any requestor, the one-port memory might be able to simulate a multiport memory. To do so it must satisfy each requestor within that requestor's cycle time, even when several requests occur simultaneously.

Arbitration Policy

The general scheme we have for sharing memory is shown in Fig. 4.14. This shows an arbiter responding to three different requests. The arbiter responds to a request either by granting immediate access to memory or, in case of conflict, by responding with a WAIT signal to all but one requester. No more than one request is granted at any time, and delayed requests are granted eventually. This presumes, of course, that the outstanding requests can be held for several memory cycles, perhaps indefinitely, by a WAIT signal.

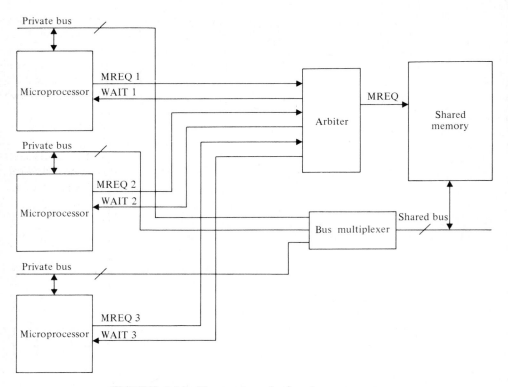

FIGURE 4.14 The structure of a shared memory system.

The arbiter shown in the figure, in general, is implemented with a protocol that treats all processors equally over the long term. When a conflict occurs between Processor A and Processor B, the arbiter grants the memory to A one time, then on the next conflict it grants the memory to B. The implementation requires that the arbiter maintain a current priority ranking of the processors, and that when a request is granted, the winning processor's priority moves to the bottom rank. With three processors there are six different priority rankings possible. So the arbiter has six states, one for each different ranking. Ties are broken on the basis of the present state of the arbiter. If Processor A has priority over Processor B when they make conflicting requests, the arbiter will grant memory to A, then change internal state so that Processor B has priority over processor A.

Table 4.1 is a state table showing the transitions made each time a request is granted. The rows of the table correspond to the present priority ranking, and the columns correspond to input conditions. The way the table is constructed is rather simple-minded. In a state in which the priority ranking is A-B-C, if A makes a request then A's request is granted, regardless of the condition of the other two processors. The next state then gives priority to the other two processors. Hence the next state is B-C-A as shown in the table. If

TABLE 4.1   A State Diagram for an Unbiased Arbiter

	Input Requests						
State	A	B	C	A, B	A, C	B, C	A, B,C
A-B-C	A	B	C	A	A	B	A
	B-C-A	A-C-B	A-B-C	B-C-A	B-C-A	A-C-B	B-C-A
A-C-B	A	B	C	A	A	C	A
	C-B-A	A-C-B	A-B-C	C-B-A	C-B-A	A-B-C	C-B-A
B-A-C	A	B	C	B	A	B	B
	B-C-A	A-C-B	B-A-C	A-C-B	B-C-A	A-C-B	A-C-B
B-C-A	A	B	C	B	C	B	B
	B-C-A	C-A-B	B-A-C	C-A-B	B-A-C	C-A-B	C-A-B
C-A-B	A	B	C	A	C	C	C
	C-B-A	C-A-B	A-B-C	C-B-A	A-B-C	A-B-C	A-B-C
C-B-A	A	B	C	B	C	C	C
	C-B-A	C-A-B	B-A-C	C-A-B	B-A-C	B-A-C	B-A-C

Each table entry indicates which processor receives a grant and which state is the next state of the arbiter.

A makes no request when the arbiter is in state A-B-C, then B is given priority over C in case of conflict, in which case the next state is A-C-B under this policy.

The policy stated is not the most general policy. It does not take into account the age of outstanding requests. Thus in state A-B-C a conflict between B and C leaves the arbiter in a state in which A still has priority over C. So if A makes a request during the next cycle, C has to wait yet another cycle before being granted access to memory. Since there are only two other processors, no processor must wait more than two cycles before being granted access to memory.

Another perfectly reasonable policy is to grant priority to the request waiting the longest and to break ties in an unbiased manner. This arbitration policy is more difficult to implement because there are more possible states. Not only do the states represent all permutations of relative priority, but they also encode the age of the request pending. The policy shown in Table 4.1 is quite adequate for most systems. If the policy fails in a particular situation because of critical timing problems, then perhaps it is best to design a specific arbitration algorithm for the application.

For more than three processors it becomes more difficult to implement the policy of Table 4.1 because the complexity of the arbiter grows much faster than the number of processors. The number of states in the arbiter grows factorially with the number of processors. For five processors there are 120 states, which is a rather substantial number for

TABLE 4.2   A State Diagram for a Rotating Priority

State	A	B	C	A, B	A, C	B, C	A, B, C
			Input Requests				
A-B-C	A	B	C	A	A	B	A
	B-C-A	C-A-B	A-B-C	B-C-A	B-C-A	C-A-B	B-C-A
B-C-A	A	B	C	B	C	B	B
	B-C-A	C-A-B	A-B-C	C-A-B	A-B-C	C-A-B	C-A-B
C-A-B	A	B	C	A	C	C	C
	B-C-A	C-A-B	A-B-C	B-C-A	A-B-C	A-B-C	A-B-C

Each table entry indicates which processor receives a grant and which state is the next state of the arbiter.

a small controller. Obviously, the complexity of this arrangement may be more than necessary to support the memory system. A much simpler arbitration scheme is based on a rotating priority. In this case the initial priority ranking is A-B-C-D-$\cdots$, and after A is granted an access the priority ranking rotates cyclically to B-C-D-$\cdots$-A. If A is idle and B is granted a request, then the priority ranking rotates cyclically so that B's priority becomes the lowest. This yields a ranking of the form C-D- $\cdots$-A-B. Since changes in priority are reflected in cyclic shifts of the ranking, there are only N distinct states in a system with N requesters. Moreover, no request can be outstanding more than N cycles, so the worst-case latency is no worse than in the scheme described in Table 4.1. A rotating priority scheme for three processors is shown in Table 4.2. The rotating priority scheme is, then, a much more practical scheme to implement than the general scheme and the differences in system behavior may be negligible.

Synchronization

The difficulty with arbiters is not in the implementation of the basic functions, but rather in the problem of accepting signals from processors that are running asynchronously with respect to each other. We discussed this problem earlier and indicated that the best way to solve the synchronization problem is to use a common clock for all processors. In this way we can be sure that all request signals are stable at the time an arbitration decision is made. If the requests are truly asynchronous then all requests have to be synchronized to the same clock through the use of the techniques described earlier. Inevitably there is a time penalty in synchronizing signals because a synchronizing flip-flop might enter the metastable state, and the interfacing circuitry has to delay long enough for the flip-flop to become stable again.

Figure 4.15(a) shows typical timing for arbitration in relation to timing for a memory cycle. Note that the requests for memory access have to be stable for the arbitration, and

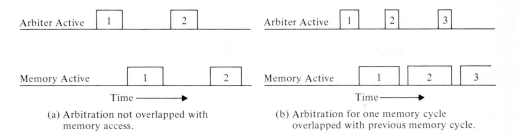

(a) Arbitration not overlapped with
memory access.

(b) Arbitration for one memory cycle
overlapped with previous memory cycle.

FIGURE 4.15   Relative timing of arbitration and shared memory activity without and with the overlapping or arbitration and memory access.

that this occurs in advance of the main memory cycle. If the requests to the arbiter have the timing of normal memory requests, then arbitration has the effect of lengthening memory cycle time. That is, a request to a private memory can be granted in the time shown as the memory cycle time, whereas requests to shared memory have to pay the penalty for arbitration.

A better approach is to overlap arbitration for the next memory cycle during the present memory cycle. The timing for this is shown in Fig. 4.15(b). Requests to the arbiter for memory access are generated one or more clock cycles before the actual memory request is issued. The arbiter operates on these advanced requests and issues a grant in time for the winning processor to make a memory access using normal timing. The problem, then, is how to generate the requests one cycle sooner than they normally would appear. The problem cannot be solved by the system designer. It has to be solved on the chip itself.

To give some idea of the solution to this problem consider the relevant signals for the MC6809E microprocessor, shown in Fig. 4.16. (The ''E'' designation stands for ''external clock.'') This version of the processor is intended for multiprocessor applications. Two features shown in the figure support this application. One feature is that the four-phase clock for the processor is generated externally from a source that can drive multiple processors in synchronism. The four-phases of the clock are generated by a pair of square-wave clock signals that are 90° out of phase with each other. These are labeled CLOCK and QUADRATURE CLOCK in the figure. The second feature is a signal labeled ADVANCED REQUEST (called AVMA for ''advanced valid memory access'' by the manufacturer). This signal is produced one cycle earlier than a normal memory request. Its purpose is to facilitate arbitration that must occur prior to memory access. The normal signal for the 68XX family that denotes MEMORY REQUEST (called VMA for ''valid memory access'') is not produced directly by the 6809E. However, the designer can generate VMA as a delayed version of the ADVANCED REQUEST produced by the winner of a bus-arbitration cycle.

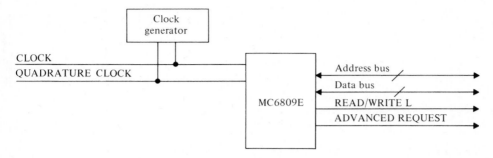

FIGURE 4.16   Interface signals for the 6809E showing a shared clock and ADVANCED REQUEST to facilitate early arbitration of an access to shared memory.

4.3 DMA CONTROLLERS

To complete our description of memory interfacing, we discuss the design and use of DMA controllers. These controllers were once expensive and complex subsystems, whose complexity was comparable to that of a small central processor. LSI implementations of DMA controllers have been as successful in shrinking DMA functions onto a single chip as they have been in shrinking the processing unit of a computer onto a single microprocessor chip.

The basic structure of a DMA channel is shown in Fig. 4.17. Because the DMA controller must issue commands to memory exactly the way the processor does, the controller has a full bus interface. Over this bus, the DMA receives control information from the microprocessor and transfers data to and from memory. This DMA controller has three independent channels. Each channel contains an address register, a control register, and a byte counter. The objective of a DMA operation is to transfer a block of data between an external device or I/O port and memory. To do so, the processor stores initial values in the address, control, and byte-count registers. The DMA channel then transfers the block of information from or to memory according to the direction of the transfer encoded in the control register. The starting address of the block in memory is given by the address register, and the length of the block is given by the byte count. To make this transfer, the DMA controller has to synchronize the activities of the processor to the external device. Basically, before it performs each transfer, the controller has to wait for both the external device to be ready and the processor to be idle.

The interface with the I/O port requires two signals per port (TRANSFER REQUEST and TRANSFER ACK), plus the ability to generate I/O READ/WRITE L to indicate to the port the direction of the transfer. The DMA controller accepts a TRANSFER REQUEST from the port when the port has data ready to write into memory or has an empty buffer that can accept data from memory. When a transfer is to take place, the DMA outputs the control signal TRANSFER ACK, which indicates that the port should receive data from or write data into memory. TRANSFER ACK functions like a CHIP SELECT

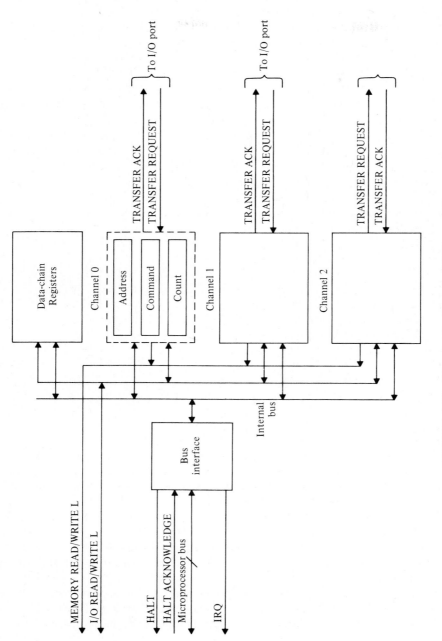

FIGURE 4.17   The structure of a typical DMA controller.

signal because when TRANSFER ACK is asserted, the port responds on the memory bus interface. The response is almost the same response as though the port had been selected by a CHIP SELECT. The major difference between a DMA-controlled response and a normal response is that the port responds in the opposite direction of the transfer indicated on the READ/WRITE control lines on the memory bus. If the control lines indicate a READ, then the READ is *from* memory *to* the I/O port. That is, the operation is a WRITE to the port if it is a READ from memory; and, conversely, a READ from the port is a WRITE to memory. Consequently, the I/O subsystem and the memory require distinct READ/WRITE L controls. Therefore the figure shows the normal control line to the memory system designated as READ/WRITE L and a second independent line to the I/O subsystem designated I/O READ/WRITE L. The DMA controller exercises both of these lines simultaneously in opposite polarity during a DMA transfer. The microprocessor, however, exercises only one of the two lines at a time, and therefore for microprocessor-controlled activities the two lines can be tied together.

This peculiarity of DMA systems raises an interesting question. How do we use I/O ports in a memory-mapped I/O system? In such a system there is usually a single bus to carry the READ/WRITE L control signal. Clearly the READ/WRITE L signal either has to be inverted externally to the I/O port or on the I/O chip itself. If the logic is external, the logic required is rather simple and is shown in Fig. 4.18. The READ/WRITE L signal is gated through an EXCLUSIVE OR with TRANSFER ACK, and passed to the I/O port. This inverts the polarity when TRANSFER ACK is asserted during DMA transfers. The chip select for the I/O port is the logical OR of a memory-mapped chip select and TRANSFER ACK.

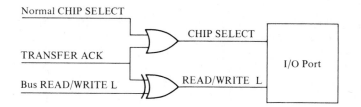

FIGURE 4.18   Control signal logic for an I/O port that runs under the direct control of a microprocessor and a DMA controller.

Because it is necessary to correct polarity of READ/WRITE L at the I/O ports for DMA transfers, a number of I/O ports have an internal mode in which the role of READ/WRITE L is reversed. For microprocessor-controlled transfers, the ports are operated in a normal mode. For DMA-controlled transfers, the microprocessor first places a port of this type in the DMA mode, then initiates the DMA controller. Then for the duration of the DMA transfer the complement of READ/WRITE L controls the direction of the data transfer.

The interface between the processor and the DMA controller is described in Chapter 1. The controller has a HALT request output signal and a HALT ACKNOWLEDGE input pin. During the byte-by-byte transfer of a block of data, the controller waits for a TRANSFER REQUEST on a channel. Then the controller asserts HALT and awaits HALT ACKNOWLEDGE. This instructs the processor to relinquish the memory bus. Within a few clock cycles, the processor asserts HALT ACKNOWLEDGE, and places all of its output drivers to the bus in high-impedance state. Now the DMA controller has access to memory. The controller simultaneously

1. places an address on the bus,
2. sends TRANSFER ACK to the requesting I/O port, and
3. sends the proper polarity of READ/WRITE L to memory and the complement of this signal to the I/O system.

The I/O port and memory respond to these actions in opposite ways so that data moves from one to the other depending on the polarity of READ/WRITE L. At the completion of the memory cycle, the DMA controller removes all of the signals it has placed on the bus, then places its bus drivers in high-impedance mode. When HALT is deasserted, the processor can continue its operation from the point of suspension. Because the DMA shown in Fig. 4.17 has three channels, the operations described can be multiplexed among three separate I/O ports.

Placing a HALT request on the bus causes some latency and overhead in the DMA operation. Usually one bus-clock cycle is lost each time the bus mastership changes hands, so that for each cycle of DMA transfer, two additional cycles may be lost through HALT and HALT ACKNOWLEDGE overhead. Moreover, some microprocessors continue to the end of the present instruction before relinquishing the bus, and this occupies as many as 10 to 15 cycles. To reduce the overhead and latency for high-performance transfers, the DMA controller usually has a burst mode in which the DMA controller retains control of the bus through the entire block transfer, and relinquishes the bus back to the processor only at the end of the block transfer. The selection between block mode and single-byte transfers is determined by the control word passed to the DMA from the processor.

The microprocessor can be interrupted by the controller at the end of a block transfer. When the processor responds to the interrupt, it can reload the DMA registers for a new block transfer and thereby maintain the continuity of the I/O flow. Another way to achieve continuous operation is to provide a means for the "chaining" of block transfers within the DMA controller. The box labeled "data-chain registers" in Fig. 4.17 holds an address, byte count, control word, plus a channel ID. These registers hold data to be used to reload the designated channel's registers when that channel completes a transfer. In many systems, the contents of the data-chain register can be used repeatedly for a sequence of transfers. Then after each transfer completes a new one can be begun without intervention by the processor. If the data-chain register must be reloaded, the processor can query the DMA controller periodically by reading its status. If the status indicates that a transfer has completed and used the data-chain registers to initiate a new transfer, the processor reloads the data-chain registers with the parameters for the next block transfer.

4.4 EXAMPLES OF DMA CONTROLLERS

This section discusses three different DMA controllers. The i8257 and Am9517 are designed for 808X-style buses. The MC6844 is used for the 6800 family of buses.

The i8257 DMA Controller

A block diagram of the i8257 appears in Fig. 4.19. This controller has four independent channels, each of which contains an address register and a counter. The counter decrements as each transfer occurs, and forces termination of the DMA operation after the last transfer. The controller increments the address register after each operation, so that successive data transfers are made at contiguous ascending addresses.

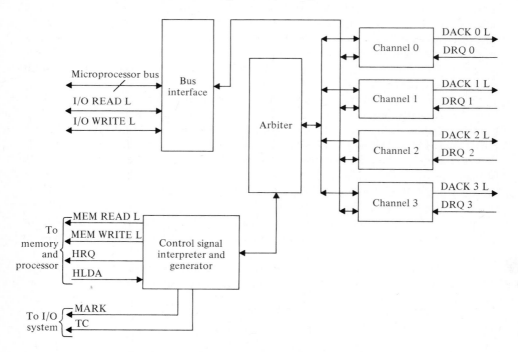

FIGURE 4.19   Structure of the i8257 DMA controller.

The arbiter in the figure resolves conflicts among the channels for access to memory. Two different arbitration schemes, selectable by the microprocessor, have been designed into the i8257 in order to make the chip useful in a variety of different applications. In one mode, the channels have a fixed priority and conflicts are resolved according to this priority. In this case Channel 0 has the highest priority and Channel 3 the least priority, so that Channel 0 should attach to the most critical I/O devices. The second arbitration mode is a rotating-priority scheme in which priority rankings are the four cyclic shifts of 0-1-2-3. When a channel is granted access to the bus, the priority ranking shifts cyclically to place the channel in the lowest priority position for the next arbitration cycle.

The remainder of the block diagram shows the interface with the microprocessor, memory, and I/O systems. In keeping with the requirements of the 808X family, this chip has four signals associated with the READ and WRITE operations. MEM READ L and MEM WRITE L are signals produced by the DMA controller to exercise memory. The two signals I/O READ L and I/O WRITE L are bidirectional, however. They are inputs from the microprocessor when the microprocessor sends commands to the 8257 and reads back the 8257 status. During I/O operations these signals are outputs from the 8257, and they are functionally opposite to the memory signals for reasons mentioned earlier. The 8257 takes control of the bus by exercising HALT (HRQ in the manufacturer's notation), and receives back the "go-ahead" signal on HALT ACKNOWLEDGE (denoted HLDA by the manufacturer).

Two signals produced by the DMA controller can be used by I/O ports to assist in controlling the transfer process. One signal, TC for terminal count, is asserted during the last cycle of a DMA block. This signal can be used to disable a DMA mode on an I/O port or to reset the port's internal state to indicate the end of a transfer. The second signal, MARK, is asserted when the remaining count on a channel becomes a multiple of 128. Hence MARK provides a convenient timing signal for an external device.

The microprocessor accesses specific registers on the chip through the use of four address lines decoded on chip. This yields 16 addressable locations. Eight of those are the four pairs of channel registers. Two other addresses are assigned to a control register and status register while other addresses are unused. All registers are 16 bits in length, but the data bus for the chip is only 8 bits wide. How does a microprocessor read and write the 16-bit registers over an 8-bit bus? Obviously, two bus operations are required per 16-bit register. The state of an internal flip-flop determines whether the low byte or the high byte is the byte being accessed. Each time an access occurs, the state of the flip-flop changes, so that on subsequent accesses the chip alternates between high byte and low byte. The state of the byte flip-flop is reset to the low-order byte during a system reset operation and by writing into the command mode register. Otherwise, register READs and WRITEs to the chip should always be made in pairs.

The internal byte flip-flop has a hidden software overhead associated with it. The problem is that a pair of accesses to a register must be uninterruptible. If for some reason an interrupt occurs between the accesses, then a side-effect of the interrupt program may be a change of the byte flip-flop. For example, the interrupt program may initiate an I/O operation on the DMA controller chip, or may interrogate the status register, both of which involve operations that must reset the byte flip-flop. Therefore whenever the 8257 registers are accessed by a microprocessor, the microprocessor must first turn off interrupts, then access the 8257's registers, then reestablish interrupts. The programming and performance burdens are small but annoying penalties. More disastrous are the consequences of failing to turn off the interrupt system. The resulting system errors are extremely subtle and difficult to analyze.

Another critical hazard created by the addressing facility is due to chip selects asserted during a DMA cycle. In theory, when the DMA controller has taken over the bus, the controller will not produce an address that selects the controller itself. However, should such a chip-select be generated, that chip select will change the state of the byte flip-flop. Then subsequent WRITEs of low and high bytes of addresses and counts will reverse these items in the registers. A failure of this type from a spurious chip select is extremely difficult to diagnose.

Chaining of successive DMA operations is provided in a somewhat limited fashion. One of the control modes of the chip is an autoload mode, in which Channel 2's registers are automatically reloaded from Channel 3's registers when Channel 2 completes its operation. In this mode, Channel 3 is essentially dedicated to the autoload function, so the effective number of channels is reduced from four to three. A status bit in the status register indicates when Channel 2's registers have been reloaded. By examining this bit, the microprocessor can determine when transfers have been completed, and when to reload the registers in Channel 3 for a subsequent automatic reload.

This DMA controller is inherently a burst-mode device, because the chip will not remove its bus request once the request has been granted until all block transfers in progress have been completed. However, through the use of external logic, the block transfer can be forced out of the burst mode to permit the microprocessor or other DMA controllers to access memory. The peripheral device (or other external logic) normally responds to a DMA request with a DACK L as shown in the I/O port interface of the 8257 in Fig. 4.19. If the signal HALT ACK (or HLDA in the manufacturer's notation) is forced low, indicating that the microprocessor is no longer halted, then the 8257 will automatically relinquish the bus at the end of the current memory cycle. When the next request for service appears on a DRQ line, the 8257 continues the block transfer.

The Am9517 DMA Controller

A somewhat more advanced DMA controller for 808X and other microcomputer systems is AMD's Am9517. Its block diagram is almost identical in structure to the 8257. In fact, the 9517 performs essentially all of the functions of the 8257 and more. Our discussion here highlights the differences in the chips, and omits discussion of points of similarity.

One difference is that the 9517 has four registers per channel rather than two per channel as in the 8257. Two of the channel registers hold the block address and block count, and the other two hold the initial values of these registers. When an address or block count is written into a channel register by the microprocessor, the datum is copied into both the intended destination register and the corresponding initial-value register. At the completion of a channel operation, the address and block counts can be reloaded automatically from the initial-value registers, and a new block operation will begin without intervention by the processor.

Of the sixteen port addresses selectable on the 9517, eight of them are used by the four channels in much the same way that the 8257 uses eight addresses for eight 16-bit registers. At the remaining eight addresses the 9517 has six registers, as compared to only two registers for the 8257. In addition to addresses used for registers, two other addresses are interpreted as chip commands ("reset" and "initialize the byte flip-flop").

We noted above that external logic dictates whether or not the 8257 operates in burst mode or in single-byte mode when it performs a block transfer. These modes are controlled by mode bits on the 9517 chip for each individual channel. Actually there are three distinct transfer modes built into the 9517:

1. A single-byte mode in which the 9517 releases the memory bus after each transfer.
2. A block mode, in which the 9517 retains control over the memory bus throughout the block transfer.
3. A demand-transfer mode, in which the 9517 retains control over the bus while a device continues to assert DREQ, and the 9517 releases the bus when DREQ becomes passive or when the block transfer completes.

Another capability of the 9517 is the capability to increment or decrement the address during a block transfer. The 8257 can only increment addresses; it never decrements them.

The mode control, autoload control, and increment/decrement control for each channel is stored in a mode control word for each channel. But the chip has but a single address for all the mode registers. The mode word itself supplies the channel number in its first two bits. Hence, when a mode word is written to the mode-register address, the mode word steers itself to the correct channel.

The MC6844 DMA Controller

The block diagram of the 6844 controller in Fig. 4.20 shows that it follows our general description of DMA controllers, but also that it differs somewhat from the 8257 and 9517. The major difference at the interface level is that the 6844 controls only one READ/WRITE L signal that is common to both memory and I/O ports. Therefore, logic in the I/O port chip or external to it must complement this signal during DMA operations.

The device has four ports, each containing a byte count, address, and control register. Data transfers can be one of three different modes described as follows, and are specified in the control register for each port. A separate register is used for chaining block transfers. It contains a 2-bit field that selects one of Channels 0, 1, or 2 for an automatic reload when that channel completes its present block transfer. The reload transfers the contents of the registers of Channel 3 to the designated register, so that the automatic-reload mode effectively reduces the number of available channels from four to three. The priority control register contains the enable (start) bits for the channels. Setting an enable bit for a channel initiates a transfer on that channel. The register contents also determine if requests are to be resolved by a fixed priority scheme (Channel 0 highest, Channel 3 lowest) or by a rotating priority scheme that was described earlier.

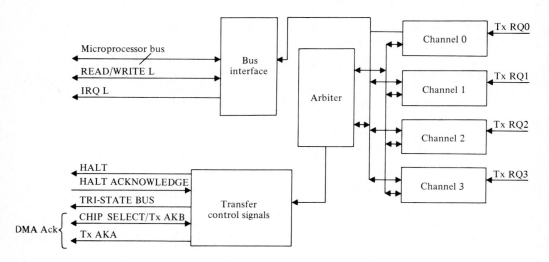

FIGURE 4.20   The structure of the MC6844 DMA controller.

Interface signals with I/O ports and memory are somewhat different for this chip than for others described because the modes available for block transfer are slightly different. The 6844 transfers data in any of the following modes:

1. A byte mode using HALT, in which the DMA controller halts the processor before each byte transfer, then allows the processor to restart after the transfer.
2. A byte mode in which clocks are stretched, leaving enough time for a normal processor access and a DMA access.
3. A burst mode, in which the processor is halted during the entire block transfer before it is restarted.

The clock-stretch mode is new to this discussion. It is a mode that appears to be peculiar to the 6800 family because the family lacks the READY/WAIT control signals. The controller uses the familiar HALT and HALT ACKNOWLEDGE handshake-control signals for modes in which the processor is stopped, and uses the signal called TRI-STATE BUS for the clock-stretch modes. This signal forces a 6800-family processor to release all tri-state signals on its memory interface, and simultaneously holds the system clock in a level state. There should be sufficient time while the clock is high for both a DMA access and a processor access to memory, but the clock cannot be held constant indefinitely because the 6800-family microprocessors require a clock cycle to refresh critical information.

The CHIP SELECT signal does double duty on this device. It functions as an input when the device is a passive listener on the bus. After the device takes over the memory bus, the CHIP SELECT signal becomes an output. Hence the CHIP SELECT signal should be driven externally by a tri-state or open-collector device. The output on the CHIP SELECT pin is denoted Tx AKB, which together with Tx AKA form a pair of signals that acknowledge transfer requests. These two signals encode four states, such that each state is a handshake acknowledge for a request on one channel. Both the 9517 and 8257 produce unencoded acknowledge signals for this purpose, which eliminates the need for off-chip logic to decode the state of these pins.

All other aspects of this chip are sufficiently similar to the ones previously described in this section to make additional discussion unnecessary.

OTHER READING

Practical implementations of memory systems and DMA controllers are described in detail in reference material published by semiconductor manufacturers. Intel's *Memory Design Handbook* (1977) is a particularly good source of information in that it covers the problems of power distribution and noise control, as well as the basic principles of interfacing to memory chips. It contains detailed logic schematics and printed circuit board layouts of memory designs for various types of memory chips. Techniques for programming PROM and for designing PROM programmers are also covered in this handbook. Metzler and Oliphant (1978) provide details on interfacing to the 16 K 2118 dynamic RAM and include oscilloscope traces of waveforms that compare the 2118 to the 2117 (MK4116). Altnether (1980) covers the design of memory systems that use the high-speed 2147H static RAM. Osborne and Kane, vol. 3 (1978), covers the full spectrum of RAM, ROM, and PROM. In this same volume they also treat the 8257 and 9517 DMA controllers, and the 6844 is covered in vol. 2 (1978).

EXPERIMENTS

4.1 For this experiment you will need a dual-trace oscilloscope and a microcomputer. You should have the full logic schematics for the computer, but it is sufficient to have the chip specifications for the microprocessor and the memory chips to carry out the experiment.

a) Write a brief program loop, as described in Table E–3.1 of Chapter 3, that places your computer in a tight loop. Be sure that your program is written to access a RAM location, not ROM or a nonexistent address. With this program running, connect the oscilloscope external sync input to the WRITE line. This will lock the oscilloscope to the repetitive signals.

b) Locate the RAM chip that your program accesses. Connect one probe to a CHIP SELECT line and the other to an address line. For dynamic RAM use ROW SELECT (RAS) for the CHIP SELECT. If the chip has more than one CHIP SELECT, use one that is produced from a decoded address. In this configuration measure the address setup time prior to the leading edge of CHIP SELECT, and the address hold time after the trailing edge of CHIP SELECT. Compare these times to the chip specifications. (If the address bit you probe does not change at the beginning or end of a cycle, probe various address lines until you can observe both the leading and falling edges of addresses relative to the leading and falling edges of the CHIP SELECT.)

    c) Measure the relative time difference between WRITE and CHIP SELECT. Which signal reaches its active state first during a WRITE cycle? Compare your measurements with the chip specifications.

    d) If the chip is a dynamic RAM, measure the setup and hold time for the column addresses relative to COLUMN SELECT (CAS). Compare these measurements with the chip specifications.

    e) Measure the access time for data read from the chip; then measure the data hold time. You may not be able to measure the access time directly because doing so depends on the timing of the output enable as well as the true access time. Nevertheless, measure the apparent access time, including the effects of the delay in enabling the output drivers. Compare your measurements to the chip specifications.

    f) For a WRITE cycle, measure the input data setup time and hold time, and compare them to the chip specifications.

4.2 This experiment repeats the previous experiment, but uses ROM instead of RAM.

    a) Enter your tight program loop as you did for the previous problem, except that the instruction that loads data should load data from a ROM, not RAM, location. The program should continue to write to a RAM location.

    b) Connect one probe to a CHIP SELECT on the ROM that you access. If there is more than one CHIP SELECT, then connect the probe to a CHIP SELECT that is produced by an address decoder. Select the INTERNAL SYNC mode on the oscilloscope and sync the display to the CHIP SELECT signal.

    c) Measure the address setup time relative to the CHIP-SELECT. This is usually not a critical time, and many manufacturers do not specify it in their reference documentation.

    d) Measure the access time of the chip relative to the point at which the addresses stabilize. Compare this time to the manufacturer's specifications.

    e) Measure the delay in the enabling of the output drivers of the chip relative to the OUTPUT ENABLE. If the chip does not have an OUTPUT ENABLE then find a CHIP SELECT that turns on the output drivers, and measure the driver delay with respect to this CHIP SELECT. Compare your observations with the manufacturer's specifications.

4.3 For this experiment you will design and construct a 1 K-byte memory expansion to an existing computer.

    a) You will need a microcomputer that has a memory-expansion bus. Find a region of memory in which there is no installed RAM, and verify that addresses in this region do not activate any memory cell, I/O port, or tri-state buffer that drives the microprocessor bus. You must be absolutely certain that you can install the memory without a tri-state conflict on the bus.

    b) Design a 1 K-byte RAM using two 2114s, address decoders, and other random logic as required. Interface the address lines of your memory to the memory-expansion bus through tri-state buffers in the 74LS24X family (or their equivalents) that have hysteresis for noise immunity. Interface the data bus through an 8-bit bus transceiver such as 74LS245s, or through tri-state buffers such as 74LS241s connected back-to-back. Carefully design the ENABLE inputs on your memory so that there is a dead time in the transition between a bus READ and a bus WRITE.

c) Construct your memory on a project board. It is essential that the memory chips be mounted on sockets or on a breadboard so that they are both insertable and removable.

d) Construct a short cable to extend the bus to your project board. If you use flat cable, there should be a ground wire between every signal wire. If you use discrete wires, use one ground wire for every signal wire, and twist each signal with its corresponding ground. Connect together all ground wires at both ends of the cable to signal ground points. Bring +5 V to the project board through hefty power conductors in order to minimize power drops on the lines. Use decoupling capacitors on your project board, at least one 0.1-μF capacitor for every two chips and two 10-μF capacitors on opposite sides of the board.

e) The next several steps are checks for common problems that can cause serious damage to the project board and the microcomputer. *Never apply power to a computer connected to a project board without first performing these tests or their equivalents.* Recheck your design, your project board, and your cabling.
   - Remove the cable between the project board and the computer temporarily.
   - With no chips plugged into the board, measure the impedance across the project board power supply and verify that the supply is not shorted.
   - Apply power to the project board, and verify that the power reaches 5 V and remains constant.

f) With power off, connect the cable between the project board and the microcomputer. Apply power to both the computer and the project board and verify that the 5 V supplies to both remain at 5 V in this configuration.

g) With power off, insert all chips into the project board, except for the memory chips and the data bus drivers. Turn on the power, and enter a program that reads from a location on your board within a tight, endless program loop. Connect an oscilloscope to the ENABLE lines of the data bus drivers. Verify that the data bus "turns around" only during the READ, and at all other times the data bus drivers are either in a WRITE state or in a high-impedance state.

h) Change your program to write to your memory instead of reading from it. Probe the ENABLE lines of the data bus driver and verify that bus drivers are in a WRITE state during the WRITE cycle. At all other times the drivers should be in a high-impedance state or in a WRITE state.

i) With power off, insert the data bus drivers and the memory chips. Turn on power and test the memory.

If you have thoroughly checked your design and followed these procedures, you should be able to run diagnostic programs with your project board connected to the computer. If for any reason the microcomputer fails to execute normal programs, turn off the power immediately and recheck your work with power off. If you can execute programs, but the memory diagnostics indicate that the memory is not working properly, probe your project board for correct logic and correct timing at the memory chips.

4.4 This experiment requires a small memory on a project board for which wiring can be easily changed. The project board of Experiment 4.3 is quite suitable for this purpose. The objective of this experiment is to examine failure modes of static RAM when setup times fail to meet chip specifications.

a) Disconnect one address line, A9, from the address driver output. All chips should have this pin floating. Exercise your project board and determine the effects of this change.

b) Create a delay by passing A9 through a series of six inverters of a 7404 chip. The lead inverter should be driven by the address-bus driver, and the last inverter in the chain should drive the address lines of the memory chips. Observe the effect of this change on an oscilloscope and determine whether the address setup time has been violated. Add another six gates in the chain if necessary so that the address A9 definitely changes state during a period when it should be stable. Exercise the memory and observe the effects of this change.

c) Remove the delay from A9 and insert the delay into the WRITE line so that WRITE changes at the 2114 after CHIP SELECT. Observe the effects of this change.

5 / SERIAL INTERFACING

This chapter is the first of the chapters that cover detailed information on interfacing microcomputers to specific devices. A natural starting point is the serial interface because it is probably the least complex electrical interface to implement. It requires only one signal wire to carry all data flow in one direction. (Two wires are required for two-directional flow—that is, one wire for input data and one for output data.) Serial interfaces do, however, have some logic to convert between parallel and serial data streams, and this logic is not necessary for other types of interfaces. But because serial links have a small number of wires and a correspondingly low cost, they are standardized into a few widely used protocols for which there exist LSI interface chips. The large volume of production for these interfaces has reduced the cost per serial port to a few dollars for parts in spite of the additional logic required for transforming data between parallel and serial data streams.

The structure of a typical serial I/O port is shown in Fig. 5.1. Note that the structure is similar to the general port structure outlined earlier in this textbook. That is, the port contains a bus interface through which the microprocessor can send commands to the port, read port status, and access input/output data registers in the port. An interrupt line notifies the microprocessor of the completion of an operation. What distinguishes this port from the general structure of an I/O port is the conversion that occurs between serial and parallel data streams. The bus interface with the microprocessor is a parallel interface through which eight (or sixteen) data bits are transmitted in a single transaction. The interface with the outside world is a serial interface, in which those same data bits are transmitted on a single output wire or received on a single input wire, with the bits appearing on these lines sequentially in time.

The figure shows an output register XMIT loaded in parallel from the microprocessor data bus. This register, in turn, is connected in parallel to a shift register. Data loaded into XMIT are subsequently passed to the shift register, then shifted serially onto a single output line. Input data are received sequentially and passed to a shift register, which collects the bits until the register is full. Subsequently, the input data are passed in parallel from the shift register to the register identified as RCV, and from there to the microprocessor bus.

The reason that both the transmit and receive sections have two registers relates to the need to buffer data in transit through the port. It is possible, for example, to combine RCV and its corresponding shift-register into one register, but this creates a serious timing constraint in the port. There may be an indefinite delay between the receipt of a full 8-bit datum from the outside world, and the availability of a bus cycle during which that datum can be transferred to the microprocessor. Unless the port can safely buffer a received datum for a short period of time, there is a very high risk that a received datum will be overwritten by the leading bits of the next arriving character. Hence, RCV gives the

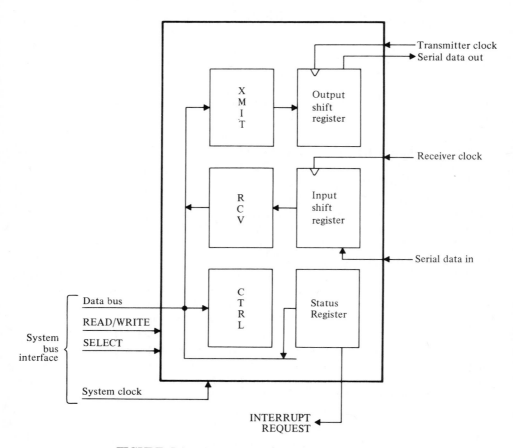

FIGURE 5.1   The structure of a typical serial I/O port.

necessary additional buffering for input data. As each successive bit of the input stream appears, the shift register shifts to make room for it. When the last bit of a character is received, the completed character moves to RCV, from where it is eventually moved to the processor. Thus, by buffering a received datum in RCV, the shift register is free to accept the next byte of information from the serial data stream.

Once a character is transferred to the buffer register RCV, the microprocessor has an opportunity to remove the character from the I/O port and copy it to memory where further operations can be done. The microprocessor can determine the availability of the character either by testing the status bit of the port, which distinguishes between a full buffer and an empty buffer, or by fielding an interrupt generated at the completion of character reception. In the latter case, the microprocessor must distinguish the interrupting port from all other ports by testing port status or by accepting a transfer vector from the port in response to an interrupt-acknowledge signal.

Although we have focused on the input stream to indicate why a buffer register is commonly used, the output stream also benefits from a buffer register configured as in the figure. In this case, the microprocessor can fill the output buffer while the last character is still being shifted out of the shift register. If the output buffer XMIT is full when the shift register empties, the XMIT datum is automatically transferred to the shift register, thereby freeing XMIT for another datum. The buffering of the output register improves performance, but is not essential for the correct operation of the interface. If XMIT and its corresponding shift register are combined into a single register, then when that register empties, it remains empty until reloaded from the microprocessor bus. This leaves the transmit line in an idle state until the microprocessor services the transmitter again. To eliminate the idle period in the absence of buffering, the microprocessor must respond to a service request in the very brief interval between the end of one character and the beginning of the next. With buffering as shown in the figure, when an output datum is transferred from XMIT to the shift register for output, XMIT can accept the next datum from the microprocessor at any time during the transmission of the datum from the shift register. When the shift register outputs the last bit of its datum, it reloads from XMIT, and transmits the first bit of that datum with no idle time between data. Thus, this scheme eliminates idle time on the output line, provided that the microprocessor reloads XMIT before the shift register empties again, but this reload interval is at least one 8-bit character interval, and not just the brief period between characters that is available in an unbuffered transmitter.

Because buffering is so important to correct operation and good performance, virtually all forms of serial I/O ports use buffering as shown in Fig. 5.1. The cost of buffering is negligible when implemented in LSI form; and, in fact, some interface devices contain several buffer registers per port in order to attain additional reliability and higher performance.

5.1 SERIAL I/O PROTOCOLS

A *communications protocol* is a convention for data transmission that includes such functions as timing, control, formatting, and data representation. Protocols generally fall into two categories depending on the clocking of the data on the serial link:

1. *Asynchronous protocols:* Successive data appear in the data stream at arbitrary times, with no specific clock control governing the relative delays between data.
2. *Synchronous protocols:* Each successive datum in a stream of data is governed by a master data clock and appears at a specific interval in time.

Commonly used synchronous and asynchronous protocols deliver serial data in 8-bit characters. Asynchronous protocols treat each character as an individual message, and the characters appear in the data stream at arbitrary relative times. Within each character, however, the bits are transmitted at a fixed predetermined clock rate. Hence these protocols are actually synchronous within a character and asynchronous between characters, but they are called asynchronous because the asynchronous timing between characters is their distinguishing characteristic.

Synchronous protocols produce a stream of data at a fixed clock rate with the clock governing not only the bits within a character but the character-to-character timing as well. Asynchronous protocols tend to be simpler, slower, and more widely used than synchronous protocols. In asynchronous protocols, since each character in the data stream is independent of the preceding and following characters, neither the transmitter nor the receiver needs to retain state information while processing a sequence of characters in a message. Although simplicity has its attractions, the asynchronous protocols have at least a 20% overhead per character of control information transmitted with each character. This overhead is substantially lower in synchronous protocols where control information is not required on a per-character basis. These protocols group characters into blocks of characters and place the control information at the beginning and end of blocks. Hence the control information per data byte can be made much smaller, provided that blocks are long; however, the consequence is that the receiver and transmitter must retain more state information. The synchronous protocol also has hardware to extract a synchronous clock from incoming data, which is a more demanding operation than the edge detection performed by an asynchronous receiver. So synchronous protocols tend to require more complexity in the transmitter and receiver than do asynchronous protocols, but they lead to greater effective use of communications bandwidth.

Another important difference between the protocols is the error correction and detection capability of the basic protocol. In the asynchronous protocols each message is a single 8-bit datum. Some protection from errors is available through the use of one of those 8-bits as a parity check. With one parity check, any single-bit error or odd number of bit errors is detectable, but not correctable. But when an even number of bits is incorrectly received, the parity check is "satisfied," and the errors are thus undetectable. Although it is possible to impose error-correction and detection capability on sequences of characters through the use of parity checks over blocks of data, such a capability is outside the specifications of the asynchronous protocol, and is therefore incorporated into system firmware or software and not into the I/O port itself.

However, synchronous transmission protocols, for messages that are typically tens or hundreds of bytes in length, usually include sufficient redundancy to detect the most probable errors in any given block of data; moreover these protocols provide additional information for other control purposes. The use of redundancy at the block level instead of at the character level gives higher error-protection for a given percentage of check bits in the data stream, and thus makes more efficient use of the communications bandwidth. Moreover, with additional control information in each block of synchronous data, higher-level functions can be defined as part of the synchronous protocol and built into the I/O port. One such function, for example, is automatic retransmission of a block of data when a receiver discovers an error in the block. In contrast, retransmission of individual characters sent on an asynchronous channel is very difficult because there is no easy way for a receiver to tell the transmitter which character to retransmit, nor for the transmitter to distinguish between a new character or a retransmitted character. For synchronous protocols, control information in each block can contain the sequence number of the block, so that the receiver can request retransmission of specific blocks. The retransmitted blocks are readily identified by their sequence numbers.

5.2 ASYNCHRONOUS PROTOCOLS

To study asynchronous protocols, we separate the timing conventions from the electrical connection requirements. There is only one timing convention in widespread use, but electrical connections usually follow any one of three systems:

1. RS-232-C.
2. 20 mA current loop.
3. RS-422, RS-423, and RS-449.

RS denotes "recommended standard" and refers to official published standards of the Electronic Industries Association, or EIA. Each of the three interconnection systems is described in detail after we examine timing conventions that apply to all three systems.

Figure 5.2 illustrates the bit timing for a single data byte transmitted serially on an asynchronous link. The idle line is assumed to be in a high or 1 state. Each character begins with a 0 bit, followed by 8 data bits, then followed by 1, 1½, or 2 closing 1 bits. A bit interval is a fixed period of time governed by a local clock in the transmitter and receiver. Signaling frequencies common today are 300 Hz, 600 Hz, 1200 Hz, etc., up to 19.2 kHz. Slower, obsolescent equipment runs at 110 Hz, 134.5 Hz, and 150 Hz. Interfaces often support these rates for the purposes of compatibility, even though new equipment rarely signals at these rates. Within the 8-bit data portion of a character, the data are transmitted least-significant bit first. Hence, the figure shows the pattern in time 1000 0010 for the ASCII (American Standard Code for Information Interchange, pronounced "ask-ee") encoding of the letter A, which when written with the least-significant bit on the right is $0100\ 0001 = 41_{16}$, which readers should recognize as the correct encoding of the letter A. (See Appendix A.)

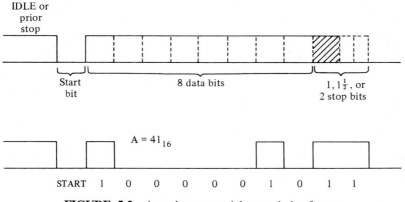

FIGURE 5.2 Asynchronous serial transmission format.

The start and stop bits serve a very important purpose. Obviously they identify the beginning and end of each character; but more important, they permit a receiver to resynchronize a local clock to each new character. Since a character can begin at an arbitrary time, the receiver has to discover when that edge occurs with such accuracy that it is able to sample the next 10 to 11 bits correctly. The receiver's clock is not identical to the transmitter's clock, so sample points at the receiver will, in general, be spaced less than or greater than a bit period as defined by the transmitter clock. A fast receiver samples successive bits earlier and earlier in a bit period. A slow receiver does the opposite. The receiver must not let its relative clock speed cause it to sample the wrong bit. The best strategy is that the receiver samples each bit as closely as possible to the center of the bit period. If the receiver makes a good estimate of the start of the first bit, then it can sample this bit after waiting for one-half of a bit period after the leading transition on the start bit. Thereafter the receiver waits one bit period and samples again until it reaches the last bit.

This strategy works correctly when the opening transition is known accurately, provided that the receiver clock is close enough to the transmitter clock in frequency that the last bit is sampled within one half-period of its true center position. This means that the receiver clock, in relation to the transmitter clock, cannot gain or lose more than half a bit in position over 10 to 11 clock periods. Hence, we require both clocks to be accurate within a 5% error margin, which is easily realized with today's technology. But this sampling strategy depends on discovering the leading edge of a character, then timing all subsequent samples from this point. To make the leading edge discoverable, the start bit is made different from both the idle-line state and the closing bit of a character. Hence, the leading edge can be observed when the new character occurs on an idle line, or when one character immediately follows another. Because of the skew of the bit transitions caused by variances in thresholds and rise/fall times, the 5% margin of error is a greater margin of error than actually required, but the error margin is still a few percentage points at slow clock rates.

Assuming that the leading transition of a character is readily observable, the next problem is to use this as a time base for sampling the following bits. Most receivers use a fast clock for this purpose. Figure 5.3 shows a receiver clock that runs at 16 times the bit frequency. With this clock, the receiver can determine the beginning of a character to within $\frac{1}{16}$ of a bit period. All sampling is done on the basis of the $16\times$ clock in the following steps:

1. When the leading transition of a character occurs, a counter register is cleared.
2. The counter increments for each tick of the $16\times$ clock.
3. When the counter first reaches the value 8, it has reached the middle of the start bit. At this point, the start bit is sampled, and the counter is cleared.
4. Subsequently, each time the counter reaches the value 16, the waveform is sampled, and the counter is cleared. The sampling is repeated until the last stop bit is sampled.
5. If the stop bit (or bits) is correct, the character is accepted, loaded into a buffer, and the process begins again at Step 1.

Although this example uses a $16\times$ clock at the receiver, the receiver clock can be other multiples of the bit rate. Higher receiver clock rates yield greater resolution, but the resolution is not particularly advantageous beyond the resolution available with a $16\times$ clock.

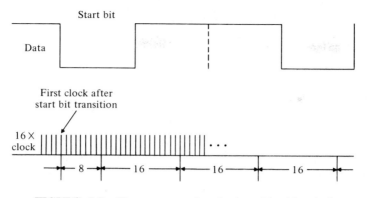

FIGURE 5.3   Character resynchronization with a 16× clock.

Note that the timing constraints are not very critical. The limit on the timing variation between receiver and transmitter is easily met with crystal-controlled clocks, since these circuits have a stability of at least one part in 10^5. Less accurate but acceptable clocks can be implemented with simple RC timing circuits. Of course there is a cost for making the protocol relatively insensitive to clock speed. This is the cost of using a start and stop bit of opposite polarity, which uses at least 20% of the available communications bandwidth. Even this 20% overhead is not quite sufficient to achieve the clock insensitivity required. When transmitting a long sequence of characters without idle time between them, a transmitter that is slightly faster than a receiver may eventually overrun the receiver by one bit, thereby losing a whole character or worse. It is necessary to insert idle periods every so often in the transmitted bit stream to prevent this occurrence, which reduces useful bandwidth even more. We address this topic in greater depth later in this chapter.

The RS-232-C Interface

The RS-232-C Interface Standard is a widely used popular standard of the Electronic Industries Association. The EIA RS standards cover a very broad range of areas, going well beyond communications and computers. The RS-232-C standard was originally developed to foster data communications on public telephone networks. The interface to a telephone network is normally made through a device known as a *modem*, from *mo*dulator-*dem*odulator. This device translates 0s and 1s from a sequence of high and low voltages into a sequence of high and low frequencies, which are compatible with telephone networks. At the other end of a connection, another modem retranslates the frequencies back into a sequence of high and low voltages. The RS-232-C standard, then, originally provided a specification for connecting remote devices together by using the telephone network as an intermediate medium, with interfacing accomplished by modems. In the mid-60s during the early phases of the development of time-shared computers, remote access over serial links was done almost exclusively through telephone connections. The RS-232-C standard then became widely adopted in both terminal and computer equipment. In the 1980s, with the proliferation of microcomputers, terminals are usually connected directly to computers through RS-232-C ports, and do not use the telephone network or modems except for truly remote connections.

The original use of the standard is strongly reflected in the implementation shown in Fig. 5.4. On the left in the figure is an interface for a computer or terminal that connects to a modem interface on the right of the figure. Conspicuous in the figure are the two grounds defined in the RS-232-C standard. One ground is a chassis ground that is tied directly to the shields in the systems. This ground connection should be made between two devices only if it is safe to connect the chassis grounds together. The other ground is a signal ground that provides a common reference point for all other signals. This connection is mandatory. But because the signal grounds are not necessarily isolated from the chassis ground, RS-232-C has an inherent potential ground-loop problem. While the standard is quite useful for short distances, for longer distances it becomes unreliable and hazardous. The published standard recommends that each device should have a cable not in excess of 50 feet, which permits the total cable length between a pair of devices to reach 100 feet. For longer cables, the standard strongly recommends that other means of interconnection be used. The RS-232-C standard describes 21 signals and a 25-pin physical connector for asynchronous communication. Details of the signals are in Appendix B. The following discussion highlights the more important signals.

Returning to Fig. 5.4, we see that the terminal/computer interface on the left and the modem on the right have a pair of wires dedicated to TRANSMIT and RECEIVE functions. These are compatible signals because TRANSMIT is a modem input and a

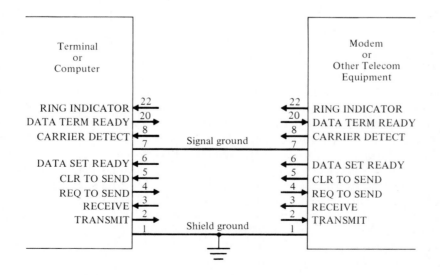

FIGURE 5.4   RS-232-C interface with communications equipment.

computer/terminal output; the converse applies to RECEIVE. Other signals reflect the telephone protocol of the modem. Specifically, REQ TO SEND and CLR TO SEND relate to the characteristics of half-duplex telephone lines. Such lines are capable of bidirectional traffic, but they can send in only one direction at a time. The terminal signals a modem with REQ TO SEND when it has a character to transmit, but the character has to be queued until the modem changes from a receive to a transmit mode. When transmission is possible, the CLR TO SEND signal is returned to the terminal, and transmission can begin. The modem can also turn off CLR TO SEND if the modem moves into the receive mode from transmit mode.

The CLR TO SEND and REQ TO SEND lines are held to a constant voltage when the telephone connection is full-duplex—that is, when transmit and receive functions can oocur simultaneously on independent wires. Full-duplex links are commonplace today so that the half-duplex protocol is seldom used with modems; the protocol, however, is built into the serial-interface devices widely available for RS-232-C use, and the control signals are occasionally used for purposes other than the one originally intended.

Two READY signals are included in the RS-232-C standard. DATA SET READY signifies that the modem is operational, and DATA TERM READY is the corresponding signal for computers and terminals. These signals are sometimes connected to the power supply and become asserted when the device is powered on. The DATA SET READY signal for a modem indicates more than just a power-on condition; the modem is actually connected to a communications line, and is not in a test mode or a disconnected state. The READY signals are then passed across the cable link so that the equipment on the opposite end of the cable can sense the condition.

CARRIER DETECT and RING INDICATOR are related to telephone functions. The RING INDICATOR is asserted during the period that a ringing tone is present on the communications line. When ringing is sensed at a computer I/O port, the port should post an interrupt, at which point the computer can initiate a connection to the caller. CARRIER DETECT is a signal that indicates that a remote connection is currently active. If the connection should break for any reason, the CARRIER DETECT signal is lost, and this too should cause an interrupt at a computer I/O port.

The standard incorporates other signals not shown in the figure. These relate to testing and to secondary channels. For interconnections between computers and terminals that do not use a telephone network, the signals in the figure are sufficient for nearly all functions.

Now we come to an interesting problem. Figure 5.4 shows that a computer or terminal can be wired to connect directly to a modem. But when wired in this fashion they cannot be connected directly to each other. The connections show both the computer and terminal transmitting on the same pin and receiving on the same pin. It is obvious that these pins cannot be connected directly together. There are several ways to solve the problem. One way is to build terminals that have the same interface as the modems. Then they can connect directly to computers. But unfortunately these terminals are incompatible with the modems and the telephone network. Another common solution is to correct the problem in the interconnecting cable as shown in Fig. 5.5. Note that the TRANSMITTED DATA and RECEIVED DATA lines are crossed so that the devices can, at least, transmit

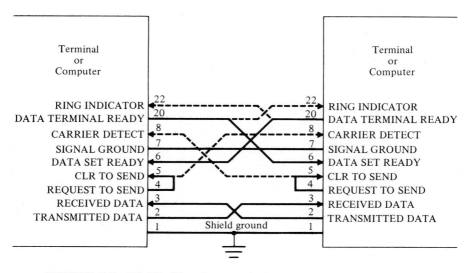

FIGURE 5.5   RS-232-C interface, terminal/computer to terminal/computer.

and receive properly. Given the full-duplex nature of the hard-wired connection, RE-
QUEST TO SEND and CLR TO SEND no longer serve a useful modem-like function.
Hence, REQUEST TO SEND is folded back as CLR TO SEND, and a transmission request is thereby always granted. The dotted line shows this signal used as CARRIER
DETECT at the other end, since the presence of REQUEST TO SEND is functionally
similar to the detection of a carrier in a communications channel. The last set of signals,
DATA SET READY and DATA TERMINAL READY are crossed in the cable so that
each end of the link can detect the presence of a ready condition on the other end. Note the
dotted line that carries the READY signal to the RING INDICATOR input. Dotted lines
in this drawing signify connections that are sometimes made in practice, but are less common than the connections, as represented by solid lines, that cross couple or feed back
pairs of signals.

Electrical conventions for RS-232-C circuits are shown in Fig. 5.6. The voltage levels are quite different from the TTL and MOS voltage levels. Voltages in RS-232-C systems are symmetric with respect to ground, and are at least 3 V for a logic 0, and −3 V or
less for a logic 1. (The standard occasionally uses the terms "Mark" and "Space" to
denote logic 1 and logic 0, respectively.) In actual practice, the voltage levels are
powered by ±12-V and ±15-V supplies, so that the voltage swing between logic 1 and
logic 0 may be 20 or more volts. Inexpensive translator circuits are available for changing
the voltage levels. The MC1488 transmitter accepts TTL input levels and produces RS-
232-C output levels. The actual output voltage is a function of the supply voltage on the
MC1488, and these are usually set at ±15 V or at ±12 V. The MC1489 receiver uses a
standard 5 V supply for signal receiving; and this is all that is necessary, although an additional small voltage supply can be connected to the receiver to alter the switching thresh-

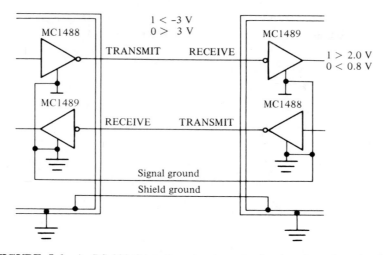

FIGURE 5.6   An RS-232-C interface showing gates for changing voltage levels.

old. Although the switching threshold with a 5 V supply is above 0 V, and not symmetric with respect to the signaling voltages, it is well within the specifications for RS-232-C voltages. The receiver also has about 1 V of noise protection through hysteresis.

The large voltage swing on RS-232-C signals is required for noise immunity on the communications link. With a common signal-ground between transmitter and receiver, there is no opportunity for double-ended signaling, and therefore common-mode noise is inherently coupled into the signaling system. TTL voltage levels are simply too sensitive to noise to work over long distances unless the common-mode noise can be eliminated. TTL has at best 1.2 V between the logic 0 (0.8 V or less) and logic 1 (2.0 V or greater), so noise voltages of the order of 0.5 V can be severely disruptive. But common-mode noise voltages easily climb to a few volts in the presence of electric motors, photocopiers, typewriters, and the like. Thus the common signal-ground is largely responsible for forcing the higher transmission voltages found in the RS-232-C standard. Even for these voltages the standard covers signaling rates only up to 20 kHz and at distances on the order of 30 m, the maximum distance at which signal grounds can be safely connected.

The 20-Milliampere Current Interface

Another popular serial-interconnection methodology is current controlled, rather than voltage controlled, as in the RS-232-C standard. The current control relies on currents of 20 mA to encode a logic 1, and zero current to encode a logic 0. The basic idea of the electrical connection appears in Fig. 5.7. The transmitter on the left side of the figure is shown with a 20 mA current source and a switch. The receiver on the right-hand side of the figure has a current detector. The transmitter simply opens and closes the switch, which pulses current through the loop and which is sensed by the receiver. The reverse

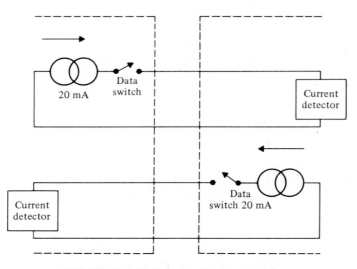

FIGURE 5.7   Full-duplex 20-mA current loop.

link is symmetric as shown in the figure; but in reality, many implementations are not symmetric. Note that in the figure the current source need not be located at the transmitter. For example, it is perfectly acceptable for the device on the left to have current sources for both its receiver and transmitter loops, and for the device on the right to have neither. The requirement is that a loop have one and only one current source; whether that source is at the transmitter or receiver end is not important.

The current-loop interface originated, as did the RS-232-C standard, in a context of telephone equipment. In this context, the equipment interfacing the serial link was a standard mechanical teletype. The current detector in a teletype is simply a coil that is energized by current (or a current amplifier that detects current flow and drives a coil). A succession of 1s and 0s set up internal electro-mechanical linkages in the teletype; and when a full character is received, those linkages force the teletype to print that character. For standard teletypes, the encoding of bits on the serial-data stream follows the same conventions as RS-232-C encoding, with a start bit, 8 data bits, and 2 stop bits. The transmitter in a teletype is passive, and consists only of a switch that opens and closes according to the bit encoding of a character depressed on the keyboard. The receiver has to supply the current source for a teletype keyboard.

The teletype that fostered the current loop interface has long been obsolete, so one might expect that the original reasons for using a current loop are no longer valid. However, the current loop is superior to the RS-232-C interface in many applications because it is inherently double-ended with common-mode noise rejection, and can be easily connected over much longer distances than the RS-232-C because isolation can eliminate problems caused by ground loops.

Figure 5.8 shows a typical receiver for a current loop, and also shows where the isolation capability arises. The receiver in this instance is an optical isolator. This is a device that contains in a single package both a light-emitting diode and a light-sensitive transistor. When the diode fires, it emits light that causes the transistor to conduct, so that the signal travels from the input lines to the output lines over an optical path, and not over a direct electrical connection. The isolator appears in the figure within the dotted lines. The components outside the dotted lines are required to make the isolator into a full receiver. Note that there is a series resistor in the loop because the LED offers essentially no resistance when it fires. The current loop must have a load impedance to drop the source voltage, for otherwise all of the source voltage would be dropped across the LED in the isolator. Typical source voltages run as low as 10 V and as high as 15 V; and there is no official standard that sets these voltages. Some implementations of a current source are nothing more than a voltage source and a series resistor that limits the current to about 25 mA when the terminals of the current source are shorted. The presumption is that additional impedance in the receiver circuit can limit the current even further.

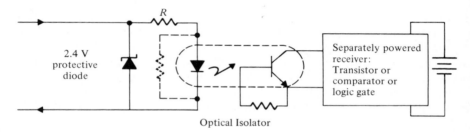

FIGURE 5.8   Current detector and isolator for 20-mA current loop.

In the absence of specific information about what voltages are likely to appear across the terminals of a 20 mA receiver, the receiver in the figure uses a Zener diode to limit this voltage to a maximum of 2.4 V (any voltage in the range from 2 to 3 V, and possibly even higher, will work acceptably). Then the resistor R in series with the LED, together drop 2.4 V when the isolator fires. If the LED voltage is known (say, 0.8 V), the voltage drop across R is then 2.4 V minus the LED voltage, or 1.6 V in this example.

It is not necessary to funnel the full 20 mA current through the LED. In the example, if the LED is designed to run at, say, 10 mA, then two resistors in the detector loop are required. The resistor R shown in the figure passes the full 20 mA, while a second resistor in parallel with the LED accepts that portion of the 20 mA that is not passed through the LED. In this example, the series resistor R drops 1.6 V at 20 mA and is, therefore, an 80 Ω resistor. The shunt resistor across the LED drops 0.8 V, if one is required; and the resistance value is selected to shunt the portion of the 20 mA current that is not accepted by the LED. Any current that reaches the receiver in excess of 20 mA passes through the Zener diode shunt. Note that we assume that the interface threshold is 20 mA; that is, the receiver should fire at 20 mA and not at lower currents. Actually, because we have to consider noise problems in a serial link, the firing threshold should be set lower than 20 mA, say at about 10 mA. Then the threshold lies halfway between a logic 0 and logic 1, and the noise margin is symmetric with respect to the signaling current.

The light-sensitive transistor is very easily coupled into a TTL gate through an external amplifier transistor or comparator gate. Hence, one component is all that is necessary to convert voltage and current levels to TTL-compatible signals. Across the gap between the LED and the light-sensitive transistor, the isolator is built to withstand voltages that are in excess of 1 kV, and as high as 2 or 3 kV. With this level of protection, it is quite possible to run a serial link from one location to another a few kilometers away. The RS-232-C interfaces do not directly offer this capability because of the direct connection of signal ground across the link. The direct connection defeats isolation and becomes a very serious electrical hazard when the connection is made over long distances.

Another advantage of using the current loop rather than the RS-232-C is the inherent common-mode rejection offered by the light-emitting diode receiver. The diode reacts to a differential voltage across its terminals. Common-mode noise raises or lowers both LED terminals equally so that this noise is canceled out by the diode. However, if the current source for the loop is at the receiver, a bad design may couple the common-mode noise back into the receiver circuit. In order to achieve the desired insensitivity to common-mode noise, the receiver current source must be electrically isolated from local ground. This is also a requirement for proper isolation of the receiver from the transmitter. If the current source at a receiver has any direct connection whatsoever with local ground, then there is a direct path from the remote transmitter ground to the local ground, and the isolator function is defeated.

Because the current loop has at least two major advantages over the RS-232-C in its common-mode rejection and isolation, we might expect it to be preferred over RS-232-C. Indeed, it is preferred in long-distance applications where the RS-232-C cannot be used. However, for short distances the RS-232-C signal levels provide more than adequate protection from noise, and isolation is unimportant. Moreover, EIA maintains a standard for RS-232-C interfaces, and the documentation for the 20 mA current loop is only informally standardized at this time. Therefore, most manufacturers supply at least the RS-232-C serial interface; and as a result, these connections are the most widely used. Because the differences between RS-232-C and current loop interfaces are strictly in the electrical connections, both interfaces can share a common I/O port interface. Designers often take advantage of this commonality by providing two different connectors for serial ports, one to a current loop and the other to an RS-232-C link. This lets the equipment owner decide which of the two types of serial interfaces to use in any particular installation.

The RS-422, RS-423, and RS-449 Interfaces

Three new standards incorporate new interface technology designed to overcome the shortcomings of RS-232-C. The major need is to achieve a higher signaling rate bandwidth over longer distances than the RS-232-C provides. To this end, the RS-422 standard defines a double-ended electrical interface module that can signal at rates well in excess of the 20-kHz limitation of RS-232-C. The mechanical connections for this interface are provided by the RS-449 and covered in its standard. This latter standard provides for a 37-pin connector as opposed to a 25-pin connector for RS-232-C and has caused quite some concern in the industry. One of the primary advantages of a serial link should be the lower cost of cables and connectors as compared to a parallel link. A connector with 37 pins that carries only one bidirectional channel on a serial link can be an excessive burden. The RS-449 standard addresses this problem by providing for a 9-pin connector for secondary channels. Each additional channel of a multichannel link requires only the 9-pin connector, provided that the primary channel of the link is connected through the full 37-pin connector.

Compatibility with existing standards is extremely important. The single-ended electrical standard RS-423 is intended to achieve this compatibility, while simultaneously conforming to both the RS-422–type electrical conventions and the RS-449 mechanical standards. Specifically, an RS-423 link is designed to connect to both the RS-232-C and the RS-422 links, thereby providing a means for making a transition from the old technology to the new. The electrical specification of the RS-423 standard is almost identical to that of the RS-232-C standard, with differences too small to dwell on here, but still of importance to designers who wish to build interfaces that satisfy both standards. The major thrust of the new standards is to move to RS-422 balanced transmission and to more reliable, higher-speed communications.

The electrical aspects of RS-422 and RS-423 appear in Fig. 5.9. Compatibility between the unbalanced and balanced interface is achieved through the use of the same type of differential receiver, as specified in both standards. When used in double-ended mode, the receiver accepts signals of opposite polarity from a double-ended driver. When used in single-ended mode, the receiver accepts a signal on one input and SEND COMMON, the transmitter reference voltage on the other input. SEND COMMON is isolated

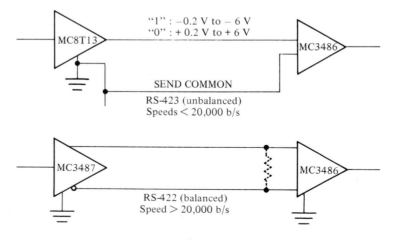

FIGURE 5.9   RS-422 and RS-423 electrical characteristics.

from the receiver ground, so that it provides an estimate of the actual reference voltage at the transmitter. When an RS-423 device is connected to an RS-232-C device, it is obvious that the SEND COMMON connection of RS-423 is tied to SIGNAL GROUND of RS-232-C, with proper precautions taken regarding the isolation of equipment. The single-ended mode shown in Fig. 5.9 is rated for signaling speeds up to 20 kHz. To go beyond this frequency, it is mandatory to used double-ended signaling as defined by the RS-422 standard.

Mechanical connections for the RS-423 are made according to the RS-449 standard as shown in Fig. 5.10. Note that the ground reference point for SEND DATA is carried to the receiver as SEND COMMON and coupled to the differential receiver. Similarly, RECEIVE COMMON is carried from the right-hand device to the left-hand device, and coupled into the differential receiver.

The interface standard requires that SIGNAL GROUND between the two units be connected in order to provide a ground reference point, but it also provides for the isolation of SIGNAL GROUND from SHIELD GROUND. The RS-449 standard limits cable lengths to 60 m, primarily because of the lack of isolation. It does, however, provide for "tailored" operation in which cable lengths can greatly exceed this limit. Presumably in

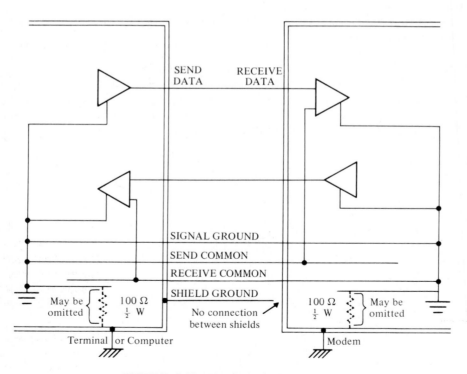

FIGURE 5.10   Unbalanced RS-423 signals.

tailored circumstances, precautions can be taken to limit the hazards by isolating SIGNAL GROUND from SHIELD GROUND, and perhaps by isolating the signal paths themselves with optical isolators. RS-422 interfaces are connected together by connections similar to those given in Fig. 5.10. Since RS-422 transmitters are double-ended, the negative-polarity active signal is used in place of a SEND COMMON or RECEIVE COMMON signal. Otherwise the connections are as shown in the figure.

The signal definitions for the most important signals in the RS-449 standard appear in Fig. 5.11. We have already discussed the functions of RECEIVE DATA, SEND DATA, CLEAR TO SEND, and REQUEST TO SEND. DATA MODE and RECEIVER READY correspond, respectively, to DATA SET READY and DATA TERMINAL READY of the RS-232-C standard. TEST MODE is a new mandatory signal for RS-449, which in conjunction with other optional signals provides a means for testing the communications equipment. The idea is to be able to jumper the SEND output to the RCV input temporarily, and to create a loopback connection. This permits links to be partitioned selectively, and to exercise individual transmitters and receivers in the links in order to discover failing equipment with a minimum of difficulty. Note that two pins per signal are allocated to those shown in the figure, which accounts for the majority of the extra pins in RS-449 interfaces. Not shown are the optional circuits for transmitter and receiver clocks, switched telephone-network control signals, and control signals to be used for testing. The secondary channel that uses a 9-pin connector carries only the SEND, RECEIVE, CLEAR TO SEND, REQUEST TO SEND, and RECEIVER READY, plus four extra

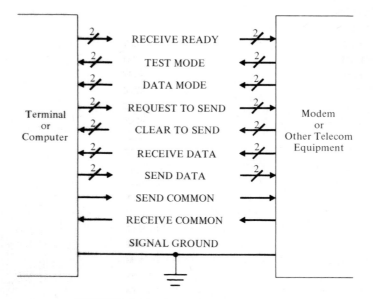

FIGURE 5.11   RS-449 mandatory signals.

lines that carry the grounds for the shield, the SEND and RECEIVE signals, and the signal-reference ground. All signals for the 9-pin connector are single-ended, and therefore this type of channel loses the advantages of the RS-422 standard.

The future of RS-449 connections, and specifically balanced RS-422 signaling, is clouded by other competitive methods for high-speed serial interconnection. Changing over to a new standard from an old one is a costly and lengthy process. The RS-232-C standard is so widely used that most new designs will continue to supply this type of interface until there is a clear advantage for supplying an RS-422 interface. The very simple expedient of using a completely passive adapter cable that mates with RS-232-C on one end and with RS-423 on the other end is an effective means for connecting the devices and conforming to the two standards in both new and old equipment if, and only if, both implementations use electrical conventions that conform to both standards. The move to the RS-422 standard, which is not directly compatible with the RS-232-C standard, is a more difficult and costly step to take. Other schemes for high-speed serial interconnections are being pursued, most notably ones that use coaxial interconnections at bandwidths that range from three to several hundred megahertz. If standardization efforts produce an acceptable coaxial-type of interconnection scheme, designers may choose to use this interface standard in lieu of the RS-422. Hence, a possible scenario for the long-term future may be the widespread use of the RS-232-C standard for low-speed interconnections and a new standard coaxial scheme for high-speed interconnections, with the RS-422 standard used rather rarely.

5.3 SYNCHRONOUS INTERFACES

Synchronous links use a clock to control character-to-character timing within a block of characters. The principal advantages of this convention over the asynchronous protocols studied earlier are as follows:

1. The synchronous clock eliminates the need for start and stop bits, and thus increases the bandwidth available for data.
2. Protocols are inherently block-oriented, rather than character-oriented, which provides an efficient means for incorporating control and redundancy information into the communication link.
3. It is possible to run a communications link at a higher bit rate over longer distances.

The motivation for moving to synchronous protocols from asynchronous protocols is higher communication speed. Links for asynchronous systems run at speeds as high as 19.2 kHz, but rarely above 9600 Hz. With proper electrical connections, a synchronous link can easily run at 500 kHz, which is a substantial increase over the asynchronous link. Because of the high data rates, recommended practice for electrical connections is to use a double-ended transmitter/receiver, such as an RS-422 link, or to use a coaxial cable link with special drivers and receivers.

The main difference between synchronous and asynchronous interface designs lies in the treatment of the clocking hardware and in the logic required to maintain character-to-character synchronization. Figure 5.12 shows the structure of a simplified synchronous system to illustrate these differences. Note specifically that the received clock is extracted from the received data stream. That is, the receiver locks onto the frequency of the data it receives, rather than relying on an independent local clock whose timing cannot be made precisely coherent with the received clock. The interface contains the familiar shift registers and buffer registers to facilitate conversion between parallel and serial data streams. Because characters do not have start and stop bits, additional logic is required to synchronize the receiver to the beginning of a character. The means for achieving character synchronization differs from protocol to protocol; but the idea, in any case, is the same. Special sequences in the stream of data bits indicate the beginning of a character. These sequences are inserted at the transmitter and detected by the receiver. When detected, the receiver then has achieved character synchronization, and then can partition the succeeding data bits into 8-bit characters at the correct boundary points. Since synchronization sequences occur at the beginning of a block of data (although in some protocols they can occur within the block as well), it is possible to establish block-to-block synchronization while simultaneously establishing character-to-character synchronization.

One other difference between asynchronous and synchronous interfaces is often required. That is, synchronous interfaces typically use more than one register to buffer incoming and outgoing data, with typical interfaces using three registers in a queue, known as a FIFO (first-in, first-out) arrangement. Data flows through the buffer automatically, so that the microprocessor interfaces only with the register at the input end of the transmit FIFO and at the output end of the receiver FIFO. Similarly, the transmit and receiver shift registers connect only to the registers at the opposite ends of their respective FIFOs. The transmitter shift register reloads from its FIFO whenever a new character is to be sent. With a FIFO available, the microprocessor can preload it with several characters at one time to reduce the burden of maintaining a constant stream of output characters. Similarly, an input FIFO permits a microprocessor to unload several characters at one time, and again reduces the overhead required to service the receiver. Most interfaces provide control options that raise READY indications or assert interrupts when a FIFO has a specific number of registers available for service, with this number settable to 1, 2, or more depending on the depth of the FIFO.

Synchronous protocols have evolved naturally from protocols that specify only character synchronization to protocols that specify both block and character synchronization. The three most widely-used protocols today are

1. BISYNC (Binary Synchronous Communications), an older, obsolescent protocol used in IBM equipment,
2. DDCMP (Digital Data Communication Message Protocol), a protocol used primarily in DEC equipment, and
3. HDLC (High-level Data-Link Control), a protocol used in most new synchronous equipment across the industry.

Because LSI chips are widely available for BISYNC and HDLC protocols, we limit our attention in this discussion to these two techniques. HDLC has evolved from two earlier

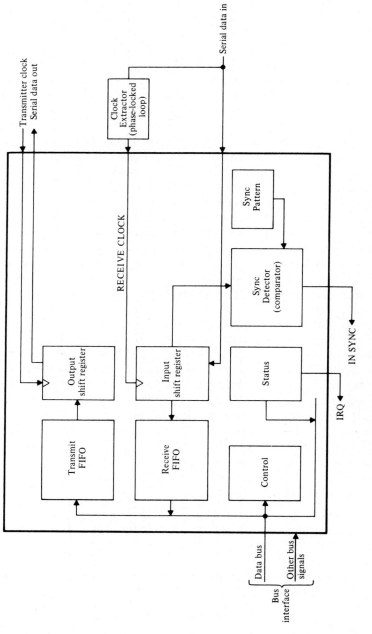

FIGURE 5.12   The structure of a typical synchronous I/O port.

standards, the SDLC (Synchronous Data Link Control) and the ADCCP (Advanced Data Communications Control Procedure). Because of the close similarity of the three, we discuss only HDLC in this text.

The BISYNC Protocol

BISYNC protocol relies on one or two successive sync characters to identify both character and block synchronization. The idea is that the receiver establishes synchronization by searching for the special synchronization pattern by inspecting each successive bit that appears at the interface. Presumably, before synchronization has been established, the transmitter sends the sync pattern continuously, while monitoring its own receiver for a sync pattern sent on a reverse channel. Handshake messages between two transmitters then confirm to each other that both are synchronized. Synchronization is thereafter maintained by the protocol.

A typical message structure for BISYNC appears in Fig. 5.13. Although this structure is widely used by convention, the common interface chips that implement BISYNC do not require this message format. LSI interface chips typically implement the character synchronization function and the conversion between parallel and serial data streams with FIFO buffering, but leave the higher-level functions on blocks of data to software control. The figure shows that immediately following the sync characters is a header that starts with SOH (Start of Header). SOH and all other characters we name for BISYNC are ASCII control characters. This header is used for control purposes, and can contain a source and destination address, and a message sequence number. In case of an error in the reception of a block, the receiver transmits a message back to the source (as identified by the source address in the message) with the sequence number of the message in error. The source then retransmits the message. Because each message has a sequence number, the receiver recognizes when a message has been retransmitted, and can then reassemble a sequence of messages into their correct order. The data block begins with STX (Start of Text) and ends with ETX (End of Text) or ETB (End of Transmission Block), and is followed immediately by a redundancy check over the block. Individual characters in the block can also be checked by a single-parity bit if the characters are 7-bit ASCII codes.

SYNC	SOH	Header	STX	Data block	ETX	Check bits	SYNC	SOH	

FIGURE 5.13   The structure of a BISYNC block.

With this basic idea, the BISYNC protocol appears to be rather simple. There are additional problems, however, that complicate the protocol. The structure of the protocol places a special status on ETX and ETB. In general, if the data block (or control information) contains either of these characters among its data, the characters can be misinterpreted. For example, if the datum happens to be an 8-bit pattern identical to the ASCII pattern for ETX, this datum character could deceive the receiver into taking an end-of-block action when actually the block has more characters to follow. Thus there is a need for the protocol to distinguish specific patterns as data characters, when they need to be treated as data. This ability to treat control patterns either as control information or as data is often called *data transparency* and is implemented in various ways across the range of protocols.

BISYNC uses another character, DLE (Data Link Escape), to obtain the necessary transparency. When a control symbol is to be treated as data, it is preceded by DLE. The receiver then is armed by the receipt of a DLE to accept the next character as a data character, without taking any control action. (LSI chips usually do not have this ability built onto the chip. Therefore, the control software normally performs this function.) The use of DLE is somewhat more complicated than described here because of other special considerations. For example, to maintain synchronization in the absence of data in the transmitter queue, the protocol provides for an automatic insertion of sync characters, which are then removed by the receiver. But it is quite possible that a sync character might be inserted between a DLE and a control character that follows it. This situation forces the receiver to interpret the sync character as if it were data, rather than accepting the next character as data. In this case, the transmitter cannot simply send a sync character after a DLE. The transmitter should queue the DLE, and should then send sync characters until both the DLE and its corresponding data character are ready. If buffering is not available, the transmitter might have to send DLE, and then stay idle on the line. In this case, it should transmit in the idle state the pairs of characters (DLE, sync), which the receiver can ignore as pairs of characters. Note that because DLE is a control character with special significance, the DLE pattern in the data stream must be treated the same way that ETX and ETB are treated, and must be preceded by a DLE when transmitted over the link.

There are, therefore, two independent and important characteristics of BISYNC:

1. BISYNC depends on a sync pattern to establish character synchronization.
2. BISYNC uses a transmission protocol for block structure and transparency.

An implementation of a BISYNC-like protocol need not implement both the synchronization technique and the block format, because these two protocol characteristics are indeed independent. For this reason, BISYNC interface chips are mostly oriented to synchronization, and they leave the block formatting up to the user.

The HDLC Protocol

HDLC, like BISYNC, uses a special pattern to maintain character synchronization. However, this pattern is unique, and can never occur anywhere in a bit stream other than at the beginning of a block (which is also the beginning of a character). Hence the HDLC receiver maintains a constant scan of the input stream, and automatically resynchronizes to the sync pattern whenever that pattern appears. The pattern is the bit sequence 01111110 and is called a *flag*. The flag sequence contains six successive 1s, and no data sequence can contain this many 1s in a row. To ensure that the sync sequence is not transmitted as part of a data sequence, whenever the transmitter has transmitted five successive 1s, it automatically inserts a false 0, then sends the succeeding data bits. The receiver reverses this process by removing a 0 that appears after a sequence of five 1s. The inserted and deleted 0s have no effect on the transmission of arbitrary information other than to guarantee that the sync pattern occurs on the communications link only at sync points. The data stream that enters the transmitter can contain the sync pattern, and the receiver produces this pattern at its output if the pattern is in the data stream input to the transmitter. The fact that the transmitter adds some additional bits and the receiver removes these bits has no net effect on the data stream itself, although it may reduce the average data rate slightly.

An HDLC block has the structure shown in Fig. 5.14. The format is quite similar to the BISYNC format in terms of the information passed within a block, but the specific fields are encoded differently. HDLC avoids the use of special characters to bracket fields, and thereby greatly simplifies the problem of transmitting data that might contain these characters in the data stream. An HDLC block begins and ends with a sync pattern that is labeled "flag" in the figure. Address and control information appears immediately after the flag. As in BISYNC, the address and control information typically contains a source and destination address and a sequence number. Since a block terminates at a flag, there is no need to have a different special symbol close a block. Block length need not be an integral number of bits either, because the flag pattern is accepted as a block end regardless of where it occurs in relation to the beginning of a character. When a flag is discovered, the immediately preceding 16 bits are treated as cyclic redundancy checks to determine if any errors are likely to have occurred in the previous transmission. The next block can use the ending flag as its initial flag, and thereby move directly into address and control information.

01111110	1 byte	1 (or 2) bytes	Variable length	2 bytes	01111110
Opening flag	Address	Control	Information	Check	Closing flag

FIGURE 5.14   Frame structure of HDLC.

The synchronous nature of the link forces the transmitter to have data ready in a buffer at the beginning of a block transmission. If it is not ready, and the software fails to produce the data in time for transmission, the transmitter will run out of data to transmit. The HDLC protocol does not provide for an "idle" character within a block, so that typical implementations abort an entire block transmission when the transmitter runs out of data before the end of the block. The abort code is a sequence of eight 1s.

HDLC protocols are suitable for point-to-point links commonly used for RS-232-C links. However, serial bandwidth is potentially much higher for HDLC than for the RS-

232-C standard, and more likely to be used in short bursts of transmissions, followed by relatively lengthy idle periods. A more efficient means for using the available bandwidth is to connect several synchronous devices together on one line, and to share the bandwidth. Such a scheme is presented pictorially in Fig. 5.15, which shows a loop connection with N devices connected together around the loop. At each device is a receiver/transmitter interface that can receive a message and retransmit the message to the next node on the loop. Here the idea is that a receiver retransmits messages intended for other nodes, but does not retransmit a message if the receiver node is the message's destination point. In this way a message can be injected into the loop by the transmitter and removed from the loop by the receiver at the destination, so that messages do not, in general, travel repeatedly around the loop. A variation of this idea is to remove a message only after it travels around the loop one full cycle and returns to the originating transmitter. The source, not the destination, then removes the message. The destination usually alters the message just slightly by returning it with a code that indicates the message successfully reached its intended destination. This gives the transmitter a positive acknowledgment of message receipt (or a negative acknowledgment if transmission is unsuccessful).

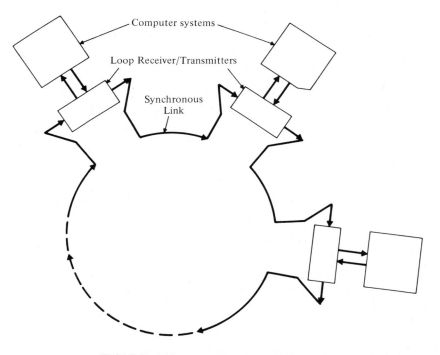

FIGURE 5.15   A synchronous loop network.

Two ways to operate the loop depicted in Fig. 5.15 have been presented in the literature. One way is for one transmitter to gain control of the loop, then transmit all messages
it has enqueued, then pass control to the next node on the loop. Loops of this type are
called *Newhall loops* after the work of Farmer and Newhall [1969]. This type of loop is
very simple to implement, but has the problem that some messages may be enqueued for
lengthy times while waiting for their respective transmitter to gain control of the network,
as only one transmission can take place at any given time.

The *Pierce loop* (Pierce *et al.*, 1971) reduces this latency somewhat by breaking messages into small packets. The packets are transmitted individually and reassembled at the
receiver. The idea is for a transmitter to transmit briefly, and then pass control to another
transmitting node. In fact, the loop is frequently operated in multiplexed mode with
specific ''slots'' assigned to specific transmitters, each transmitter placing data onto the
loop only at its designated slot. It is possible to operate the loop in this way and have
several transmitters actively inserting data packets onto the loop at various points. If the
loop protocol cannot prevent a local message transmission from colliding with a received
message, the transmitter has to have a local buffer space large enough to hold the incoming packet, which is then retransmitted when the local-packet transmission has been
completed.

It is quite clear that synchronous interfacing schemes are of great importance in systems in which a great deal of information has to be transmitted.

5.4 IMPLEMENTATIONS OF SERIAL INTERFACES

In this section we examine three general problems related to serial interfacing that arise
with sufficient frequency to warrant a separate discussion of each. Two are electrical
problems, namely, cross talk and isolation. The third problem is primarily a software
problem and is related to the flow control of communications signals.

Rise -Time Control for Cross -Talk Reduction

A typical serial link carries data as voltage or current changes, and thus a typical
waveform for data is the one shown in Fig. 5.16(a). The sharp edges of the pulses indicate
that there are high frequencies present in the signal, where these high frequencies are high
harmonics of the basic signaling rates, and lie well outside the range of frequencies useful
for carrying serial information. The problem with these high frequencies is that they couple readily into nearby signal wires and cause a noise disturbance commonly known as
''cross talk.'' Cross talk between adjacent signal runs is caused by coupling energy from
one wire to another, where the coupling mechanism is either inductive, due to mutual inductance of nearby loops, or capacitive, due to wire-to-wire stray capacitance. Insofar as
the use of twisted pairs and balanced signaling can reduce cross talk, a serial link can be
made less sensitive to the problem. But as cable lengths become long, other steps are

RISE-TIME CONTROL

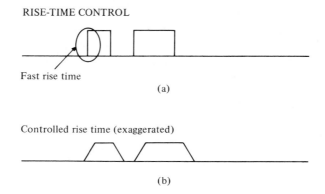

Fast rise time

(a)

Controlled rise time (exaggerated)

(b)

FIGURE 5.16   Examples of waveforms without and with rise-time control.

helpful in reducing the cross-talk problem. For capacitive coupling effects, high frequencies are worse offenders than low frequencies. Cross talk can be reduced, in fact reduced substantially, by eliminating unnecessary high frequencies on the signal line.

Figure 5.16(b) shows an effective means for dealing with cross talk. The waveform in the figure uses rise-time control to prevent fast changes of the signal voltage, and the resulting sloped waveform has a diminished high-frequency content. With less energy at higher frequencies, the waveform produces less cross talk across adjacent cable runs. Hence, rise-time control is a practical and important method for improving the reliability of a communications link.

The RS-232-C standard specifies rise-time control, but the standard is relatively weak in this regard. The standard permits slew rates up to 30 V/μs, which therefore permits rise times to be roughly as small as a microsecond for signals that change from +15 V to −15 V. There is no particular reason that the change must take place in so small a time segment. A 10-μs rise time, or even a much longer rise time, is quite adequate for slow signaling speeds. At high signaling speeds, however, a slow rise time may result in a signal skew large enough to throw off the receiver's sampling points. At these clock rates, there is justification for having a relatively fast rise time.

To control rise time, a very simple technique used in many interfaces is to limit the current flow as shown in Fig. 5.17(a). The current limiter in this figure delivers a fixed maximum current when the current turns on. With a constant current charging the line capacitance, the voltage increases linearly in time until the line is charged high enough to reduce current flow. Without current limiting, the line is charged exponentially to its final value.

Another recommended scheme for RS-232-C–type interfaces is to load the output of an MC1488 transmitter with a capacitor. This device has a current-limited output and, therefore, has a bounded slew rate, but the rate is well over 30 V/μs. When the capacitor is added to the output as shown in Fig. 5.17(b), the slew rate diminishes and can be set to

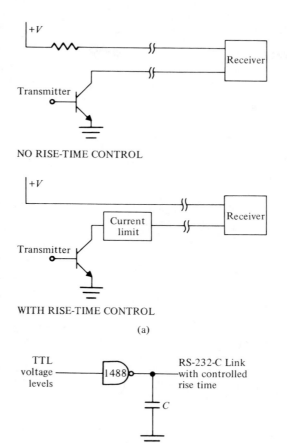

NO RISE-TIME CONTROL

WITH RISE-TIME CONTROL

(a)

(b)

FIGURE 5.17 (a) A 20-mA loop without and with rise-time control; (b) rise-time control for an RS-232-C driver.

any desired value. The internal-current limiting of the MC1488, together with the load capacitor, results in a waveform similar to that in Fig. 5.16(b). With C in the region of .01 to .001 μF, the slew rate of the transmitter drops to between 1 and 10 V/μs.

Isolation

Isolation is treated here in the context of current loop interfaces. In Fig. 5.18, we see a bi-directional link with isolation at the receiver end for one direction and at the transmitter end for the other direction. The link is somewhat simpler when isolation is at the receiver, because the LED of the optical isolator is very close to being compatible with the link

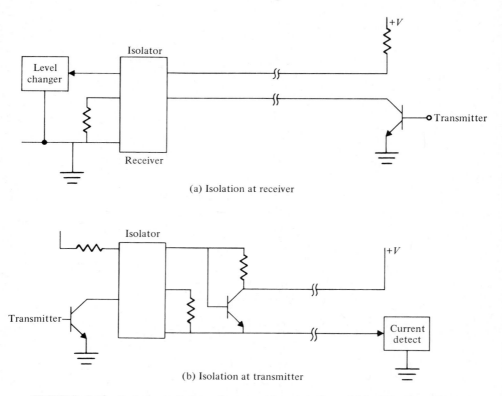

(a) Isolation at receiver

(b) Isolation at transmitter

FIGURE 5.18   Isolation techniques for current-loop interfaces: (a) Isolation at receiver; (b) Isolation at transmitter.

characteristics. We still need some extra logic at the receiver (not shown in the figure) for overload protection and for interfacing the LED in the isolator to the 20 mA current as we discussed earlier in the chapter.

When the isolator is at the transmitter end, it is necessary to drive the transmitter with an independent power supply in order to achieve the isolation desired. We show that supply as being located in the receiver, and use this supply to power the photo-transistor and a transistor line driver. This general scheme can be used to isolate RS-232-C interfaces where the driver transistor is replaced by an MC1488 driver operating at RS-232-C voltage levels. Since the MC1488 draws more power than the transistor shown in the figure, it is desirable to develop that power locally rather than to draw it from the receiver. If local supplies are used, they must be isolated from ground and from all other supplies. Hence if a computer has several RS-232-C channels, each going to a different remote location, then each of these channels must have an independent, isolated power supply if the RS-232-C lines are themselves to be isolated. Obviously, the problem of isolating these

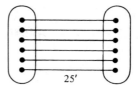

6-wire RS-232-C cable
(supplied by manufacturer)

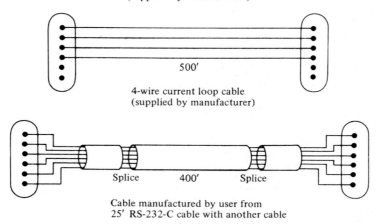

Cable manufactured by user from
25′ RS-232-C cable with another cable

FIGURE 5.19　Cable configurations for the case study.

power supplies adds to the expense of the interface and makes this arrangement unattractive. Nevertheless, given both proper isolation of RS-232-C links and rise-time control, it is possible to signal safely and correctly over links up to a few kilometers. Unfortunately, the temptation is to make such connections without proper isolation, with disastrous results.

A case study of an actual problem of this sort is shown in Fig. 5.19 and Fig. 5.20. A computer manufacturer supplies two different types of cables for interconnecting terminals to the main frames of a particular family of computers. The 6-wire cable carries the essential RS-232-C signals, and the 4-wire cable carries a pair of 20 mA current loops. The manufacturer happens to use identical connectors for the RS-232-C and current-loop systems. Terminal equipment has two mating connectors, one for each type of communications link. For RS-232-C interfaces, only the 6-wire cable is available, and it is limited in length to 25 feet, per the constraints on RS-232-C interconnections. Longer lengths of 500 feet are available in a 4-wire configuration that is intended for 20 mA use where the links are properly isolated. The figure shows how a customer purchased 6-wire cable for a long interconnection run, and then spliced this cable into the 6-wire connectors used for both RS-232-C and current loop interfaces. The splice was a very simple way of obtaining

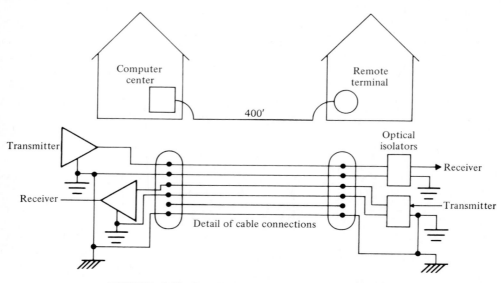

FIGURE 5.20   Detail of cable installation for case study.

compatible connectors for 400-foot cable. Since the customer knew that the long interconnections had to be made through current loops, these long cables were then connected to
the current loop by 6-pin connectors at the terminal and computer ends of the line. Figure
5.20 shows these lines running underground from the computer center to a computer
room, with four of the current-loop wires properly isolated. However, in adding the fifth
and sixth wires, the customer did not realize that a hazardous ground loop had been
created on the sixth connector pin, which was connected to the chassis at the respective
ends of the cable. During an electrical disturbance in which lightning strikes were observed within a short distance of the buildings, the computer and terminal equipment sus-
tained severe damage. All drivers and receivers at the computer end of line burned out,
and the electrical overload extended beyond these points into other regions of the I/O system. At the far end of the line, damage was limited mainly to the circuits surrounding the
isolators and to the power supplies. With a direct connection from ground to ground
across the buildings, the isolators became ineffective. Differences in potential between
the two buildings were coupled directly into both systems, and the resulting stress des-
troyed large portions of the interfaces. One integrated circuit in the receiver section of a
terminal interface exploded from the stress. The lesson to be learned here is to respect the
need for isolation and to be extremely careful when cabling remote systems together.

Flow Control on Serial Links

No matter how one builds a serial interface, the amount of buffering available is a fixed,
finite amount. However, transmitters can run faster than receivers, especially in an asynchronous system where the local and remote clocks inherently run at different speeds.
What prevents a buffer overflow?

Figure 5.21 shows two situations, one involving two clocks and one involving three clocks. In the system with two clocks, when the transmitter runs slightly faster than the receiver, it might eventually overrun the receiver, except that the receiver in most asynchronous systems can start hunting for a new character before the completion of the last stop bit of the present character. Hence the receiver can resynchronize its activity to the beginning of the next character, even when the received character time is slightly less than the expected character time. For this reason two-clock systems are usually safe from overflow, provided that the receiver at the slow-clock side of the system empties the buffer register in the interface at a fast enough rate.

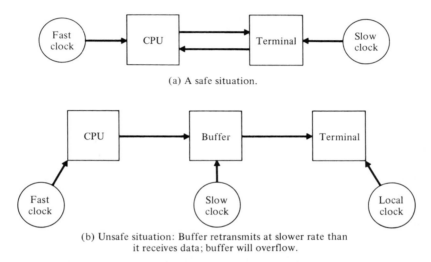

(a) A safe situation.

(b) Unsafe situation: Buffer retransmits at slower rate than
it receives data; buffer will overflow.

FIGURE 5.21   Buffer-overflow considerations in asynchronous systems.

The three-clock system is a system in which an intermediate processor receives and retransmits data. Here there is a very real problem because the retransmission is limited by the rate of the local clock. Hence characters cannot pass through the interface faster than the local clock, while they enter at the rate of the remote transmitter clock. Eventually, the input from the fast clock will overrun the slow receiver, and a character will be lost.

On a more general basis, even in two-clock systems, received data must pass through all buffers and queues at an average rate at least as high as the input rate, for otherwise the system will experience buffer overflow at the receiver. There are several ways to solve this problem, of which the simplest is to slow down the transmitter every so often and to prevent buffers from filling. Specifically, the transmitter can be adjusted to run at, say, 95% full data rate by sending data in bursts of 19 characters, and then waiting one character time before sending the next character. If the system does not buffer and is insensitive to particular characters such as the ASCII null character (all 0s), then the transmitter can send a null every 20 characters. Another way to attain this same functional behavior is to transmit with two stop bits, but to set the receiver for one stop bit. Then the receiver can start looking for the next character roughly one bit time sooner than if it were looking for two stop bits.

More complex ways of controlling data flow require passing information on queue lengths over a transmission link to the sender. When the information indicates that buffer space is filled (or nearly filled), the transmitter stops transmitting. Some implementations use CLR TO SEND and REQ TO SEND signals for this purpose.

When the receiver is a line printer, there is usually a slightly longer delay for carriage return and line feed than there is between characters. To prevent buffer overflow in this case, conventional interfaces transmit three to six nulls after a line feed (or carriage return) to allow time for the printer to adjust to the next line. This function can be implemented in the transmitter software very simply. To use CLR TO SEND and REQUEST TO SEND requires compatible hardware as well as the capability to set a signal at one interface and to sense it at the other. This may require special software drivers at both ends of the link. This is more difficult to implement if the designer has access to software at only one end of the link and is not able to modify the software at the other end.

5.5 INTERFACE DEVICES

In this section we examine LSI peripheral devices that implement the various protocols considered in this chapter.

Asynchronous Interfacing with the MC6850

The MC6850 interface device follows the general plan of a serial interface as discussed earlier in this chapter. External connections for the device are shown in Fig. 5.22. The 6850 uses a standard microprocessor-bus interface for the 6800 family, and produces or receives the basic RS-232-C control signals. The signaling rate is controlled by separate transmitter- and receiver-clock inputs, which can be set internally to be $16\times$ or $64\times$ the data rate. (The rate can be also set to be equal to the clock rate; but, in this case, the received clock must be synchronized externally to each character received.) To obtain software-controlled signaling rates, we simply multiplex several different frequencies to the 6850 and select the multiplexer output through a software-settable control vector. This device contains four registers accessible by the microprocessor—a control register for commands, a status register, an input register, and an output register. The command register is used to configure the transmitter mode as to parity and the number of stop bits, and to arm or disarm the interrupt output. The REQUEST TO SEND output is a single bit in the control register whose value is set by software. The status register reflects the current status of the interrupt request, the input and output registers (full or empty, respectively), and of the CLR TO SEND and CARRIER DETECT inputs to the chip from other interfaces. The receiver overrun condition, parity errors, and framing-error (missing stop bit) condition are also reported in the status words. The figure shows the 6850 driving both the

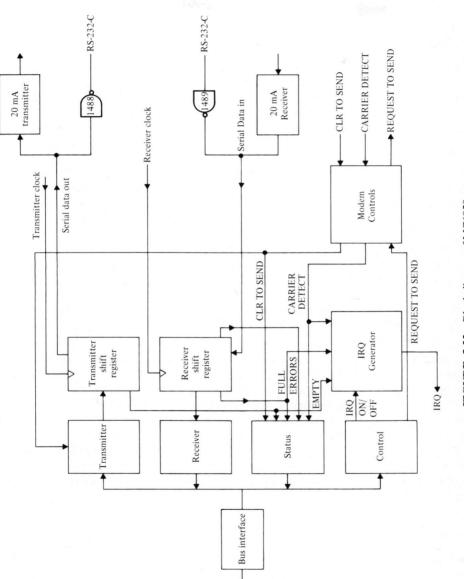

FIGURE 5.22   Block diagram of MC6850.

current-loop and RS-232-C interfaces, which is possible because these two types of links are compatible at the data-signal level even though they are not electrically compatible.

The BISYNC Interface

The MC6852 is a close relative of the 6850 that is used for BISYNC protocols. Its interface signals are shown in Fig. 5.23, where we see the similarity with those of the 6850. The main difference in the function of the two devices is that the 6852 has a built-in capability that establishes character synchronization by searching for a 1- or 2-character sync pattern in the serial-bit stream. The pattern can be loaded into the port from the microprocessor, and the micro can also instruct the port to initiate a search for synchronization. A SYNC MATCH output indicates that the 6852 has found the sync pattern and established the character synchronization. Almost all aspects of BISYNC relating to the structure of a BISYNC block are not implemented, and are left to microprocessor software. These include the functions relating to transparent transmission and reception of data, which is a nontrivial task for the support software. The maximum data rate of the 6852 is much higher than that of an RS-232-C link, and is roughly 600 kHz.

The extra complexity of the BISYNC protocol requires three control registers in the 6852 as opposed to a single register in the 6850. Among the functions controllable by these registers are those of the 6850 (word length, parity selection, and interrupt control), as well as such functions as sync mode (1 or 2 characters), start search, and individual start/stop controls for the receiver and transmitter. Although the 6852 does not implement all of the functions required for transparent data, it can strip out all instances of the sync pattern that it finds in received data.

Synchronization with a two-character pattern is a little tricky with this device. There is but a single 8-bit register for holding the pattern, so after the first character is matched, this register has to reloaded on the fly. An interrupt generated at the first match can be used to notify the micro to reload the register with the second sync character. A FIFO with three stages is built into the receiver to give extra time to make this match and to buffer received data that is en route to the main memory.

Receiver clock generation must be done off-chip, using techniques such as the phase-locked loop technique that is described later in this textbook. The receiver clock must be derived from the incoming data stream, and should not be generated by an independent local oscillator.

The i8251 for Asynchronous and Synchronous Links

There is a good deal in common between asynchronous and synchronous links because both have similar logic devoted to the bus interface and to conversion between serial and parallel data streams. Intel's 8251, shown in Fig. 5.24, is suitable for both synchronous and asynchronous links. Specifically it implements the synchronization requirements of

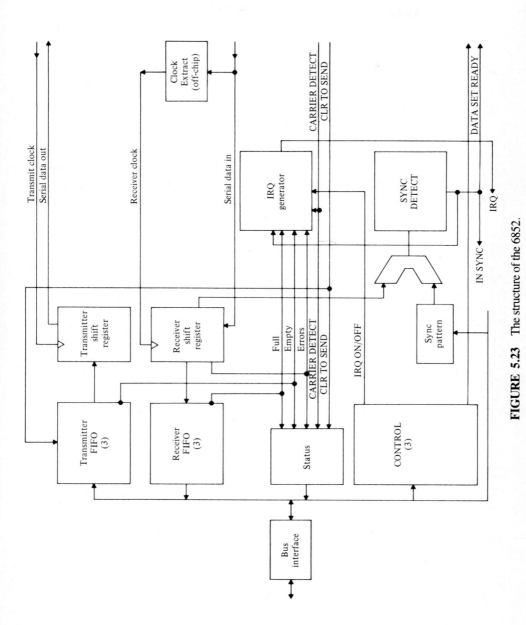

FIGURE 5.23   The structure of the 6852.

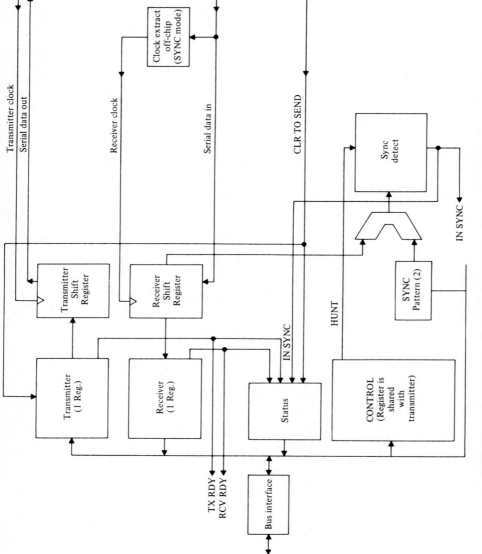

Transmitter clock

Serial data out

Receiver clock

Serial data in

CLR TO SEND

Clock extract off-chip (SYNC mode)

Sync detect

IN SYNC

SYNC Pattern (2)

HUNT

Transmitter Shift Register

Receiver Shift Register

Transmitter (1 Reg.)

Receiver (1 Reg.)

IN SYNC

Status

CONTROL (Register is shared with transmitter)

TX RDY
RCV RDY

Bus interface

FIGURE 5.24   Structure of the i8251 synchronous/asynchronous receiver/transmitter.

BISYNC, together with all asynchronous protocol requirements. For the RS-232-C proto-col, the device connects to transmitted and received-data signals — REQ TO SEND, CLR TO SEND, DATA SET READY, and DATA TERMINAL READY. Like the 6850 and 6852, the 8251 has clock inputs for transmitter and receiver clocks that determine the data rate for both synchronous and asynchronous links. The asynchronous clocks can be set to be 16× or 64× the data rate. An external clock detector must be used to derive the clock from incoming synchronous data, just as for the 6852.

The 8251 has four register addresses whose functions are similar to those of the 6850. However, the 8251 does not contain an addressable control register as the 6800-family de-vices do. Rather the 8251 has a control address to which a program outputs a sequence of commands. These commands then affect many different aspects of machine state. A typi-cal sequence of control directives passes two to four control words to the interface. At sys-tem reset or after the microprocessor writes a sync character to the 8251, the 8251 reini-tializes its state to expect the next command byte to be the first byte of a sequence.

The first control byte sets the chip into an asynchronous or synchronous mode, and determines the character length, parity check format, and stop-bit format (for asynchro-nous mode) or sync-pattern format (for synchronous mode). The remaining functions are set by the second control byte. These functions include the ability to start and stop the transmitter and receiver, to initiate a synchronization search (in the synchronous mode), and to output REQ TO SEND to the modem interface. Interrupt-control signals are com-mon to both asynchronous and synchronous operation, and both operations are also armed or disarmed through the control words. A status register gives error indications for parity, overrun, and framing errors, and also gives the state of the system. State information in-cludes a detailed description of the transmitter FIFO and the receiver state, and provides information as to whether or not the device has been synchronized with an incoming syn-chronous bit stream. In the synchronous mode, one or two additional bytes are inserted between the opening mode-setting byte and the closing command byte. These inserts con-stitute the sync pattern.

The only BISYNC function actually performed on chip is the BISYNC synchroniza-tion function. All other requirements, particularly the transparent data requirement, must be implemented in software elsewhere in the system. Recall that the 6852 implements a small portion of the transparent data requirements by deleting received sync patterns from the data stream. But in both the 6852 and 8251 interfaces, a substantial amount of over-head is left, and external software must implement the block-oriented functions of a BISYNC protocol.

HDLC Interfacing

The Intel 8273 is a very sophisticated link controller designed for the 808X family of pro-cessors. It performs most of the essential HDLC functions, while providing interfaces to a microprocessor, an RS-232-C modem, and to a DMA controller. The Motorola MC6854 is an HDLC peripheral for the 6800 family that has a similar capability. Both devices im-plement portions of the HDLC protocol that were once implemented in software or firmware in a central processor. Hence, both devices provide an economical means for interfacing to high-speed links, with little risk of overloading the computational capacity of a microprocessor.

The complexity of the protocol leads to high chip complexity, which prevents this discussion from doing more than touching on the highlights of the device capabilities.

Starting with the 8273, we note the structure of the interface as shown in Fig. 5.25. A major feature of this chip is an on-chip digital phase-locked loop for clock recovery and the synchronization of received data. But this chip requires an externally generated clock at $32\times$ the nominal clock rate of the receiver data stream, and also severely restricts the operating range of the system to 64 kHz data rates. By contrast, the 6854, with off-chip synchronization, permits data rates up to 600 kHz.

The command structure of the 8273 is quite rich; and, in fact, the 8273 can be viewed as an independent processor dedicated to the HDLC function. Communication with the 8273 is through control and parameter registers. Commands issued to the control register are usually followed by a sequence of transmissions to the parameter register, depending on the control function. The chip is sufficiently powerful to accept a single command to write a frame, with all pertinent parameters of that frame provided to the chip. Thereafter, the chip can generate the full frame, including the flag, address and control bytes, the data field, and the closing bytes. Because the chip interfaces to an external DMA controller, it can access data from local memory as needed to fill the data field of the frame. The chip can also operate in non-DMA mode, in which interrupts or status signals report back to the microprocessor whenever a FIFO needs to be filled (for transmit) or emptied (for receive). Loop operation is provided automatically by tying the receiver input directly to the transmitter output with a one-bit delay.

The computational power of the 8273 is quite astounding, which is surely indicative of the directions of multiprocessor development in the next decade. We can expect the I/O functions of a system to migrate gradually over time to a collection of intelligent peripherals that like the 8273 have the preprogrammed capability of performing standard operations. While the 8273 has the necessary functional capability, its performance dictates that its use be limited to low-speed synchronous links. As the technology improves, we can expect to see similar chips appear with performance rates as much as 10 to 50 times as high as that of the 8273.

The 6854 is a high-performance HDLC interface that implements the most important HDLC functions, but does not quite have the functional capability of the 8273. Note that the received-clock generator in Fig. 5.26 is off-chip, not on-chip. The 6854 contains both a DMA interface and modem control functions, although there are fewer pins dedicated to these functions than in the 8273, which yields slightly less flexibility. With regard to the low-level functions of the HDLC protocol, the 6854, like the 8273, automatically inserts and deletes bits in the data stream to establish the uniqueness of the flag sequence 01111110 for synchronization. It also, like the 8273, produces the redundancy check bits automatically in the transmitted data stream and checks them in the received data stream. FIFOs in the receiver and transmitter sections can hold up to three bytes of data, and thereby provide some degree of buffering of high-speed data. It is possible to operate the

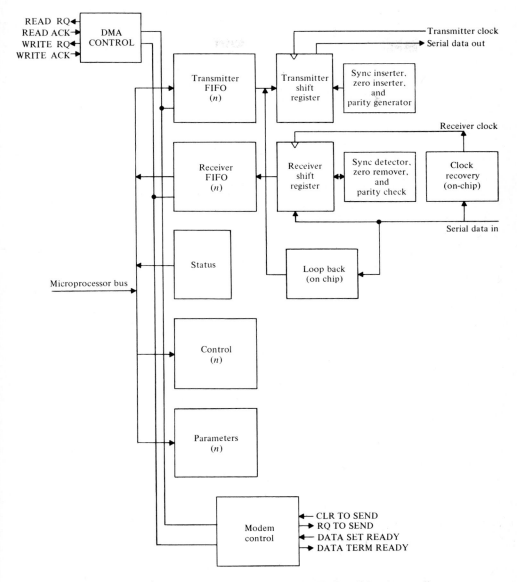

FIGURE 5.25　Block diagram of the i8273 HDLC peripheral controller.

6854 under the control of an external DMA controller to attain high-speed memory access without microprocessor intervention. Or, with less logic required, the DMA controller can be omitted, leaving the processor with the burden of loading and unloading data from

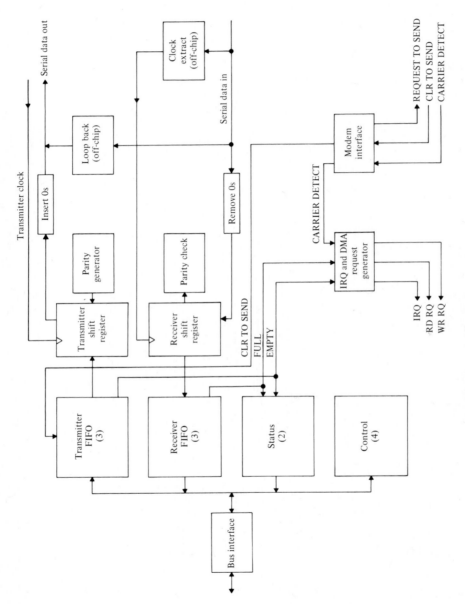

FIGURE 5.26 Block diagram of the MC6854.

the chip. Loop operation is provided externally by tying received data to transmitted data, using gates not provided on-chip. Because the device can transfer data at about 1 byte per 15 μs, the I/O rates possible are at the upper limit of the ability of a processor to service the I/O chip. This limits link performance by software delays rather than by the electrical interface. Gross data rates with the 6854 are about 10 times higher than for the 8273, but when the effects of software delays are factored in, the ratio may be somewhat lower. With either the 8273 or 6854, the cost of an HDLC link is substantially smaller than the cost of constructing the link out of discrete hardware; moreover the performance is far higher than is attainable with conventional software-intensive techniques.

OTHER READING AND SOURCE MATERIAL

An excellent treatment of the full range of data communications protocols appears in McNamara (1981), which covers such diverse topics as the hardware design of 20 mA interfaces through standard protocols such as HDLC. Material on DEC's DDCMP protocol, which has been omitted in this textbook, also appears there.

Another textbook of equal quality is Tanenbaum (1981). Tanenbaum covers system aspects of high-speed communications between computers. Among the topics of interest in his textbook are flow control methods, network topology, methods for controlling SDLC protocols, and a very comprehensive treatment of packet-switching networks.

For implementation of the RS-232-C interfaces, there is no better source of information than the standard itself (Electronic Industries Association, 1969). Copies of the standard can be obtained by writing to the Electronic Industries Association in Washington, DC. Newer standards such as those for the RS-422, RS-423, and RS-449 are available from the same source.

In spite of the advantages that the double-ended signaling of RS-422 has over the single-ended signaling of RS-232-C, the RS-422 standard has appeared at a time when competitive methods of communication are being developed. Specifically, Ethernet, a multiaccess, high-bandwidth communications system, and other similar communications techniques are undergoing standardization. Metcalfe and Boggs (1976) describe the principles of Ethernet but they leave the implementation unspecified. LSI implementations of Ethernet interfaces are becoming widely available, and may become a more attractive alternative for high-speed communications than the RS-422 interfaces.

The case study in this chapter that related the problems and consequences of improper grounding is a true and certainly not rare example of grounding implementations. Many installations violate electrical codes for grounding. As the case study illustrated, manufacturers' equipment and installation procedures do conform to grounding codes, but on-site modifications by the equipment owner can upset the codes. It would be an interesting and valuable exercise for the reader to examine the grounding and signaling connections of a local computer installation, paying particular attention to hard-wired communications lines that are over 30 to 60 m long.

EXPERIMENTS

5.1 For this experiment you will need a microcomputer or terminal with an RS-232-C communications link.

a) Configure the communications link for 8-bit data, two stop bits, and no parity. Connect oscilloscope probes to pins 2 and 3 of the RS-232-C connector. If the link is connected to a computer, program the computer to transmit the character A continuously; otherwise at a terminal depress the letter A in a repeat mode so that the character is continuously transmitted. One or both of the channels will display the signal. If you observe the signal on both channels, explain why it appears on both. Draw the waveform, and identify the start bit, stop bits, and data bits.

b) The letter X has the ASCII code 58_{16}. Draw the RS-232-C waveform for this character, then transmit the character X over the link, observing its waveform on the oscilloscope to confirm the accuracy of your drawing.

c) Reconfigure the link for 7-bit characters, even parity, and one stop bit. Retransmit the character A and explain what you observe on the oscilloscope screen. Then transmit the character B. Is the parity bit different from that of an A? Next transmit the character C. Is its parity bit different from that of an A? Explain your observations.

5.2 This experiment requires a logic analyzer and a computer with a serial port. The purpose is to explore the effects of double buffering. Connect the logic analyzer to the serial I/O chip to display the READ and WRITE controls of the chip. Trigger the analyzer from the CHIP SELECT pins of the chip so that it samples READ and WRITE each time the chip is selected. Configure the port to run at the highest possible baud rate.

Write a serial-port output program for the chip that uses a wait loop to test the status of the chip before each output. The wait loop should read the status register until the status indicates the chip is ready for a new output. Test this program to be sure that it works correctly.

The main program that you will use to exercise the chip is the following:

```
JSR     OUTPUT     OUTPUT A CHARACTER
JSR     OUTPUT     OUTPUT A SECOND CHARACTER
JSR     DELAY      DELAY ABOUT 80% OF A CHARACTER TIME
JSR     OUTPUT
JSR     DELAY
JSR     OUTPUT
JSR     DELAY
JSR     OUTPUT
JSR     DELAY
JSR     OUTPUT
HALT
```

The objective of the program is to count the number of times that the program executes the status check in the wait loop. The DELAY subroutine eliminates about 80% of the checks that would otherwise be made so that the buffer of the analyzer does not overflow. Note that no delay occurs between the first two outputs. If the chip is double-buffered, the wait loop will execute only once during the second call to OUTPUT.

Now start the trace mode of the analyzer and start to execute the program. Display the contents of the analyzer buffer. You may have to adjust your delay subroutine to be longer or shorter in order to obtain usable data. Verify that the first two characters are accepted immediately by the port. Are all other characters accepted by the port after equal delays? It is very likely that the third character is accepted after a shorter delay than subsequent characters. Verify whether this is true or false for your port. Explain why the third character might be accepted sooner than one full character delay after the second character is accepted.

5.3 For this experiment you will need a computer with a serial port that has CLEAR TO SEND and REQUEST TO SEND modem controls. A logic analyzer will be helpful, but not necessary.

a) Write an interrupt-driven program that receives characters from the serial port. Write a second program that uses a program-controlled wait loop to transmit characters over the serial link. Then connect the transmitter to the receiver on the link, and test your programs to be sure they work correctly. For this test, the port should have its CLEAR TO SEND input tied to a voltage level that asserts the signal.

b) Write subroutines that assert and deassert the REQUEST TO SEND output, and verify that they operate correctly.

c) Modify the receiver program so that it calls the subroutine to deassert REQUEST TO SEND immediately after an interrupt invokes the receiver program. Also, modify this program to increment a counter each time it is invoked. Then tie the transmitter output of the serial port to the receiver input by bridging pins 2 and 3 of the RS-232-C port connector. Similarly, tie REQUEST TO SEND to CLEAR TO SEND by bridging the corresponding pins on the RS-232-C connector. (Examine the specifications for your computer just in case these pins do not conform to the standard.) Write a driver program that does the following:

i) Initializes the interrupt system and interrupt vectors for the RS-232-C receiver.

ii) Turns on REQUEST TO SEND.

iii) Clears the counter for the receiver program.

iv) Outputs a continuous stream of As.

When you execute this program the computer will hang up in the transmit wait loop waiting for CLEAR TO SEND to be reasserted. Execute the program and verify that this occurs. Reset the computer and examine how many characters were received before the program permanently entered the wait loop. Note that the REQUEST TO SEND was turned off immediately after receipt of the first character. You might expect that no additional characters are received from that point on. How many were actually received?

d) Repeat the experiment using two computers instead of one. The first computer executes the transmitter program, and the second executes the receiver program. How many characters are received in this case? If the number is different, explain why it is different.

e) Connect a logic analyzer to the REQUEST TO SEND line and to the transmitted-data line, and repeat the experiment with either one or two computers. Examine carefully the relative timing of the transition of the REQUEST TO SEND line as compared to the timing of the individual bits on the data line. After which bit is the REQUEST TO SEND line deasserted? What is the state of the transmitter buffer and shift register at this time? How does this timing explain your observations of the previous steps?

5.4 The purpose of this experiment is to examine differences in ground potential between two pieces of equipment. Obtain a computer, a CRT terminal, and a long RS-232-C cable. Disconnect the interconnecting cable to be sure that there is no direct connection between the two pieces of equipment. Connect the computer and terminal into different AC power outlets. Use power outlets in the laboratory that are physically as far apart as possible and that, preferably, are controlled by different circuit breakers. Connect the RS-232-C cable to one piece of equipment and bring it to the other piece of equipment without making an electrical connection. Connect a voltmeter from pin 7 of the RS-232-C connector on the cable to pin 7 of the connector on the equipment. Measure AC and DC voltage. Connect an ammeter across the same pins if the voltage is less than 1 V, and measure the AC and DC current flow. (*Caution*: Use a high-current scale at first, and be prepared to break the connection quickly if the flow is unexpectedly high.) Report and explain your observations. Return the equipment to their original configuration, and do not attempt to operate them in their experimental configuration.

PROBLEMS

5.1 Draw a circuit for optically isolating a 20 mA current loop at the receiver end of a serial interface. The optical isolator LED has a 1.2 V nominal drop and can accept up to 30 mA safely. The phototransistor in the isolator has an emitter-to-collector voltage of 0.3 V when the LED is drawing 20 mA. At this voltage, the collector current is 7 mA when the LED is drawing 20 mA.

5.2 Repeat Problem 5.1, showing isolation at the transmitter end of the loop. Why is it better in this circuit to power the 20 mA line from the receiver rather than from the transmitter?

5.3 Draw a circuit for optically isolating an RS-232-C serial line at the transmitter end of the line. The circuit should accept TTL levels in and produce RS-232-C levels out. Assume the same isolator as in Problems 5.1 and 5.2.

Since your interface must produce RS-232-C levels out, it has to have power supplies for $+12$ V and -12 V. Show how to connect the reference grounds for these supplies with respect to the reference ground for $+5$ V, as well as with respect to the shield ground.

If your computer interface drives more than one RS-232-C port, and each port is connected to a remote terminal on a potentially different chassis ground, then you must not only isolate the computer from each port, but isolate each port from each other. Does your design isolate the ports from each other? If not, then what must you do to achieve the necessary isolation?

5.4 Show a *passive* (no transistors, no power source) circuit for isolating an RS-232-C line at the receiver end of the line. (Use the optical isolator from Problem 5.1.) Calculate the power dissipated in your circuit for a 50% duty cycle signal. Your circuit should accept RS-232-C levels in and should produce TTL levels out.

6 / PARALLEL INTERFACING

In this chapter we discuss the interfacing of external equipment to a microprocessor through a parallel I/O port. With this type of port, a microprocessor can control or sense virtually any digital signal, provided that the sample/control rate does not exceed the rate at which the microprocessor can access the port. With microprocessor clock times on the order of 1 to 4 MHz, and about 10 to 20 clock times required between port accesses, signaling through a parallel port can attain a maximum of about 100,000 to 200,000 transfers per second. But each transaction transfers one byte of data, so that the actual information rate is on the order of 1 megabit per second. Note that this rate is about 50 times faster than the maximum bandwidth of 20 kHz for an RS-232-C link, and about 1000 times faster than typical serial links. The parallel interface, then, is well suited to high-speed requirements and to requirements where the response time is critical.

But parallel ports are widely used in low-speed applications, too. For these applications it is the versatility of the parallel port that promotes its use because the port greatly simplifies interfacing to various types of digital devices. The parallel port is commonly used for sensing switch closures, driving output indicators, interfacing to elaborate digital devices, and even implementing serial links. Many manufacturers of modular microprocessor systems have discovered that system users invariably want to interface their systems to many kinds of exotic devices, and the manufacturers usually offer for this purpose an I/O board that is packed with as many parallel ports that can fit.

In this chapter we first look at the general structure of a parallel I/O port, and examine its use for interfacing to various kinds of digital devices. The asynchronous handshakes studied earlier play an important role in parallel I/O because external devices are unsynchronized to the microprocessor clock. When such devices are interfaced through a parallel port, data transfers are normally controlled with asynchronous handshakes, as described earlier in this textbook. For this reason, parallel ports usually have on-chip logic for implementing these handshakes.

As with serial interfacing, standards play an important part in parallel interfacing. It is wasteful and costly to design a unique interface for each possible type of device that can be connected to a microprocessor. To a certain extent, the parallel I/O port reduces this cost by being almost universal, but the designer still has to devote some effort to adapting a universal interface to an individual application. With a standard parallel interface, much of this work is unnecessary. Two different devices, both of which interface to a particular I/O standard, can be connected directly together without having to customize the interconnection. One of the most popular parallel I/O standards today is the IEEE-488 standard, which provides for the immediate interconnection capability of a wide variety of digital test instruments.

Early in this chapter we examine the electrical connections available on typical ports, and show schemes for putting the ports to work in useful applications. The IEEE-488 standard is the focus in the middle of this chapter, and the chapter closes with a discussion of ports available for the 6800, 6500, and 808X microprocessor families.

6.1 PARALLEL PORT CHARACTERISTICS

The external signals for a parallel I/O port are shown in Fig. 6.1. On the left in the figure is a standard microprocessor bus interface, usually directly compatible with a particular family of microprocessors. On the right are three types of signal lines that tie to the outside world. All three types can act as either input or output lines, and in some implementations the lines can be set by program control to be input, output, or bidirectional lines. The three types of lines are

1. data I/O with tri-state output,
2. data I/O with open-collector output, and
3. a control line for handshaking signals.

Each type of signal line is useful in specific instances, so that normally all three types of lines are included in an LSI parallel I/O port to provide the greatest possible versatility.

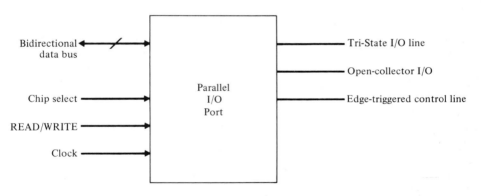

FIGURE 6.1   Structure of a typical I/O port. The three common types of I/O pins are shown on the right.

Open-Collector Outputs

An electrical model of one open-collector circuit in Fig. 6.2 shows an open-drain circuit of a field-effect transistor as an ''open collector.'' When the gate of the transistor (the input driven by the NAND) has a voltage above threshold, which represents a logic 1, the transistor conducts and there is a low impedance path from the I/O pin to ground through

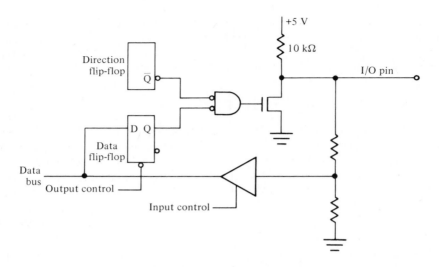

FIGURE 6.2   An open-collector I/O pin.

the transistor. When the transistor gate-voltage drops below threshold to logic 0, the transistor opens. Now the path from the I/O pin to ground through the transistor is open, and the I/O pin is pulled high to 5 V by the 10 kΩ resistor. The I/O pin, when programmed as an output pin by setting the direction flip-flop, carries the value of the bit in the data flip-flop, provided that no other open-collector output attached to the same pin is also active.

Many designers use open-collectors for signals asserted in the low state, in which case the open-collector performs an OR function of the active low signals. That is, the node voltage at the junction of several active, low open-collector gates is asserted (in the low state) if any open-collector gate is asserted. For example, an interrupt request signal is often implemented as an active low signal. Then the devices that produce interrupt requests generate the requests on open-collector gates whose outputs are simply tied together with a pull-up resistor and connected to an IRQ L signal line. IRQ L is low if any device asserts its active low output.

In the output mode, the present value of the data bit is gated to the output pin through an open-collector driver. Because the output is an open-collector, the voltage on the output pin is pulled low if any open-collector output tied to that same pin is low. Hence the output pin may have a low voltage (0) when the data bit value is a 1.

The input-control signal shown in the figure gates the present value of the I/O pin onto an internal data bus, and the output-control signal latches the value of the internal data bus into an output flip-flop. The control signals shown are raised and lowered by the microprocessor through instructions that output commands to the parallel I/O port. Note that while the port is set in the output mode, with the output register loaded with data, the port can still be asked to input the value of the I/O bit by asserting the input-control line (with an IN instruction or a LOAD instruction directed to the data register of the port). The value of the data read is the actual value on the output pin, and this may not agree with the value in the data register. Note also that the port can report misleading information on the input line if the port is in the output rather than input mode. In order to avoid spurious interference with the value of the external data that result from interactions with the output-data register, it is essential to disconnect the data register from the output pin by resetting the direction flip-flop. The pull-up resistor guarantees that the output value is high rather than undefined when no output devices actively drive the output node. The pull-up is set at a rather high value, in this case 100 kΩ, because many different open-collector lines can be tied together, and the net parallel impedance of this connection must not load the output drivers.

Having the output voltage pulled up to logic 1 when the output is passive benefits output ports that control critical devices. Without this feature, an undefined value on an output control line of an open-collector gate could possibly appear to be low when the port is first powered up. For this reason, typical I/O ports react to RESET and power-on conditions by making all I/O pins inputs, and by relying on internal resistors to pull up open-collector I/O pins to a logic 1. Then the devices controlled by a parallel I/O port should treat a logic 1 as an inactive signal during the power-on period. After power is turned on successfully, system software can reconfigure I/O pins as output pins while holding the output register at logic 1. This guarantees that control is inactive during and immediately after port configuration. Because tri-state and other types of output gates might not have internal pull-up resistors, their outputs may be undefined after a power-on sequence, which means that the outputs may be in a state that could accidentally activate external equipment. Therefore, as a general rule, safe practice requires external pull-up resistors on tri-state gates or open-collector gates with internal or external pull-up resistors on all critical control signals.

Figure 6.3 shows a simple way to interface four input switches to a computer without additional circuitry other than an I/O port. Each signal line is connected to a switch that grounds that line when the switch is closed. The corresponding open-collector pins are programmed to be in the input mode. Until the switch is thrown, the pins are at logic 1 because of the internal pull-up resistor. A closed switch pulls the voltage at the pin to logic 0, which can be sensed by the microprocessor.

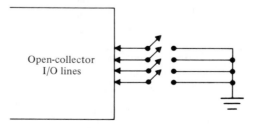

FIGURE 6.3   Interfacing simple switches to an open-collector port.

669

888

This is rather simple, almost deceptively so, because the circuit lacks the usual flip-flop or Schmitt trigger to protect against spurious signals caused by contact bounce. In fact, when the switch is closed, the switch does not close cleanly; it bounces open and shut a number of times. The desired waveform is a step in time, but the actual waveform produced is a series of pulses that eventually decay to a constant voltage. The trick is to use software to do the debouncing as the program fragment of Prog. 6.1 does. (This fragment uses a pseudo-high-level language whose meaning is clear without further explanation.)

PROGRAM 6.1   Software Debouncing of an Input Switch

```
begin initialize port;  (* Set I/O bits to input mode. *)
   REG_0 := SWITCH_DATA;
      (* Read the instantaneous value of the switch lines.
         This reads eight bits. The least significant four bits are input lines. *)
   REG_0 := 0F16 AND NOT REG_0;  (* Mask out leading bits. *)
      (* Switch closures show up as 0s when they are copied to REG_0.  The NOT opera-
         tion causes active lines to show up as 1s in the statements that follow. *)
   if NOT (REG_0 = 0) then  (* Process data if there is a 1 bit. *)
      begin DATA_IN := REG_0;  (* Report data just read. *)
      DELAY;  (* Wait for contact bounce to subside. *)
         (* Now the switch is depressed. Accept the input when the switch is
            released. *)
      while NOT ( (DATA_IN AND NOT SWITCH_DATA) = 0) do;
         (* Read the port repeatedly until bits in positions that are active in the
            DATA_IN byte become passive. *)
         (* At this point the switch has just been released. *)
      DELAY;  (* Wait for contact bounce to subside. *)
      ACCEPT (DATA_IN);  (* Report back the data read. *)
      end;
   end;
```

The program uses a mask with a value $0F_{16}$ to mask out high-order bits, leaving only the four least-significant bits of the data retrieved from an I/O port. These four bits are connected to the four I/O switches shown in the figure. The mask operation is a logical AND operation, and is available in some fashion in all microprocessor instruction sets. The result of the masking operation is tested to see if any switch is depressed; and if so, the microprocessor delays further action until contact bounce has finished. A simple way to do this is to place the program in a loop that decrements a counter until the counter reaches 0. However, this does not permit any other useful work to proceed while the delay is in progress. A better way is to set a timer interrupt to return the processor to this point in the program at a predetermined time in the future and, meanwhile, to exit the program in order to do other useful work. The size of the delay is somewhat dependent on the switch, but a delay of 10 to 50 ms is usually sufficient for mechanical switches, and quite tolerable with respect to human reaction time.

After the first delay, this program waits for the switch to be released before accepting the data. Since a switch can bounce when it is released, just as it bounces when closed, there is a second delay when the program detects the switch release. The data can also be accepted immediately after the first delay, which corresponds to accepting the data when a switch is depressed, if the human factors in the system dictate this to be the more desirable mode. In any event, before any new data can be accepted there must still be a delay after the release of the switch is sensed.

The program is written for applications in which only one switch at a time is closed (as in a hand calculator). If multiple switches can be thrown, and they do not all close at once, the program has to be modified to detect changes in the input data and to debounce each new bit that changes.

Because multiple switch-closures are difficult for humans and awkward to process correctly with software, many switch interfaces rely on a single switch closure, and use a matrix of many switches to facilitate data entry. Figure 6.4 shows a 4 × 4 matrix (such as a hex keypad) interfaced to a parallel port. Four pins of the 8-bit port are output pins, and the remaining four are input pins. Switches are placed across the intersections of the output and input lines so that each switch ties one output line to one input line. The microprocessor senses which output line is connected to which input line, and thereby determines which key is depressed. To do so, the microprocessor energizes one output line at a time, and observes the input lines. With the input lines tied to an internal pull-up resistor, the data read is a logic 1 unless the input line is held down to a logic 0 by a switch closure.

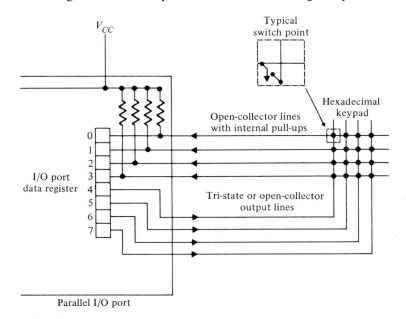

FIGURE 6.4   Interfacing a hexadecimal keypad to an open-collector I/O port.

The microprocessor program energizes each output line in succession by driving that line with a logic 0, and is able to discover which, if any, switch is closed. Program 6.2 implements this function in a high-level language.

PROGRAM 6.2   Software Interface to a Hexadecimal Keypad

```
begin initialize port; (* Set the 4 high-order bits to output mode, and the 4 low-
   order bits to input mode. *)
   OUTPUT_MASK := 7F₁₆;
      (* The leading bit of OUTPUT_MASK is zero. This is used to deassert the lead-
         ing bit. Subsequently OUTPUT_MASK is shifted right to deassert the other
         output bits, one at a time. *)
   for I := 0 step 1 until 3 do
      begin SWITCH_PORT := OUTPUT_MASK;
         (* Output the mask and make one output line active. *)
      OUTPUT_MASK := rightshift (OUTPUT_MASK);
         (* Rotate OUTPUT_MASK to make ready for the next active bit. The opera-
            tion is a right shift with a 1 bit shifted into the sign bit position. *)
      INPUT_MASK := 1;
      for J := 0 step 1 until 3 do
         begin if (INPUT_MASK AND SWITCH_PORT) = 0 then
            begin (* Found a 0 bit; this switch is closed. *)
            delay; (* Debounce. *)
            while (INPUT_MASK AND SWITCH_PORT) = 0 do;
               (* Switch has been released. *)
            delay; (* Debounce after switch release. *)
            DATA_IN := 16 * (I) + J; (* Encode the switch data. *)
            exit; (* Exit the loops. *)
            end
         else
            begin (* Prepare to examine the next input bit. *)
            INPUT_MASK := leftshift (INPUT_MASK);
            end;
         end;
      end;
end;
```

The program reads the port data and looks for a switch closure, which is evidenced by a 0 among the four input bits. When a closure is discovered, the program delays for a debounce period and reads the input bits one at a time. When it finds the nonzero bit, the datum accepted is a composite of the value of I and J calculated as shown in the program. This example should be sufficient to clarify the general use of both inputs and outputs for parallel ports, and to show specifically how to take advantage of the internal pull-up resistor to minimize external parts.

Tri-State Outputs

The second type of pin used in parallel interfacing is the tri-state, which has a driver/receiver circuit similar to that shown in Fig. 6.5. It is similar to the open-collector circuit in that the circuit contains two flip-flops, one for directional control and the other

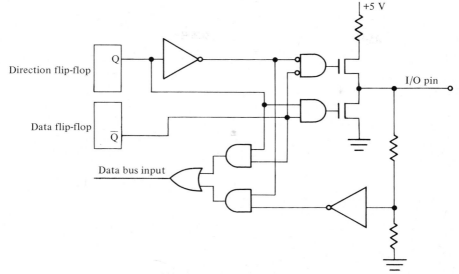

FIGURE 6.5   A tri-state I/O pin.

for the data bit. In input mode, the direction flip-flop disables the output circuit completely, and the pin is free to be pulled high or low by an external source. (In the absence of an external source, the figure shows the pin pulled low by the voltage-divider circuit to ground. This circuit is not necessarily present in every chip, and the input pin may actually float freely if an implementation omits the divider circuit.) Since the output is disconnected from the input when the port is placed in the input mode, there is no interaction with the output bit when the input bit is read, and the port returns the value of an external bit. In the output mode, the line is driven by a data register. Note that when the port is read in the output mode, the value of the data register, and not the data on the external I/O pin, is read. The I/O pin may actually have a different value if an external source is driving the bus simultaneously, although multiple sources should never be active simultaneously on a tri-state signal line.

A typical use of a tri-state line is demonstrated in Fig. 6.6. In this case the port is interfaced to a relay or light-emitting diode through the collector circuit of a Darlington transistor. In order to drive the Darlington transistor, the output pin must deliver enough current to turn on the base of the input transistor of the Darlington driver. Since open-collector outputs have a high impedance to the 5 V supply, the open-collector output is unsuitable for this purpose. The tri-state output normally delivers a very small current in its high output state, usually approximately 0.05 mA at about 3.5 V. As the current delivered increases, the voltage output diminishes. The question is whether an output line can deliver sufficient current to a Darlington driver to drive a device like a relay or LED, and still maintain a voltage high enough to maintain the necessary base-to-emitter voltage of the Darlington input circuit. In Fig. 6.6, the voltage requirement to keep the Darlington driver on is at least two diode-voltage drops because a Darlington, when active, has one

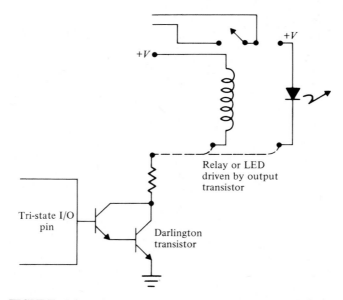

FIGURE 6.6   Driving high-power devices with a tri-state I/O pin.

diode-voltage drop from the base to emitter of each of its internal transistors. Hence the voltage should be about 1.5 V when the Darlington circuit conducts. Tri-state outputs of I/O ports are designed specifically to drive Darlington transistors, and are usually rated to deliver several milliamperes of current at 1.5 V, which is sufficient for the applications depicted in Fig. 6.6. Because these ports can drive a Darlington transistor directly, there is no need for other external gates to buffer or amplify output signals.

Another important advantage of tri-state outputs over open-collector outputs is in the speed of the transition from logic 0 to logic 1. Tri-state outputs charge the output line to a high output voltage by connecting the line to the power supply through a conducting transistor and small load resistor. Open-collector outputs charge the output line through a load resistor that has a relatively high value. Since tri-state outputs offer an inherently lower impedance to the power supply through the conducting transistor, they charge the output line much faster than the open-collector outputs.

Another type of output pin has qualities similar to both the open-collector and tri-state outputs. This type of output, known as *pseudo-bidirectional*, is shown in Fig. 6.7. The lower gate in the output totem pole is driven from the current value of the stored output datum. This gate fires when the stored datum has a 0 value, and after firing, the gate pulls the port output to 0. When neither gate in the output totem pole is on, the port output is pulled up to a high value by the internal resistor. Input signals sample the output line, and read a true value only if the value of the output datum is 1; for otherwise the output datum brings the line to logical 0. Hence, before reading from the port, the system interfacer has to be sure that the output data register is loaded with a value of 1. The advantage

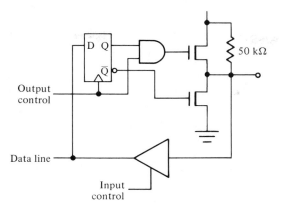

FIGURE 6.7   Equivalent circuit of the pseudo-bidirectional I/O port.

of this type of port is that there is no direction register that dictates whether the port is in the input or output mode. In fact, the port can either write data to or read data from external devices without changing from one mode to another.

Control Lines

The last type of output interfacing signal line is a control line used for handshake signals that control data transfer into and out of parallel ports. The purpose of these lines is to implement control signals in the data-transfer process by using the principles of handshake control, as we outlined in Chapter 3. Since fully interlocked asynchronous control is quite generally and widely used, the control lines for I/O ports tend to have built-in features that support this function. The way the protocol is usually implemented is to provide at least two control lines per 8-bit data port, one for MASTER and one for SLAVE handshake-control signals. The I/O port can be either a master or slave for an external transaction; thus the control logic in the port usually can be programmed for either function. As a master, the port outputs a MASTER signal and responds to changes on the SLAVE line. Conversely, as a slave, the port samples the MASTER line and drives the SLAVE line. In either case, the port can be programmed to change its control-signal output automatically in response to a change on its control-signal input per the conventions of MASTER/SLAVE handshakes. More details on the facilities available for specific I/O chips for parallel I/O interfaces appear later in this chapter.

6.2 THE IEEE-488 INSTRUMENT BUS

Parallel I/O interfaces throughout the 1960s and early 1970s were usually defined on an *ad hoc* basis, specific to a peripheral device and to a computer system. Rarely, if ever, could one find a computer-interface module manufactured by Company A that could drive a peripheral manufactured by Company B—except where the interfaces were specifically designed for plug-to-plug compatiblity. Most of the larger companies adopted in-house standard interfaces for parallel I/O, no two of which were compatible with each other; and even within these companies there were deviations between in-house standards for one reason or another. The situation across the industry was chaotic in comparison to the rigid RS-232-C standard that was already in use for serial interfaces. Whereas interfacing to a common telephone network was the driving force that led to industry-wide compatibility for serial links, no equivalent motivation promoted similar standardization for parallel links. (Actually, the large market for IBM peripherals stimulated many companies to manufacture equipment that interfaced directly to the IBM System/360 channel interface. This channel interface has recently been the subject of a National Bureau of Standards (NBS) standardization process, but the resulting standard is not particularly useful, since the channel interface is obsolete and is no longer used on new designs, not even by IBM.)

In the early 1970s, Hewlett-Packard (HP) recognized the problems created by the lack of standardization in its own product line because of the difficulty in interfacing peripherals for one family of computers to newer families, as well as the problems, in general, of interfacing its test equipment to its own and other manufacturers' computers. HP developed an in-house parallel interfacing standard for an 8-bit data path, and found the resulting standard to be quite versatile and powerful. The interface required more control logic per device than most of the earlier parallel interfaces in use, but the cost of the extra control logic diminished rapidly with the development of LSI and VLSI technology. The HP standard became the basis of a standard adopted by IEEE (IEEE Std. 488–1975, "Standard Digital Interface for Programmable Instrumentation"). This has also been approved by the American National Standards Institute as ANSI Standard MC1.1–1975. The original standard was released in 1975, and a revised standard was released in 1978.

With this standard in place, several integrated-circuit manufacturers initiated the development of LSI interface chips, while the instrument and peripherals manufacturers began the development of IEEE-488–compatible products. At this writing several hundred different products are available that interface together through the IEEE-488 bus, with nothing more than cabling required to make the connection. For new designs, the logic designer can choose from no fewer than four companies offering IEEE-488–type interface chips. And more offerings are likely to appear in the future. Manufacturers of micro- and minicomputers as a rule supply IEEE-488–compatible interface cards, and an IEEE-488 port is a standard feature of all Commodore PET microcomputers.

The original standard was stimulated by a company that makes both test instruments and computers, so that the first peripherals for the bus were largely test instruments. Although the majority of peripherals offered today still are test instruments, the bus also supports the more conventional computer peripherals such as terminals, disk drives, printers, and plotters. For high-speed devices such as disks, the IEEE-488 bus is of somewhat marginal utility because its maximum bandwidth is just barely sufficient for floppy disks and too low for faster devices. Nevertheless, there are major cost advantages in adopting the IEEE-488 bus rather than other types of interconnections, even for low-speed devices for which RS-232-C interfaces are acceptable. Figure 6.8 illustrates one of

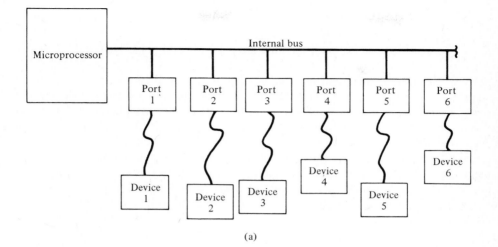

(a)

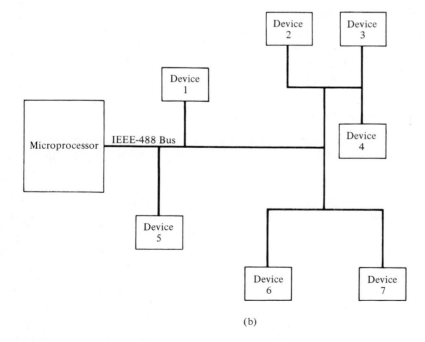

(b)

FIGURE 6.8 (a) Interfacing structure with one device per port. (b) Interfacing structure with IEEE-488 bus; each peripheral and the microprocessor must have IEEE-488 interfaces.

the benefits of the IEEE-488 bus over RS-232-C channels other than its obvious benefit of a higher transfer rate. For the RS-232-C interconnections shown in Fig. 6.8(a), each link requires a separate channel, since the links are point-to-point links. Therefore, if a computer drives N peripherals over N RS-232-C links, it requires N different RS-232-C I/O ports. The cost of a single port may be less than that of an IEEE-488 port because the complexity is less; but as the number of ports increase, the cost of board space, cabinet space, connectors, interface chips, and cabling mounts higher and higher, to the point that it becomes less expensive to interface all devices to a single IEEE-488 bus as shown in Fig. 6.8(b). Note that all bus cables appear to be tied together in some fashion. In fact they are tied, because the cables share connectors in a very clever interconnection arrangement. The IEEE-488 cable connector is a piggy-back type of connector. The cable connector contains both a socket and jack, so that when the cable-jack is mated to a socket on a peripheral device, the piggy-back socket on the cable can accept the jack of another cable. Hence, each device needs to supply only one IEEE-488 socket connector, and all devices can be cabled together by using the piggy-back connectors on the cables to tie two or more cables together.

The signaling speed of the IEEE-488 bus is 500 kHz for standard applications, and can go to 1 MHz if special conventions are followed. Since each transaction carries 8 bits, the maximum data bandwidth is on the order of 4 to 8 megabits per second. This is sufficiently fast to run several different low-speed devices concurrently over the shared-interconnection path, although during a disk transaction, a high-speed block transfer may temporarily cut off a low-speed one from the computer. If this is a serious problem, it might be wise to use two separate buses, one for high-speed block transfers and the other for multiplexing among various low-speed devices.

Functional Description of the IEEE-488 Bus

To understand the detailed operation, electrical conventions, and transaction conventions of the IEEE-488 bus, let us first start with a description of the electrical signals on the bus, and then move to a functional description showing how these electrical signals exercise the bus functions. The electrical interface is shown in Fig. 6.9, where it is shown point to point. In reality the IEEE-488 is a bus to which many similar modules can directly connect. A total of 16 wires are shown in the figure—eight data lines and eight control lines. Bus cables actually have 24 wires, providing eight additional wires for shielding and grounds. To understand the control lines, it is best to observe their use for specific functions, which we do later in this section. For the purpose of the present discussion, the four lines that are the most pertinent are ATTENTION, which is used by a controller to issue a command, and the three handshake lines READY FOR DATA, DATA ACCEPT, and DATA AVAILABLE. These handshake lines are similar to the MASTER and SLAVE lines that we have examined earlier in regard to the asynchronous transmission of data. In fact, DATA AVAILABLE corresponds to MASTER, and the pair READY FOR DATA and DATA ACCEPT correspond to the single SLAVE line. The IEEE-488 bus uses two lines for the SLAVE function in order to permit broadcast operations to the slaves on a

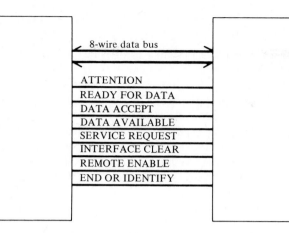

FIGURE 6.9   IEEE-488 bus configuration.

bus. In fact, these two control signals are asserted as active low signals in order to use the open-collector bus to perform an OR function when two or more signals are asserted simultaneously. In our notation system the controls would be labeled NOT READY FOR DATA L and NOT DATA ACCEPT L, but the standard chooses to call them NOT READY FOR DATA and NOT DATA ACCEPT, which is the notation used in the remainder of this chapter. DATA AVAILABLE is also an active low signal.

The operation of the three control lines for a bus handshake is shown in Fig. 6.10. Although the figure shows the behavior for the broadcast mode, let us assume for the moment that there is only a single slave respondent, that the width of the shaded area has

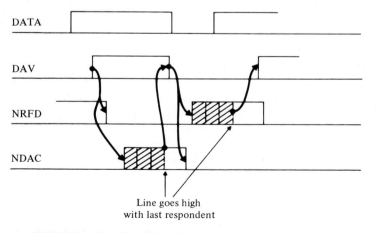

FIGURE 6.10   The IEEE-488 3-wire data transfer handshake.

shrunk to zero, and that the handshake is a generalization of the familiar fully interlocked handshake. The main difference between the two-wire and three-wire handshake is that in the latter, the MASTER responds only to a rising edge of a SLAVE signal. Hence, NOT READY FOR DATA (NRFD in the figure) and NOT DATA ACCEPT (NDAC) are essentially complementary signals with NDAC supplying the active transition at the beginning of the handshake and NRFD supplying the active transition at the end of the handshake. Note that NDAC has the general appearance of the 2-wire handshake-control signal SLAVE, and that NRFD looks something like the complement of SLAVE. Transitions on DATA AVAILABLE (DAV), the MASTER signal, cause transitions on both NRFD and NDAC, so they both react to DAV in the way that SLAVE reacts to MASTER except for the timing delays at which the transitions take place. Note carefully how the transitions are interlocked, and observe how DAV responds to the rising edges of NRFD and NDAC. Visualize the drawing with the shaded region collapsed to zero.

Now consider how a broadcast mode is implemented. When MASTER is asserted, MASTER can be released only after SLAVE responds with a message DATA ACCEPTED. NDAC is an open-collector line that stays low as long as any slave has not accepted the data. Only after the last slave accepts data does the open-collector line go high. The leading edge of the shaded area of NDAC indicates when the first responding slave releases the handshake line. The trailing edge of the shaded area indicates when the last slave releases the line, and the line relaxes to a high voltage. At this point MASTER can be deasserted, which is indicated by the rising edge of DAV. Dotted vertical lines in the shaded region indicate when other slaves respond.

MASTER can be reasserted when all slaves are in a "ready for data" state. NRFD is an open-collector control line so that NRFD rises only when all slaves are ready. This is shown as the rising edge of NRFD at the right-hand edge of the shaded area. The left-hand edge of the shaded area indicates when the first slave responds.

The series of diagrams in Fig. 6.11 shows the basic principles behind the operation of the IEEE-488 bus. Figure 6.11(a) shows the bus with an active controller (Device 1). All other modules are presently inactive. These other modules, and possibly the controller as well, can either transmit or receive data over the bus. A data transmitter is called a *talker*, and a receiver is called a *listener*. Talkers and listeners do not initiate their transactions on the bus; this is the function of the controller. So the basic idea is for the controller to start a data transfer by commanding a talker to talk and listener to listen. The controller then leaves the command mode while the data transfer takes place.

In Fig. 6.11(a), the controller initiates the transaction by asserting ATTENTION, which stops all bus activity and places all devices in a state to accept commands. While ATTENTION is asserted, the controller transmits messages that select Device 3 as a talker and Device 6 as a listener. When the controller releases ATTENTION, the transaction begins as indicated in Fig. 6.11(b). Here we see a sequence of bytes transmitted over the bus through the use of the three-handshake signals. The talker asserts DATA AVAILABLE and awaits the response of DATA ACCEPT, then removes DATA AVAILABLE and waits for READY FOR DATA. This is the IEEE-488 version of the asynchronous fully-interlocked handshake.

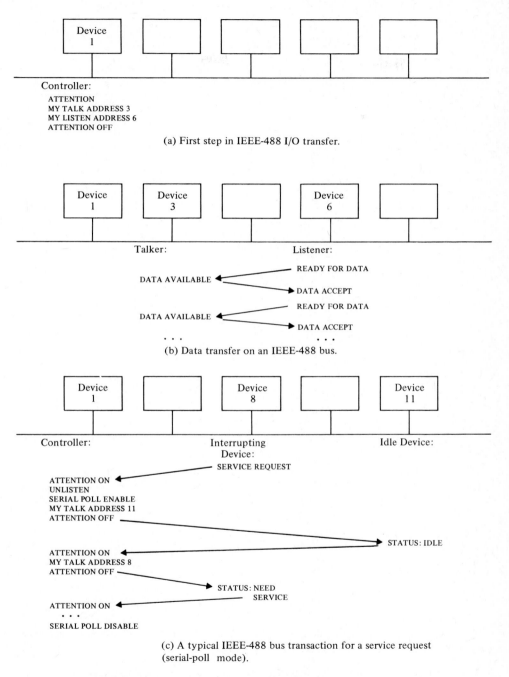

(a) First step in IEEE-488 I/O transfer.

(b) Data transfer on an IEEE-488 bus.

(c) A typical IEEE-488 bus transaction for a service request (serial-poll mode).

FIGURE 6.11   Basic principles of the IEEE-488 (continued on next page).

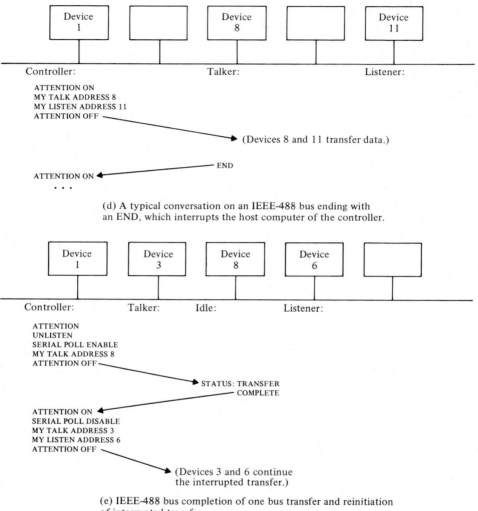

(d) A typical conversation on an IEEE-488 bus ending with an END, which interrupts the host computer of the controller.

(e) IEEE-488 bus completion of one bus transfer and reinitiation of interrupted transfer.

FIGURE 6.11   (Continued.)

In this very simple example, we did not describe how the talker was commanded precisely what data to transmit, nor did we indicate how the listener was commanded what to do with the data to come over the link. These commands can be sent to talker and listener in at least two different ways; namely, the devices

1. can accept commands as bus listeners, or
2. can be placed in a particular state through a secondary talk or listen address.

The first of these methods requires the controller to select a device to be a listener, and the controller itself becomes the talker. There follows a short transaction such as the one shown in Fig. 6.11(b), during which the sequence of data gives the device sufficient information to operate as a talker or listener for a lengthy data transaction. Many test instruments operate in just this manner, and the codes transmitted over the bus are merely codes for the corresponding buttons and switches on the front panel. Thus, it is relatively simple to convert a series of front-panel actions into a program that "pushes" the same set of buttons, but does so through a message transmitted over a parallel link.

The second scheme takes advantage of the addressing properties of the IEEE-488 bus. When ATTENTION is asserted, the 8-bit data path becomes an 8-bit command path. Five of these bits are dedicated to an address function, and the other three bits indicate a type of address function. One pattern of three bits, for example, is used to specify "talker address" and another to specify "listener address." With five address bits, up to 32 different addresses are available, but one of these is reserved to indicate "no address." The 31 different addresses should be adequate for most operations; but to provide for address expansion in case it is needed, the bus standard includes the ability to use those other three bits to indicate a secondary address. When the 3-bit group does indicate a secondary address, the remaining five data bits transmit a second address to all devices that recognized the previous primary address. In this way up to 31^2 distinct addresses can be recognized on the bus.

With secondary addresses available, a secondary address can be used to give one of 31 different commands to a device selected by the primary address. In a sense, this idea is the IEEE-488 equivalent of memory-mapped I/O, in that a particular function is invoked by transmitting to a particular address.

The first two diagrams in Fig. 6.11 reflect the usual means of selecting a talker and listener, and of transmitting a sequence of bytes from the talker to the listener. We also see how the controller sends information to the talker and listener prior to a bus transaction in order to set up that transaction. What happens if other devices, not currently active on the bus, are doing local processing and reach a point where they require service on the bus? This process is shown in Fig. 6.11(c). The device that requires service asserts the control line SERVICE REQUEST, which is clearly the IEEE-488 counterpart of an interrupt-request line. Asserting SERVICE REQUEST causes an interrupt in the controller, which then takes control of the bus by asserting ATTENTION. When ATTENTION is active, all bus activity stops, and the controller can then poll the devices to determine what caused the interrupt. There are two ways to poll the devices on the bus.

1. A slow device-by-device serial poll can cover all 31 devices.
2. A fast parallel poll can accept up to eight distinct responses simultaneously.

The serial poll is shown in Fig. 6.11(c). In this case Device 8 places a SERVICE REQUEST on the bus, and the controller asserts ATTENTION to determine what actions are necessary. With ATTENTION asserted, the controller can then request status from each device on the bus. This process is shown symbolically in the figure. In reality, the process involves sending a special command on the 8-bit data bus to place the devices in the serial-poll mode. This command is SERIAL-POLL ENABLE. Also used in the transaction are the commands UNLISTEN, which disconnects any listener previously connected to the bus, and SERIAL-POLL DISABLE, which takes the devices out of the serial-poll mode. The sequence of commands is

ATTENTION ON	Stop all activity on the bus.
UNLISTEN	Disconnect all listeners.
SERIAL-POLL ENABLE	Initiate the poll.
MY TALK ADDRESS 1	Address the first device as a talker.
ATTENTION OFF	Remove attention and let the talker talk.
Status byte	The talker sends status to controller.
ATTENTION ON	Controller takes the bus again.
MY TALK ADDRESS 2	Poll resumes with next talker.
ATTENTION OFF	Prepare for next status byte.
Status byte	Talker 2 sends status.
ATTENTION ON	The poll continues.
.	.
.	.
.	.
Status byte	The last status byte arrives.
ATTENTION ON	The controller takes control again.
SERIAL-POLL DISABLE	Leave the serial-poll mode.

Now we assume that the service request by Device 8 has high priority relative to the current transaction. In this case the controller simply suspends the current transaction and initiates a new one for Device 8 as shown in Fig. 6.11(d). Here we see the same control sequence as we saw earlier, but this time Device 8 is set up to talk to Device 11. This transaction runs to completion, and Device 8 indicates completion by asserting END, which is one of the eight control lines on the bus. This signal is asserted concurrently with the last data byte transmitted on the 8-bit data path and tells the listener that no additional bytes follow the present one. The controller takes control when the END message appears, and resumes the interrupted transaction with the message sequence shown in Fig. 6.11(e).

In the example transaction in Fig. 6.11, the polling method used is inherently slow when there are many devices on the bus and when the controller does not know in advance which device may have asserted the SERVICE REQUEST line. To speed up device identification, the bus protocol has a parallel-poll mode. In this mode, the controller asserts both ATTENTION and END, and the response is an 8-bit data byte. Each device on the bus asserts one data line if ready, so that up to eight different devices can each be identified uniquely by the status byte. If more than eight devices are on the bus, two or more devices can share a data line for reporting status, and the controller can resolve the ambiguity by following the parallel poll with a short serial poll. Since END is used for both ending a transaction or for parallel polling, it is called END OR IDENTIFY in the IEEE-488 standard.

Note that we have examined the use of six of the eight control lines shown in Fig. 6.9. The two remaining lines are REMOTE ENABLE and INTERFACE CLEAR. REMOTE ENABLE is used to place a device connected to the bus under the control of commands transmitted over the bus, and usually disconnects the device from front-panel control. INTERFACE CLEAR obviously is used to force devices into a fixed, known initial state.

Note that the IEEE-488 bus can include many devices that can talk and many that can listen, but it usually has only a single controller. It is possible to have more than one controller in a system, but at any given time only one controller has possession of control capability, whether that controller is actively giving commands or is idle in the background. When a second controller is to issue commands, the first controller passes the control of the bus to the second one through a TAKE CONTROL command.

With this overview of the IEEE-488 bus functions, we can examine the several additional functions that are provided by the bus. These are listed in Table 6.1. Recall that devices are categorized as listeners, talkers, and controllers, and any device can have the ability to perform any or all of these functions.

Consider which functions listed in Table 6.1 have to be implemented in typical devices. For example, consider the simplest possible talker. This device must have the source handshake function to transmit data on the bus and must have the talker function in order to accept commands from the controller and function as a talker. A more complex talker might include the service-request function and the remote/local function. A still more complex talker might include the parallel-poll, device-clear, and device-trigger

TABLE 6.1   IEEE-488 Interface Functions

Function	Description
SOURCE HANDSHAKE	Exercise DAV and sense RFD and DAC to transmit data on the bus.
ACCEPTOR HANDSHAKE	Sense DAV and respond with RFD and DAC to receive data on the bus.
TALKER	Respond to talker address, transmit streams of data, and return status in response to serial poll requests.
LISTENER	Respond to listener address, receive streams of data, and return status in response to serial poll requests.
SERVICE REQUEST	Exercise SRQ to notify controller of a request pending.
REMOTE/LOCAL	Accept commands from the bus when REN (Remote Enable) is sensed.
PARALLEL POLL	Respond with status word when END OR IDENTIFY is exercised by bus controller.
DEVICE CLEAR	Respond to bus command by changing to an initial state.
DEVICE TRIGGER	Respond to bus command by performing a prespecified action.
CONTROLLER	Issue commands on the bus.

functions. For greater capability, a device might be both talker and listener, and would therefore include the acceptor handshake and listener functions in addition to the talker functions. A controller, when embedded in a computer, normally includes both listener and talker functions so that external devices can transmit data to and from computer memory as bus transactions.

Each of the functions listed for the IEEE-488 standard is described in the standard by a detailed state description similar to that of Fig. 6.12, which, for our expository purposes, is somewhat simpler than its corresponding diagram in the standard for the talker function. In the figure, we observe that in the idle state, the talker is inactive. When the controller asserts ATTENTION and addresses the talker, the talker moves to a new state awaiting the opportunity to take control of the handshake lines. When ATTENTION is released, the talker then moves either to a serial-poll state or to an ordinary talk state. In either case, the talker then initiates a bus transaction through the source-handshake function (not shown in the figure), and relinquishes control of the handshake lines when the controller reasserts ATTENTION. If the controller selects a different talker (or no talker), the presently active talker returns to the idle state.

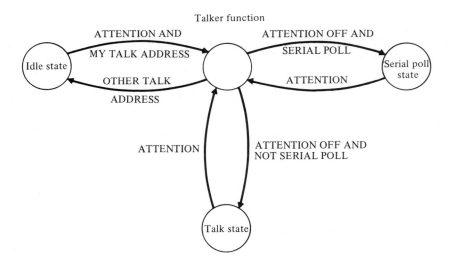

FIGURE 6.12   A greatly simplified state diagram for an IEEE-488 talker function.

At this point, we have completed a discussion of the general functions defined by the IEEE-488 standard. This standard is clearly a competitive alternative to the RS-422 standard for high-speed implementations. This follows because the IEEE-488 bus is able to provide much higher bandwidths through a 24-pin cable and connector than an RS-422 link can provide with its 37 pins. The IEEE-488 bus functions are defined in the standard at a somewhat higher level than the RS-422's functions, so that it is possible to build "smart" interfaces and reduce software loads by adopting the IEEE-488 bus.

6.3 INTEGRATED CIRCUITS FOR PARALLEL INTERFACES

In this section we discuss several different chip implementations of parallel ports; then move to chips for the IEEE-488 bus. The discussion begins with the 6800-family of microprocessor chips, and the 6821 parallel port shown in Fig. 6.13. This chip has the usual microprocessor-bus interface, plus two 8-bit ports. One port is an open-collector port, and the other is a tri-state port. For both ports, individual signal lines can be programmed to be inputs or outputs. Two control lines are available for each port, one of which is an input, and the other of which can be programmed to be either input or output. This provides a total of 20 I/O pins on this chip, which is a substantial number for most purposes.

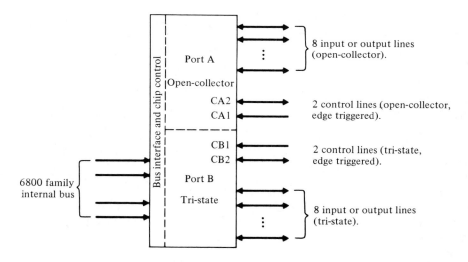

FIGURE 6.13   Structure of the 6820/6821 I/O lines.

Each port contains three registers—a data register, a direction register, and a control/status register. Each bit in the direction register indicates whether the corresponding bit in the data register is to be an input or output. Since the direction register is rarely accessed by a program once the port is initialized, the direction register does not have a separate address in the port. Instead it shares a port address with the data register. One bit of the control register determines whether an access to the direction/data address goes to the direction register or to the data register.

The two control lines in each port, when connected to external control signals, can be programmed to raise interrupts when the external signals change in a specified way. Since the control lines are edge-triggered, they are particularly useful for arbitration and handshaking functions where edge triggering is essential to distinguish the order in which events have occurred. Table 6.2 is a partial illustration of how to program the edge-sensing capability of a control input. This table describes how control line 1 of Port A (called CA1 in chip specifications) is programmed to set a flag and to raise an interrupt from the chip. There are four possibilities given in the table: The first two set the flag on the falling edge of a signal on this line; the second two set the flag on the rising edge. The second and fourth raise the interrupt, and the first and third do not. The four possible combinations are encoded by two bits stored in the control register for the port, and are set under program control. Identical control bits exist in the corresponding control register for Port B.

TABLE 6.2   Control of 6821 Handshake-Input Signal

CA1 Control Bits	Interface Mode
0 0	Sense falling edge of CA1, IRQ off.
0 1	Sense falling edge of CA1, IRQ on.
1 0	Sense rising edge of CA1, IRQ off.
1 1	Sense rising edge of CA1, IRQ on.

The other control pin, CA2, can be either an output or an input pin. It is programmed by three bits, one of which indicates whether that pin is an input or an output, and the other two of which indicate one of four possible functions for input or output. The four functions possible for the pin as an input are identical to those shown in Table 6.2. That is, an internal flag can be made sensitive to either a falling edge or rising edge, and the chip can either raise an interrupt or not when an active transition is sensed. The only difference is that the second control line, CA2, has its own flag bit, and does not affect the flag bit associated with the first control line. The two flag bits can be read by the microprocessor as the sign bit (for CA1) and the next most significant bit (for CA2) of the control word. Port B's second control pin, CB2, is functionally identical to CA2 in the input mode, and varies just slightly from it as an output control pin.

The handshaking capabilities of the port are provided through CA2 and CB2 used as outputs, with CA1 and CB1 used as inputs. Table 6.3 shows the four possible choices of

TABLE 6.3   Control of 6821 Handshake-Output Signal

CA2 Control Bits	Interface Mode
1 0 0	Reset CA2 to 0 after READ; set CA2 to 1 on active edge of CA1.
1 0 1	Reset CA2 to 0 after READ; set CA2 to 1 after the next clock cycle.
1 1 0	Reset CA2 to 0.
1 1 1	Set CA2 to 1.

function for CA2. Note that two of the states force the output pin high or low. These states can thus be used to raise or lower a MASTER output after specific transitions on the SLAVE input are sensed. (CA2 can also be a SLAVE output with CA1 a MASTER input.) The program fragment in Program 6.3 shows how one might implement the asynchronous handshake in a port operating as a master. The program is somewhat more awkward than necessary because it does not take advantage of the automatic handshaking controls described later.

PROGRAM 6.3   Handshaking for a Parallel Port

```
begin
    (* This program outputs a datum, and exercises a MASTER signal as part of an
        asynchronous handshake. It assumes that the program is entered with SLAVE
        in a logic 0 state. *)
    Set CA1 flag to be sensitive to a rising edge on CA1;
    Output the datum;
    Set CA2 to 1; (* MASTER is high indicating data available. *)
    Await interrupt (if armed), or test CA1 flag and continue after a rising edge on
        CA1; (* Wait for SLAVE response. *)
    Read the data port to reset the control flag for CA1;
    Set CA1 flag to be sensitive to a falling edge on CA1;
    Set CA2 to 0; (* MASTER is low. *)
    Await interrupt, or test CA1 flag and continue after a falling edge on CA1;
    Read the data port to reset the control flag for CA1;
    Exit ready to output the next datum;
end;
```

The required waiting by a program can be done elsewhere if the program is interrupt driven. If the program is not interrupt driven, waiting can be done by tight loops that continually check the control flags. Note that the act of reading the data buffer in the port clears the flags associated with the control lines and arms the flags to respond to the next active transition of the control signal.

Two other control modes for CA2 as an output provide additional useful capabilities. One is a pulse mode in which the user can force the output low by programming the microprocessor to read from a data register; the output is returned high about one clock cycle later. (For Port B, the output is forced low by an instruction that writes to the data register instead of reading from it.) Some external devices require pulses on the control lines to indicate the presence of data or completion of a transfer, and this mode provides the necessary capability to generate those control pulses.

The most interesting mode is that in which the port operates a MASTER or SLAVE handshake signal in response to the transitions on a control input line. For Port A the mode lowers CA2 after the microprocessor reads data from Port A and raises CA2 after an active transition on CA1 is sensed. For Port B, CB2 drops on a write to the data register rather than a read from the register, but otherwise the function is similar to Port A. To use this mode to facilitate an interlocked transfer, consider the Program 6.4, which works with Port B.

PROGRAM 6.4   Automatic Handshaking for a Parallel Port

begin
(* Assume the port is initialized to handshake mode, and that CB2 is currently high. The port writes data to an asynchronous link and acts as a master on the link. Assume that the CB1 flag is sensitized to interrupt when a SLAVE transition indicates that the slave is ready for a new datum. *)

•
•
•

Interrupt entry-point:
Read data register of Port *B*;
(* This clears the interrupt and associated flag. *)
Obtain next output datum;
Write datum to Port *B*; (* This lowers MASTER. *)
Return from interrupt;
(* Exit. When the next reentry occurs, the interrupt from the SLAVE will automatically raise MASTER from this port in preparation for the next cycle. *)
end;

The timing of the MASTER signal with respect to the SLAVE signal is shown in Fig. 6.14. MASTER and SLAVE are shown to be active in the low state because this is the way they are controlled in the automatic handshake mode. Observe how MASTER is brought low by program control and then changed to high when an active transition on SLAVE occurs. Astute readers will observe that the handshake is not fully interlocked because the interface responds to only one transition of SLAVE. To be fully interlocked the chip must respond to both transitions, and this requires reprogramming the sensitivity of CB1 between each transition as the chip specifications now stand. A more useful chip specification, which is a slight deviation from Table 6.3, is to post an interrupt when CB1 moves in one direction, and to respond with a change in CB2 when CB1 moves in the op-

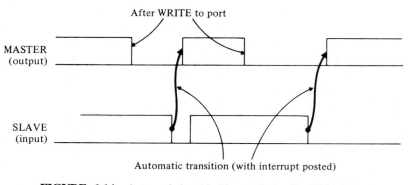

FIGURE 6.14   Automatic handshaking mode for the 6821 I/O port.

posite direction. This gives the required sensitivity to both edges of CB1. The interrupt should occur when CB1 indicates the slave is ready for data, and this should not change MASTER. MASTER changes when a new datum is placed in the output register. Unfortunately, the chip is not manufactured with this behavior.

The 6500 family uses the 6821 chip for parallel I/O functions, since the bus interface is identical; or it uses a compatible version numbered 6520. Several parallel I/O chips in both the 6500 and 6800 families offer other capabilities. For example, the 6530 and 6846 both contain one I/O port plus read-only memory and a timer. The 6522 has an I/O port, two interval timers, and serial-to-parallel and parallel-to-serial converters. Handshaking functions for these chips follow the general scheme for the 6821.

Intel's i8255 is a parallel-interface device that has capabilities somewhat similar to those of the 6821, with differences worth describing here. The chip has 24 interface pins that can be programmed to be in one of three functional modes, namely,

1. Basic I/O without handshaking.
2. Unidirectional I/O with handshaking.
3. Bidirectional I/O with handshaking.

For the basic-I/O mode, the I/O port is essentially a buffer/repeater for data that move between the microprocessor and the external world. Output data are latched in the port to be held constant for external sensing, and input data are sampled under microprocessor control without latching. Since no control signals are required, the 24 I/O bits are organized into three ports of eight bits each as shown in Fig. 6.15(a). The direction of the signal wires is controlled in groups of four or eight pins, and not individually controlled as for the 6821. Ports A and B are treated as 8-bit ports, and each port has all of its pins set simultaneously to be inputs or outputs. The third port C is made up of eight pins that are control signals in the other modes. In the basic I/O mode this port has two 4-bit groups, and each group is set as a group to be an input or output group, but the two groups need not have the same direction.

The next mode, which has strobed handshake-control, utilizes external control signals to latch input data and to generate interrupts. The act of latching data also returns an acknowledgment, which thereby provides for automatic handshaking for MASTER/ SLAVE signals to control asynchronous transfers. An equivalent logic diagram for this type of control signal appears in Fig. 6.15(b). In the figure, the control lines STB, IN-TERRUPT REQUEST, and IBF are three handshake signals configured from three pins of Port C. A total of five lines of Port C are used this way—three lines to control Port A and two more to control Port B. The INTERRUPT REQUEST line is common to both ports. The remaining three lines of Port C are usable as general I/O lines in this mode. Ports A and B act as independent 8-bit data ports. The INTERRUPT ENABLE in the figure is produced by an internal control bit of the 8255, which is set and reset by the processor through commands sent to the 8255. The last control line, READ L, is the familiar bus-control line that determines the direction of a data transfer.

The 8255 functions are sufficient to implement the fully interlocked, asynchronous protocol because the control logic is sensitive to both edges of MASTER, and each transi-

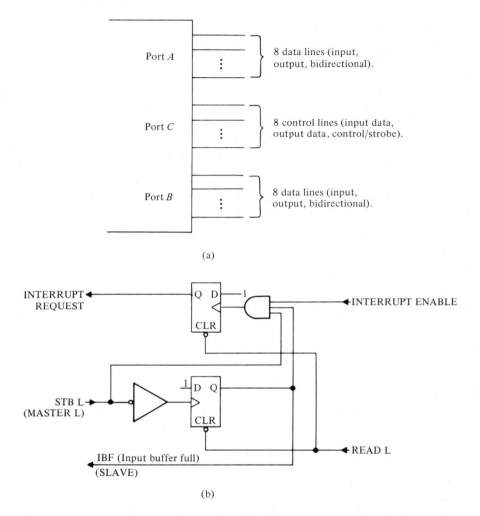

(a)

(b)

FIGURE 6.15   (a) The structure of the i8255 I/O pins; (b) equivalent logic diagram for the i8255 handshake control lines.

tion of MASTER triggers a corresponding transition of SLAVE, either directly or indirectly. Note from the schematic in Fig. 6.15(b) that the falling edge of STB L (the MASTER signal) causes IBF (the SLAVE signal) to set to 1. The rising edge of STB L does not directly trigger a change in IBF, but it does raise an interrupt if the interrupt is enabled. In response to the interrupt, a READ issued by the microprocessor accepts data from the port, and clears IBF, thereby completing the fully interlocked transaction. A similar behavior for the output configuration of the ports guarantees that both MASTER and SLAVE functions are compatible with the specifications of an 8255 I/O port.

The last mode, bidirectional mode, provides for bidirectional transfer on Port A. To control transfers on this port, the 8255 uses five bits of Port C for handshaking and interrupt generation. Two lines control input handshaking, two lines control output handshaking and the fifth line is the interrupt request line. When Port A is used in a bidirectional mode, Port B is still available for use in either basic-I/O mode or unidirectional mode with the remaining three pins of Port C used for handshake control and interrupt generation.

Programmable control of the configuration of the 8255 is accomplished through an 8-bit control command that the microprocessor issues to the peripheral chip. There are two types of commands, and these are distinguished by the most significant bit of the control word. A 1 in this position identifies the command as a mode-configuration command, and a 0 in this position indicates the command sets or resets control bits in the 8255.

For mode configuration, there are seven bits remaining in a command word other than the 1 bit in the most significant position, and these select one of 128 possible configurations. The mode control specifies which direction the various ports will take and which functional modes of data transfer are to be used. When the command word from the microprocessor has a 0 in the most significant position, four of the remaining bits of the command set or reset a bit in Port C. Of the four command bits, three bits select a bit in Port C and the fourth becomes the new value of that bit. This capability is required so that specific bits of Port C can be changed without affecting other lines when Port C is controlling asynchronous transactions. With conventional access to Port C, all bits are altered simultaneously, and it is impossible to change a single bit without affecting all others. Restoring the previous values of bits to be left unchanged is unsatisfactory, because those bits may have changed since they were last read.

The data registers of Ports A, B, and C are each individually addressable, as is the control word address, so that the 8255 occupies four bytes of port-address space.

Interface Chips for the IEEE-488 Bus

The appearance of the IEEE-448 bus standard in 1975 stimulated several integrated-circuit manufacturers to investigate the feasibility of implementing LSI chips for the IEEE-488 bus. Hewlett-Packard, with a head start in the use of the major portion of the standard, was able to fabricate a custom-LSI chip that implements the entire functional protocol (except for the bus drivers) and to release it in various products starting in the late 1970s. This chip is not sold separately outside HP, so that other interface designers were on their own until the integrated-circuit manufacturers could produce the necessary LSI components. Motorola and AMI in the late 1970s announced the manufacture of the 68488 chip that implements the functions required for talker/listeners. Intel announced two chips in roughly the same time period: the i8291, which implements the talker/listener functions; and the i8292, which implements the controller functions. Most peripherals that attach to the IEEE-488 bus are talker/listeners and, therefore, require only the 8291. However, the microcomputer interface to the bus normally is a controller and functions as talker/listener as well, so this interface requires both the 8291 and the 8292. The Intel devices are themselves single-chip microcomputers in the 8041 family, each containing a small memory, an 8-bit processor, and a limited I/O interface all integrated on a single circuit. The on-chip read-only memory is preprogrammed to perform the required bus functions. A third member of this family, the i8293, is a bus-transceiver chip that contains half the drivers necessary to connect an 8291 or 8292 to an IEEE-488 bus.

As the popularity of the bus standard increased, other integrated-circuit manufacturers began to offer competitive devices. The 96LS488 from Fairchild is one such device that is distinguished for its on-chip bus drivers, which makes it a truly single-chip interface for talker/listener functions. With the low-cost of the IEEE-488 interface today, and still lower costs as integration density becomes higher, the advantages of the parallel high-speed I/O bus may displace such well-entrenched serial links such as the RS-232-C.

A schematic diagram of the 8291 appears in Fig. 6.16. The diagram shows 16 interface registers connected to an internal bus of a microcomputer. These registers are actually part of an on-chip RAM of that microcomputer. The IEEE-488 data bus connects to the interface registers through the internal bus, and the command signals for the IEEE-488 bus are controlled and sensed through other I/O lines on the internal microcomputer. The interface to an 808X family bus provides a way to connect the IEEE-bus chip to a host microprocessor, and thus the 8291 functions very much like any other peripheral chip. The

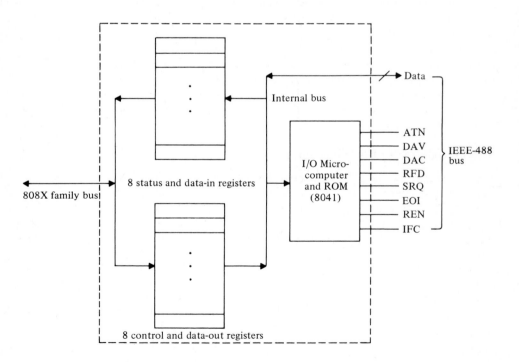

FIGURE 6.16   Structure of the Intel 8291 talker/listener.

system designer may be totally unaware that the internal architecture of the 8291 is that of a microcomputer.

The 8291 interface registers are shown in two groups—namely a group of eight status and data-input registers, and a group of eight control and data-output registers. The 808X host microprocessor reads and writes these registers to transfer data to and from the IEEE-488 bus. The functions controlled by these registers are as follows:

1. There are two registers that buffer data onto and off the IEEE-488 data bus.
2. Two registers arm and disarm individual interrupts. Among the conditions recognized are a full input buffer, empty output buffer, end of information, serial-poll mode, and device-address recognition. Each of these conditions on the IEEE-488 bus can invoke software routines in the host (808X) microprocessor when they occur.
3. Two registers hold the state of the interrupt signals. The host microprocessor can sense these bits to determine which condition triggered an interrupt and which did not.
4. Two registers hold control and status information for the serial-poll function. One register, an output register, holds a service-request bit and a 7-bit status word that is sent to a controller on the IEEE-488 bus in response to a serial poll. Setting the service-request bit in this register sends a SERVICE REQUEST to the system controller. The other register, an input register, contains the present value of the serial-poll status word.
5. Five registers control the address-selection function of the interfaces. Of these, one register controls the selection mode. The interface can respond to a single primary address or to primary/secondary pairs of addresses issued sequentially. Control bits in the mode register determine which of several possible response modes is active. A status register indicates the present state of the selection logic so that the host microprocessor can determine whether the device has been selected and, if so, whether that selection has been as a talker or listener. One register, an output register, carries both the primary and secondary addresses. The data passed to this register is routed to one of two input-registers that hold, respectively, the primary and secondary addresses.
6. One register holds a special character that acts as an END OF STRING (sometimes called END OF SEQUENCE). When a listener discovers this character in an incoming data stream, the listener responds as if the END control line has been asserted, and performs the normal actions for an end of message.
7. One register is a command pass-through register and holds any command transmitted on the bus that is not recognized by on-chip logic. This permits software in the host to interpret such commands in nonstandard ways, and thereby permits extension of the bus capability in system-dependent ways.
8. One register controls miscellaneous auxiliary functions.

To understand how the 8291 is used to interface to an IEEE-488-bus, consider a system with a host microprocessor and an 8291 in which the host microprocessor is to "talk" to the bus. Elsewhere on the bus is a bus controller. Consider what happens when the controller requests the host microprocessor to send a string of bytes on the bus. The following actions occur:

1. The talker address in the primary-address register of the 8291 matches the talker address received from the IEEE-488 bus. This match raises an interrupt, which eventually initiates the talker program in the host microprocessor.
2. After the controller has set up the listeners, the talker program in the host initializes the 8291 for the transmission of data. To do so, it sets the state of the interrupt masks and of other control bits in the 8291 to control the activity during the data transfer. A typical set of actions is the posting of an interrupt at the end of each byte transferred, and the transmitting of the END signal when the END OF STRING character appears in the output data stream.
3. The talker sends a sequence of characters that terminates with END OF STRING.
4. The bus controller should be conditioned to recognize when the EOI or end-of-string character is transmitted. The controller detects this condition, becomes active, and asserts ATTENTION.
5. The talker goes to the idle state.

The listener function operates in a very similar manner, with the data-flow direction being the major difference between the two types of interface. The talker/listener functions require substantial program control as we have described them here. If the interrupts are left unarmed, then the talker and listener have to monitor bus events to be sure that they can react to changes of state.

The most usual type of implementation of bus interfaces with the 829X family is to use the 8291 and two 8293s in peripheral devices, with the idea that the talker/listener functions are sufficient for most peripherals. A system controller does all these functions and more, and therefore the controller for the IEEE-488 bus contains the 8292 controller chip plus the other chips. Programming this particular interface is an interesting challenge because it involves enabling and disabling the 8291 and 8292 chips repeatedly, as the instructions shift between those functions that are to be performed by the controller and those that are to be performed by the talker/listener. A DMA-controller chip in the system further complicates the programming complexity because, in this instance, the software has to multiplex its capabilities among the DMA controller, the 8291, and the 8292. In spite of the complexity of the program required to control the multiplicity of functions of the 829X family, the bus-interfacing problem is very much simpler than it might otherwise be.

The 6800-family interface is the 68488 chip manufactured by Motorola and AMI. It is functionally similar to the 8291 talker/listener, but differs considerably in the details of its operation. The 68488 implements the principal functions to be performed by talkers and listeners, and it does so with the same general technique of the 8291. The 68488 has 16 registers in its address space, of which 8 can be read and 8 can be written. (Not every one of these addresses corresponds to a physical register.) Given the requirements of a talker/listener, it is clear that the 68488 must be similar to the 8291 in at least the following ways:

1. There are two registers for data transmission. One holds input data from the bus, and the other holds data to be output to the bus.
2. An interrupt-mask register controls the conditions that can post interrupts.
3. Two registers hold interrupt status. One of these has bits that correspond to the mask-register bits. The other has additional status bits that are used to distinguish among several possible conditions that are OR'ed together in the first register.
4. Four registers are used for address selection. One register determines the mode and primary address. This controls whether the chip will respond to talker or listener addresses, and whether a primary address or a primary/secondary pair of addresses is required. A second register holds a primary address that is read from external switches or an external register. A status register indicates what modes are in force, and what address selection has occurred most recently. The last register, a mode register, controls other address-selection functions.
5. Two registers are used for the serial-poll function. These are essentially the same as the registers in the 8291. One register (an output register) holds a service-request bit and a 7-bit word for response to a serial poll, and the other register (an input register) holds the present values of these bits.
6. One register holds the 8-bit word delivered to the bus in response to a parallel-poll command.
7. One register is dedicated to holding the status response to a serial-poll request.
8. One register is a command pass-through register, and holds any unrecognized command received on the bus. Its function is essentially identical to the corresponding register in the 8291.
9. One register, the auxiliary-command register, controls other miscellaneous functions.

The major differences between the 68488 and the 8291 are in the treatment of interrupts. Because there are a very large number of possible interrupts, it is convenient to organize them hierarchically. For example, three different but related conditions can be OR'ed together on one interrupt bit. Then setting or resetting the corresponding mask bit respectively arms or disarms the three interrupt conditions. If the interrupt is armed, then the chip posts an interrupt if any one of the three conditions occurs. When the microprocessor responds to the posted interrupt, whether the interrupt is vectored or not, the microprocessor cannot determine from the external interrupt precisely which bus condition caused the interrupt. The microprocessor must "poll" the chip in some sense. For the case where three interrupts are OR'ed on one bit, the microprocessor first must sense the interrupt bit that is the logical OR of the three conditions. When it discovers that the OR has caused an interrupt, the microprocessor must then determine which of the three conditions has occurred. Therefore, there must be yet another status word that contains the individual conditions, and indeed the 68488 is organized in just this way. Hence, the interrupt software first determines which of the interrupt bits at the first level has triggered an interrupt; then if a bit that represents a composite signal has done so, the software next interrogates the status bits for the individual control signals. The 8291 interrupt scheme is not organized in this hierarchical fashion, so that the decoding of the interrupt is more direct for the 8291 than for the 68488, but the interrupts are slightly more time-consuming to interpret.

At this writing, the 6800-family has only the 68488 chip for the talker/listener function, and no chip for specifically implementing the controller function. However, since the controller function does nothing more than assert (or sense) the 8 control lines and issue commands on the 8 data lines, the controller can be implemented with a parallel I/O chip that has two 8-bit ports. A suitable candidate for this implementation is the 6821. But the 6821 has very little on-chip logic to assert and deassert specific control signals in response to status sensed on the bus. Hence, when the 6821 is used as a controller, a good deal of the bus control must be implemented in the software. Consider, for example, how a 6821 and support software can implement the SERVICE REQUEST function. The SERVICE REQUEST should ordinarily post an interrupt. Hence this control line is connected to a handshake line on the parallel port, and the port is armed to interrupt an active transition.

When a SERVICE REQUEST interrupt occurs, software initiates a serial poll. To do so it first asserts ATTENTION by setting the corresponding bit in the parallel port. Then it sends a sequence of commands on the data port, doing so by transmitting the commands to the data port of the 6821. After each command is sent, the controller has to manipulate the DATA AVAILABLE handshake line and sense DATA ACCEPT and READY FOR DATA signals. It is possible to perform these functions through software control of the 68488; but if the 68488 is a talker or listener active on the bus at the point of the SERVICE REQUEST, there is some danger that its state will be lost if the chip is used to respond to the SERVICE REQUEST. For this reason, it may be better to do all of the control functions through the parallel port, and thereby preserve the present state of the 68488 chip. Then after each command is output to the parallel port, software has to exercise the control port to handshake on DATA AVAILABLE and to sense the incoming handshake lines. The 6821 chip is general enough to be able to perform the controller task, but the related software becomes more difficult to write and debug, and its performance is lower than it might be if the controller were an LSI chip specifically designed for the IEEE-488 bus.

A totally different approach to the problem has been taken in the Fairchild 96LS488. This device has essentially no addressable registers and is, in effect, preprogrammed to do a specific set of talker/listener functions. Its interface signals are shown in Fig. 6.17. These signals include the 16 signals for the IEEE-488 bus, plus four mode-control lines, five device-address lines, and six lines for controlling the transfer of data between the IEEE-488 bus and a device attached to the 96LS488. The address lines are presumably connected to switches whose settings establish the talker/listener address. The mode switches set the interface chip into one of 16 preprogrammed modes that dictate whether the chip is a talker, listener, or both, and whether the device responds to one or to two ad-

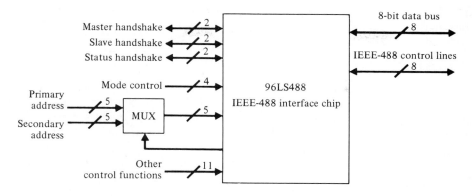

FIGURE 6.17   Interface signals for the 96LS488.

dresses. (If it requires two addresses, external logic has to multiplex two addresses onto the 5-bit address port. Multiplex control is developed on-chip by an address-select signal.)

To interface this chip to an instrument or to a microprocessor, it is necessary only to write data into the chip or read data from the chip, and to perform a minimum of status sensing. Two of the handshake lines control the transfer of data when the 96LS488 acts as a bus master. The transfer protocol is a fully interlocked asynchronous handshake. Two additional handshake lines control data transfers when the chip is a bus slave. The remaining two lines are used to pass a status byte to the 96LS488 during a serial-poll sequence, and they too follow the same interlocked handshake protocol.

Figure 6.17 is somewhat simplified because other functions are not shown individually. Among the miscellaneous control lines is a signal to the 96LS488 that forces it to issue a SERVICE REQUEST on the IEEE-488 bus. Other control lines are used for specific functions in a similar fashion. The reason for bringing the control lines to boundaries of the chip and for eliminating the need to access internal registers is that the 96LS488 need not be associated with a microcomputer. It is readily interfaced to instruments that have digital logic, but not necessarily a digital microcomputer contained within them. When this chip is to be interfaced to a microcomputer, the easiest way to do so is to connect it to a parallel port such as the 8255 or 6821 because the handshake lines on the 96LS488 follow the same or similar protocols to those followed by the 8255 and 6821. Since all bus drivers are contained on-chip, the 96LS488 is very close to an ideal one-chip bus interface. Software required to drive this chip is negligible as well, because the functions are preprogrammed. In using this chip the designer gains a great deal in speed and integration level, but may give up something in flexibility.

This completes our discussion of the interfacing to the IEEE-488 bus. The designer who implements such an interface is best advised to study the IEEE-488 bus standard well and to be thoroughly familiar with it before initiating the design. This discussion is intended to give such a designer basic information as to what functions are performed in interface chips and how the chips are controlled. In working out the details for any specific interface, the designer must work from the chip specifications and the documentation for the standard.

OTHER READING AND SOURCE MATERIAL

For information on parallel interfaces, the most detailed sources are the manufacturers' specification sheets. Osborne and Kane, vol. 2 (1978), cover the major parallel interface chips and give many practical tips for putting the chips to use. Ebright's application note (1976) shows several uses for the 8255, including the schematics and assembly-language driver programs.

With the introduction of the LSI interface chips for the IEEE-488 bus, an extraordinary amount of information has become available. The primary source of documentation is the published standard (IEEE, 1975, revised 1978.) An overview of the interface standard by Knoblock, *et al.* (1975), is somewhat broader and less detailed than the material in this chapter. The 1975 Wescon Proceedings carries four papers by implementers of the standard (Knoblock, 1975; Lee, 1975; Coates, 1975; and Fluke, 1975) that give interesting insights into considerations and recommended approaches for commerical implementations. The papers are, in general, written with instrumentation applications in mind, and they were written before LSI chips appeared.

To assist designers in the use of LSI chips, several manufacturers have released detailed application notes that are excellent sources of information. Forbes (1980) shows logic diagrams and programs for the Intel family of chips (on the cover, this application note credits T. Voll with authorship but internally the authorship is credited to Forbes). Intel Corporation makes available source listings of the programs in the 8291 and 8292 controllers for implementers who have very specific questions on their operation.

Motorola offers two application notes of interest. "Getting aboard the 488-1975 bus" (undated) is a very readable discussion of the standard and relates the standard to the MC68488 interface chip for the standard. Kryka (1979) shows how to implement the standard with the use of an MC68488 for talker/listener functions and a parallel I/O chip for the controller functions. Summers (1980) describes applications of Fairchild's 96LS488. In the microcomputer system area, Fisher and Jensen (1980) cover techniques for controlling IEEE-488 devices on the Commodore PET and CBM computers. The primary I/O bus for these systems is the IEEE-488 bus, as is the case for several families offered by Hewlett-Packard. Compatible peripherals including printers, floppy-disk drives, and modems are marketed by Commodore and Hewlett-Packard, as well as by numerous independent suppliers.

EXPERIMENTS

6.1 This experiment constructs a square output from a parallel port. Obtain a microcomputer with a user-programmable parallel port. If your microcomputer does not have an available parallel port, then obtain a parallel I/O chip and interface it to your microcomputer. For 808X microprocessors use the 8255, and for 68XX and 65XX microprocessors use the 6821.

a) Write a program that does the following:

    i)   Initializes the I/O port so that a specific bit is an output bit.

    ii) Alternates the output value of that bit between 0 and 1 at the maximum rate permissible by the microcomputer. To alternate between 0 and 1, execute the following loop.

For 808X microprocessors:

```
LOOP    XRI    0FFH    COMPLEMENT THE ACCUMULATOR
        OUT    PORT    OUTPUT THE ACCUMULATOR
        JMP    LOOP
```

For 68XX microprocessors:

```
LOOP    COM A          COMPLEMENT THE ACCUMULATOR
        STA A   PORT   OUTPUT TO PORT ADDRESS
        BRA     LOOP
```

For 65XX microprocessors:

```
LOOP    EOR    $FF     COMPLEMENT THE ACCUMULATOR
        STA    PORT    OUTPUT TO PORT ADDRESS
        JMP    LOOP
```

b) On a dual-trace oscilloscope observe the waveform of the output pin you have programmed, and verify that it is a square wave.

c) Probe the system clock on the second trace, and find the number of clock cycles per square-wave cycle. Calculate the number of clock cycles required to execute the three-instruction loop, and verify that this number agrees with your observation.

d) Expand the scale of the output pin, and observe where the transitions on this waveform fall relative to the system clock. Find the delay between the completion of the OUT or STA instruction and the transition on the output of the parallel port. Compare this delay to the minimum delay in the manufacturer's specification for the I/O chip.

6.2 Connect two computers together through a parallel port. You should use MASTER and SLAVE handshake lines to control data transfers. The data bus for the transfer should have eight data lines. For the interconnecting cable, keep the cable as short as reasonable, and include in the cable one ground wire for each signal wire. Twist the ground wires around the signal wires to form twisted pairs, and connect all ground wires to logic grounds at their respective microcomputers. Before powering up the dual-processor system, be sure that the two systems have a common earth ground at the AC power source.

a) Write a program that transfers data across the link with a fully interlocked handshake protocol. Generate the bytes at the transmitter as a sequence of alternating 00s and FFs, and discard the data at the receiver without attempting to buffer it. Find the rate of data transfer that you have achieved. How many times faster is this than the RS-232-C connection on the same computer?

b) Measure the skew time of the data by probing the data bus at the receiving microprocessor. To do so you will have to sync the scope to the chip select of the parallel port receiver or to an equivalent periodic signal. (Or you can use a logic analyzer.) Find the delay of each data and handshake line relative to a transition of the system clock, and find the maximum observed skew among the signals on the bus.

6.3 Create an interrupt-driven transmitter programmer for the parallel link described in Experiment 6.2, and use the automatic handshake lines to the greatest possible extent so that the program does the minimum amount in a data transfer after having initialized the interrupt system and the port. Observe the MASTER, SLAVE, and data lines on an oscilloscope. For the 6821, the transfer may not be fully interlocked because the 6821 does not easily support this type of transfer in the automatic-handshake mode.

6.4 From the manufacturer's specifications for a 2732 or 2716 PROM, find what is required to build a PROM programmer from a microcomputer and parallel port. Design and build such a PROM programmer. Test the programmer by running it without a PROM plugged in, and verify that all WRITE control signals, data signals, and address signals follow the manufacturer's specifications.

6.5 Obtain a music synthesizer chip such as the General Instrument AY3-8910. Interface this chip to a microcomputer through a parallel port.

6.6 Interface a hexadecimal keypad to a microcomputer through a parallel port, and write a program that uses software to debounce the key switches and to encode the keys depressed.

6.7 Interface a 4-digit, 7-segment display to a microcomputer by using a parallel port and external latches. Your interface should use only 7 output lines for data to the latches, and should use other control lines to multiplex the seven signals to the storage logic for the corresponding digit. If you use external BCD-to-7-segment decoders, then you may reduce the number of digit output lines from seven to four.

6.8 Find a system that contains an IEEE-488 bus, and program the system to "talk" continuously. Then initiate a perpetual data transfer and monitor the bus handshake signals DAV, NRFD, and NDAC. Observe these signals on an oscilloscope, and determine the maximum data rate for such a transfer. Verify that the signals conform to the shape and timing that you anticipated.

PROBLEMS

6.1 Table P–6.1 is an abbreviated table that shows how particular bits in a control register govern the behavior of signals CB1 and CB2, the handshake control pins for Port *B* of a 6821. This table is quite similar to, but not identical to, Tables 6.2 and 6.3, which give the behavior of the handshake lines for Port *A* of the same type of chip. The control bits are identified as CRB-0 through CRB-7, where CRB designates Control Register *B*, and the bits of the register are numbered from 0 to 7 from least significant bit to the most significant bit. CRB-7, the sign bit, is a status bit that can be read by a microprocessor to determine what events have taken place as reported by pins CB1 and CB2.

TABLE P–6.1   CB1 Control Function for a 6821 Parallel Port

CRB-1	CRB-0	CRB-7 Setting
0	0	Set on CB1 falling, no interrupt.
0	1	Set on CB1 falling, with interrupt.
1	0	Set on CB1 rising, no interrupt.
1	1	Set on CB1 rising, with interrupt.

CB2 Output Behavior for a 6821 Parallel Port

CRB-5	CRB-4	CRB-3	CB2 Behavior
1	0	0	CB2 goes high when CRB-7 signals an event, and drops low when data are written into data register of port.
1	0	1	CB2 goes low during a clock transition after data are written into the port, and goes high after the write is completed and the chip is disabled.
1	1	0	CB2 is forced low.
1	1	1	CB2 is forced high.

Write a brief program that works with this type of port and implements a fully interlocked asynchronous handshake as automatically as possible. Assume that the computer controls the port to write to a parallel device such as a printer. Assume that the printer READY signal is connected to CB1 as an input, and that the CHARACTER READY signal is CB2. READY and CHARACTER READY are to be fully interlocked, and the program is supposed to set up the control register to simplify the software that controls the handshake.

In your program, when you read or write a control register, assume that it has a memory address (or port address) CRB. The corresponding data register has a memory (or port) address DATAB.

6.2 Consider the same problem as the previous one; but for this one, the port is used to read data instead of to write data. For reading, use Port *A* on the device in place of Port *B*. The two ports are, in general, identical in function except that control output CA2 behaves as indicated in Table 6.3, which is different from the behavior of the corresponding control output CB2.

6.3 The Intel 8255 I/O port has three modes of operation, one of which (Mode 1) is a handshake mode of operation. In this mode, Port *A* can be configured either for input or output. When configured for input, Port *A* carries data in, whereas bits 3, 4, and 5 of Port *C* control a handshake for Port *A*. When Port *A* is configured for output, bits 3, 6, and 7 of Port *C* control a handshake for Port *A*. The function of the handshake bits is given in Table P–6.2. The interrupt outputs of the 8255 can be used to interrupt a microprocessor to service the interrupt.

TABLE P−6.2   Intel 8255 Port *C* Functions (Mode 2)

Port *C* Bit	Type	Pin Function
4	STROBE L	This signal is generated externally to the 8255 and fed to the 8255, where it triggers a latch on-chip to capture external data in Port *A*. A 0 on this signal latches the data.
5	INPUT BUFFER FULL	The 8255 produces a 1 on this pin to acknowledge a response to an external STROBE signal that latches external data into the data register. A 0 is produced when the processor reads the data register.
7	OUTPUT BUFFER FULL	The 8255 outputs a 0 on this line to indicate the processor has filled the buffer, and a 1 when an external ACK is received to indicate the contents have been read.
6	ACK L	A 0 on this input indicates that the output of Port *A* has been accepted externally.
3	INTERRUPT	If the Port *A* interrupt is enabled for input operations, the 8255 produces a 1 on this pin when a STROBE returns to 1 after filling an input buffer. This output returns to 0 when the input buffer is read. For output operations, this signal becomes 1 when an ACK is sensed by the 8255, and becomes 0 when the data buffer is rewritten.

Show a strategy for interconnecting computers with a pair of parallel I/O ports. Assume that data flows in one direction from Computer 1 to Computer 2, and that the transmission is interrupt driven. Assume specific port addresses for setting the mode and direction of the 8255, and for accessing the I/O buffer in Port *A*. Show the interconnections and signaling behavior required to attain a fully interlocked asynchronous handshake.

7 / MAGNETIC-RECORDING TECHNIQUES

This chapter covers the basic principles for interfacing microcomputers to magnetic-recording devices such as cassette tapes, cartridge tapes, floppy disks, and hard disks. Although this material is oriented toward microprocessors, the information is of more general interest as well, since the principles hold for larger and faster computer systems, except for additional complexities in very high-performance systems. Because cost is a major factor in microprocessor systems, the usual design practice is to sacrifice high performance in return for low cost.

This chapter describes two types of recording devices—the tape medium as found in cassettes and the disk medium as found in flexible (floppy) disks and rigid (sometimes called "hard") disks. For tape media with low bit density, particularly for cassettes, the critical part of the interfacing problem is to eliminate sensitivity to the mechanical speed of the recorder. Home recorders are quite adequate for microprocessor applications, but the speed variations from recorder to recorder or in a given recorder over a period of time are rather substantial. The device interface must be insensitive to minor speed variations in order to assure reliable recovery of data, especially when tapes are to be used by different recorders. The discussion in this chapter shows two different techniques for data recovery, one of which is a software self-timing technique and the other is the use of a feedback circuit known as a *phase-locked loop*. Besides its use in magnetic recording and playback, the phase-locked loop has many other computer applications such as receiving circuits that must adapt to the signaling frequency of a particular peripheral device or communications channel. So, although the material is focused toward magnetic recording, the content is generally useful for such other applications as clock recovery for high-speed HDLC data channels, which were discussed earlier in this textbook.

The latter part of this chapter treats disk interfacing techniques. For disks the data density is usually high enough to interfere with the ability to lock on to the frequency of the recovered data stream. While phase-locked loops are useful for recovering data from disks, they are normally used for long-term stability, and other techniques are used for short-term timing. A digital form of a phase-locked loop is used to give gross estimates of the average clock rate, and fine tuning is done through timing compensation, amplitude compensation, or other analog techniques.

Other recording media commonly used for microprocessor systems are data cartridges, reel-to-reel tapes, and video cassettes. While recording densities and data transfer rates may be quite different for these media than for other devices discussed in this chapter, the principles are the same. A designer will find this chapter useful background for interfacing to virtually any magnetic recording device.

7.1 TAPE INTERFACES

A tape interface must be insensitive to speed variations in the mechanical tape drive, and therefore the interface must, as part of the data recovery operation, be able to detect the frequency of the recovered data. Under ideal circumstances, a local clock in the data recovery portion of a tape interface supplies the basic timing for the incoming data stream. However, if the local clock is slightly different from the frequency of the recovered data, then eventually the local clock will lose synchronization with the incoming stream, and the result will be loss of data.

A costly way to solve the problem is to use very tight frequency control for recording and playback and to resynchronize the data stream at regular intervals, so preventing the inevitable loss of sync that otherwise occurs when two clocks are slightly different in frequency. Since the frequency of the recovered data stream is directly related to the mechanical speed of the tape drive, the implication is that the mechanical portions of the drive must be built to very high precision to satisfy the frequency control problem. This obviously is an unsatisfactory solution where cost constraints preclude precision mechanical devices. There are, in fact, very simple electronic techniques for eliminating problems caused by mechanical speed variations.

What is necessary is a signaling scheme that not only presents data as a sequence of 1s and 0s, but encodes them in such a way that it is possible to recover the underlying clock frequency of the transmitter from the data stream. Such signaling schemes are said to be "self-clocking," and they are used in virtually every digital magnetic-recording device. As a first, simple example of a self-clocking signaling scheme, consider the signals shown in Fig. 7.1. A 0 is encoded as a signal that oscillates at a high frequency f for the

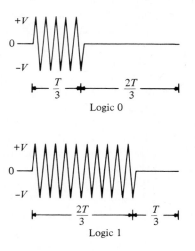

FIGURE 7.1 A signal encoding scheme for a simple self-clocking magnetic tape system.

first third of its duration and thereafter is constant. A 1 bit is recorded as a signal that oscillates at f for the first two-thirds of its duration, and is constant after that. A stream of bits encoded this way is easily decomposed back into 0s and 1s. Assume that a new bit starts at each transition from no oscillation to oscillation. Within each bit time the receiver has to determine if the datum is a 1 or a 0, and to do so the receiver simply has to determine if the oscillation occupies one-third or two-thirds of the bit duration. A suitable way of doing this is to measure the time for the oscillation and the time of no oscillation. If the oscillation time is longer than the constant-voltage time, the bit is decoded as a 1; otherwise it is decoded as a 0. This scheme is rather tolerant of variations between playback and recording speeds.

Figure 7.2 shows a block diagram for a tape interface built on this principle. The interface contains a local oscillator that produces the recorded frequency f_c, and a lower frequency f_b that determines the recording rate for information. For simplicity, the data-rate clock is typically obtained by dividing frequency f_c by some convenient integer. For home recorders, frequency f_c should be under 10 kHz; but as f_c decreases, then so does the basic data rate. A reasonable choice is to make f_c approximately 4.5 kHz, and set the data rate f_b at 300 Hz, which is $f_c/15$. Then a 0 is encoded as 5 cycles of f_c, followed by no signal for a duration equal to 10 cycles of f_c; a 1 bit is encoded as 10 cycles of f_c followed by a duration equal to 5 cycles of f_c. The divisor 15 can be reduced to 9 or to 6, or f_c can be increased above 4.5 kHz, with a resulting increase in the recorded data rate and a reduction in noise rejection capability. The recorder in Fig. 7.2 can be any home-quality recorder; high precision is not required. While the signal oscillates, the recorder stores magnetic transitions on the tape. These transitions are recovered on playback. The absence of transitions results in the recorder producing only background noise (such as tape hiss) from the tape or noise from its own amplifier. Typically, the voltage excursion on playback from noise is much less than that of the signal, so that the recorded signal can be

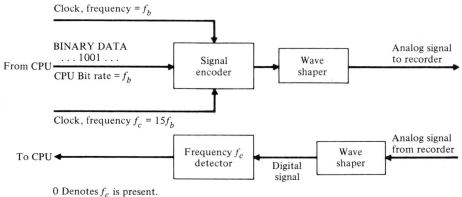

0 Denotes f_c is present.
1 Denotes f_c is not present.

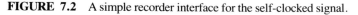

FIGURE 7.2　A simple recorder interface for the self-clocked signal.

used to trigger a flip-flop or a one-shot and produce a logic 0 as shown in the detector module when f_c is present and a logic 1 when f_c is not present (or conversely). There are various ways that the original data can be recovered from this encoded form of signal. A purely hardware approach uses an integrator at the detector output. It is cleared at the start of each bit and sampled at the end. If the average value of the detector voltage is greater than half of the value produced by a signal that oscillates during the entire bit duration, then the signal is decoded as a 1; otherwise the bit is decoded as a 0. Another purely software approach is worth illustrating here. An integrator is simulated by incrementing a counter when the detector indicates that f_c is present and by decrementing the counter when f_c is not present. If the counter has a positive value at the end of a bit time, the signal is decoded as a 1. An example of a short program in a high-level language for this purpose is Program 7.1.

PROGRAM 7.1   Cassette-Reader Program

```
begin counter := 0;
    while detector output = 1 do counter := counter + 1;
    while detector output = 0 do counter := counter − 1;
    if counter > 0 then accept a 1 else accept a 0;
end
```

This program looks deceptively simple. But if the program is compiled into machine language and executed, the user may discover a built-in bias toward accepting a 0 or a 1, depending on the specific instructions that are used to implement the statements given. In order to set the decision threshold halfway between a 0 and 1, the two loops must each take the same amount of time per count, and the overhead of entering and leaving a loop must be carefully programmed to eliminate bias that may creep in from this source. A satisfactory implementation in machine language for a typical microprocessor is Program 7.2. For the microprocessor in question, we presume that the DEC and INC take equal time to execute, as do BNZ and BRZ.

A number of minor details have been omitted from the program for the sake of clarity. The output bits have to be concatenated into a buffer by instructions that use indexing or shifting in some combination. In addition, the initial value of the counter should be set to a value that accounts for the presence of frequency f_c when the program first enters the loop. Note that the two loops in the program are equal in length, and both contain instructions whose execution times are also equal. The overhead of accepting a bit requires the execution of possibly many instructions whose time may bias the timing for the receipt of the next bit. To remove this bias, a nonzero value is used for the initial value of the counter to reflect the time spent in accepting and storing a new datum.

At this point we turn our attention to a much higher performance tape interface based on principles developed for very high-speed devices. The recorder interface is compatible with the popular Kansas City Standard (KCS) for cassette recording. While this system is used by many manufacturers, the standard is not recognized by any official standards organization and is far from being universally accepted in the industry.

PROGRAM 7.2　Assembly-Language Version of Cassette-Reader Program

NEWBIT	CLEAR	COUNTER	Get ready for next bit.
	BRA	L2	Enter loop looking for f_c.
L1	INC	COUNTER	Increase count.
L2	INPUT	TAPEIN	Test to see if frequency f_c is present.
	BNZ	L1	If not 0, go back, and look for f again.
L3	DEC	COUNTER	Count down because f_c was not there.
	INPUT	TAPEIN	Test to see if frequency f_c is present.
	BRZ	L3	If 0, branch to loop beginning.
	CLEAR	R	Initialize the output bit to 0.
	TST	COUNTER	Decide whether data was a 0 or 1.
	BMI	L4	If negative it was a 0.
	INC	R	Make the bit a 1.
L4	...		Output the bit in R, typically using indexing or shifting. At this point, test to see if more bits should be received. If so, initialize COUNTER and return to L2 to obtain them. If not, then exit.

The encoding technique used by the Kansas City Standard is shown in Fig. 7.3. Figure 7.3(a) shows a 0 recorded as four full cycles of a 1200 Hz square wave. A binary 1 is recorded as eight full cycles of a 2400 Hz square wave as shown in Fig. 7.3(b). Note that the time duration of a 0 and a 1 are equal, and that certain transitions appear in both the 1200 Hz and the 2400 Hz square wave. With this encoding scheme, the transmission rate for a single bit is 1/4 of 1200 Hz, or 300 Hz. The transitions common to both the binary 0

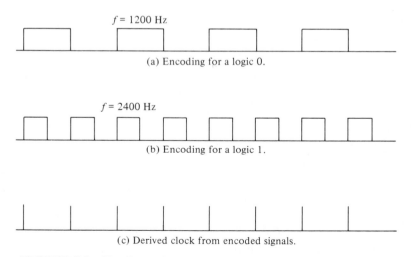

$f = 1200$ Hz

(a) Encoding for a logic 0.

$f = 2400$ Hz

(b) Encoding for a logic 1.

(c) Derived clock from encoded signals.

FIGURE 7.3　Signal encoding and derived clock for Kansas City Standard recording systems.

and binary 1 are used to lock a local oscillator to the incoming data rate when the data are recovered from the recording. Figure 7.3(c) shows the derived clock from the waveforms for 0 and 1. Note that the clock "ticks" occur during the transitions common to both the 0 and 1 signals, whether the transitions are in phase or not. So the clock detector must look for the presence of a transition, and ignores the polarity of the transition. If a transition occurs between clock ticks, the detector assumes that a 1 is encoded; otherwise the detector assumes the code is a 0.

To increase the information transmission rate of the Kansas City Standard, we simply use fewer transitions to encode each datum. The normal rate for the interchange of information is 300 Hz, but minor changes to the basic interface produces higher nonstandard transmission rates. At an information rate of 1200 Hz, the sequence 1100 is encoded as shown in Fig. 7.4(a). Here the binary 0 requires one full cycle of 1200 Hz, and the binary 1 requires two cycles of 2400 Hz. This might appear to be the highest limit of a modified standard if the recording technique is to use 1200 and 2400 Hz as its basic frequencies. But the standard can be pushed to 2400 Hz as shown by the encoding scheme in Fig. 7.4(b). In this scheme, a binary 0 is half a cycle of 1200 Hz, and a 1 is one full cycle of 2400 Hz. Each digit, whether a 0 or 1, begins with a transition. A binary 1 is a full cycle of a 2400-Hz signal whose phase depends on the final voltage of the immediately preceding bit. Likewise the phase of the ½-cycle pulse of 1200 Hz that represents a 0 depends on the final voltage of the preceding bit. Two successive 0s are therefore encoded as pulses of opposite polarity. This coding scheme is what is obtained when an encoder for 300 Hz is used with a data rate of 2400 Hz.

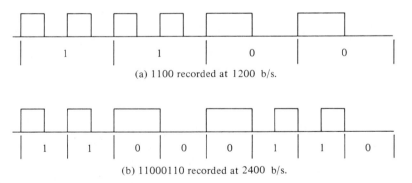

(a) 1100 recorded at 1200 b/s.

(b) 11000110 recorded at 2400 b/s.

FIGURE 7.4   Maximum data rate recording in the Kansas City Standard.

A block diagram of a cassette interface is shown in Fig. 7.5. The output of a serial-interface chip is a serial bit stream running at the clock rate of the output data (300 bits per second for the standard transmission rate). This bit stream modulates a 4800-Hz clock and divides it by two or four, depending if the output data is a 1 or 0, respectively. A wave shaper takes off the sharp edges of the output data, removes the DC component, and

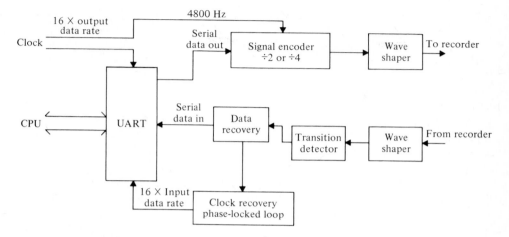

FIGURE 7.5   Block diagram of tape interface for Kansas City Standard.

drives the cable to the recorder. On playback, the analog signal is amplified and limited to create a reproduction of the modulated signal that was originally recorded. This signal passes through a transition detector that finds the edges of the signal. The output of this stage is a pulse train similar to the one in Fig. 7.3(c). The pulse train drives a one-shot that is designed to retrigger for pulses created by transitions in a 2400-Hz signal, but will time-out for pulses derived from a 1200-Hz signal. The fall of the one-shot denotes a 0 received, and the retriggering of the one-shot denotes a 1 received.

The one-shot would be sufficient for recreating the recorded data, were it not for the possible variations in data rate on playback due to fluctuations in the speed of the playback mechanism and other sources of data distortion in the data recovery electronics. A good interface can take advantage of the self-clocking nature of the recorded signal to derive a clock useful for sampling the recovered data at the playback rate, which is not necessarily at the exact data rate of its original recording. In Fig. 7.5 the data detector produces a clock output as well as a data output. The clock output is a pulse at the beginning of each bit period. This pulse drives the clock recovery circuit. The clock-recovery circuit is a phase-locked loop that oscillates at a multiple of the data rate of the clock, which is the usual requirement for a clock input to a serial port. Figure 7.5 shows the recovered data and the recovered clock combined together at the serial port, which transforms the serial input into a byte-parallel stream for transmission to computer memory.

Software control of data rate is readily available quite simply for the type of interface shown in Fig. 7.5. The idea is to select the transmit and receive clocks to the serial port under software control. For example, two control bits developed at the output of an I/O port can drive a pair of four-to-one multiplexers—one stage for transmit and one for receive. The transmit clock simply selects from 300, 600, 1200, and 2400 Hz, which may be produced at successive stages of a counter. (Actually these clocks are a fixed multiple of the serial-port data rate, typically 16 or 64 times the data rate.) The receive clock is connected to successive taps of a counter that counts the pulses produced by the phase-locked loop. The phase-locked loop in this diagram oscillates at 38.4 kHz, or 16 times the 2400 Hz maximum data rate of the system. This, then, is the correct clock for recovery of a 2400-Hz data rate. Clocks for data rates 1200, 600, and 300 Hz are available at the outputs of stages of a frequency divider internal to the phase-locked loop.

The self-clocking of the recorded data substantially improves the ability to interchange cassette tapes from one recorder to another in spite of variations in mechanical-transport speeds. However, there is a hidden cost in going to this level of sophistication. Since the interface requires the phase-locked loop to lock onto the clock of the incoming signal, the signal must be recorded synchronously, that is, locked to a particular clock rate. Data must be produced in bursts that can be recorded as contiguous blocks. Should there be idle time between bursts of data, then the data should be recorded with one or more synchronizing characters prefixed to each burst to permit the phase-locked loop to acquire the clock for the burst. The interface may also introduce a continuous stream of null characters to maintain phase lock between blocks. Data cannot simply be recorded one byte at a time whenever a program produces an output byte. Rather, data must be buffered into blocks when they are generated and then recorded as blocks with no gaps between bytes.

Speed variation may not be a problem if data are recorded and played back on the same cassette recorder, provided that the recorder has good speed stability. In this case, the receive clock of the serial port can be connected to the transmit clock, and the phase-locked loop can be eliminated. This reduces the cost of the interface, and eliminates the need to record data according to strict timing rules. But the recovery of data will be more sensitive to speed variations, and reliability can be a problem if an aging recorder changes in speed over a long period of time.

Principles of Phase-Locked Loops

The use of the phase-locked loop in a cassette interface is just one of its many important applications. Because the phase-locked loop appears so frequently in computer interfaces, we devote this subsection to the detailed principles of its design, and show some simple ways of implementing the circuit for a cassette interface.

The basic structure of a phase-locked loop is shown in Fig. 7.6. The circuit consists of a phase detector that compares an incoming signal with a reference signal. A voltage proportional to the phase difference is produced, filtered, and then fed to a voltage-controlled oscillator. For the cassette interface, this oscillator operates at 32 times the nominal 1200 Hz clock rate of the input signal to provide the receive clock for the serial port. Since the oscillator operates at a much higher frequency than the incoming signal, the oscillator output is not directly compared to the incoming signal, but is first divided down to the correct frequency, and then compared.

The role of the filter in the design of the loop is critical in terms of determining the ability of the loop to lock onto a signal, reject noise, respond to transient changes, and

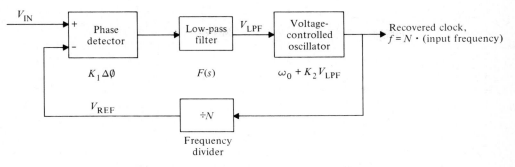

FIGURE 7.6   Block diagram of a phase-locked loop.

stay in lock as an input signal deviates above and below the ideal center frequency. To understand the operation of the filter, we first examine the output of the phase detector so that we can determine the requirements for the filter output.

There are a number of very simple phase detectors that are suitable for measuring the phase of a square-wave clock. One of the most simple is the EXCLUSIVE OR-gate detector whose behavior is illustrated in Fig. 7.7. Consider what happens when two clocks of equal frequency but different phase are fed to the respective inputs of an EXCLUSIVE-OR gate. The gate output is the difference signal shown in Fig. 7.7 for various phase shifts

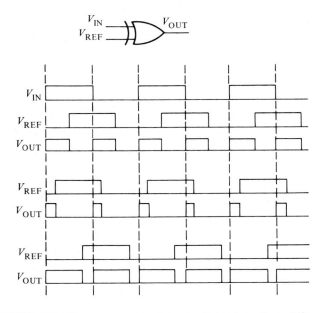

FIGURE 7.7   Phase-comparator behavior for various phase differences.

between input and reference clocks. Note that the difference signal is a signal of twice the frequency of the clocks, and it spends proportionately greater time at 1 or at 0, depending on whether the clocks have equal polarity or opposite polarity for the majority of a clock period. The output is identically 0 when the two clocks are in exact phase, identically a logic 1 when the two clocks are in exact opposite phase; and it is an oscillating signal with a 50% duty cycle when the two clocks are 90° out of phase.

The average value of the difference voltage is the key parameter because it indicates the true phase difference of the signals. Figure 7.8 is a plot of the average value of the difference voltage as a function of phase difference. This plot presumes that the input signal and the reference signal are both clocks with a 50% duty cycle. If either or both have a duty cycle other than 50%, the plot retains the same general shape, but the slope of the lines is reduced. For the 50% duty-cycle case in the figure, the average voltage moves from 0.3 V for 0° phase difference to 3.6 V for 180° phase difference, so that the slope is approximately $3.3/\pi$ V/rad. Since we wish to maximize the slope to maximize the sensitivity of the phase-locked loop, it is a good idea to ensure that the clock has a 50% duty cycle. Indeed, this is the case in the block diagram of the system shown in Fig. 7.5. The clock ticks fed to the phase-locked loop are derived from the transitions of a 2400-Hz signal, two per cycle, so that the basic rate is 4800 Hz. However, clock ticks at a 4800-Hz rate cannot be recovered directly from the transitions of a logic 0 that is encoded at a 1200-Hz frequency. The missing clock ticks for a logic 0 are regenerated by the fall of the one-shot that detects the presence of a 1200-Hz pulse. Unfortunately, the tick inserted does not come midway in a 2400-Hz cycle. The tick depends on when the one-shot falls, which should be roughly three-quarters of the way through a 2400-Hz cycle. By dividing down the nonuniform 4800-Hz signal through a two-stage divider, we guarantee that the resulting square wave has a 50% duty cycle. The idea is to use every fourth clock tick out

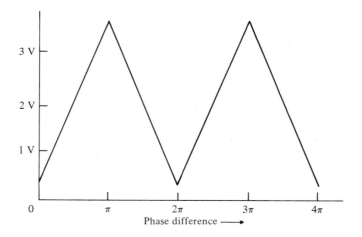

FIGURE 7.8   Average output voltage of phase comparator.

of the detector, and to be sure to discard the ticks generated by the one-shot when counting down the frequency.

At this point, we see that the average voltage from the EXCLUSIVE-OR gate has the proper information to drive the voltage-controlled oscillator. In the loop's quiescent state, the input signal clock leads the reference clock by 90°, so that the average difference voltage is halfway between logic 1 and logic 0. If the input signal clock drifts to a slightly higher frequency, the change will show up initially as an input signal phase leading the reference signal by more than 90° and, as a result, an average difference voltage that will increase toward logic 1. This voltage increase speeds up the oscillator and causes it to reach a steady-state frequency equal to that of the input frequency. The phase error will be just enough greater than 90° so that the filtered error voltage will maintain the higher frequency. (Alternatively, one can build a voltage-controlled oscillator whose frequency decreases with increasing voltage. In this case, the loop automatically assumes a quiescent state in which the reference leads rather than lags the input by 90°.)

Now the problem is to pass the average voltage of the phase-detector to the voltage-controlled oscillator; to do so, it is necessary to filter the phase-detector output. For our purposes a simple RC filter is sufficient to do the job. The circuit is shown in Fig. 7.9. Just how this filter affects the behavior of the phase-locked loop is detailed below.

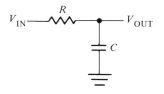

FIGURE 7.9 An RC low-pass filter suitable for a phase-locked loop.

To analyze the transient behavior of the loop to a step change in the input frequency, we use the appropriate mathematical tool, the Laplace transform. The phase-locked loop is a feedback-control system that cannot follow sudden changes in the input frequency, but rather settles over a period of time to its steady-state behavior. Either this settling behavior may oscillate above and below the asymptotic output frequency with the oscillations eventually dying out, or the circuit may settle exponentially to the steady-state value with no oscillations at all. We use Laplace transforms to find the transfer function of the loop. From this we can discover the natural frequency of oscillation about the steady-state output and the damping factor that dictates how long the loop takes to settle to its steady-state output. Table 7.1 contains a brief list of Laplace transforms of common functions to assist the reader in recalling the details of the technique.

To begin, let K_1 be the gain of the phase-detector in volts per radian, K_2 the gain of the voltage-controlled oscillator in rad/s·V, N the divisor of the frequency divider, and

TABLE 7.1   Table of Laplace Transform Pairs

Function	Transform
$u(t)$, the unit step	$\dfrac{1}{s}$
t, the unit ramp	$\dfrac{1}{s^2}$
$\delta(t)$, the unit impulse	1
e^{-at}	$\dfrac{1}{s+a}$
$\sin \omega t$	$\dfrac{\omega}{s^2+\omega^2}$
$\cos \omega t$	$\dfrac{s}{s^2+\omega^2}$
t^n	$\dfrac{n!}{s^{n+1}}$
$e^{-at}f(t)$	$F(s+a)$
$e^{-at}\sin \omega t$	$\dfrac{\omega}{(s+a)^2+\omega^2}$
$e^{-at}\cos \omega t$	$\dfrac{s+a}{(s+a)^2+\omega^2}$

note that the filter transfer function is $1/(1+RCs)$. This latter follows because the transfer function is $F(s)=Z_C/(Z_R+Z_C)$, where $Z_R=R$ and $Z_C=1/Cs$. To compute the behavior of the loop, observe that the reference frequency is given by the equation

$$V_{REF}(s)=K_1K_2F(s)\frac{\Delta\phi}{N},$$

where $\Delta\phi$ is the phase difference between the input and reference voltages. Since phase is the integral of frequency, we use the relation

$$\Delta\phi=\frac{V_{IN}-V_{REF}}{s}$$

We can solve for the ratio of output to input to obtain the transfer function

$$\frac{V_{REF}(s)}{V_{IN}(s)}=\frac{K_1K_2/NRC}{s^2+s/RC+K_1K_2/NRC}.$$

This is the equation of a second-order system. If we write the equation in the form of a general second-order system, the right-hand side becomes

$$\frac{K}{s^2+2d\omega_n s+\omega_n^2},$$

where ω_n is the natural frequency of the system and d is the damping factor. For the phase-locked loop we have

$$\omega_n = \sqrt{\frac{K_1 K_2}{NRC}}$$

and

$$d = \frac{\sqrt{N/K_1 K_2 RC}}{2} = \frac{N \omega_n}{2 K_1 K_2}.$$

To complete the design of the filter, we simply have to pick R and C so that we obtain a desirable natural frequency and damping factor.

To understand the effects of the selection of R and C, consider the behavior of the second-order system for this example as shown in Fig. 7.10. This shows the transient response to a sudden shift of frequency. The response calculation is made by treating the shift in input frequency as a step change, which has a Laplace Transform of $1/s$. Then the response is given by the inverse Laplace transform of $1/s$ times the transfer function

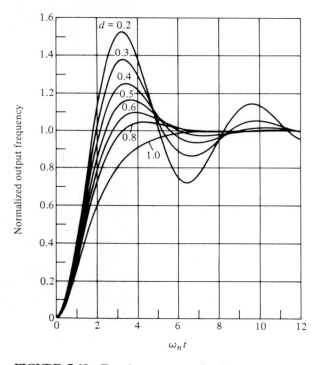

FIGURE 7.10 Transient response of a phase-locked loop to a step change in input frequency.

V_{REF}/V_{IN}. The response has two components—one the inverse transform of $1/s$, which is the unit step, and the other the inverse transform of the transfer function, which is a damped sinusoid. The shapes of the curves in Fig. 7.10 clearly show the combination of a damped exponential and unit step, with the amount of damping and the frequency of the damped sinusoid varying with the parameters of the RC filter. Note that the lightly damped systems have severe overshoot, indicating that if the input shifts suddenly, as it does during initial synchronization, lightly damped systems will not track for a short period of time. Consequently, they require longer synchronization periods. Heavily damped systems are sluggish in response, and have narrower bandwidths of operation. For most purposes, it is best to select damping factors so that the system responds to a step input with a small overshoot followed by fast settling. For our purposes, a damping factor of $d = 0.7$ is adequate, but it can be a little higher or lower without a serious consequence.

The natural frequency and the damping factor are determined solely by the gain factors, K_1 and K_2, and the time constant of the filter, RC. The constants K_1 and K_2 are determined by our choice of the EXCLUSIVE-OR gate as phase detector, and by the selection of a suitable voltage-controlled oscillator. These constants are usually not alterable by the designer once a specific device or devices for the phase-locked loop are selected, except for small variations due to differences in devices, aging, and temperature. Consequently, once we have set the damping factor, we have uniquely determined the time constant RC, and this constant, in turn, uniquely determines the natural frequency of the loop.

Since the choice of damping factor for our simple RC filter determines the natural frequency, we must investigate the way that the natural frequency is related to loop behavior. In general, the lower the natural frequency, the slower the loop in response to transients and the smaller the range of frequencies over which the loop will acquire lock. In Fig. 7.10, at a given settling point, the product of natural frequency and time is a fixed value. Hence if natural frequency decreases, then time increases; and we have to wait longer to reach this settling point as a result of a transient. The interaction of damping factor with natural frequency complicates the situation somewhat. For the RC filter, the damping factor increases with natural frequency, which lengthens the settling time as the damping factor grows larger than unity. Consequently, it is best to select the RC time constant for a suitable damping factor, and verify that the transient behavior is acceptable. The natural frequency must, of course, be lower than the input frequency of the loop, say to $1/10$ the input frequency, to prevent the input signal from setting up a stable oscillation in the loop. If it is impossible to choose R and C to meet these conditions, then the designer should use a more complex filter, like one of those shown in Fig. 7.11 that permits the designer to set both the damping factor and loop frequency independently.

As an example of a check on the transient response of a loop, suppose we wish for the loop in Fig. 7.5 to settle into phase lock after receiving two synchronizing characters at the beginning of a transmission. Also suppose that the choice of R and C for a damping factor of 0.7 leads to a natural frequency of 120 Hz. The sync characters are each encoded with 10 bits, and therefore the synchronization should be achieved within 20 cycles of

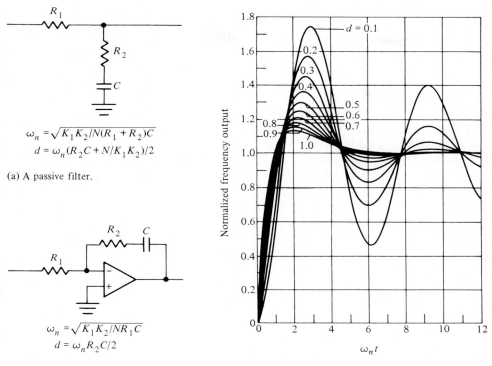

$$\omega_n = \sqrt{K_1 K_2 / N(R_1 + R_2)C}$$
$$d = \omega_n (R_2 C + N/K_1 K_2)/2$$

(a) A passive filter.

$$\omega_n = \sqrt{K_1 K_2 / NR_1 C}$$
$$d = \omega_n R_2 C/2$$

(b) An active filter.   (c) Transient response of both filters.

FIGURE 7.11   Useful filters for phase-locked loop systems.

2400 Hz, which is the information rate for the system and twice the phase-locked loop input frequency. At 120 Hz, the system must stabilize within one cycle. Figure 7.10 shows that for a damping factor of 0.7 the loop frequency settles to within a few percent of the signal center frequency after one cycle, which meets the design constraint. If the transient response is too slow, it can be improved by choosing a filter with a higher natural frequency and the same damping factor (0.7), but there is some risk in moving too close to the input frequency of the loop. The alternative is to use a longer synchronizing sequence and to accept a poorer transient response.

Loop performance is often characterized in terms of hold-in and capture capability. The *hold-in range* is the range of frequencies for which the loop will stay in lock once it is locked. This is solely a function of the maximum tolerable error signal at the output of the low-pass filter. Note that as the input frequency deviates farther and farther from the loop's center frequency, the phase shift between reference and input increases until the shift reaches the point at which the maximum error voltage is generated. Any additional frequency difference will cause phase lock to be lost. Since the maximum phase difference is 180°, the average error voltage at this point is $K_1\pi/2$, and the frequency of the voltage-controlled oscillator is $K_1K_2\pi/2$ away from the center frequency. The reference frequency is then $K_1K_2\pi/2N$ from center and this is ½ the hold-in range. Hence the hold-in range ω_H is given by

$$\omega_H = \frac{K_1K_2\pi}{N}.$$

The *capture range* is the frequency range over which the loop will achieve phase lock. When the loop is out of phase lock, the reference-signal frequency is determined by the average voltage output of the phase detector. Since the reference frequency of an unlocked loop is not phase coherent with the input signal, the phase detector output has frequency components at the difference of the input and reference frequencies, and the difference frequency is passed by the filter while the other components are filtered out. The difference frequency voltage when applied to the voltage-controlled oscillator supplies a voltage that can bring the loop into lock. Consequently, the bandwidth of the loop determines the highest difference frequency that can be passed through to the reference signal. Because the filter is not ideal and attenuates signals near the upper end of its bandwidth, the actual capture frequency is less than the bandwidth of the filter. For the simple *RC* filter the capture range is given approximately by the equation

$$\omega_C \simeq \sqrt{\frac{\omega_H}{RC}} < \omega_H,$$

where ω_H is the hold-in range.

There are a number of phase-locked loop devices available as integrated circuits. Some devices have all of the necessary parts of a loop, except the loop filter. Other devices have specific sections of the loop, and must be used in conjunction with implementations of the missing sections. The CD4046 phase-locked loop integrated circuit contains everything except the filter and frequency divider. Its block diagram is shown in Fig. 7.12. It is quite adequate for the cassette interface, and needs only the *RC* filter, an external 5-stage binary counter, and a pair of resistors that define the voltage-controlled oscillator center frequency.

Although this analysis assumes a particular form of the filter, the general principles are valid regardless what kind of filter is used. Only the specific equations for the loop behavior, damping factor, and natural frequency differ in their dependence on the loop parameters. Two other types of popular filters for phased-locked loops appear in Fig. 7.11, together with the loop transfer function for that type of filter. The transfer function in both cases has the same form, and it yields a transient behavior that is similar in structure but different in detail to the curves shown in Fig. 7.10. The active filter, in general, tracks the input more closely than the passive filter because of the gain in the filter, but the gain may also lead to instability of the loop if it moves the poles of the second-order equation for the loop to the right half-plane. A good reference for the derivation of the phase-locked loop behavior is Moschytz (1965), and several semiconductor manufacturers summarize the pertinent equations, typical loop behavior, and filter design criteria in their

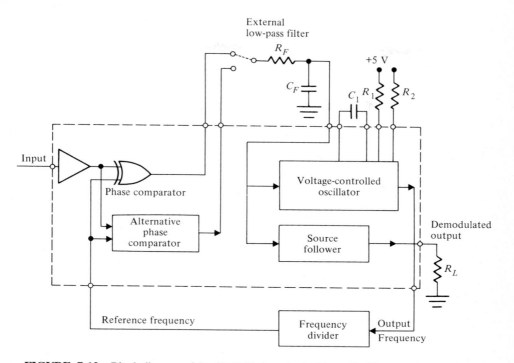

FIGURE 7.12   Block diagram of the CD4046 phase-locked loop; R_1, R_2, and C_1 determine the center frequency and the limit frequencies of the voltage-controlled oscillator.

literature for phase-locked loop devices. Gardner (1979) is a general reference text on phase-locked loops that includes material on other important questions such as noise rejection and stability. Many texts examine the second-order linear systems from the Laplace transform viewpoint; and in particular, Dorf (1980, pp. 110–119) describes the transient behavior analysis pertinent to our discussion here.

Example of an Interface with a Phase-Locked Loop

A complete schematic for a cassette interface with a phase-locked loop, clock-recovery circuit appears in Fig. 7.13. The interface is an adaptation of a circuit manufactured by Percom Data Company (Garland, Texas) and illustrates all of the principles described above. The output of the serial port controls a J-K flip-flop so that the J-K flip-flop divides the input frequency of 4800 Hz by 2 if the port output is a 0, and does nothing if the port output is a 1. This flip-flop in turn drives a second divider so that the net output frequency is either 1200 or 2400 Hz, depending on whether the first flip-flop divides the input frequency by 2 or by 1. The result is the phase-encoded signal of the Kansas City Standard.

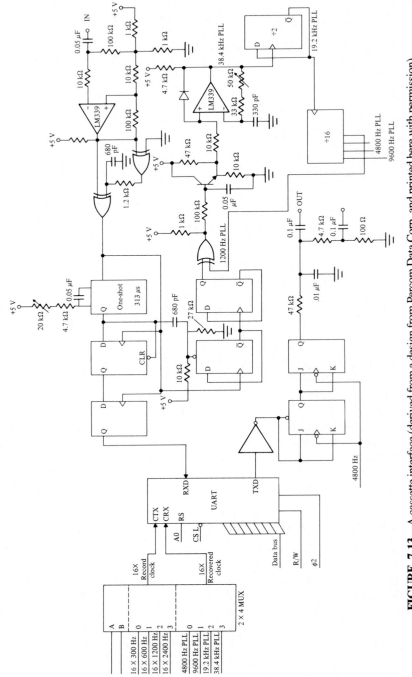

FIGURE 7.13 A cassette interface (derived from a design from Percom Data Corp. and printed here with permission).

The *RC* network filters out the sharp edges in the signal and reduces the voltage so that the signal is compatible with the signals accepted by cassette recorders.

For signal recovery this interface uses a comparator to shape the input signal to a "squared-up" signal that is a replica of the phase-encoded signal before filtering. Two EXCLUSIVE-OR gates act on this signal to produce a sequence of pulses that indicate where the transitions occur in the input signal. Note that the first gate in the pair is simply a buffer that drives an *RC* filter. The filtered signal has slightly rounded edges that, when compared with the original signal, is different only during the rising and falling edges of the original signal. Hence, the output of the second EXCLUSIVE-OR is a positive spike for both the rising and falling edges of the original signal.

The one-shot is tuned to retrigger when pulses come close together, as they do for encoded versions of logic 1, and to time-out when pulses are separated by longer periods, as they are for logic 0. Specifically, at 2400 Hz, a logic 1 produces pulses spaced at intervals of $1/4800 = 0.208$ ms, and a logic 0 produces pulses spaced at intervals of $1/2400 = 0.417$ ms. The one-shot should time-out about halfway between these values, or at about 0.313 ms. The output of the one-shot, when sampled at the end of a bit-period, contains the correct value of the recovered data, but the 0 levels occupy only about $\frac{1}{4}$ of a bit period instead of a full bit period. The one-shot output advances through two flip-flop stages that detect the correct value of the input data and stretch the 0s so that they occupy the full bit-time. The output from the second of these two stages is a faithful replica of the original data stream that was produced at the output of the serial port.

The recovered data can be sampled with an estimate of the correct clock; but to take advantage of the self-clocking nature of the signal encoding, the received clock should be generated from a phase-locked loop. The stream of pulses derived from the transitions in the encoded input data is fed to two D flip-flops that drive the phase-locked loop. The first of the flip-flops triggers a clock input twice for a logic 1, and once for a logic 0. To obtain a second count for a logic 0 (and thus produce a constant frequency output that is independent of the input data stream), a logic 0 sets the flip-flop, and thus supplies a second transition for 0s. The output of this flip-flop does not have a 50% duty cycle, however, because the logic 0 that sets the flip-flop is low for only about $\frac{1}{4}$ cycle instead of for $\frac{1}{2}$ cycle. But the next stage counts down again by 2, triggering only on the rising edge of the signal because this edge occurs consistently at the $0°$ and $180°$ phase points of a 1200-Hz signal. The falling edge is ignored, since its phase depends on whether the bit detected is a 0 or 1. The output of this stage is a 1200-Hz square wave with a 50% duty cycle.

The remainder of the circuit is a phase-locked loop. The input gate is an EXCLUSIVE-OR, which produces a 2400-Hz difference frequency. After filtering through an *RC* network, the resulting voltage is nearly constant, and about half of the peak-to-peak voltage at the EXCLUSIVE-OR output. Note that the resistor pulls up the EXCLUSIVE-OR gate output to nearly 5 V from a normal output of about 3.5 V. The effect of this change is to increase the gain factor K_1 or, equivalently, to increase the slope of the curve in Fig. 7.8. The change also increases the possible excursion of the filtered error signal to a range of 0–5 V from 0–3.5 V.

The *RC* filter produces the DC level required to drive the voltage-controlled oscillator, and this level is nominally at 2.5 V when the loop is operating in the middle of its range. The transistor circuit is an emitter-follower that isolates the filter output from the oscillator. At the emitter of this transistor, the signal is essentially identical to the input signal at the base, except that the voltage is reduced by one diode drop of about 0.7 V. Hence, the emitter voltage is approximately 1.8 V. Since the *RC* circuit cannot remove all AC components of the 2400-Hz difference frequency, there is a small triangular-shaped ripple voltage impressed on the DC component at the input and output of the emitter-follower. The ripple voltage does not affect the average frequency of the oscillator, but it does lead to nonuniform spacing of the transitions of the oscillator with observable jitter on the output waveform.

The oscillator in the diagram is of the relaxation type. The idea is that the positive input of the comparator is held to some fixed voltage while the negative input follows an exponential decay curve upward or downward, depending on the phase of the oscillation cycle. As the negative input reaches a voltage equal to the positive input, the output of the comparator suddenly switches, producing two different effects on the circuits. The change in output voltage causes the voltage at the negative input to decay in the opposite direction. Hence if the voltage is rising, it then begins to fall, and conversely. Meanwhile, the voltage at the positive input switches suddenly because the diode connected to the comparator output conducts when the comparator output drops. If the output is high, the positive-input voltage is high and equal to the emitter-follower output voltage. If the comparator output is low, the positive-input voltage is low and equal to one diode voltage drop above the comparator output.

The frequency of the relaxation oscillator thus depends on the time constant of the *RC* filter in the comparator's negative-input circuit. Assume initially that this circuit is discharged, so that the comparator output is high. The positive input is then at the emitter-follower voltage of about 1.8 V, and the negative input begins to charge to an asymptotic value of about 5 V. Later, the negative input reaches 1.8 V, and the comparator output drops to 0.3 V. Now the positive-input voltage is about 1.0 V, and the negative input begins to discharge toward 0.3 V. When the negative-input voltage reaches 1.0 V, the comparator output goes high and the cycle repeats. Note that the constant K_2 is negative for this oscillator because, as the emitter-follower voltage rises, the relaxations take longer and the frequency decreases.

The loop is adjusted to oscillate at 16 times 2400 Hz, which is 32 times the loop-input frequency of 1200 Hz. A D flip-flop followed by a 4-stage binary counter divides the loop output by 32 to produce the reference frequency to compare to the loop input. The oscillator output can be fed to a serial port as the recovered clock for 2400-Hz signals, and taps from other stages in the frequency divider provide recovered clocks for other data rates down to 300 Hz.

By using a CD4046 in place of the comparator and EXCLUSIVE-OR gate, a designer can make the phase-locked loop slightly more compact. The voltage-controlled oscillator shown with discrete components in Figure 7.13 is substantially the same as the oscillator on the CD4046 as well as other integrated-circuit oscillators.

7.2 MAGNETIC-DISK RECORDING TECHNIQUES

The previous section treats low-performance magnetic recording, with an emphasis on techniques suitable for cassette recording. In treating disk systems we find that the problems are much more complex because of the higher bit densities on the recording medium. In this case the recovered bit stream has a substantial amount of phase noise, often called *bit shifting*, which can cause severe problems in data recovery unless the disk interface compensates for or eliminates the phase noise. The magnetic tape medium, too, is subject to this problem in high-performance, high-density systems. So in this section we investigate what these problems are, and how today's designs treat and solve the problems. A phase-locked loop by itself is insufficient for clock recovery in high-performance magnetic-memory systems because the phase-locked loop tends to compensate incorrectly in the presence of bit shifting. However, phase-locked loops, in conjunction with other techniques, are widely used. The phase-locked loop extracts the clock and operates in a manner analogous to a flywheel, maintaining a constant frequency in spite of observed local deviations from the long-term average frequency. The other techniques compensate for the local deviations and enable the receiver to recover data information in spite of the phase noise in the input stream.

The structure of a floppy-disk controller is shown in Fig. 7.14. It bears a striking resemblance to that of the cassette-recorder controller: the recorded signal contains both signal and clock, and the interface produces the clock and data information from recorded data. The floppy-disk interface is somewhat more complex than a cassette interface because of the additional logic required for the sensing and control of the head's position. The data separator portion of the controller analyzes recovered data and produces two different outputs. One output is the recovered data itself, and the other is the clocking for the data. The recovered data stream is rarely an exact replica of the recorded data stream; it is made into an exact replica by using the associated clock to control the points at which the recovered data are sampled. The data separator is essentially identical in function to the cassette interface we discussed previously, but the two implementations of that function are considerably different.

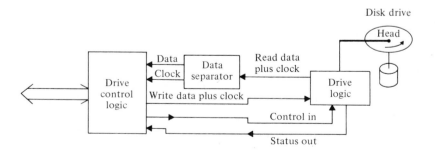

FIGURE 7.14 Floppy-disk interface structure.

Data recorded on floppy disks is magnetically recorded in essentially the same fashion as required by the Kansas City Standard for the cassette tapes described previously. Specifically, transitions of a magnetic field are recorded on the disk and observed during playback. The way that flux transitions encode data is shown in Fig. 7.15. Each pulse in the diagram corresponds to a flux change on the magnetic medium. The diagram shows a series of pulses transmitted to a floppy disk that control the points where a flux change is recorded. This figure shows one bit recorded every 4 µs. At the beginning of each 4-µs interval, a flux transition (or *clock* transition) is recorded. Halfway through the interval, the datum for that period is recorded either through the recording of a transition if the datum is a logic 1, or through the absence of a transition if the datum is a logic 0. The clock transitions guarantee that at least one transition occurs in each bit interval so that the receiver will be able to recover the apparent clock for the recorded data. Although we found that it is useful to extract the clock from a cassette's low-performance tape recorded data, the cassette interfaces will often work correctly even when the received clock is developed from a local oscillator and not locked onto the phase of the recovered data. In disk recording, however, it is absolutely essential to recover the clock from the recorded data because the data-recovery circuits must sample at intervals that have a tightly controlled tolerance with respect to the clock of the incoming data.

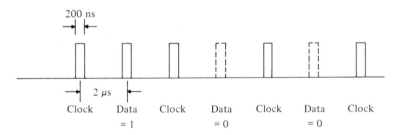

FIGURE 7.15   Data encoding for FM (single-density) recording.

We mentioned that the disk-recording scheme is essentially the same as the Kansas City Standard for cassette tapes. But Fig. 7.15 seems to contradict this statement. Instead of recording a logic 1 at double frequency, a logic 1 appears to be encoded as the presence of a bit. Similarly, a logic 0 is encoded as the absence of a transition, rather than as one cycle of a nominal frequency. But, by comparing this technique with the Kansas City Standard, we discover that the two are essentially the same. The information in Kansas City Standard recordings is in the transitions of the recorded data. A double frequency cycle has a transition in the middle of its cycle. This is a logic 1. Similarly, logic 0 is represented by recording half as many cycles at the nominal carrier frequency, which is the equivalent of recording no flux transition in the middle of a cycle. The disk-recording system is more widely known as *Manchester encoding*, and is sometimes called FM (frequency modulation) or *single density* to distinguish it from other schemes that achieve higher bit density.

The Manchester-encoding scheme is about 50% efficient in the encoding of raw bits. Assume that the clock rate is chosen so that bits are packed as closely as possible on the disk; and note that at this packing density only half of the bits contain information, while the remaining bits are used for clocking. If there were a way to recover clocking without wasting half of the bits, then it would be possible to double the number of information bits on a disk. Indeed, such an encoding scheme exists and is widely used today. This scheme is shown in Fig. 7.16 and is often called *double-density* or *MFM* (modified-FM) encoding. The idea is to assign a bit window for each bit, where the bit window is half the size of the window for single-density encoding. A logic 1 is encoded as a flux transition in the middle of that window, and a logic 0 is encoded as no flux transition in that window. But the clocking has to be encoded in some fashion as well, because otherwise the controller could not be sure where each 0 lies in a long string of 0s. To solve the clocking problem, a clock transition is recorded *between* two adjacent 0s as shown in the figure. No two transitions are closer than 2 μs apart, which is the same minimum spacing as in single-density recording. Moreover, each double-density bit occupies half the space of a single-density bit, and no bit cells are set aside for clock bits. But the controller is more complicated because it has to recognize clock bits that occasionally appear midway between data bits, whereas the single-density controller can presume there is always a clock bit and can trigger its recovery circuitry from that clocking point.

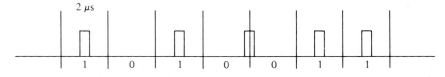

ENCODING STRUCTURE:

A 1 bit is encoded as a pulse in the middle of a bit window.

A 0 bit is encoded as the absence of a pulse in the middle of a bit window.

Insert a clock pulse at the transition of two windows if no pulse occurs in the middle of either window.

FIGURE 7.16   Modified FM (MFM) data-encoding double density.

While single-density encoding techniques have been informally standardized as Manchester encoding, double-density encoding is less uniformly accepted. Manufacturers have invented other techniques to achieve higher density, and there tends to be much less interchangeability for media recorded at densities higher than single-density. One scheme that is used by several manufacturers is the *group-code recording* (GCR) scheme shown in Fig. 7.17. In this scheme a group of four data bits is encoded as a block of five code bits. In each block of five bits a 1 is recorded as a flux transition, and a 0 is encoded as the absence of a flux transition. It is not necessary to record clock transitions in this scheme, since the 5-bit code groups are carefully selected so that the transitions in a continuously

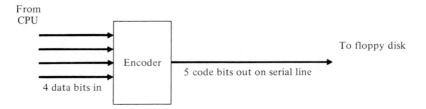

From
CPU

To floppy disk

Encoder

5 code bits out on serial line

4 data bits in

FIGURE 7.17   GCR encoding.

encoded bit stream will be spaced neither too closely nor too far apart. This scheme, then, uses 5-bit windows to encode four information bits, and is thus about 80% efficient. The encoding scheme must also lend itself to group synchronization so that the controller can break up a stream of recovered bits into groups of five bits at the correct 5-bit boundaries.

Disk recording, unlike tape recording, permits access to a specific block of information without requiring the reading of all other blocks that come before it. We say that access to data on magnetic tape is *serial access* because the controller must read $n - 1$ records before accessing the nth record, whereas disk access is sometimes called *random-access* or *direct-access*. In this context "random access" has a different connotation than the same term used in conjunction with semiconductor memory, where it means that the access time to any *individual item* is independent of the sequence of accesses. Disk systems do not have this property, so that the term "direct access" is more appropriate to them than "random access."

Figure 7.18 shows how direct access to information is aided by addressing information on disks. Two different methods for storing this information are commonly used for floppy disks, and variations of these methods are used in most other disk systems. In Fig. 7.18(a) we see a method, called "hard-sectoring," for dividing a disk into regions known as *sectors*. The disk has sector holes spaced around it at uniform intervals. One additional hole is placed at a nonuniform spacing with respect to the others to identify an index

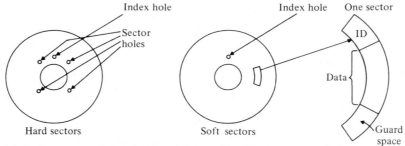

Index hole

Index hole   One sector

Sector
holes

ID

Data

Hard sectors

Soft sectors

Guard
space

(a) Only data are recorded.   (b) Data and sector identification are recorded.

FIGURE 7.18   (a) Hard sector and (b) soft sector recording.

point. As the disk spins on a drive, an optical device can detect the holes passing through its aperture, and thereby detect which sector is currently passing the read/write head. The figure shows four sectors located by sector holes, plus one index hole that identifies the adjacent sector hole as sector 1.

Access to data on a disk is essentially two dimensional for a single-sided floppy disk, and is three dimensional for disk systems that have several readable surfaces on a common spindle. One of the two dimensions of a floppy-disk is the sector position; the other is the track position. By placing the movable read/write head at a particular distance from the disk center, the head traces out a *track* of data as the disk spins beneath it. Mechanical positioning moves the head from track to track. Electronic circuitry senses the sector holes and identifies when a particular sector of the disk passes under the head. Thus by a combination of mechanical and electronic means, any given track/sector pair can be read or written.

Another means for achieving this same end is shown in Fig. 7.18(b). In this scheme there are no sector holes, but a single index hole provides a physical reference point. Sector information is encoded magnetically on the disk within each sector. That is, each sector contains an identifier field that appears on the data stream just before the data field. To read data, the head is first positioned at the correct track, where it reads the data stream continuously. When the head detects an identifier with the correct sector number, the data block that follows the identifier is accepted. To write a new data block, the disk controller first reads data continuously until it finds a matching sector number in an identifier, and then rewrites the new data over the existing data block as that block passes under the head. During normal operation the identifiers are never rewritten, although the controller has the capability to write those identifiers onto a blank disk when initializing a disk for its first use. This technique is called *soft sectoring* because the sector format of a disk can be freely changed by rewriting the sector identifiers on a new disk.

The soft-sectored format provides slightly less density than the hard-sectored, because the identifier field occupies space that is otherwise usable for data. But the soft-sectored format offers much greater versatility, since the user is free to format the disk in ways that are sensible for particular applications. The user can choose to have many short sectors per track or fewer sectors of longer length. The user can also number the sectors arbitrarily or interlace them around the track to minimize the rotational delay between sector accesses.

Figure 7.19 shows the structure of a typical sector in soft-sectored format. The leader, gap, and trailer region are regions of data padded with 00_{16} or FF_{16} whose function is explained later. The sector begins with a 6-byte leader, and then has a special byte called an *address mark*. This must be distinguishable from all other data patterns, including any arbitrary pattern that can appear in user data. To make the address mark distinguishable, some clock bits are dropped from the mark. Except for this mark and a few other control marks, all other patterns must have all clock bits present. Hence, a user cannot write a pattern that can be mistaken for a control byte.

The address mark is the pattern FE_{16}, and the corresponding clock pattern is $C7_{16}$. Since clock bits are dropped, the mark contains 1s in the data pattern between the missing

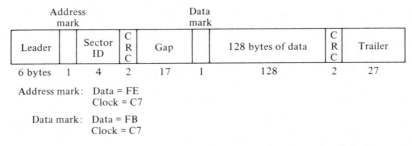

Address mark: Data = FE
Clock = C7

Data mark: Data = FB
Clock = C7

FIGURE 7.19   IBM 3740-compatible sector format (FM encoded): 188 bytes per sector, 68% data bytes.

clock bits in order to maintain clocking synchronization. Following the mark are four bytes of identifier. These give, respectively, the track, sector, side (top or bottom), and block-length code for the following data block. The CRC bytes shown in the figure are a cyclic redundancy check on the identifier block so that a controller can be sure that the identifier is read correctly. After the identifier block there is a gap of 17 bytes, a data mark, and the block of data, followed by two CRC bytes and a trailer.

The leader, trailer, and gap are embedded in the sector for several reasons. Because data blocks are written and rewritten from time to time, the identifier and data blocks are not synchronized to the same clock. The leader and gap provide additional bytes that can be used by a phase-locked loop to acquire the recorded clock. Quite apart from synchronization, the physical length of a data block depends on the speed of the drive and the exact clock rate of the controller that writes the data on the drive. Hence speed and clock variations from drive to drive are reflected in a variation in the physical length of a sector. But a sector must fit within a specific space; it cannot be so long as to overlap the identifier of the next sector. Hence the padding after the data block allows for some variation in the physical length of a data block.

In addition to these factors, the head geometry is a principal factor in determining the length of the padded areas. The geometry is shown in Fig. 7.20, where we see three physical gaps in the head. (These gaps are not the same as gaps between data blocks written on magnetic disks.) The center gap is the read/write gap, and it is sandwiched between two

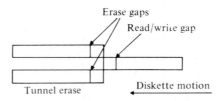

FIGURE 7.20   The tunnel-erase head.

erase gaps that form a "tunnel" for it. The magnetic field of the read/write head is generally wider than the read/write gap, and thus results in track widths that are larger than the mechanical geometry permits. The purpose of the tunnel-erase gaps is to trim the recorded track to the nominal track size. Trimming is an effective means of reducing track widths, and thereby decreasing the track-to-track spacing.

Padding between data blocks is required because there is a significant variation in time between the point at which the read/write head records a transition and the time that same transition reaches the erase gaps for trimming. The gaps are a fixed distance apart, but the linear speed of the medium depends on the track radius and instantaneous motor speed. Hence, the minimum time between read/write gap and erase gap is as small as 213 μs (on an outer track with a "fast" motor), and can be as large as 528 μs (on an inner track with a "slow" motor). It is not possible for a controller to turn the erase gap on at precisely the correct time to trim the first bit written on the disk. Hence the controller turns on the erase gap and the read/write gap at the same time (within a few microseconds), and relies on the leader, gap, and trailer bytes to provide the necessary protection against accidental erasure of identifier-block data. The identifier blocks cannot be tunnel-erased after their initial writing and tunnel erasure. A second tunnel erasure degrades the recorded signal because it is extremely unlikely that the second-round tunnel-erase gaps will be aligned to the data exactly as they were when the data were first erased.

We mentioned earlier that some disk systems have multiple recorded surfaces so that surface selection is a third dimension of a memory system. Typical systems of this type select one surface at a time by electronic means, although the mechanical positioner may drive several heads simultaneously to corresponding points on their respective surfaces. The advantage of this type of design is to reduce mechanical costs by sharing the positioner mechanism with many recording surfaces. Some high-performance memory systems of this type can read or write simultaneously through several recording heads.

Thus far we have discussed the major features of magnetic disk recording, but we have not yet addressed the question of the design of a disk interface. Most of the following information applies not only to floppy-disks, but to all types of disks in use today (except in specific details).

Disk-Controller Design

One of the major differences between a floppy-disk controller and a cassette controller is the clock-recovery circuit. As bit densities become greater and greater, there are various factors that cause the recovered data to appear shifted from their nominal position. Figure 7.21 shows the phenomenon as it appears to a disk controller. In the upper trace we see five transitions recorded on the disk at the positions shown. When these transitions are read back from the disk, the pulses are shifted in time from their apparent recorded position: Some pulses appear earlier and others appear later. What is happening is a combination of many factors, including magnetic interactions and nonlinearities in the pickup electronics. An oversimplified model gives an intuitive view of why the bits are shifted. The flux transitions recorded on the disk are very much like small magnets. In the upper

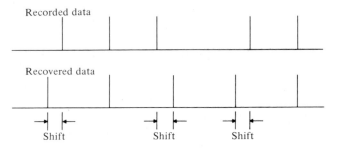

FIGURE 7.21   Problems of data recovery: Bit shifting.

diagram of Fig. 7.21, the transitions shown in time are associated with a small magnetic domain on the disk. Consider the group of three recorded bits on the left of the diagram. The leftmost one has a bit on its right but not its left. Hence, its corresponding magnetic domain is influenced by a like magnetic pole on its right, but not on its left. Thus the magnetic flux lines are distorted and bend away from the nearby right pole, and the magnetic domain itself may shift to the left slightly in the magnetic medium. The drive electronics senses the first transition as it passes under the read head; but because of the field distortion, the possible shift of the actual recorded domain, and the electrical response properties of the read/write head, the apparent position of the first bit transition has been shifted to the left, as if repelled by the flux transition on its right.

Carrying this reasoning further, we can see that the middle of three flux transitions is affected equally by flux transitions on the left and right, and is therefore not shifted from its nominal position. The rightmost flux transition of the three is shifted to the right because it is repelled by a flux transition on its left. Hence, transitions appear early or late in a completely predictable fashion depending on other transitions in their immediate vicinity. The amount of the shift depends on the bit density and on the flux per transition. Single-density recording is sufficiently dense that bit shifting is a major factor that has to be addressed in the data-recording and recovery process.

There are at least three different techniques that are used to treat the problem of bit shifting: One can

1. control the flux density of the read/write head during recording to compensate for the increased bit density on inner tracks,
2. adjust the window during which bits are detected to compensate for bit shifting, and
3. compensate during writing by writing bits earlier or later than their nominal writing time so that bit shifting will tend to put the bits into their normal position.

Of these methods the first two are commonly used for single-density recording; but for double-density recording, the problems are just sufficently more complex to require the third technique as well. Single-density recording on 8" disks is normally made at two different flux levels. Normal current is used on tracks 0 through 43, which are the outermost 44 tracks on a disk. For track numbers 44 through 76, the recording current is reduced because of the greater density of the bits on the inner tracks and the correspondingly higher flux densities. Timing precompensation for double-density recording is accomplished by detecting the specific patterns that lead to bit shifting while the bits are passed through a serial buffer. When offending patterns are discovered, the corresponding bits are delayed or written early.

A very simple, but workable scheme for the data recovery of a single-density recording is shown in Fig. 7.22. This is a data separator that works with a phase-locked loop to break a composite clock/data signal into a clock-only and data-only signal. The idea is to use the phase-locked loop to generate a 2 μs window during which a data bit is expected, and to gate the data line from this window. Then the window changes to a clock window and gates the clock line. The controller cannot determine at first if a pulse is a clock or a datum, so the controller has to guess one or the other. If it guesses a clock pulse and if after a period of time there are missing clock pulses, the controller changes its guess. Note that up to three clock pulses can be missing for mark bytes, so the controller has to await four or more missing clocks before changing its guess. For this reason, sequences of 0s are recorded as part of the leader, gap, and trailer bytes, in order to be sure that the controller locks onto the correct clock/data phase of the incoming data stream. In the figure, the phase-locked loop oscillates at 16 times the clock rate of the incoming data, so that 8 counts of this loop apply to the clock window and 8 counts apply to the data window. Hence the window generator is nothing more than a 4-bit counter whose most significant bit is the window-control bit. This bit is fed in true form to the data-window gate, and in complemented form to the clock-window gate.

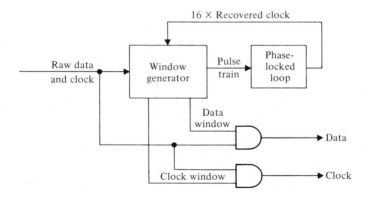

FIGURE 7.22   Structure of typical FM data separator.

The phase-locked loop discussed in Section 7.1 is more complex than what we need for single-density recording. In fact, the phase-locked loop tends to compensate incorrectly for bit shifting; and therefore we have to use it for long term stability only, seeking other techniques for treating bit shifting. Figure 7.23 shows a very simple digital version of a phase-locked loop. This scheme works perfectly well in the absence of bit

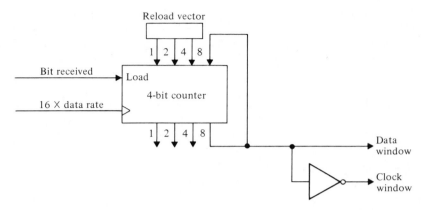

FIGURE 7.23   A digital phase-locked loop.

shifting, and can be used for single-density data recovery without resorting to preshifting data during writing. The idea is very similar to the behavior of a serial data port that uses a transition to resynchronize to each new character. In this case the digital phase-locked loop resynchronizes to an input stream by reloading a 4-stage counter whenever a received bit is observed. If the counter is reloaded with a fixed nominal value, then the counter produces a change on the high-order bit of the count at a time that is fixed in relation to the reload point. This gives the timing behavior shown in Fig. 7.24. The first clock has appeared later than the nominal point, which results in the data window being delayed to a fixed time after the clock transition. The second clock transition comes early, which results in the next data window coming early. Note that the window shifting is in the proper direction for compensating for fast and slow clocks, but is in the wrong direction to compensate for bit shifting. If the first clock is late because of bit shifting, the window has to be moved to an *earlier* time, not to a later time, to catch the next data bit.

A better way to run the phase-locked loop is to reload the counter with a value that depends on how far the observed clock time differs from its nominal value. The idea is to

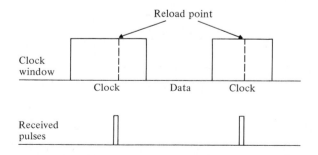

FIGURE 7.24   Window adjustment by a digital phase-locked loop.

make no adjustment if the difference is small, say 1 or 2 counts, and to adjust partially if the difference is large, say 6 or 7 counts. For example, the reload vector might adjust by 2 counts if the difference is as high as 6, and by 1 count for differences between 3 and 5; it would make no adjustment for smaller differences. In this way the digital version of the phase-locked loop will track the average value of the clock frequency over long periods of time.

With the growing popularity of floppy disks for microprocessors, a number of semi-conductor manufacturers have introduced LSI floppy-disk controller chips to perform the bulk of the disk-interfacing function. Most of these chips require off-chip data separators, phase-locked loops, and timing precompensation circuits; but otherwise the majority of the logic required for a controller is on a single chip. A typical controller of this type is shown in Fig. 7.25, which represents the Western Digital family of interface chips num-bered WD177X and WD179X, where the final digit X designates a member of the family. (Differences among chips in this family are related to the bus interface or to other specific chip functions.) The figure shows that this chip can control head motion by issuing step pulses and head-load commands to the drive. Step pulses move the head from track to track. The head-load command forces the head to contact the disk surface. When the head is not loaded, it is physically lifted from the disk surface. The controller also combines clock and data to form a composite serial data stream, and is able to assemble separated data and clock signals into 8-bit bytes to transmit back to a microprocessor. The index-hole signal is used by the drive to count revolutions and thereby permits the drive to time-out if a command fails. The controller also issues a command to lift the head from the disk if no activity occurs during a few revolutions.

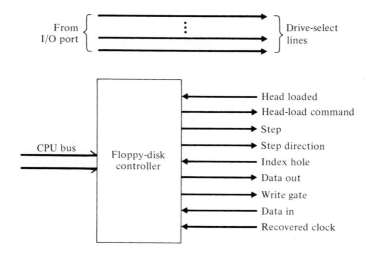

FIGURE 7.25   A typical LSI floppy-disk controller chip in the WD177X or WD179X families.

Data bytes are transmitted at the rate of one byte per 32 μs for single-density data on standard 8'' floppy-disk drives. At this rate, a typical microprocessor operating with a 1 to 2 MHz clock is quite taxed if the data are transferred under the control of the microprocessor. In nearly all instances, transfers must be made in a program-controlled mode rather than in an interrupt mode, because the overhead of the interrupt is unacceptable. A much safer but more complex method is to transfer data under DMA control, in which case it is quite feasible to interface a floppy disk to a microprocessor with a 1 MHz clock. Double-density recording doubles the data-transfer rate, and therefore almost surely requires a DMA controller.

Examples of Practical Disk Interfaces

Figure 7.26 is the schematic of a full, single-density disk interface. This particular interface is designed to connect to an MC6800 memory bus, which is a challenging problem because this bus does not have a WAIT signal to stop the microprocessor for slow memory devices. Hence, there is some difficulty in synchronizing the MC6800 to the floppy-disk controller chip. (The technique for solving this difficulty is explained later in this section.)

On the left in the figure we see the bus interface. Note that an external parallel port develops signals that are used as select signals for individual drives. Hence, the controller chip is not concerned with which drive is active. It simply issues commands to the connector on the right-hand side of the figure, and system software has the responsibility of selecting the particular drives to respond to the commands.

The floppy-disk controller chip in this diagram is the WD1771, a single-density controller that has now been replaced by the WD179X series of chips. The latter chips have the capability to read and write in single or double density, but they are otherwise essentially identical to the chip shown in the figure. Note that only a few external chips are required to interface to a floppy disk, since almost all aspects of disk control are embedded in the controller chip. It operates on its own 2 MHz clock, and has an on-chip processor that is designed for floppy-disk control. Figure 7.27 shows the register arrangement on the disk controller chip. Note that the chip occupies four port (or memory) addresses. The track, sector, and data registers each have unique addresses, and the registers can be both read and written. The track register holds the track number of the arm position of the disk that is presently selected. If a new disk drive is selected, the track register will be incorrect momentarily, until software commands from the host microprocessor instruct the controller to read the disk and load the track register from the track identifier as it passes under the read/write head.

The purpose of the sector register is to indicate to the controller which sector is to be read or written. When the controller executes a READ or WRITE instruction, it first places the head in contact with the floppy disk (which is called a *head load*), and then reads the sector IDs at the present arm position. As each ID passes under the head, the controller checks the ID for a match against the contents of the track and sector registers. If the track register fails to match, the operation is aborted because the arm is in the wrong position on the disk. Eventually, as the disk rotates the correct sector comes under the

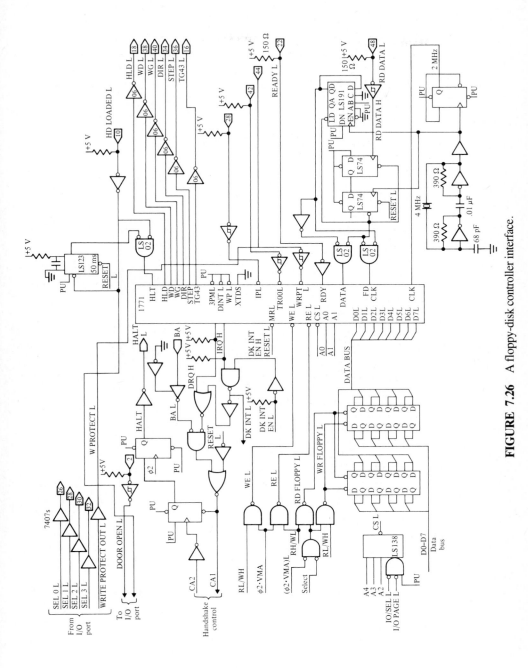

FIGURE 7.26 A floppy-disk controller interface.

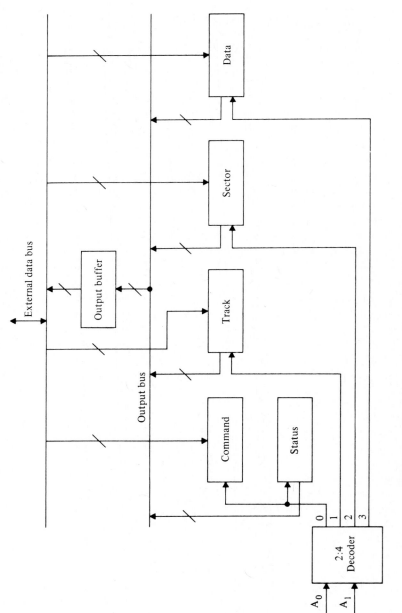

FIGURE 7.27   Register layout for the WD177X and WD179X families.

head. This is indicated by a match of the ID to the track and sector registers. At this point the controller is ready to read or write the data that immediately follows the sector ID. The data read from the disk are accumulated bit by bit in the controller until a full byte is available. This byte appears in the data register of the chip and is passed to the microprocessor over the memory bus. Data to be written on disk flow in the opposite direction, from the microprocessor to the controller over the memory bus. These data are stored into the data register by parallel 8-bit writes, and are then output as a serial bit stream to the disk drives. Note that the output stream has clock bits inserted between data bits, and that the input stream from the drive contains the same clock bits. Clock and data bits in the input stream pass through the data separator, and are passed to the controller chip as two distinct streams of bits.

The last two registers shown in Fig. 7.27 are the COMMAND and STATUS registers, which occupy a single address in the port-address space. Data written to this address are commands to be interpreted by the controller, whereas data read from this address are status reports to be returned to the microprocessor by the controller. Commands available on the WD family of controllers are listed in Table 7.2. The Type I commands are the commands that move the arm to the correct track. The STEP IN and STEP OUT commands move the arm one track in or out, respectively; and the STEP command moves one track in the same direction as the last arm movement. When the arm has to be moved several tracks in a single step, it is somewhat faster to use the SEEK command. This command accepts a target track number in the data register, then issues the correct number of step pulses to move the arm from the present track to the target track. At the conclusion of this command, the arm is directly above the target track and the track register has been updated to show the correct present position of the arm. Commands labeled Type II are the commands used to read and write data. These commands function correctly when a drive as been selected, the arm has been moved to the correct track, and the track and sector registers have been loaded with track and sector numbers of the data to be accessed.

TABLE 7.2   **Commands for the WD177X and WD179C Families**

Type	Command
I	RESTORE
I	SEEK
I	STEP
I	STEP IN
I	STEP OUT
II	READ SECTOR
II	WRITE SECTOR
III	READ ADDRESS
III	READ TRACK
III	WRITE TRACK
IV	FORCE INTERRUPT

Two other types of instructions appear in the table. The Type III commands are used more rarely than the others, but serve an important purpose. The READ ADDRESS reports back the sector ID of the first sector that passes under the read/write head. From this information the microprocessor can determine both the present track and sector passing under the head, and can then use this information to allocate disk memory in a manner that tends to minimize rotational delay and arm movement. The WRITE TRACK command writes an entire track, including the sector IDs. This command is typically used on an initially empty disk to write sector IDs, and thereby prepare the disk for future reads and writes. The READ TRACK command is the inverse operation, and used primarily for diagnostic purposes because it is the only command that reads and reports disk data in the exact image of the data on the disk.

The last type of command, Type IV, is the FORCE INTERRUPT command. This command can be used to halt operations in progress, or to halt operations when certain selected events occur, such as the removal or reinsertion of a disk into the drive.

The command structure of the WD177X and WD179X families of controllers is quite similar to that of other controller chips, although there are differences in details. Other disk controller chips available from Intel, Motorola, and NEC are described and compared in Table 7.3.

TABLE 7.3   Comparison of Floppy-Disk Controller Chips

Characteristics	WD177X	WD179X	MC6843	i8271	NEC372	NEC765
Single density	Yes	Yes	Yes	Yes	Yes	Yes
Double density	No	Yes	No	No	No	Yes
Pins	40	40	40	40	42	40
Voltages	3	2	1	1	3	1
IBM 3740 format	Yes	Yes	Yes	Yes	Yes	Yes
Other format	Yes	Yes	No	Yes	Yes	Yes
Drive select	No	No	No	Yes	Yes	Yes
Side select	No	No	No	Yes	Yes	Yes
Key-compare mode	No	No	No	Yes	No	Yes
DMA controls	No	No	Yes	Yes	No	Yes
Interrupt lines	2	2	1	1	1	1

This brings us to a discussion of the operation of the interface in Fig. 7.26. First we note the signal buffers: The drivers are open-collectors, which normally drive 150-Ω, 50-conductor flat cables; the receivers—Schmitt triggers because the hysteresis of the Schmitt trigger is an excellent mechanism for removing noise introduced through the cabling— are terminated with 150-Ω resistors in order to eliminate reflections on the cable. The far end of the cable has similar resistors terminating lines driven by the open-collector gates on the controller interface. Most signaling on the cable is in short pulses, 200 ns in length, with a pulse-repetition rate of no greater than one pulse in 2 μs. Because of this low duty cycle, the pulses are asserted in low polarity—that is, as logic 0s, so that while the signals are unasserted no power is consumed in the load resistor. Some disk systems take advantage of the open-collector drivers to do "wired-OR" logic of status signals from multiple drives.

The basic signals produced by the controller are the signals for moving the arm (STEP and IN), for writing data (WRITE DATA, WRITE GATE, and TG43), and for sensing external status (WRITE PROTECT, WRITE FAULT, INDEX PULSE, TRACK 0, and READY). The WRITE DATA signal contains both clock and data interspersed, and the WRITE GATE signal is asserted when WRITE DATA contains a serial bit stream to be written. The signal TG43, which means "track greater than 43," is asserted as the arm moves inward on the disk. The function of this signal is to force the drive to reduce the recording current on tracks 44 and higher in order to reduce the effects of bit shifting. The status signals report the condition of the drive or of the disk in the drive. If the disk is protected, that is, if it is physically notched in a manner that triggers a protect circuit, then WRITE PROTECT indicates this condition to the controller, which then aborts any attempt to write on the disk. TRACK 0 status is asserted when the arm is moved to the outermost track on the disk. The INDEX PULSE signal triggers each time an index hole passes under a photosensitive diode. This enables the controller to count disk revolutions and to abort incomplete operations if they do not complete within a fixed number of revolutions. The READY signal is usually connected to the drive power or to the door of a disk drive and indicates READY when power is applied and a disk is properly mounted in the selected drive.

Only two nontrivial circuits connect the controller chip to the disk drives. One circuit is responsible for head-load timing and the other for data separation. Head loading refers to the process of forcing the head to contact a disk in preparation for a read or write operation. In current practice, heads are lifted from a disk when the disk is inactive. This reduces wear on both the head and the magnetic media. In order to perform an access, it is necessary to load the head, and then to follow the normal procedures for read or write. Unfortunately, the time required for the head to reach its functional position is rather lengthy, so that the controller must delay operations until the head responds to a HEAD LOAD command. In the interface shown, the disk drives report back that the head-load solenoid is active. A one-shot delay triggers when a HEAD LOAD signal is issued. The HEAD LOAD signal travels to the disk drive where it initiates the head loading, while the one-shot prevents any further action from taking place. After the one-shot times-out (in about 50 ms in the design shown), the operation can continue. The WD chip family removes the HEAD LOAD signal after about three revolutions of inactivity, although the drives may hold the heads loaded for some time after the HEAD LOAD signal is removed. In the figure, we see the HEAD LOADED status signal returned from the drive, where it is used to keep the one-shot from retriggering while the head is still loaded. Hence, if the drive happens to have the head loaded when a new HEAD LOAD command is issued, a READ or WRITE operation can begin immediately instead of waiting for 50 ms before beginning. Not all drives have the capability shown, but it is generally a good idea to leave a head loaded from 3 to 10 s after the HEAD LOAD command is removed if this is possible. The additional wear caused by this extra loading is negligible, but the advantage of avoiding unnecessary HEAD LOAD commands is extremely worthwhile. Each HEAD LOAD command produces a pulse that drives the head ''crashing'' into the disk. Users of disk-based microprocessors hear this operation as a rather loud ''clack, clack, clack,'' where each clack is a HEAD LOAD. The wear and damage produced by the unnecessary loads is far more serious than the wear produced by holding a loaded head on the disk for a few seconds longer than necessary. (The discussion here is relevant to 8'' disks; the smaller 5¼'' diskettes are usually loaded during the entire time that motor power is on. But motor power is turned off after accesses are complete in order to conserve power and limit head wear.)

This brings us to the data separator. Figure 7.28 shows the separator in somewhat greater detail. Note the pair of 74LS74 flip-flops that are used to synchronize an incoming pulse to the local clock. The first of these flip-flops receives the incoming pulse and holds it for the second flip-flop. This is necessary because clock pulses occur every 250 ns, but the pulse width of an incoming pulse may be less than 200 ns so that data storage is required in the data separator. The second flip-flop can enter the metastable state, but presumably it will do so only if the input pulse and the clock change at approximately the same time. When this happens, the output of the flip-flop is unpredictable. If the output should report no pulse received, then in 250 ns the clock pulse that occurs should bring the flip-flop out of the metastable state where it recognizes a pulse received. Note that only one of the two outputs of this flip-flop is used elsewhere in the circuit because the complementary outputs need not be complementary in the metastable state. Therefore a design that relies on the complementary nature of the outputs will fail.

In addition, the circuit illustrated relies on the assumption that if any gate interprets the output of the second flip-flop as a logic 0 then all the gates it drives will also do so. A safer approach is to use yet another clocked flip-flop stage following the series of two stages. This third stage presumably will not let the third flip-flop enter the metastable state if the second-stage flip-flop has had 250 ns in which to settle out of its metastable state. All signals for the other portions of the data separator are derived from the third stage of the modified design rather than from the second stage.

The output of the last flip-flop is gated either to the CLOCK input or to the DATA input, depending on the state of the digital phase-locked loop. When a pulse is received, the phase-locked loop counter is reset to 2, and thereby has its window adjusted for the next pulse. Because the high-order bit of the counter determines whether the pulse is to be routed to the clock or the data pins, we discover that the clock and data windows are each eight clocks, or 2 μs in width. This is the correct width for single-density recording, which encodes one byte every 32 μs, each byte consisting of eight clock and eight data windows. The middle of the window occurs just when the fourth clock appears, and a perfectly centered pulse straddles this clock. Hence, when a bit falls in the exact center of the window it arrives when the counter has a count of 3, and this is the value to which the counter is reset when a pulse is sensed. In the figure, the reload value is 2 rather than 3, which delays the window slightly from the nominal center value. This delay is inserted because of other timing factors such as bit shifting and propagation delay, and it adjusts

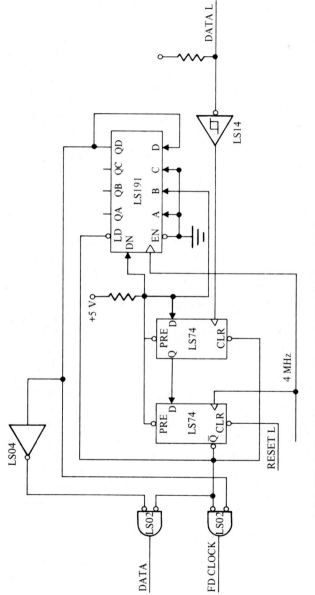

FIGURE 7.28   Data separator for the WD1771.   (From SD Systems Versafloppy interface.)

the window so that the window is more nearly centered about the expected positions of pulses. Note that the reloading of the counter affects the three least significant bits only, so that the high order bit, which controls whether the bit is a clock or a data bit, is not altered.

One of the puzzling aspects of this separator is that it contains no circuitry to distinguish between clock and data bits. The decision made by the separator appears to be arbitrary. Intuition suggests that this is wrong, and that the data separator should detect missing clocks. If four or more clock bits in succession are missing, it should change its decision as to which bits are clocks and which are data. (Recall that sector IDs are special data marks with three missing clocks to distinguish them from ordinary data. Hence up to three clocks can be missing under normal circumstances.) It turns out that this particular controller chip detects missing clocks, and switches clock and data lines internally in the event of an incorrect guess. Hence, it is not important that the separator guesses wrong as to which bits are clock and which are data. If the guess is wrong, it is corrected by the controller. The important function of the separator is that it must break up the incoming bit stream into two independent streams. If the clever designer wishes to design a separator that changes its guess when the original guess turns out to be incorrect, that designer may discover that the separator no longer works with this particular controller chip. For just when the separator switches the external data streams between the clock and data pins, the controller is making the identical switch internally, and the net result is that the controller and separator are "fighting" each other. When both the controller and the separator make a correct decision to change, they nullify each other.

This brings us to the microprocessor portion of the interface shown in the left half of Fig. 7.26. Apart from the usual bus-interface signals the controller chip produces two different REQUEST signals. One is DATA REQUEST, which is asserted during transfer of each byte of a sector. The other is INTERRUPT REQUEST, which is asserted at the end of an operation. The problem is to move one byte every 32 μs between the microprocessor and the controller chip. In general, interrupts are much too slow for this type of transfer, so we need to use either program-controlled I/O or a DMA-controlled transfer. Interrupts take several machine cycles to store processor state and several additional cycles to restore that state at the end of the interrupt. Processors with clock rates of 1–2 MHz may require on the order of 15–20 μs just for the process of entering and leaving the interrupt program. Too little time is left for moving data.

For program-controlled I/O, consider what is involved in a transfer of data through the controller chip. Program 7.3 is an example of a wait loop used for this purpose. The high-level language form of the algorithm shows the general structure of the program. Following that is an example written in the machine language of a typical microprocessor in the 6800 and 6502 families. With small changes, the code is readily adapted to the 808X and Z80 families. The cycle counts shown in the program are each 1 μs long, so we see that the program just fails to meet the requirement of processing 1 byte every 32 μs. If the microprocessor timings are shorter than those shown, the processor might actually meet the requirements. (Permissible timing variations actually reduce the available time between bytes to as little as 30 μs. This places an even stricter timing constraint on the program.)

PROGRAM 7.3   Wait-Loop Program

COUNT := BLOCK LENGTH;
INDEX := STARTING ADDRESS;
do begin
    while not READY **do**; (* Wait for READY. *)
    MEMORY [INDEX] := DISK BYTE;
    INDEX := INDEX + 1;
    COUNT := COUNT − 1;
end until COUNT <= 0;

CYCLES	LABEL	CODE	OPERAND	COMMENTS
	START	LDA A	BLOCKLENGTH	COUNT := BLOCK LENGTH;
		STA A	COUNT	
		LDX	STARTADDR	INDEX := START ADDRESS;
4	LOOP	LDA A	STATUS	READ STATUS OF DISK CONTROLLER
4		AND A	#READY	IS THE READY BIT SET?
4		BRZERO	LOOP	IF NOT SET, READ AND TEST AGAIN
4		LDA A	DATA	CONTROLLER IS READY AT THIS POINT
4		STA A	0,X	MEMORY [INDEX] := DISK DATA;
4		DEC	X	INDEX := INDEX + 1;
5		DEC	COUNT	COUNT := COUNT − 1;
4		BGT	LOOP	
33	TOTAL CYCLES			

The timing estimates given in the program make the possibly incorrect assumption that the wait loop is executed only once. Actually the program may pass through the wait loop two or more times. The extra passes through the wait loop might add just enough cycles to the critical loop to cause a failure in the data transfer if the program otherwise meets the critical timing constraint. To be on the safe side we need to have a much larger margin of safety. If we cannot find a means to obtain that margin of safety, we must resort to DMA for the data transfer.

The most obvious way to reduce the critical timing path is to eliminate the wait loop in the program. Two different ways of doing so both make use of facilities on typical microprocessors. The most direct way is to use the READY signal produced by the controller to hold the processor in a wait condition until the transfer can take place. In this case the wait loop disappears completely from the program, and the instruction that accesses the floppy-disk controller simply suspends itself until the controller reports READY. When this method is used with a processor such as the Z80 that has a block-repeat instruction, the entire data-transfer loop of Program 7.3 reduces to a single instruction executed in the block-repeat mode.

The second method uses a HALT instruction to stop the processor, and the READY status triggers a restart. This method is widely used on 808X and Z80 processors, which can be interrupted after executing a HALT instruction and then will restart execution. In this case, the wait loop is replaced by a HALT instruction. Both methods replace the programmed testing of the controller status with continuous hardware testing of the status. But the hardware costs essentially nothing because it is embedded in the microprocessor.

The controller interface shown in Fig. 7.26 uses a variant of the HALT-instruction method. The external hardware creates a HALT instruction for a microprocessor that has none. The processor is an MC6800, and the code for the data transfer is shown in the Program 7.4. In this case, an external I/O port is preset to drop the voltage on a handshake line when the port is read. This handshake line is brought to the controller interface, where it is synchronized to the 6800 clock and output as a HALT signal, as though a DMA process were being requested. The microprocessor halts at the end of the following instruction, then continues when the DRQ signal removes the HALT request. This program executes comfortably within the 32-cycle constraint. The external hardware required in this design for the HALT function is not extensive, and even this much hardware can be eliminated if the microprocessor has a HALT instruction or a slow-memory interface. Note that the hardware makes use of the handshake lines on a parallel port and requires clock synchronization as discussed earlier in Chapters 6 and 3, respectively.

PROGRAM 7.4   Stop-and-Start Program

```
COUNT := BLOCK LENGTH;
INDEX := STARTING ADDRESS;
do begin
    HALT until READY;  (* Stop processing until READY. *)
    MEMORY [INDEX] := DISK BYTE;
    INDEX := INDEX + 1;
    COUNT := COUNT − 1;
end until COUNT <= 0;
```

CYCLES	LABEL	CODE	OPERAND	COMMENTS
	START	LDA A	BLOCKLENGTH	COUNT := BLOCK LENGTH;
		STA A	COUNT	
		LDX	STARTADDR	INDEX := START ADDRESS;
		LDA A	#HALTCODE	THIS BIT PATTERN HALTS THE MICRO
		STA A	PORT CMD	OUTPUT TO HALT THE PROCESSOR
4	LOOP	LDA A	PORT DATA	THIS HALTS THE PROCESSOR
4		INC	X	INDEX := INDEX + 1;

(* The HALT occurs at this point. *)

CYCLES	LABEL	CODE	OPERAND	COMMENTS
4		LDA A	DATA	CONTROLLER IS READY AT THIS POINT
4		STA A	0, X	MEMORY [INDEX] := DISK DATA;
5		DEC	COUNT	COUNT := COUNT − 1;
4		BGT	LOOP	
25	TOTAL CYCLES			

Double-density interfaces are more complex than the single-density interfaces discussed here for several reasons. Because the data transmission rate is double that of single-density recording, it is extremely difficult to implement a double-density interface without a DMA controller. Timing constraints require one byte to be transferred every 16 μs, which is insufficient time for most microprocessors with clock rates up to about 4 MHz to execute the program loop in Program 7.4. (A microprocessor with the Z80-type block-repeat instruction may be an exception to this statement.) For newer microprocessors that have clock rates between 8 and 10 MHz, program-controlled I/O is again a possibility, but the higher clock rate does require more careful design than does a slower system with DMA.

The problem of bit shifting is much more severe in double-density interfaces than in single density. Consequently, the data separator is more critical, and it is necessary to pre-shift data written to compensate for the shifting anticipated when the data are read. The circuits for precompensation and data separation are sufficiently widely used to be suitable functions to implement in LSI. This has the additional advantage that the system designer who draws upon packaged versions of these functions need not be concerned about the tricky details of compensation and data separation. Some examples of chips that implement these functions are shown in Figs. 7.29 and 7.30. Figure 7.29 shows a circuit precompensating data written on a floppy disk. In this case the controller is in the WD179X family, and produces signals that determine what precompensation is to be used. Since the controller buffers the serial bit stream, it can determine from that stream which bits will suffer from bit shifting. For example, in single-density recording a data bit has a clock bit on each side; and therefore if the data bit is a 0, the neighboring clocks will

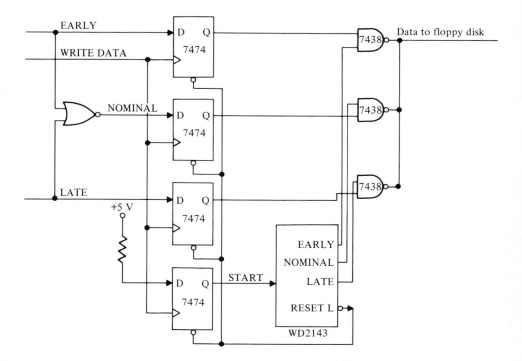

FIGURE 7.29   Timing precompensation with the WD2143 clock generator.

be shifted toward the missing data pulse. Hence, the first clock should be written early and the second clock should be written late to compensate for the shifting. The amount of the precompensation is determined by the WD2143 clock generator. Each time a pulse appears from the controller chip, that pulse latches the EARLY and LATE signals, then initiates the clock cycles of the WD2143. This chip then emits a sequence of four pulses— one each for early, nominal, and late pulses, and the last to reset the control latches. The pulses are combined with the decoded EARLY and LATE signals to create a single pulse to the drive that is the data actually recorded.

For the tricky problem of data separation of double-density data, the WD1691 support-logic chip produces a recovered clock from the composite data/clock signal that is read from a disk. This chip contains an internal frequency divider and phase-comparator for a phase-locked loop as shown in Fig. 7.30. The internal divider is set to maintain an oscillation at 4 MHz. This reference frequency is compared to the incoming data stream to produce three outputs from the phase-comparator. The PUMP UP and PUMP DOWN L outputs, when filtered, are used to drive a voltage-controlled oscillator. PUMP UP is a signal that tends to increase the average frequency, and PUMP DOWN L indicates that the frequency is to be decreased. This is a slightly different scheme than used in the example of a voltage-controlled oscillator earlier in this chapter. The reason for the difference is that the input signal to this phase-locked loop is not a square wave with a 50% duty cycle, but rather a stream of narrow pulses, with many pulses missing from their nominal locations. Hence, it is not clear how to measure phase differences between the input signal and the reference frequency when pulses are missing. For this reason the comparator produces both a PUMP UP and PUMP DOWN L, a pair of interlaced pulse trains. The difference in the average voltages of these signals determines the output frequency of the oscillator. Also shown as part of the WD1691 is the interface with the WD2143 clock generator. The WD1691, then, contains both the bulk of the data separator except for an external

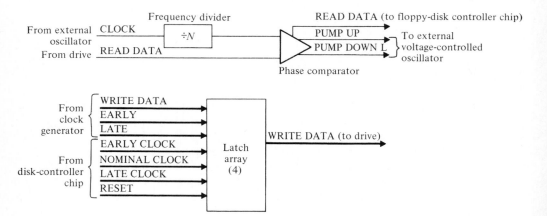

FIGURE 7.30 Functional components on a WD1691 floppy-disk controller support chip. The phase comparator can be coupled to an external oscillator to form a phase-locked loop. The latch array implements write-precompensation logic.

voltage-controlled oscillator, and the latch circuitry and logic required to drive the clock generator to obtain write precompensation.

OTHER READING AND SOURCE MATERIAL

Within this chapter we have cited material relating to phase-locked loops and linear systems. The technique for cassette recording with a tone burst is described by Wharton (1977). Several single-board computer systems use a similar technique. The SYM-1, for example, switches between two tones, one at 3600 HZ and one at 2400 HZ, to construct each bit. The distinction between a 1 and a 0 depends on the relative lengths of the 3600 HZ and 2400 HZ tones.

Floppy-disk recording techniques have been the subject of many articles, particularly because new methods are increasing the recording density 10 to 20 times that of the first-generation floppy disks. Hoeppner and Wall (1980) describe various common recording techniques, and touch upon the requirements for the controller to record and recover data. Harman (1979) shows how the structure of the gap for soft-sectored disks is related to the geometry of the recording heads. Many different application notes from Western Digital cover the behavior and the applications for their family of disk-controller chips. Interested readers should contact Western Digital for their most recent publications.

EXPERIMENTS

7.1 For this experiment you will need a microcomputer with a cassette interface. Write a program that outputs a series of FF_{16}s (all 1s) to a cassette recorder. Connect an oscilloscope to a pin that carries the output in digital form prior to waveshaping for recording. If you can discover the break between bytes, you may be able to determine the encoding of a 1 bit. It may be helpful to write your program to pulse a parallel-port output bit to provide a sync signal for the oscilloscope at the start of each byte output. Modify the program to output sequences of FE, F7, EF, and 7F bytes. These bytes have a single 0 bit. By comparing these sequences with each other and with the FF byte, you may be able to discover the encoding of both the 1 bit and 0 bit. Connect a second oscilloscope probe to the analog output to the recorder and compare the analog and digital forms of the output signals. Describe your observations.

7.2 Using the cassette interface and recording technique of the previous problem, design and construct a simple interface that recreates the digital version of the recorded signal from the recorded analog version of that signal. Connect the digital output to one pin of a parallel port. Then write a program that samples the parallel port pin and successfully recovers recorded data. Test your program on recorded data.

7.3 Your recovery program undoubtedly contains constants that are related to the expected transmission rate of the incoming data or to the recorded frequencies on the cassette tape. Vary your constants until you discover the range over which you can correctly recover data from the cassette tape. What causes the failures to read correctly at the extremes of your range?

7.4 Construct a breadboard of the interface for the Kansas City Standard that appears in this chapter. Jumper the output to the input, attenuating—if necessary—the output voltage. Adjust the one-shot time out to fall ¾ of the way through one cycle of 2400 HZ. Adjust the oscillator in the phase-locked loop to oscillate at 38.4 kHz. Output a continuous sequence of data bytes and verify that you can recover them. With the continuous stream running, probe the signals in the interface and explain what you see.

7.5 For this experiment you will need a microcomputer with a floppy-disk controller and the schematics for the controller. Write a program that reads a particular disk sector continuously. Connect one oscilloscope probe to the incoming data stream and another oscilloscope probe to a signal that defines whether a bit is a data bit or a clock bit. This is the clock "window." With the oscilloscope synchronized to the clock window, execute your program and observe the incoming data bits. Measure and describe the bit shifting that your observe. Execute your program with the head located on different tracks and plot the maximum shift observed as a function of track. Is there a discontinuity anywhere? Can you explain the discontinuity?

PROBLEMS

7.1 Consider the oscillator circuit for a phase-locked loop shown in Fig. P–7.1. The voltages shown at the test points are the steady-state DC voltage components of time-varying signals. The LM339 comparator is an open-collector device that has a typical low saturation voltage of 0.3 volts. The NPN transistor is in an emitter-follower circuit whose gain is essentially unity, and may be treated as unity gain in your analysis.

a) Draw a timing diagram that shows the general shape of the voltages at points A, B, C, D, and E. Describe for each voltage the underlying principles that give the voltage signal the characteristic shape you have shown.

b) The voltage at point E increases to what asymptotic voltage? What is the initial voltage at E when it begins to rise? At what point does the comparator fire while E is rising? What is the time constant that governs this increase? What is the mathematical expression that describes E while it is increasing? How long does it take for E to reach the firing voltage from the time it starts to rise?

c) Repeat the answers to Part b for the portion of time that E is decreasing instead of increasing.

d) What is the constant K_2 for the voltage-controlled oscillator? (This is the derivative of frequency out with respect to voltage in expressed in rad/s·V. To calculate K_2, you can differentiate a messy expression, or use a hand calculator and see how much the frequency output shifts for a small change in voltage input.)

e) Assume that the frequency output is divided by 32 and fed back as the reference voltage of the loop. Calculate the natural frequency and damping factor for the loop from the values of K_1 for the phase comparator and the K_2 that you have already calculated. Then use the plots in the notes to estimate the settling time of

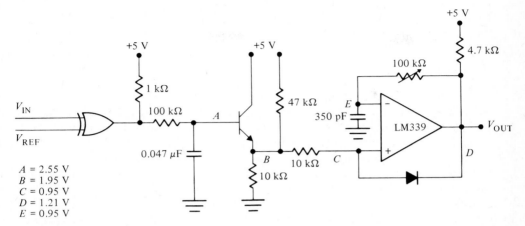

FIGURE P−7.1 The phase comparator, low-pass filter, and voltage-controlled oscillator of a phase-locked loop. (Adapted from Percom Data Corporation's interface CIS-30+, courtesy of Percom Data Corporation.)

the loop. Assume this is the time for the frequency response to a step change in voltage to reach and stay within 5% of its final value.

7.2 The damping factor for the phase-locked loop in Problem 7.1 is not 0.7 for the components given. Redesign the filter to achieve a damping factor of 0.7 and a reasonable natural frequency for the feed-back loop.

7.3 In Chapter 7 are equations for the natural frequency and damping factor of a phase-locked loop with a passive filter composed of two resistors and one capacitor (see Fig. 7-11). Derive this equation.

7.4 Some microprocessors can be externally controlled to wait an extended length of time for a slow memory or slow I/O device. Such microprocessors include the Intel 8080 family and the DEC LSI-11 family. Work out a scheme for interfacing a Western Digital type of disk controller to such a microporcessor so that the micro automatically waits for the controller whenever the micro stores or fetches a data byte during a block data transfer. Estimate how much execution time per byte is saved by using the automatic wait mode of operation instead of a program loop that tests the controller DRQ signal.

7.5 Design a simple sequential-logic circuit that passes a bit stream to a floppy disk, and detects bit patterns that will be shifted early or late when read from the disk. The controller delays each bit it passes by a nominal amount if the bit will not be shifted on playback, or by a shorter than nominal amount if the bit will be delayed on playback, or by a longer than nominal amount if the bit will be read early. Thus the controller precompensates for bit shifting on playback. In this design problem assume that bit shifting is a 1-unit delay, regardless of the head position. (Many commerical disk controllers actually use precompensation of this type only on inner tracks where bit shifting is most severe.)

8 / CRT-CONTROLLER DESIGN

This chapter covers the microprocessor-based design of cathode-ray tube (CRT) terminals. Such terminals became popular when breakthroughs in the cost of memory made it possible to hold a screenful of characters in a stand-alone terminal at reasonable cost. With this capability it became possible to use existing low-cost video technology to display text while refreshing the display from local memory. Prior technology depended on the more expensive storage display to serve the dual purpose of display and memory. Memory technology breakthroughs also provided low-cost read-only memory (ROM) to hold the displayable bit patterns for each character. In early terminals, the cost of the character generator was a major portion of the terminal, whereas today the character ROMs cost only a few dollars. As terminal technology developed in the 1970s, early terminals did not make use of microprocessors because the micros themselves were relatively new to the design scene. By the end of the 70s, virtually all terminal designs incorporated microprocessors, sometimes two or more per terminal, to take advantage of the great flexibility and low cost of these devices. There also emerged special video-controller chips that were designed to perform the processing-intensive task of video refresh, and thereby free the microprocessor for higher-level control functions. Because of microprocessors, the ''dumb'' terminal—that is, the terminal that can only display text and receive and transmit data—has given way to terminals with varying degrees of intelligence. These new terminals contain expanded memory storage and powerful functional capability such as insertion and deletion editing functions. The most sophisticated terminals in this class are full-fledged, multiprocessor computer systems. Yet the cost of these devices is no more than the cost of the most primitive display terminal of the early 1970s. In this chapter we examine the techniques for implementing a CRT terminal, paying special attention to the types of video-controller chips available to support the control function.

8.1 SYSTEM DESCRIPTION OF A TYPICAL CRT CONTROLLER

To appreciate how a CRT controller operates, we first examine characteristics of video displays to obtain an understanding of the special requirements for this type of system. A typical video screen is depicted in Fig. 8.1. We see that characters are printed on the screen in a familiar format, usually with 24 lines each with up to 80 characters. (Newer high-resolution CRTs have increased these dimensions to roughly 200 lines with 132 characters each.) Each character is made up of dots that are illuminated by the video beam as it scans each row on the face of the tube.

A brief calculation gives some idea of the high data rate required to run this type of system. Let's assume that each character is made up of dots arranged in a matrix 9 dots

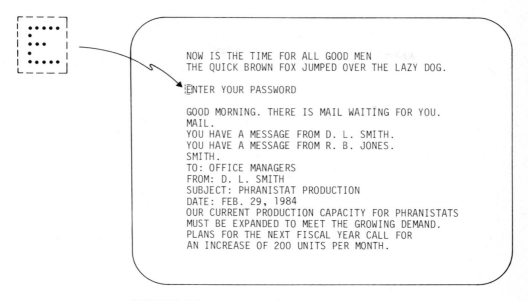

```
NOW IS THE TIME FOR ALL GOOD MEN
THE QUICK BROWN FOX JUMPED OVER THE LAZY DOG.

ENTER YOUR PASSWORD

GOOD MORNING. THERE IS MAIL WAITING FOR YOU.
MAIL.
YOU HAVE A MESSAGE FROM D. L. SMITH.
YOU HAVE A MESSAGE FROM R. B. JONES.
SMITH.
TO: OFFICE MANAGERS
FROM: D. L. SMITH
SUBJECT: PHRANISTAT PRODUCTION
DATE: FEB. 29, 1984
OUR CURRENT PRODUCTION CAPACITY FOR PHRANISTATS
MUST BE EXPANDED TO MEET THE GROWING DEMAND.
PLANS FOR THE NEXT FISCAL YEAR CALL FOR
AN INCREASE OF 200 UNITS PER MONTH.
```

FIGURE 8.1   A character display on a typical CRT.

high by 7 dots wide. To leave space between characters, we assume that each character field is actually 10×8, with the extra row and column left blank. Then the video beam has to touch each of the 80 dots per character for each of the $24 \times 80 = 1920$ characters during one scan of the display. This means that the controller must transmit at least $1920 \times 80 = 153,600$ bits per frame. To obtain a flicker-free image, each frame must be repainted roughly 60 times per second. (A lower quality image produced by refreshing every other line in each scan permits the refreshing rate to be dropped to 30 Hz.) This forces the information rate from the memory to the display to be at least 9.22 MHz. Because of other overhead in the transmission process, data rates frequently climb to 15 MHz, although this can be reduced somewhat by using lower quality characters and smaller display formats. The very high-resolution displays now becoming popular have data rates approaching 60 MHz. With data rates running from about 10 MHz to 60 MHz, the microprocessor in a CRT terminal would quickly be saturated were it not for special support chips to handle the high data-rate functions. These chips are essentially special-purpose processors that can meet the speed requirements of the refresh circuitry.

    With these ideas in mind, consider the block diagram of a typical controller shown in Fig. 8.2. The familiar parts of this diagram are the microprocessor, the memory, and the serial and parallel I/O ports that connect the system to keyboard, printer, and modem (or host computer). The aspects of the controller that reflect the CRT function consist of the dual-ported memory, the CRT-controller chip, the character-generator chip, the DMA controller, and the video shift-register.

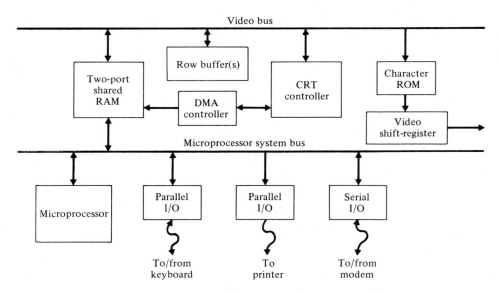

FIGURE 8.2   The structure of a typical microprocessor-controlled CRT terminal.

In this block diagram we see that both the CRT controller and the microprocessor have access to the data memory. The microprocessor stores new characters to display in the memory, but otherwise performs very little processing on the characters. The CRT controller reads the memory on a continuous basis, and uses this data to generate the data stream for the video display. Because of the very high data rate, the video memory bandwidth is almost fully utilized. In the block diagram we show an extra memory buffer that helps reduce accesses to data memory in order to maintain a high data rate.

The general flow of information from data memory to the video display is interesting in itself. Each scan line on the video display traces one of the rows that make up each character. If characters are 9×7, then 9 distinct horizontal traces are required to draw a character. Of course, every character in one row of 80 characters is drawn during the time it takes to scan one character, so the writing time per character is small. But unless the row of characters is held in a separate buffer, each character displayed on the screen has to be read once for each of the 9 scan lines that make up the character. Rereading from main memory takes excessive bandwidth and results in poor performance or costly memory. Hence, a typical CRT controller reads a line of text into a buffer. From this buffer the controller generates the scan lines transmitted to the video monitor, and reading from the· buffer does not conflict with processor accesses to shared memory.

The bit patterns for scan lines are stored in a video shift-register that performs the parallel-to-serial conversion of the data stream. The shift register need not hold an entire scan line, since the controller can insert additional data into the scan line "on the fly" as the shift register empties. In the block diagram we show the buffer memory data path passing through a ROM character-generator en route to the shift register. In this system the ROM holds the bit patterns for each character and reports these bits in response to each access request. Since our presumed character size is 9 scan lines by 7 columns, a ROM access yields 7 bits per access, and 9 different accesses (one for each scan line in a character) are required to build up a character. The address field for an access consists of the character code (usually 7-bit ASCII) concatenated with the scan line number. The bits reported change as the scan line increases, and thus the character form is gradually scanned from top to bottom

To meet the speed requirements, the bulk of the activity in the system operates in a concurrent (parallel) mode. Each character written on the screen requires

1. access to data memory to find the character code,
2. a subsequent access to the character generator ROM for each of the horizontal scan lines in the character,
3. a parallel access to store the bit image of each line in the video shift-register, and
4. serial access to the video shift-register output to stream the data to the video display.

These operations are usually performed as concurrently as possible to increase the performance of the system. For example, all activity involving the character translation in the character-generator ROM is performed in parallel with the activity of the microprocessor. The buffer and translation activity can also be done in parallel. Let us presume that the access time to the buffer is approximately equal to the access time to the character-generator ROM. Then both memories can be operated in parallel from a common clock. The idea is that an access to the buffer for character $i + 1$ occurs at the time of the access to the ROM for the bit pattern of character i.

The Controller Software

The microprocessor functions as a high-level controller in Fig. 8.2. It manages the data entering and leaving the system via the low-speed serial ports, and maintains the data in the screen memory. All of these operations constitute a relatively light load that is well within the capability of 8-bit microprocessors. The heavy load is associated with refreshing the video display, and all of this load is assumed by the video-controller chip and the buffer memory. A typical set of actions performed by the microprocessor is described in Program 8.1. This description is representative of actions of a basic terminal, and does not address the higher-level functions of advanced terminals. The program is structured as a continuous loop during which the microprocessor polls each I/O port and performs the processing for functions specific to each port. Except in unusual terminals, the data rates for the I/O ports are slow enough to permit the processor to deal with each transaction request when the request is discovered instead of queueing requests for future idle periods. Moreover, the program is greatly simplified by using a polling structure instead of an interrupt-driven structure.

The controller program loop begins with a query of the keyboard, followed by similar queries of modem output, modem input, and printer. This particular form of controller

PROGRAM 8.1   Terminal-Controller Program

```
while TRUE do (* Repeat the outer loop indefinitely. *)
    begin (* Poll the I/O ports. *)
    if keyboard status = READY then
        begin
        read keyboard; (* This reads ASCII-encoded data from the keyboard. *)
        if visible char (character) then (* Is the character displayable? *)
            begin (* For half-duplex operation, display the character. *)
            memory [display line, display column] := character;
            display column := display column + 1;
            if display column > 80 then (* Make a new line. *)
                begin
                restore cursor; (* Simulate a carriage return. *)
                newline; (* Simulate a line feed. *)
                end;
            end (* End of processing visible characters. *)
        else if character = carriage return then restore cursor
        else if character = line feed then new line
        else if . . . (* Each special character is treated by these statements. *)
        enter queue (character); (* Queue character for modem output. *)
        end; (* End of processing the keyboard. *)
    if modem output status = READY then
        begin
        character := remove queue; (* Take character from queue. *)
        if not character = NIL then modem output data := character;
        end; (* End of modem output processing. *)
    if modem input status = READY then
        begin (* Treat characters from the modem link here. *)
        (* This code is similar to the keyboard code above *)
                                                        .
                                                        .
                                                        .

        end;
    if printer status = READY then
        begin (* Process the printer port. *)
        character := memory [printer line, printer column];
        if character = carriage return then
            begin
            printer column := 0;
            printer line := printer line + 1:
            if printer line > last line then stop printer;
            end
        else (* Advance to next character. *)
            printer column := printer column + 1;
        printer port := character; (* Output to printer. *)
        end; (* End of printer processing. *)
    end; (* End of outermost loop. *)
```

shows a half-duplex operation in which characters typed on the keyboard appear immediately on the screen, and are sent to the modem output as well. Half-duplex operation forces this mode of operation on the terminal because the modem link cannot be used simultaneously in both directions. Therefore, characters typed must be displayed immediately, whereas in full-duplex operation the character typed is transmitted to the modem without displaying it first. Moreover, in full duplex operation, the output character eventually reaches a remote computer that echoes the character on the return link, and the character is displayed when it appears at the modem input.

The keyboard handler accepts a new character, which it then stores in the display memory if the character is a visible character. For control characters such as carriage return and line feed, the program moves the cursor and scrolls the screen as necessary. The response to a carriage return is a reset of the cursor to column 1, and the response to a line feed is a scroll of the display or an increment of the cursor line position.

The last action of the keyboard handler is the enqueueing of the character for the modem output. Since the keyboard is not synchronized to the modem in any way, we must in general buffer the output characters before transmitting them. When the modem output port is free to transmit a new character, it removes a character from the output buffer, always removing in first-in, first-out (FIFO) order. Hence, the buffer is a queue, and the subroutines ENTER QUEUE and REMOVE QUEUE, respectively, enter and remove data from the queue.

After processing the keyboard, the program examines the modem-output port. Here the program removes one character from the queue and outputs it, provided that there is a character present and the modem-output port is free. Following the query of the modem-output port, the program queries the modem-input port, and subsequently queries the printer port. Modem input is treated almost identically to the keyboard input, so the code for this function is not shown explicitly in the example program. The printer port is used to print a copy of the contents of display memory. Hence this program scans display memory and outputs the contents to the printer port.

To maintain good response time for all functions, it is essential that no task take too long. Hence, the polling program must reach each port sufficiently frequently to prevent lost data. The most demanding port in this example is the modem-input port, where data rates of 19.2 kHz may require service about 2000 times a second. If the polling loop requires more than 500 μs upon occasion, the modem-input port might suffer an overrun. To take the modem-input port into account, it is normal practice to operate the modem-input port (and any other heavily-used port) in interrupt mode rather than in polling mode. This guarantees that the modem-input program queries the port immediately after a datum is received. Many terminal designs drive the keyboard scanner with a timer interrupt, typically at a 60-Hz rate instead of polling the keyboard as described here.

Keyboard Scanning

Now let's look at some of the details of the keyboard handler. The keyboard is typically arranged as a matrix of switches driven from a parallel I/O port. (A typical keyboard interface is briefly described in the discussion of parallel I/O.) The scan of the keyboard switches can be made either by software or by a separate counter. With special LSI chips, keyboard scanning can be done automatically at relatively low cost. Otherwise, the microprocessor has to scan the keyboard under software control. Whereas the software method requires almost no additional hardware, it does place a greater burden on the microprocessor and reduces the processor cycles available for other purposes.

The short program for reading keyboards that was presented earlier in our description of parallel ports can be adapted in a rather interesting way as a CRT-controller program. One way to implement the program is Program 8.2. For this example we presume that a keyboard is arranged as a matrix of switches with 8 rows of 12 columns, with a total of 96 switch points. This is shown in Fig. 8.3. This arrangement supplies more than enough switch points for all standard characters, plus additional switch points for a numerical keypad and cursor control switches.

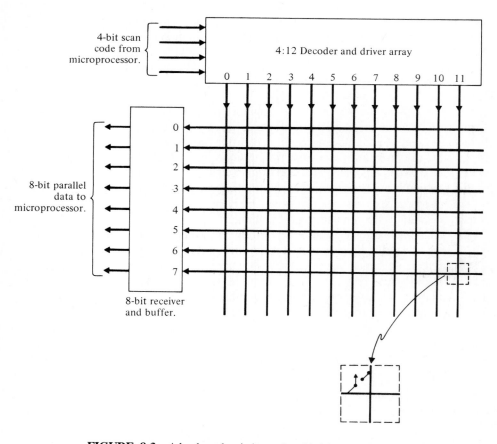

FIGURE 8.3   A keyboard switch matrix with 96 switch points.

PROGRAM 8.2   Keyboard-Scanner Program

```
NORMAL ENTRY: (* Entry point for keyboard scan. *)
keyboard column := keyboard column + 1;
if keyboard column > 11 then keyboard column = 0;
keyboard out := keyboard column; (* Activate the next column. *)
keyboard row := keyboard in; (* Read the row lines of the keyboard. *)
keyboard out := 15; (* Deactivate keyboard columns. *)
if active row then
      begin debounce counter := debounce delay; (* Alter polling address
         to return to this loop. *)
      set entry point to "DELAY LOOP";
      while debounce counter > 0 do
      begin
      keyboard status := not READY;
      return; (* Exit to main program. *)
DELAY LOOP: (* Reenter here from main program. *)
      debounce counter := debounce counter − 1;
      end;
      (* Restore the entry address of the polling routine. *)
      set entry point to "NORMAL ENTRY";
      (* Convert row vector data to binary number. *)
   for row := 0 step 1 until 7 do
      begin if (keyboard row) mod 2 = 0
         (* A 0 indicates key closure. *)
         then exit loop
         else keyboard row := keyboard row div 2; (* Shift the row
            vector right one bit. *)
      end;
   character := encode [8 * keyboard column + row]; (* Convert to ASCII. *)
   keyboard status = READY;
   return; (* Exit with character. *)
   end;
```

Recall from our earlier discussion on this topic that the software detects which key is depressed by activating one column at a time and reading the row lines concurrently. When a key is depressed it shorts a column line to a row line, which then becomes active. The software reads the row lines in parallel, and detects key closures by checking to see if any row line is active. The program then converts the 8-bit row vector into a 3-bit binary row number that corresponds to the first zero bit in the row vector. The combination of active column number and active row number uniquely identifies which has been depressed. In the figure we show the 12 column lines driven from a 4-to-16 decoder, which in turn is driven by a 4-bit scan code. The eight row lines, then, are passed to the microprocessor data bus through a parallel port or other suitable buffer.

The program as written detects only one key closure at a time. Typists often depress a new one before releasing an old one, which is easily detectable by software. Software can recognize the sequence in which keys are struck when several are in a closed state simultaneously, and thus the software can interpret the keystroke sequence correctly. The capability to accept such keystroke sequences is called *n-key rollover*. To implement *n*-key rollover, Program 8.2 should scan for every possible contact closure instead of terminating the scan when it first discovers a closure. The software keeps track of the changes that occur from one scan to the next, and thereby keeps track of the sequence in which new keys are depressed and old ones are released. This information is sufficient to interpret the keystroke sequence correctly.

The main problem for the keyboard software is to scan the 12 columns on a continuing basis while attending to other tasks. The keystrokes also have to be "debounced" in some manner to eliminate spurious pulses created just at the point of switch closure and switch opening. (The trend in terminal design favors hardware debouncing instead of software debouncing, largely because of the availability of inexpensive LSI chips for keyboard scanning that contain the necessary logic for debouncing.) Program 8.2 shows one way of treating these problems. This program advances the scan by one column each time it is called. Debouncing is treated through a delay in the program. When an active signal is discovered, the program does not accept the character immediately. Instead, it initializes a counter to a small positive number, and then exits to the main program. Each successive entry to the keyboard scanner decrements this counter until the count reaches 0, at which point the character is accepted. Typical delays that are used in practice are on the order of 10–15 ms. The idea of the debounce process is to return to the delay loop on the next entry rather than to the start of the program. In this way the debounce program returns to where it left off, and immediately decreases the debounce counter. This is a crude form of a coroutine call, which we describe at greater length later in Chapter 9. The general idea is that there is a state associated with the keyboard-scanner process. When this process is invoked, it starts up in its prior state. Hence polling the keyboard while the debouncing delay is running can be done with very low overhead and is quite efficient when compared to other ways of doing the same thing. In the example given, the state of the process is the state of the program counter at the point of exit. The state of the program counter is restored to its prior value when the program is reentered.

CRT Timing Considerations

Now that we have an overview of the system and have examined the role of the microprocessor, we move to the CRT-controller functions. To understand these functions, we need a brief introduction to video waveforms so that we can understand the requirements by the controller on the serial data-stream output. A video monitor requires control signals and one data signal to generate a raster display. These appear in Fig. 8.4. The first waveform, Fig. 8.4(a), is the video signal that modulates the scanning beam to produce light and dark spots on the screen. The second waveform, Fig. 8.4(b), is the horizontal sync signal that controls the beam's horizontal repetition rate. The sync pulses in this signal lock an oscillator to the sync frequency, and the oscillator in turn generates a ramp signal at the sync frequency that sweeps the beam across the screen. Similarly, the vertical sync shown in Fig. 8.4(c) determines the vertical repetition rate, which is the rate at which frames are repainted on the screen. The last waveform, Fig. 8.4(d) is a blanking waveform that turns off the monitor beam during horizontal and vertical retrace. This sig-

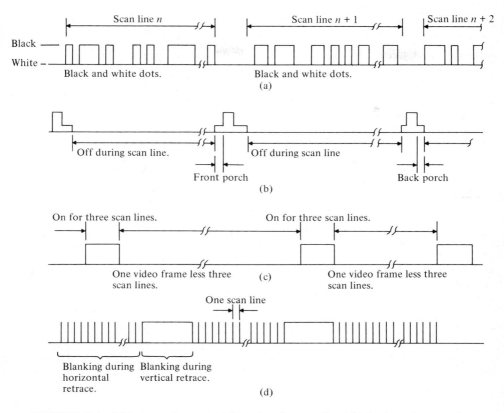

FIGURE 8.4 Video waveforms: (a) Video data for scan lines; (b) horizontal sync pulses; (c) vertical sync pulses; (d) blanking waveform. Graphs (a) and (b) have the same time scale, but (c) and (d) have much coarser times.

nal is not produced as a separate signal but is combined with the video signal of Fig. 8.4(a) to produce a composite waveform for controlling the intensity of the beam.

In commercial video, frames are usually written with an interlaced scan-line technique in which the even lines are written in one frame and the odd lines in the next. The bandwidths of these systems are relatively low, and interlacing becomes necessary in order to repaint pictures fast enough to reduce flicker. CRT terminals, however, have much higher bandwidths than broadcast receivers, so that it is possible to repaint an entire frame, rather than just the even or odd lines in the frame at the vertical repetition rate. Hence, in the remainder of this discussion we will assume that the CRT-controller uses a noninterlaced scan in place of an interlaced scan to attain a higher quality image.

In Fig. 8.4(a) we see the waveform produced for a single scan line. The line consists of a data segment followed by a blank segment. The data segment contains the information painted on the video screen in the corresponding scan line, so that the time coordinate of the waveform corresponds to the horizontal position on the scan line, and the voltage indicates the brightness at that position. The "pulses" in this waveform, then, are dark regions; and the valleys between pulses are illuminated dots on the scan line. Following the data segment is a blank segment that has no information. This region of the waveform corresponds to the time during which the beam retraces to the left-hand edge of the screen to begin a new trace. Some of this blank time is neither used for information nor for retrace, but creates a blank area on each edge of the picture to center the picture horizontally away from the edges of the screen where distortion is greatest. (The left-hand edge of the scan line actually begins within the blank segment.)

The horizontal sync waveform in Fig. 8.4(b) is a pulse pattern in which the pulse appears during the blank period of the trace in Fig. 8.4(a). The pulse has three elements:

1. The "front porch," where the signal is a low voltage.
2. The sync pulse, where the signal is a high voltage.
3. The "back porch," where the signal is a low voltage.

Note that the front porch begins at the end of the information in the trace. The timing for the sync pulse elements is not standardized, and in fact, most video monitors can synchronize to signals over a broad range of timing characteristics. To simplify the design of the CRT controller, the usual choice is to make the total horizontal period a multiple of the period for the display of one character. Thus if the data portion of the scan line is 80 characters long, the sync portion can be another 20 characters long. Within the sync pattern, each component is also made an integral number of character times. In the example shown, the sync pattern is low for 4 character times, high for 8, then low for the remaining 8. (The recommended ratio for these times is approximately 1:2:2 as selected in this example.)

The waveform in Fig. 8.4(c) shows a vertical sync waveform in a greatly condensed time scale. This waveform is a periodic pulse that causes the video monitor to initiate a new frame. Each pulse is three horizontal scan lines in length. This means that the vertical size of the display is at least three horizontal lines longer than the lines required to display the text itself. Actually, there should be even more than three extra lines per frame for the vertical centering of the picture in a distortion-free display area. In our example, our characters are 9 scan lines by 7 columns. The minimum field in which these can be displayed is 10 scan lines by 8 columns. Hence, with 24 rows of characters we find that the number of scan lines in the visible display field is $24 \times 10 = 240$ lines, so that the number of lines per frame should be set to a slightly higher number, say 256.

The last waveform is Fig. 8.4(d), the blanking waveform. This waveform turns off the beam during the blank periods of each horizontal trace, during the writing of the extra horizontal lines, and during vertical retrace at the end of each frame. Typical of most CRT monitors in use today is an interface in which the horizontal sync, vertical sync, and video information are treated as three distinct signals. The blanking is added to the video information at the CRT controller to form one signal, and the horizontal and vertical sync signals are carried on two other separate signals. In broadcast receivers all four signals shown in Fig. 8.4 are combined into one composite video signal by summing their volt-ages. If a CRT controller must connect to a monitor that accepts this type of information, then the controller must combine the signals according to the broadcast standard.

Now let's calculate the precise timing for each waveform in Fig. 8.4. This calculation will determine the basic clock rate of the controller. Since the vertical repetition rate should be equal to the AC power frequency, we find that the repetition rate of the vertical sync pulses is 60 Hz in the U.S. and 50 Hz in Europe and other countries. Since there are 256 scan lines per frame, scan lines repeat at the rate of 15.36 kHz in the U.S. (or at 12.8 kHz in Europe). With 100 characters per character row, the basic character frequency is 1.536 MHz (or 1.280 MHz), and the frequency of the dots that make up each character is 8 times as great, which is 12.28 MHz (or 10.24 MHz). This highest frequency is the frequency of the master clock of the controller. All other timing is derived from this clock.

Figure 8.5 illustrates how frequency dividers operating on the master clock produce all of the timing signals for the various functions. The master clock in the example is a 12.28-MHz crystal oscillator. This clock advances the shift register of the video signal at the bit rate. When this signal is divided by 8, a signal is produced that runs synchronously with each character displayed. Then at each edge of this clock, the video shift register must be reloaded. Note that within one character time, the controller must access display memory for the next character and then use the character code to find a displayable bit pattern in the ROM. These two accesses must be completed at a 1.536-MHz rate, or in about 650 ns. This calls for rather fast memory if the accesses are made sequentially. But the requirements are reduced substantially when the accesses are overlapped. That is, character $i + 1$ is accessed from the display buffer while character i is converted to display form by a ROM memory access as we mentioned earlier.

In Fig. 8.5 we show two more clock dividers that, respectively, produce pulses at the end of each scan line (divide by 100), and at the end of each frame (divide by 256). The scan line clock is also divided by 10, the number of lines per character, to yield a clock pulse at the end of each row of characters. Note that the line buffer has to be reloaded at the end of a row. This can be done during the last (and blank) trace line in a row of characters. Since one scan line takes approximately 65 μs and 80 accesses must be made in this period of time, we have about 800 ns per access to reload the line buffer. This time is well within the capabilities of the memory system, but it cannot be done under program control of typical microprocessors. Most microprocessors must execute three to six instructions per byte or word transferred, which takes substantially longer than 800 ns.

Therefore, the CRT controller typically reloads the line buffer under DMA control. Hence a signal synchronized to the row clock of Fig. 8.5 must trigger a DMA activity which halts the processor and fetches a block of 80 characters to transfer to the line buffer. This transfer can also be made in an overlapped fashion wherein character $i + 1$ is read from shared memory while character i is written into the line buffer. It is quite effective to use two buffers instead of one for the row display. In this case one buffer can be reloaded while the second is used for the current display line. Double buffering gives the controller about 10 scan-line times (instead of a single scan-line time) in which to reload the row buffer.

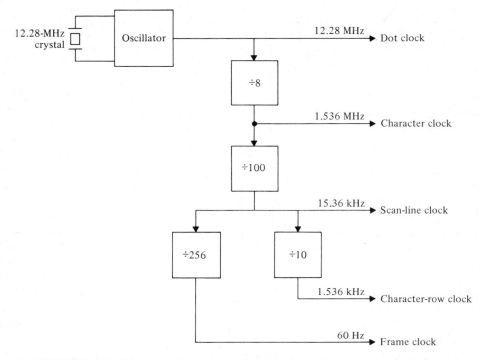

FIGURE 8.5   Frequency-divider network that generates the necessary clocks for a CRT controller.

The clocking requirements, as shown in Fig. 8.4 and Fig. 8.5, can strongly influence the design of the entire system. For the parameters that we have selected, the high-speed activity forces the use of a DMA mode for data transfer, and requires the overlapping of memory operations between the line buffer and the video shift register.

We have not described all of the activities that are triggered by the various clocks produced in Fig. 8.5. Nor have we indicated the specific phase of a clock at which an action must occur. For example, the DMA reload of the line buffer must occur at the end of the 9th line of a 10-line character scan. These other design facets are easily determined given the basic timing constraints, the system organization, and the video output requirements.

8.2 THE CRT-CONTROLLER CHIP

In this section we explore in more detail how the bulk of the display functions of a microprocessor-based terminal are implemented by a special-purpose CRT-controller chip, and Section 8.3 explores the actual structure of such chips.

The Clocking and Timing Functions

We see that all of the display functions are driven by various clocks derived from a single master oscillator. In any implementation of the display-controller logic, the basic timing must be derived by clock dividers that produce signals with the correct period and in the correct phase. Therefore, we need dividers for each of the periods shown in Fig. 8.5. Moreover, the sync and blanking signals shown in Fig. 8.4 are each produced in the same way from the master oscillator. Hence, these signals as well should be produced by a special-purpose LSI display-controller chip. Consequently, the typical controller chip is made up of banks of registers and counters that can be programmed to generate system timing signals and video interface signals as required by each individual terminal. Since such chips are usually not reprogrammed once they are embedded in a terminal, several chip manufacturers offer ''mask'' programming so that the chips are permanently specialized to particular terminals at the time of their manufacture.

What is the internal structure of a typical CRT-controller chip? A typical block diagram of the register and logic required for the timing signals is shown in Fig. 8.6. Each register holds a maximum value or a reference value for a particular counter. The counters hold the current count of various clock divider circuits. At each pulse of the master clock, the dot counter is updated and compared to the maximum number of columns per character. If the two are equal, the counter is reset and a carry is produced into the next divider/counter. In this case the counter is the *character counter*, which holds the number of characters per scan line (including the blank portion). This counter is compared with four different registers to produce a signal when the last displayable character has been reached, when the horizontal sync pulse should start and stop, and when the scan line ends. This counter resets at the end of the scan line and produces a pulse at that point that increments the character-height counter and the frame counter.

The *character-height counter* keeps track of the number of scan lines per display character, and resets when it reaches the last scan line of a character field. Each time this counter overflows it increments the *row counter*, which keeps track of the row of characters that is being displayed. This counter is compared to a register that both holds the number of character rows per screen and resets the row counter when the last displayable row has been completed.

The *frame counter* generates the vertical sync pulse. It is compared to the starting value (which determines the scan line at which the first displayable character begins) and compared to the ending value (which determines when the frame is complete and the vertical sync pulse is to begin). Vertical-sync-pulse width is typically not programmable because standards dictate that this width is three scan lines long. However, a controller chip could easily permit this width to be programmable as well if there were a need to do so.

Because of the high data rate (10 – 60 MHz) associated with the *dot counter* and limitations on the maximum clock rate of some LSI processes, LSI chips for medium and high-resolution applications normally do not have a dot counter on-chip. Hence the clock input to the chip is the character-counter clock. This is the overflow pulse from the dot counter. On the other hand, the CRT-controllers that are specially designed for

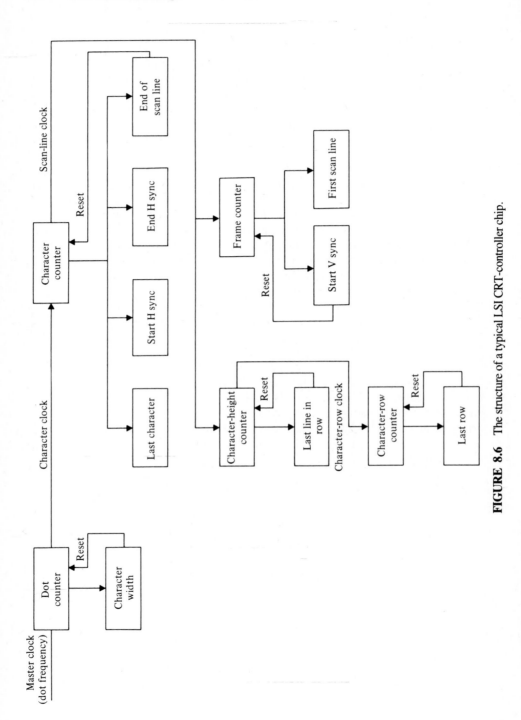

FIGURE 8.6   The structure of a typical LSI CRT-controller chip.

broadcast-type receivers with bandwidths in the 4 MHz range normally incorporate the dot counter on the chip, since the slower data rate is within the reach of LSI technology.

Given the comparators, counters, and limit registers that are on a CRT-controller chip, we can easily determine the functional behavior of the chip and the necessary interface with the remainder of a microprocessor-based controller. If the limit registers are not mask-programmed, they should be settable through the standard memory or I/O commands by the microprocessor. The outputs from the chip should consist of, at least, the following data:

1. the horizontal sync pulse,
2. the vertical sync pulse,
3. the blanking signal,
4. the character counter (which is the address of the character in the line buffer),
5. the row counter (which together with the character counter forms the address of the character to access from the shared memory during DMA operations), and
6. the height counter, (which with the ASCII character code is the address of the displayable dot code in ROM).

The counter outputs are used as addresses to access shared memory, line buffer, and character-generator ROM. If the counters, limit registers, and comparators are implemented without the benefit of LSI, the number of devices required for a controller is quite considerable. Clearly, an LSI device structured as the one shown in Fig. 8.6 has a substantial positive impact on the cost and size of a terminal.

Cursor Functions

As it becomes possible to design greater functionality into LSI chips, we must consider other functions that are reasonable for CRT-controller chips. One such function is the cursor-control function. The idea here is that the CRT-controller chip can maintain the cursor coordinates so that each time the cursor position is reached, the video signal can be treated as a special case and displayed with an inverted video signal, a blinking signal, an underline, or arbitrary cursor graphic. To implement cursor control, we require a pair of registers that give the current row and column of the cursor. These registers are compared on a continuous basis to the current row number and character counter. When both counters match their respective comparands, the chip produces a special signal used off-chip to modify the display.

A variant of this approach makes it very simple to interface a light pen to a CRT display. A light pen is a photosensitive device that emits a signal when it is illuminated. The idea is that a user points the pen at a character on the screen. As the screen is repainted, the pen outputs pulses that are synchronous with the timing of the scan line passing the viewing region of the pen. It is easy to connect the pulses of the light pen to a controller chip, so that when a pulse is detected, the controller copies the contents of the current row and character counters into special registers. Because of delays in the CRT-controller chip and the video display, the position of the beam at any given time is not identical with the current position in the controller registers; the coordinates of the light-pen registers are displaced by a few characters from the true position of the light pen. However, because they are wrong in a predictable way, delays are easily calibrated, and light-pen positions can be corrected automatically by software in the microprocessor.

Scrolling

The scrolling function is implemented in virtually every CRT terminal. Scrolling refers to the process of moving old text lines to the top of the screen as new lines are entered at the bottom. The screen at any given time displays the most recent lines entered, and the scrolling function adjusts the lines upward to fill the available display area. This gives the user a brief past history of the text that has been displayed. Some of the more advanced terminals can scroll downward as well as upward. This permits the user to examine text older than the text currently displayed. A terminal moves old data back onto the top of the screen by saving the text in a local memory or by accepting the data from a host computer under software-controlled backward-scrolling commands.

Because of the tight timing constraints that already exist in CRT displays, many terminals do not scroll displayable text by physically moving the text in memory. Instead, the rows of displayable characters are addressed with a circular numbering system that changes as scrolling occurs. Let us assume for example that the CRT has 24 displayable rows, numbered 0 through 23. Initially, Row 0 is the top row on the screen and Row 23 is the bottom row. When a new line is entered at the bottom of the screen, the screen scrolls upward one row. At this time Row 1 becomes the top row, with succeeding rows having higher numbers until Row 23. The next row below Row 23 is Row 0.

Then instead of moving data in memory, we simply have to keep track of which row is the top row on the display. This number is maintained in a separate register in the CRT controller, and it is used as the reset value of the row counter each time the bottom of a frame is reached. A separate register maintains the actual row count that is compared to the maximum row count in order to detect the bottom of a frame.

A slight variation of this idea is used to implement the pleasing version of scrolling known as "smooth scrolling." Smooth scrolling moves characters up the screen in what appears to be a smooth, continuous movement. In conventional scrolling, characters appear to leap from one row to the next in a jerky motion. The trick in implementing smooth scrolling is to treat the scan lines that make up each character in much the way that scrolling treats the rows of characters on the screen. Assume that characters are 10 scan lines high, including the blank scan line between characters. Then the character-height counter at the top of a character is 0, and at the bottom is 9 in the absence of scrolling. Conventional scrolling never uses this counter, and thus characters appear to move in discrete steps from row to row, never stopping at the intermediate positions.

To implement smooth scrolling we have the characters appear at each intermediate position between the initial and final position. To do so, we change the position of characters by one scan line for each of 10 frames. By the end of the last of the 10 frames, each character has moved up one full row. Smooth scrolling, then, requires a first scan-

line register to supplement the character height counter. The first scan-line register identifies which scan line is currently the first line in a character. Initially this number is 0;
then it increments with each frame until it reaches 0 again. The current scan-line register
is reset from the first scan-line register at the beginning of a new frame. Thereafter it
functions just as the character height counter does in determining which dots are to be
displayed. The effect of the offset produced by the current scan-line register is to adjust
the characters displayed upward by the initial value of the scan-line register. This produces the smooth-scrolling function. The total size of the frame is determined by a different counter, and therefore displacement of the text during a smooth scrolling operation does not shrink a frame's vertical size.

Other Controller Functions

The block diagram of the CRT system in Fig. 8.2 shows several different functions implemented in external devices that can also be implemented on a CRT-controller chip.
We have in that diagram the following off-chip functions:

1. the row buffer(s),
2. the video shift-register,
3. the character-generator ROM, and
4. the DMA controller.

As we see in Section 8.3, there are individual chips that perform many of these functions.

Not only is it possible to move existing logic onto an LSI chip, but it is also possible
to implement new, higher-level functions on such chips. We have mentioned already
most of the functions that appeared in the basic CRT terminal of the early 1970s. Trends
in terminals in recent years have incorporated higher-level functions that yield greater
flexibility in controlling the graphics for characters. For example, some terminals have
attributes associated with each character on the screen in order to indicate such things as
font (underlined or not underlined), highlight (normal or reversed video image), intensity
(full or half), protection (erasable or nonerasable), and emphasis (blink or no blink).
These functions require that extra bits be stored with each character to indicate the values
of the attributes. When a character is displayed the attributes modify the graphic image
of the character. Specifically, the attributes are handled as follows:

1. The font attribute adds an underline in a particular scan-line that appears below the
   graphics for the character. The dots in this scan line then are turned on for underlining and are off otherwise. (The character field must be large enough to accept underlining. Character height is usually 11 scan lines, rather than 9 scan lines in terminals
   that have this capability.) The font attribute may also select an alternative character
   ROM.
2. To reverse an image from white to black or conversely, we simply complement the
   bits obtained from the character-generator ROM. This is done with logic controlled
   by the highlight-attribute.

3. Intensity is set to half intensity by reducing the voltage level of the video signal. This can be done in the analog circuitry with a digital control signal derived from the intensity attribute of the character.
4. Protected characters are characters whose images cannot be changed on the screen through keyboard interaction, but are alterable by commands from application software. The idea is that the protected characters are headings on forms to be filled in by the user. As the user types in data, the cursor visits only the blank areas on the screen and does not overwrite the protected areas. Applications programs can transmit codes to the terminal to clear the screen and construct new forms with totally different protected characters. The protected-character function does not impact the display of the character except possibly through the highlight and intensity techniques discussed above. The function is normally implemented in the software of the microprocessor in the terminal, which examines the attribute of a character before positioning the cursor. Cursor-movement software is designed to skip these protected fields.
5. To emphasize characters by blinking, the characters are displayed successively in normal and reverse video at a rate of about 5 blinks per second. This attribute is implemented with a blink counter that determines whether or not an image will be normal or reversed during the present frame. Then the blinking attribute of each character and the blink counter together determine whether each dot is displayed in normal or reverse video.

Each of the functions described here, except for protected characters, process the display image in some fashion. Hence a number of new chips have appeared that perform these functions as well as the more standard ones described earlier. As technology advances, yet other functions will become commonplace and will find their way onto CRT-controller chips.

8.3 A SAMPLING OF CRT-CONTROLLER CHIPS

In this section we describe various implementations of CRT-controller chips, which provide a wide range of functions. Because the chips are inherently rather complex, it is beyond the scope of this textbook to describe each chip in complete detail. Designers should consult the manufacturers for complete specifications and applications bulletins.

A Basic Controller: The SMC 5027

The SMC 5027 video timer-controller manufactured by Standard Microprocessor Systems performs the timing functions illustrated in Fig. 8.6, except for the high-frequency dot counter, which must be provided off-chip. Fig. 8.7 shows most of the signals produced and accepted by the chip. The interface to a microprocessor is through an 8-bit data bus. Commands are transmitted to the controller through four address bits instead of through a command register. This yields a total of 16 distinct commands, one for each address. The chip is controlled by the *address* of their access, which makes it somewhat different from other chips described in this text.

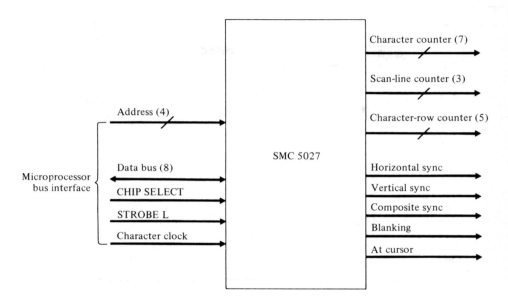

FIGURE 8.7   Major interface signals for the SMC 5027 CRT-controller chip.

Eight of the addresses refer to registers whose contents determine the video characteristics of the display. When these are accessed, the datum on the accompanying data bus is stored into a corresponding register. The microprocessor, in general, need not read the contents of video registers so these registers can be written but not read. The X- and Y-cursor address registers, however, are both readable and writable. Hence, two of the remaining commands permit the microprocessor to read the cursor row and column registers, respectively, and two other commands write into these registers. Of the remaining four commands, one is a reset, one is a scroll command, and two commands initialize the video control registers from external memory. The latter two commands are useful for systems in which there is no microprocessor to load the registers individually. The counter outputs produced by the chip are the ones discussed earlier. These are the

1. character counter (column position of present character),
2. scan-line counter (scan line of present character), and
3. row counter (row of current text).

The video signals are horizontal sync, vertical sync, blank, and a composite sync that combines the vertical and horizontal sync. The chip also produces a signal indicating that the cursor is currently being displayed, which permits external hardware to modify the cursor display.

Although the SMC 5027 implements just the timing functions, cursor highlighting, and scrolling, the high speed of the chip has led to its use in a number of popular terminals. Since the maximum clock rate for the character-counter clock input is 4 MHz, the SMC 5027 can drive high-resolution displays with formats containing up to 132 characters per row.

The Intel 8275 CRT Controller

The Intel 8275 contains all of the functions of the SMC 5027 and more. The signals it produces and requires are shown in Fig. 8.8. The bus interface shown in the figure is compatible with the 808X family of microprocessors. Note that there is one address line connected to the chip, which selects between a command and a parameter register. The microprocessor controls the functions of the chip by writing a command into the command register, followed by writing a sequence of bytes into the parameter register. (Some commands read bytes from the parameter register rather than write bytes into it.)

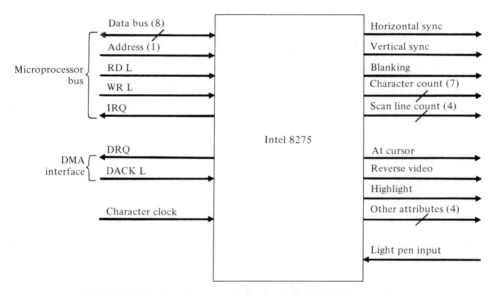

FIGURE 8.8   Interface signals for the Intel 8275 CRT controller.

The counters, limit registers, and comparators follow the general requirements of CRT controllers and are not discussed again here. Figure 8.8 shows the outputs from the character counter and scan line counter, and the video sync signals that are necessary to connect to the external world. As mentioned earlier, the dot counter frequency exceeds the limits of the chip, so that the dot counter must be implemented externally.

The major difference between the 8275 and the 5027 is the placement of the line buffer. This buffer is external for 5027 systems, but is embedded on the 8275. The 8275 therefore interfaces directly to a DMA controller, which must be used to reload the line buffer. Note that the DMA interface signals DRQ and DACK L, which respectively initiate a DMA memory fetch and sense its completion. Because of the high-performance requirements for high-resolution display systems, the 8275 reduces the DMA bottleneck by using two distinct 80-character line buffers. While a row of characters is displayed from one line buffer, the second can be filled by a DMA operation. Then the roles of the buffers are reversed. Double buffering on the chip substantially reduces the cost of the hardware and increases performance without creating significant demands on the external memory system.

In our discussion of the SMC 5027, we indicated that the chip produced the addresses necessary to obtain data from the shared memory; therefore, the 5027 takes on the role of a DMA controller with a small amount of support hardware. In a system based on the 8275, it is necessary to have an external DMA controller, as well as to enlist the services of the microprocessor. The microprocessor activity is required because there is no provision for automatic reloading of the DMA-controller parameter registers at the end of a buffer transfer. The intended way of reinitiating a buffer-filling process is through interrupt service routines. At the end of each buffer transfer, the DMA controller interrupts the microprocessor, which then sets the parameters of the DMA for the transfer of the next row of characters. The CRT controller also interrupts at the end of a frame, thereby providing a point at which the frame scan can be restarted.

The Signetics 267X CRT Chip Set

The 267X family block diagram appears in Fig. 8.9. There are four chips shown:

1. The 2672 Video-Timing Controller, which performs the timing functions for the video display.
2. The 2673 Video and Attributes Controller, which processes attributes and displayable data to produce the serial video signal.
3. The 2670 Character and Graphics Generator, which contains ROM and RAM tables for translating character codes into displayable symbols.
4. The 2671 Keyboard and Communications Controller, which contains the logic required to scan, debounce, and convert keyboard strokes, and to interface to a bidirectional serial communications link.

It is clear from our earlier discussions what functions have to be performed in a CRT terminal. The Signetics's approach in developing this chip set is to partition these functions into four LSI chips, supported with a minimum of other logic and with a microprocessor. So much of the system is implemented in the CRT-chip set that the remaining load on the microprocessor is very light. In fact the microprocessor can be used to implement functions that are not normally available in CRT terminals.

Let us start our discussion of the chip set with the 2672 Video-Timing Controller. Like the SMC 5027 and i8275, the controller contains limit registers, counters, and comparators that generate the video timing signals. The operation of the 2672 is similar to the 5027 in all of the essential details. The 2672 does, however, simplify the DMA interface because in one mode of operation it can refresh from a display buffer memory that is shared with a microprocessor. The idea is that the buffer memory contains the entire display, not just one character row. The microprocessor can read or write individual characters into the shared memory, but it must do so using the facilities of the 2672 for

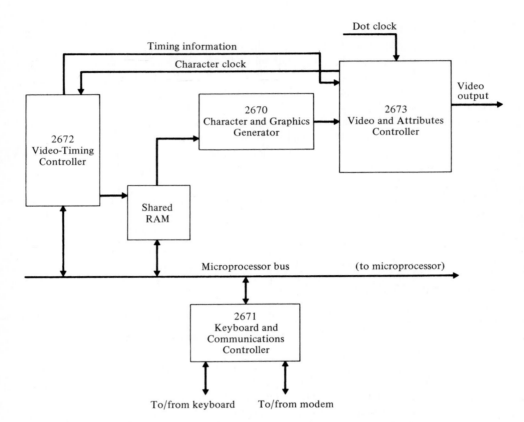

FIGURE 8.9   The Signetics 4-chip video controller system.

timing the access. When the microprocessor performs an access to shared memory, it does not supply the address of the character directly. Instead it issues the READ or WRITE command to occur at the character address currently contained in the cursor or pointer registers. The 2672 then times the access to occur during a blank period so that the visual display will not flicker during access. Status signals from the video controller are accessible from the microprocessor so that the microprocessor can determine when an access is complete.

Other modes of operation are available that enable the microprocessor to access shared memory directly rather than through addresses supplied by the video controller. One such mode is designed for a display buffer that contains a single character row in keeping with the methodology of the 5027 and other controller chips. This row must be refreshed through a DMA operation for each new row to be displayed.

The dot clock is too fast for this chip, as it is for other high-resolution controllers that we have studied, so that the input clock to this chip is the character clock. The counter outputs from the 2672 Video-Timing Controller are transmitted to the 2670 Character Generator chip where they are used to transform ASCII-encoded data into displayable symbols. The unusual aspect of the 2670 is that it contains both ROM and RAM, thereby permitting the user to load special fonts and symbols for specific applications. The symbol resolution is very high, with each character occupying up to 9 scan lines by 10 columns. The displayable field area is much higher, 16 scan lines by 10 columns. The characters are positioned vertically in this field as a function of the control signals applied to the chip. This provides for the display of subscripts and the parts of letters that descend below the base line. The output of the character generator is a parallel block of 10 bits for each character position. Not all of these bits need to be displayed. Some bits can function as attribute bits or display modifiers.

The most unusual chip in this set is the 2673 Video and Attributes Controller. This chip operates at the dot frequency and, in fact, generates the character clock for the 2672 Video-Timing Controller. The function of the 2673 is to convert parallel data to the serial video signal. It combines the video with the blanking signal to produce a composite signal for modulating the CRT beam.

The 2673 contains special logic for manipulating the displayable information. Such things as blinking, cursor highlighting, underlining, reverse video, intensity modulation, and other such operations are performed on this chip. The chip can modify the symbol displayed on a row-by-row basis as well as on an individual character basis.

The last chip in the set, the 2671, services both the bidirectional communications port and the keyboard. The chip generates internal clocks for transmit and receive data rates, and for scanning the keyboard. As keys are struck, the chip debounces the keys and encodes the raw data into an ASCII code through the use of an on-chip encoding ROM. The serial communications port is treated in a conventional fashion. The interesting aspect of this chip, of course, is the fact that it contains both the communications port and the keyboard controller, whereas earlier generations of chips performed one function or the other, but not both.

A Video Display Controller: The 6847/68047

This section treats two closely related chips, the Motorola 6847 and the American Microsystems 68047. Both chips are designed to interface to standard broadcast color-video receivers so that the timing aspects of the chips are preprogrammed and not alterable by the user. Both chips have on-chip ROMs to display standard characters encoded in ASCII. Through external control signals the internal ROM can be disabled and replaced functionally with an external ROM. The differences in the chips lie largely in the video interface and color modulator requirements.

The principal interface signals for the MC6847 are shown in Fig. 8.10. Signals for the AMI68047 are similar, but not identical. For specific details on either chip, consult the manufacturers' reference materials. The MC6847 can access memory directly through the signals shown. It produces a 13-bit address (12 bits for the 68047), and accesses successive bytes in display memory in a continuous fashion. The display

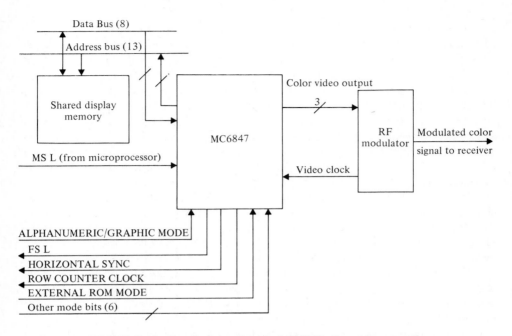

FIGURE 8.10   Interface signals to the MC6847 color-video controller.

memory is intended to be shared between an external microprocessor and the 6847. To facilitate this sharing, there is a single control pin identified as MS L (memory select), which when asserted low, forces the video controller to place its address lines into a high-impedance mode. Although the microprocessor can assert MS L at any time, it normally does so only during vertical retrace when the 6847 is not accessing display memory. No handshake is necessary to obtain access to shared memory. Immediately after asserting MS L the microprocessor can access shared memory to update displayable data.

During normal refresh operation, the video controller scans display memory, reading each byte into an internal buffer. Some internal processing of the data takes place on the chip, eventually resulting in the generation of displayable dots. These dots are passed to a shift register, where they are used to produce the color and composite-video signals that drive an external RF modulator. When new data are to be displayed, the microprocessor asserts MS L, then writes into the shared memory, releases MS L, and proceeds with other processing. The video controller does all other processing of the data.

The other inputs to controller chip are mostly mode-control signals that can be latched in an external parallel port. One control signal selects between alphanumeric and graphic display. In an alphanumeric mode, each byte input from display memory is converted in the external character-generator ROM into the graphic symbol for the character. In graphic mode, the data determine the color of a region of the display area. Additional mode bits select one of several variations of graphic and alphanumeric modes. If the chip is used only in graphic modes or with the internal ROM in alphanumeric mode, there is no need to output the contents of the internal counters. However, if an external ROM is used, the chip must indicate which scan line in a character is active at any given time. For this purpose the chip produces a horizontal sync pulse and a row-counter pulse. The row-counter pulse indicates that a new row of characters is being scanned, and this should reset an external scan-line counter. At the end of each scan line, the horizontal sync pulse increments the scan-line register, and thus the external ROM can be synchronized to the display scan. A control signal forces the chip to accept data from an external ROM, and in this case the data accepted are displayable dots rather than ASCII character codes.

The output signal FS L, field sync, is asserted during the vertical sync pulse at the end of each frame. The purpose of this signal is to provide a window during which a microprocessor can load the shared memory without disrupting the display process. If the microprocessor takes control of the shared memory during normal scanning, the video controller will fail to refresh the screen correctly while the microprocessor has control of memory. This problem is quite visible on the video screen where it shows up as flicker or other degradation of the display.

The most interesting aspects of the MC6847 is the graphic mode of operation. In graphic mode, the display screen is divided into individually displayable regions, called *pixels* for ''picture elements.'' The pixel resolution is directly related to the number of individually selectable colors that can be displayed in individual pixels. In the highest resolution mode, the screen is partitioned into a grid 256 columns by 192 rows, and each pixel can display one of two colors. In a lower resolution mode the grid is reduced to 128 by 64 pixels, but the number of displayable colors is increased to four. Since the lower resolution mode covers the same screen area, each pixel in this mode is somewhat larger than pixels in the high resolution mode. The highest resolution alphanumeric format provides for 16 rows of 32 characters. Even if the chip were to have faster timing to support higher resolution images, the limited bandwidth of broadcast receivers would preclude the display of such images. Moreover, an interesting effect of color perception is that the eye *cannot* resolve high-resolution color images. In regions where color changes rapidly the eye tends to integrate the varying colors into a single composite color.

In spite of the limited resolution available with the MC6847 and AMI 68047, they offer a very inexpensive, yet powerful way to implement color graphics in a microprocessor system. A number of low-cost ''color'' computers have appeared on the market that make use of these chips. The CRT interface requires essentially only five or six chips, including the controller, video modulator, and display buffer.

OTHER READING AND SOURCE MATERIAL

Descriptions of many of the chips covered in this chapter appear in Osborne and Kane, vol. 3, (1978). Kane (1980) covers the 8275, 6847, and 5027 that we briefly described here, plus two other controller chips. His descriptions are very detailed and include reproductions from the manufacturers' specifications. From time to time, periodicals such as *Byte*, *Microcomputing*, and *Interface Age* contain detailed schematics of a video interface designed by a hobbyist. While the designs are not always suitable for commercial manufacture, they usually contain many good suggestions for using particular features of the controller chips. The best source of information for specific controller chips are the application notes published by the chip manufacturers. Murray and Alexy (1977) describe the Intel 8275 in one such note. Signetics, Motorola, and AMI each publish application notes on their video chips as well.

EXPERIMENTS

8.1 For this experiment you will need a dual-trace oscilloscope, a video display terminal, the schematic diagram of the terminal, and chip specifications for the terminal's controller chip. Select a terminal of recent vintage that has an LSI controller chip. Earlier terminals may be designed with a hard-wired controller that will be much more difficult to analyze.

  a) Find the master clock (the dot clock) and display this clock on the oscilloscope. Measure the frequency of the oscillator with a counter or by estimating its frequency from the oscilloscope display.

  b) Find the character clock. This clock is roughly ten times slower than the dot clock. Display the character clock and dot clock simultaneously on the dual-trace oscilloscope and find the ratio between the clocks. Examine the video terminal display under a magnifying glass, and determine the width of a character in dots. Verify that the character width is equal to the ratio of the dot clock to the character clock.

  c) Find the scan-line clock. This should be about 50 to 100 times slower than the character clock. Synchronize the oscilloscope to the scan-line clock and display the video output on the oscilloscope. Most controllers combine the blanking pulses with the video output signal, so that the blanking pulses will be clearly visible on the scope. Information displayed within each line will show up as overlaid traces that are not stationary on the oscilloscope display. Program the terminal to display a blank black screen. This should eliminate the nonstationary traces on the screen except for the traces that occur during the vertical sync and retrace portion of the display. Now program the terminal to display an all white screen. How does the oscilloscope display change? Measure the ratio of the scan-line clock to the character clock. How does this ratio compare to the number of characters per row?

  d) Find the character-row clock that triggers a display-buffer reload. This clock occurs once per row of characters displayed. Display this clock and the scan-line clock together on a dual-trace oscilloscope and measure their ratio. Then use a magnifying glass to examine the terminal display to measure the character height in dots. Is the character height equal to the clock ratio?

e) Try to determine during which scan line the row buffer is reloaded. To do so, fill the terminal screen with the character *N*. Then synchronize the display to the character-row clock and probe the video output. Does the video output show that the row buffer is reloaded while displaying the character dots or while displaying a blank scan line between text rows?

f) Determine the number of character rows per vertical display by finding the ratio of the character-row clock to the vertical-sync clock. This ratio may not be an integer. If not, attempt to find the ratio of the scan-line clock to the vertical-sync clock. The ratio should be in the range from 250 to 350, depending on the resolution of the terminal.

g) Synchronize the scope to the vertical-sync clock. Probe the video output and observe the blanking that occurs during the vertical-sync and retrace period.

8.2 With advanced chips such as the 6847 and 68047, it is very simple to interface a microprocessor to a color-video receiver. You can design and build such an interface with a video-controller chip, a parallel port such as an 8255 or 6821, a 1 K × 12 memory consisting of three 2114s, and a modulator chip such as the LM1889 or MC1372. Design and build such an interface and demonstrate the interface in operation. For the design of the RF-modulator, consult the manufacturer's chip specifications or application notes.

9 / SOFTWARE DEVELOPMENT

In this chapter we investigate in some detail a methodology recommended for software development. We presume that the reader has been exposed to programming languages and software development in general, so that this material concentrates on techniques that are most relevant to the interfacing problem. High-level languages are usually not suitable for real-time programs that operate device interfaces. The reasons for this vary from language to language, but most languages fail in at least one of the following ways:

1. The code produced by a compiler is too inefficient to meet the real-time demands.
2. The code produced by a compiler is too large to fit in the available space.
3. The code produced by a compiler cannot take advantage of microprocessor facilities, such as interrupts and I/O ports that are inaccessible to the high-level language.

When no suitable high-level language exists for program development, the system engineer is forced to use assembly language. But assembly languages over the years have been shown to have several major drawbacks. They are difficult to write, debug, document, and maintain, and they are not readily transportable from one computer to another.

At this writing, there are a number of widely available high-level languages for microcomputers so that at least some, if not all, of the programming can be done in the high-level language. The languages include Pascal (for most microprocessors), C (a Bell Laboratories language available for the LSI-11 and others), and the PL languages including PLM for the 808X Family and PLZ for the Z80/Z8000 family. FORTH is a somewhat unusual language available for most micros, and has been used in various applications. And, of course, we cannot omit BASIC, which is available universally. BASIC interpreters are very powerful tools for development of small programs, and can often be used to build test software for interfaces with a minimum of effort. However, BASIC interpreters are notably slow, and are rarely suitable for running moderate or high-performance peripherals. Recent developments in the programming language Ada suggest that Ada cross-compilers will be practical tools for microcomputers. Initial releases of Ada run on large machines, with the capability of compiling for microcomputer target machines. Self-hosted compilers are becoming available for 16-bit and 32-bit micros such as the Z8000, 8086, MC68000, and the iAPX432.

The facilities that are most frequently missing in high-level languages for our purposes are

1. interrupt handling,
2. status testing of specific bits of specific machine registers,
3. concurrent control of multiple microprocessors, and
4. the ability to use specific hardware resources such as special hardware for multiplication and memory management.

What we propose is to use a high-level language where possible, and otherwise use assembly language for the remainder of the implementation. But even where the assembly language is required, a high-level language can support the development effort as we demonstrate throughout this chapter.

9.1 SOFTWARE DEVELOPMENT METHODOLOGY

In this section we review the methodology known as "top-down design" and apply it to the construction of programs in assembly language. The program example we use is a program that merges intermediate files produced by a sorting algorithm, and that exhibits all of the important facets of the design process.

Top-Down Design and Iterative Refinement

The process of top-down design involves developing a program through a succession of stages. The first stage is a top-level description of the algorithm that omits most details in order to focus on the flow and logic at the highest level. The next stage of the development process refines this description by filling in the details of supporting operations. The normal way of refining the description is to invoke the supporting operations as subroutines in the top-level description, and then to expand the descriptions of the subroutines in the refinement process. The subroutines may themselves invoke subroutines whose descriptions are expanded in subsequent refinements.

While top-down design has been an important contribution to program development, it has not been widely incorporated into the development of assembly-language code. The plan of this section is to illustrate the application of top-down design to assembly language programming, with particular emphasis on how assembly language programs can provide the benefits of a high-level language. The following is a brief statement of this method:

1. The top-level flow and logic of the algorithm is described; a high-level structured programming language is used for this description, and the language is extended where necessary to permit it to describe machine resources on the target machine.
   Since the program will be hand-translated to assembly language, it is not necessary that the programming language be a standard language, nor is it necessary to write syntactically correct programs. However, the programmer should strive to produce documentation that is readable and unambiguous. For this reason the results will be more usable and more valuable if the language is a widely used standard one and if the program adheres to the rules of syntax.
2. Subroutines invoked in the top-level description are each expanded in detail in the same manner. If these subroutines invoke other subroutines, then those subroutines are expanded as well.
3. At the end of the refinement process, the program consists of a top-level driver program and a collection of subroutines, all written in the high-level language. This

forms the primary documentation for the assembly-language program. The next step is to review the high-level description and to validate that it is a correct algorithm for the intended application.

4. Given the top-level description, the next step is a hand translation of that description into assembly language. As a part of the translation process, the original high-level description is inserted into the assembly-language code as comment lines.

5. The assembly-language program is checked against the high-level description to validate that the hand-translation process is correct.

6. The program is carefully exercised to validate that each subroutine operates correctly over the range of its possible inputs. If an error is discovered during checkout, it will either be an error in the hand-translation process, or it will be an error in the original high-level description. Translation errors are corrected at the assembly-language level. Errors in the original high-level description are corrected at that level, and the high-level description is rechecked for accuracy. When the high-level description has been corrected and validated, the changes in each subroutine are hand translated into changes into the existing assembly language for that subroutine.

If all steps of the process are made carefully, and if the errors discovered during subroutine checkout are successfully corrected, then the resulting program should run correctly with a minimum of debugging.

This author has written a number of assembly-language programs using this process and has rarely found an error in the program on the first debugging run. The errors that have appeared have largely been errors in the original high-level description, and not in the hand-translation to assembly language. Because the errors are more easily corrected in the high-level description than in the assembly-language description, having the high-level description available reduces the debugging time to a negligible fraction of the development time. The observed productivity has been between 400 to 800 lines of debugged and documented assembly language per day. This holds for programs with critical timing, interrupt-driven I/O, and tight space requirements, all of which tend to lower productivity. Since there is about a tenfold increase in the number of lines of code in the process of translating from the high-level description to the assembly-language description of an algorithm, the productivity observed corresponds to an equivalent of 40 to 80 lines of debugged and documented high-level language code per day. This level of productivity is representative of what has been achieved in industry when programmers use top-down design and a high-level language. Note that the figures quoted are for assembly-language programs that occupy from 1000 to 3000 bytes of storage. Productivity decreases as the size and complexity of programs increase, so that the figures quoted here are higher than the productivity expected for the development of large programs.

An Example: File Merging

This section illustrates the concept of top-down design in a program fragment of a sort/merge algorithm which is a standard system utility often written in assembly language. The algorithm illustrated is the merge subroutine. Merge operates on two input files and produces two output files, as illustrated in Fig. 9.1. The items in File 1 and File 2

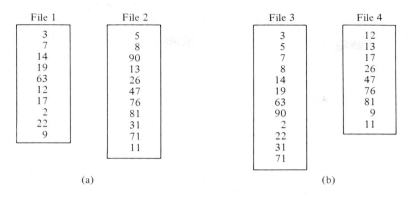

File 1	File 2	File 3	File 4
3	5	3	12
7	8	5	13
14	90	7	17
19	13	8	26
63	26	14	47
12	47	19	76
17	76	63	81
2	81	90	9
22	31	2	11
9	71	22	
	11	31	
		71	

(a)　　　　　　　　　　　　　　　　　　　　　　(b)

FIGURE 9.1　Files (a) before and (b) after merging.

are shown as numbers, but the program actually operates on any data. The files shown consist of sequences of numbers and terminate with a special mark called EOF for End of File. The merge program reads the two files, merging the successive entries from both files into one string sorted in ascending order until the string cannot be extended. This condition occurs when the last entry in the string is greater than the next entry in either input file. At this point the algorithm starts producing a new sorted string and the process repeats. New sorted strings are placed alternately in File 3 and File 4, with the file changing each time a new string is begun. At the end of the merge of Files 1 and 2, the data will have been partially merged on Files 3 and 4, with the sorted strings approximately equally distributed between the output files.

Sorting can be performed by successive calls on the merge algorithm. To sort, the output files are examined at the end of a merge phase. If neither file is empty at the end of the processing of Files 1 and 2, then the output files are swapped with the input files and the process repeats. The number of sorted strings decreases roughly by a factor of 2 during each pass of the files, and the average length of a sorted string roughly doubles during each pass. Eventually, the output becomes one sorted string on one file, and an empty file on the other. At this time the merge process has completed the sort of the input files. An efficient sort/merge package should use a fast, in-memory sort to produce long sorted strings on Files 1 and 2. The in-memory sorting algorithm operates exclusively on chunks of the input file that fit in memory, and sorts them into strings without using any external storage. Then these strings are sorted through a succession of merge phases.

The process is illustrated in Fig. 9.1 where we see the input files, Files 1 and 2, and the resulting output files, Files 3 and 4. Note that the first few numbers in Files 1 and 2 have been merged together and appear as the first sorted string in File 3. The next few numbers in Files 1 and 2 appear as the first sorted string in File 4.

The top-level description of the merge algorithm appears in Program 9.1 in a language intended to be similar to Pascal. In lines 4 through 18, the file name is declared as a record structure that contains pointers to the file, the present item now being scanned from that file, and the prior item scanned from the file. Also in the file is a status word that is used to indicate what has happened to that file. An EOF code for status indicates that we have reached the end of the file. A BREAK code indicates that we have reached a break between strings on the file. As this is sensed when the present item has a lower value than the last item, the items are in descending order at this point rather than in ascending order.

The top-level routine calls lower-level ones to implement various operations that make up the merge process. These include the system routines RESET and REWRITE that open input and output files, respectively, and the application procedures SWAP_FILE_NAME, PROCESS_ITEM, and FLUSH. (Pascal denotes subroutines as ''functions'' or ''procedures,'' depending on whether they do or do not return a value.)

By reviewing the program in a top-down fashion, the reader can quickly grasp the mechanics of the algorithm. Consider first the body of the main program loop in lines 31 through 37. It begins with a comparison of the current items in File 1 and File 2. If the value of File 1's item is greater than the value of File 2's item, the main program calls SWAP_FILE_NAME to interchange the two input files. Therefore, when control reaches the succeeding statement in line 36, the value of File 1's item is no greater than the value of File 2's.

The notation FILE1@. ITEM@ in the comparison is the Pascal notation for three distinct operations in an effective-address calculation. The @ denotes indirection. In this case the variable FILE1 is a pointer to a record. Then ''FILE1'' denotes the variable FILE1 and ''FILE1@'' denotes the record to which it points. This corresponds to an indirect access through the pointer variable FILE1. The period in the notation FILE1@. ITEM denotes an element of a record structure which in this case is the element ITEM of a file block record. Finding an element in a record structure is similar to finding an array element within an array structure. The address calculation is an indexing operation in which the base address of the record structure is increased by the offset to the ITEM portion of the structure. Since the ITEM element of a file block is itself a pointer, there is yet another indirect operation through ITEM to access the physical data.

Therefore ''FILE1@. ITEM@'' is a shorthand notation for an indirect access through FILE1, followed by an indexing operation to point to the ITEM portion of the data structure. This in turn is used as the indirect address of the data buffer. The effective-address calculations are shown later in this chapter in assembly language and should clarify the use of the Pascal notation.

PROCESS_ITEM, as seen from its call on line 37 of Program 9.1, does whatever needs to be done in the inner loop of the merge. We specify this activity in the next refinement of the program. On lines 38 and 39, the function of the procedure FLUSH is to read a file repeatedly and copy data to an output file until the READ encounters an EOF or BREAK status. FLUSH is used at the end of the main loop when one file has reached its end, and has thereby exhausted its data. Then the other file must be emptied. FLUSH acts on whichever file is nonempty. The file that triggered the loop exit will not be FLUSHed because of the tests of the file status that protect the calls to FLUSH.

With the aid of the top-level flow of the algorithm in Program 9.1, we can now refine some details by filling in the bodies of the procedures invoked by the main program. The SWAP_FILE_NAME procedure appears in Program 9.2, and is rather trivial. In this case swap-

PROGRAM 9.1   Merge Program: Top-Level

```
 1  program MERGE;
 2  (* Variables and system procedures are all printed in upper case. Reserved
 3      words are bold face. *)
 4      type FILENAME: pointer to FILE_BLOCK;
 5      FILE_BLOCK = record
 6          FID: file;
 7          STATUS:                        integer;
 8          LAST_ITEM:                     pointer to BUFFER;
 9          ITEM:                          pointer to BUFFER;
10      end
11      (* A file block is a data structure that contains:
12          a file identifier
13          a status code
14              OK    = normal status
15              EOF   = end of file encountered on read
16              BREAK = present item is less than previous
17          a pointer to the last item
18          a pointer to the present item. *)
19  var FILENAME: FILE1, FILE2, FILE3, FILE4;
20  begin
21  (* Outermost loop. *);
22      (* Open File 1 and File 2 for input. *)
23      RESET (FILE1@. FID);
24      RESET (FILE2@. FID);
25      (* If either file is empty, the merge is done. *);
26      if (FILE1@. STATUS = EOF or FILE2@. STATUS = EOF) then exit;
27      (* Open File 3 and File 4 for output. *)
28      REWRITE (FILE3@. FID);
29      REWRITE (FILE4@. FID);
30      repeat
31  (* Main loop *)
32          begin
33          if FILE1@. ITEM@ > FILE2@.ITEM@ then
34              SWAP_FILE_NAME (FILE1, FILE2);
35          (* The item for FILE1 is now the lesser item. *)
36          PROCESS_ITEM;
37      end until (FILE1@. STATUS = EOF or FILE2@. STATUS = EOF);
38  while not (FILE1@. STATUS = EOF) do FLUSH (FILE1);
39  while not (FILE2@. STATUS = EOF) do FLUSH (FILE2);
40  (* Close all files. *)
41  (* Now that both files have been exhausted, make the output
42      files into input files, and conversely. *)
43  SWAP_FILE_NAME (FILE1, FILE3);
44  SWAP_FILE_NAME (FILE2, FILE4)
45  end of program.
```

ping pointers to files is more efficient than swapping all of the information about the files. Therefore, on line 4 of Program 9.1 a FILENAME is declared to be a pointer to a FILE_BLOCK. Program 9.2 swaps two pointers of this type leaving the file blocks unchanged.

PROGRAM 9.2   Merge Program: SWAP_FILE_NAME

```
1  procedure SWAP_FILE NAME (var: FILEA, FILEB: FILENAME) ;
2  var FILENAME: TEMP;
3  begin
4      (* Interchange the pointers to the file blocks. *)
5      TEMP := FILEA;
6      FILEA := FILEB;
7      FILEB := TEMP;
8  end;
```

Now let's expand the PROCESS_ITEM procedure and determine what functions it performs. It appears in Program 9.3 that PROCESS_ITEM does little more than read one item from File 1. If PROCESS_ITEM encounters an EOF or BREAK, then on line 5 PROCESS_ITEM flushes the contents of File 2 to the output file. This advances File 2 to the next break between sequences or to its end of file if File 2 has no more breaks. Now an equal number of sorted substrings have been processed for Files 1 and 2.

PROGRAM 9.3   Merge Programs: PROCESS_ITEM, and FETCH

```
1  procedure PROCESS_ITEM;
2  begin
3      (* Read from File 1 and synchronize its BREAKs with those of File 2. *)
4          FETCH (FILE1) ;
5      if not FILE1@. STATUS = OK then FLUSH (FILE2) ;
6      (* FLUSH File 2 when File 1 has reached an end condition
7          or BREAK condition. *)
8  end;
9  procedure FETCH (WORKFILE: FILENAME) ;
10 begin
11     (* Output an item, read a new record, and record EOF and BREAK status. *)
12     OUTPUT (WORKFILE) ; (* Output and switch output files at a break. *)
13     WORKFILE@. LAST_ITEM := WORKFILE@. ITEM;
14     READ (WORKFILE, WORKFILE@. ITEM) ;
15     WORKFILE@. STATUS := read status;
16     if WORKFILE@. STATUS = OK and WORKFILE@. LAST_ITEM@ > WORKFILE@. ITEM@ then
17         WORKFILE@. STATUS := BREAK
18 end.
```

PROCESS_ITEM calls on the procedure FETCH whose Pascal program appears with PROCESS_ITEM in Program 9.3. FETCH keeps track of breaks in the input file, and it does so by buffering one input item for each input file. The opening statement of FETCH outputs the current item in WORKFILE. This item is the lesser of the two items that were previously examined in the main program. Then FETCH moves the current item for the file into the position held for the last item. (This move may be implemented as a movement of pointers rather than as a movement of the items themselves.) The next three statements, respectively, read a new item from the file, record the file status in the file block, and look for a BREAK in the file.

It is not necessary to continue the Pascal description of the example. The only missing procedures are OUTPUT, SWAP, and READ. The latter two procedures follow standard conventions, while OUTPUT outputs individual records and discovers breaks in the output stream. At each break, OUTPUT swaps the output file names, and begins transmitting strings of numbers to the output file that had formerly been idle.

Readers familiar with Pascal should have no difficulty in understanding the examples. If the notation is unfamiliar to the reader, then we invite the reader to rewrite the Pascal versions of the algorithms in a more familiar programming language. The point is to express the algorithm at the highest-possible level from which the entire assembly language can be generated mechanically. During the refinement process, as details of the algorithm are filled in, changes to the structure of top-level programs may be required. The term "iterative refinement" for this programming process is intended to convey the need to iterate through the design and programming of the top-levels of the algorithm as the details of the lower levels are specified.

In the next section we revisit the Pascal procedures and observe how they can be translated to assembly language.

Translation to Assembly Language

The first example of a translation process is shown in Program 9.4.

This is a translation of portions of the main program into assembly language for a register-oriented microprocessor. Among the microprocessors for which this type of translation is pertinent are the 808X family, the Z80, Z8000, and MC68000. Since industry has followed no particular standard in the use of assembly language, our example tends to follow Intel's conventions for the 808X family.

In the assembly language in Program 9.4, we have chosen to follow the conventions outlined as follows:

1. Assembly directives begin with a period. We use the directives .ORG (origin), .EQU (equate), .BYTE (reserve block storage, bytes), and .WORD (reserve block storage, words). A word of storage is 16 bits (two bytes).
2. The machine instructions are MOV DEST, SRC (move data from SRC to DEST), JSR (jump to subroutine), RTS (return from subroutine) CMP (compare and set condition codes), and the conditional branches BEQ (branch if equal), BNE (branch if not equal), BLE (branch if less than or equal, signed comparison), and BLO (branch if low, unsigned comparison).
3. The addressing modes are direct, register indirect, and immediate. The instruction MOV DEST,SRC has both addresses in direct mode. Indexed mode is indicated by parentheses as in the instruction MOV DEST, (SRC). In this case the operand address is taken from the contents of machine register SRC. Immediate mode is represented by the use of the # in front of an operand as in the instruction MOV DEST,#FILE1. This instruction moves the immediate operand (the address of File 1) into DEST.

This very limited instruction set and addressing capability is sufficient to illustrate all of the ideas involved in translating algorithms into assembly language. The reader can easily create the assembly-language program for virtually any other microprocessor by following principles exhibited in Program 9.4.

The first section of the example, lines 9 through 26, shows how to create data structures in assembly language. In this section, the program creates the data structure for a FILENAME record. The purpose of the assembly language code is to create the symbols FID, STATUS, LAST_ITEM, and ITEM with values equal to their offsets in a record. To do so, the program defines the values of the symbols through the .EQU directive.

In lines 27 through 37 the program reserves space for the pushdown stack and for the FILENAME pointers. As other details of the main program are filled in, declarations of other variables, particularly temporary variables, will be made in this region. Note that there is space left for four records of seven bytes each. An initialization procedure not shown in the example sets the initial values of the pointers to addresses of the file region.

Line 41 fixes the main program origin at 2000_{16}. The main program starts with code for initializing variables and pointers and for opening the four files. The Pascal code for this process is shown on lines 42 through 53. Initialization code in assembly language has been omitted from the example because the initial values of variables do not appear in the Pascal descriptions of the algorithms. These values should be determined by analyzing the algorithms, and the code to create the initial values should be incorporated into the assembly language. File-handling procedures have been omitted because they are quite dependent on the system software and executive program. It is not particularly illuminating to include such details in this discussion.

The next portion of the example in lines 55 through 97 is the body of the REPEAT loop of the main program. A rather interesting address calculation takes place in the first few statements of this iteration as shown in lines 60 through 67. The objective of the instruction sequence is to calculate the addresses of operands specified in the form FILE@. ITEM@. The calculation begins by defining registers ITEM1 and ITEM2. Symbols are used here instead of register identifiers to increase the readability of the program, and to facilitate reassignment of registers if program optimization requires such an action to be taken. The statement

```
MOV      ITEM1,FILE1
```

performs the first access by copying the file-block pointer into the machine register ITEM1. Now the address of the file block is in a register where it can be manipulated by the program, and the code has implemented FILE1@. When the next instruction, an ADD, is executed, ITEM1 is increased by the amount of the offset to ITEM in a file block. Now ITEM1 points to the item pointer, and the code has implemented FILE1@. ITEM. The last indirection requires one more MOV instruction on line 64, which leaves in ITEM1 the pointer FILE1@. ITEM@. A similar calculation deals with the pointer to the other record, and the two pointers are passed to a procedure COMPARE that determines which of the two items has the smaller value.

PROGRAM 9.4　　An Assembly Language Version of the Main Program

```
 1  *******************************************************************************
 2  *    THIS IS AN EXAMPLE OF AN ASSEMBLY LANGUAGE                                *
 3  *    IMPLEMENTATION OF PORTIONS OF THE MAIN PROGRAM                            *
 4  *******************************************************************************
 5
 6
 7
 8
 9  *******************************************************************************
10  *    PROGRAM MERGE;                                                            *
11  *    TYPE PTR: POINTER TO CHARACTER ARRAY                                       *
12  *         FILENAME = RECORD                                                     *
13  *              FID:        FILE                                                 *
14  *              STATUS:     INTEGER                                              *
15  *              LAST_ITEM: POINTER                                               *
16  *              ITEM:       POINTER                                              *
17  *******************************************************************************
18  *    DECLARE THE RECORD STRUCTURE FOR A FILENAME
19  *        THE OFFSETS ARE RELATIVE OFFSETS
20  FID        . EQU     0     ONE-WORD FILE POINTER
21  STATUS     . EQU     2     STATUS BYTE
22  LASTITEM   . EQU     3     POINTER TO LAST ITEM
23  ITEM       . EQU     5     POINTER TO PRESENT ITEM
24  *******************************************************************************
25  *    END OF FILENAME DEFINITION                                                *
26  *******************************************************************************
27             . ORG     1000H    PROGRAM ORIGIN FOR VARIABLES AND STACK
28  STACK      . WORD    256      RESERVE 256 WORDS FOR THE STACK
29  *******************************************************************************
30  *    VAR FILENAME: FILE1, FILE2, FILE3, FILE4;                                 *
31  *******************************************************************************
32  FILE1      . WORD    1              FILE 1 POINTER
33  FILE2      . WORD    1              FILE 2 POINTER
34  FILE3      . WORD    1              FILE 3 POINTER
35  FILE4      . WORD    1              FILE 4 POINTER
36  FILES      . BYTE    4*7            RESERVE SPACE FOR THE FILE RECORDS
37  *                                   4 RECORDS WITH 7 BYTES EACH
38  *******************************************************************************
39  *    CODE FOR MAIN PROGRAM BEGINS HERE                                         *
40  *******************************************************************************
41             . ORG     2000H    ORIGIN FOR PROGRAM CODE
42  *******************************************************************************
43  *    INITIALIZE VARIABLES AND RECORDS;                                         *
44  *    RESET (FILE1@. FID) ;                                                      *
45  *    RESET (FILE2@. FID) ;                                                      *
46  *    REWRITE (FILE3@. FID) ;                                                    *
47  *    REWRITE (FILE4@. FID) ;                                                    *
48  *******************************************************************************
49
```

(Continued on next page.)

```
50  *************************************************************************
51  *    (* INSERT THE MACHINE-DEPENDENT CODE HERE FOR THE                 *
52  *       STATEMENTS ABOVE *)                                            *
53  *************************************************************************
54
55  *************************************************************************
56  *    REPEAT                                                            *
57  *    BEGIN                                                             *
58  *            IF FILE1@. REC@ > FILE2@. REC@ THEN                       *
59  *************************************************************************
60  ITEM1      . EQU      REG4             REGISTER 4 WILL HOLD THIS POINTER
61  ITEM2      . EQU      REG6             REGISTER 6 WILL HOLD SECOND POINTER
62  MAIN1      MOV        ITEM1, FILE1     ITEM1 := FILE1 (* COPY THE POINTER *)
63             ADD        ITEM1, #ITEM     ITEM1 := ITEM1 + ITEM; (* ADD THE OFFSET *)
64             MOV        ITEM1, (ITEM1)   LOAD THE BUFFER POINTER
65             MOV        ITEM2, FILE2     ITEM2 := FILE2 (* COPY THE POINTER *)
66             ADD        ITEM2, #ITEM     ITEM2 := ITEM2 + ITEM; (* ADD THE OFFSET *)
67             MOV        ITEM2, (ITEM2)   LOAD THE BUFFER POINTER
68             JSR        COMPARE          SUBROUTINE CALL TO COMPARE RECORDS
69             BLE        MAIN2            BRANCH IF ITEM1 IS NOT GREATER THAN ITEM2
70  *************************************************************************
71  *            SWAP_FILE_NAME (FILE1, FILE2);                            *
72  * (* PARAMETERS ARE PASSED IN REGISTERS ITEM1 AND ITEM2 *)            *
73  *************************************************************************
74             MOV        ITEM1, #FILE1    COPY ADDRESS OF FILE POINTER TO ITEM1
75             MOV        ITEM2, #FILE2      AND SIMILARLY FOR FILE2.
76             JSR        SWAPFILE         SWAP THE FILE NAMES
77  *************************************************************************
78  *    PROCESS_ITEM;                                                     *
79  *    (* FILE1 AND FILE2 HAVE BEEN UPDATED IN MEMORY                    *
80  *       BY THE PROCEDURE "SWAPFILE" *)                                 *
81  *************************************************************************
82  MAIN2      JSR        PROCESS
83  *************************************************************************
84  *    END UNTIL (FILE1@. STATUS = EOF                                   *
85  *        OR FILE2@. STATUS = EOF)                                      *
86  *************************************************************************
87             MOV        ITEM1, FILE1     ITEM1 := POINTER TO FILE BLOCK
88             ADD        ITEM1, #STATUS   (* POINT TO STATUS WORD *)
89             MOV        ITEM1, (ITEM1)   (* LOAD THE STATUS WORD *)
90             CMP        ITEM1, #EOF      IS IT AN END OF FILE?
91             BEQ        MAINEXIT
92             MOV        ITEM2, FILE2     ITEM2 := POINTER TO FILE BLOCK
93             ADD        ITEM2, #STATUS   (* POINT TO STATUS WORD *)
94             MOV        ITEM2, (ITEM2)   (* LOAD THE STATUS WORD *)
95             CMP        ITEM2, #EOF      IS IT AN END OF FILE?
96             BNE        MAIN1            IF NOT AN END FILE, LOOP AGAIN
97  MAINEXIT   . EQU      *
98  *************************************************************************
99  *    THE REMAINDER OF MAIN PROGRAM GOES HERE                           *
100 *************************************************************************
```

```
101
102 ************************************************************************
103 *    PROCEDURE SWAPFILE (FILEA, FILEB)                                 *
104 *      (* PARAMETERS ARE PASSED IN ITEM1 AND ITEM2 *)                  *
105 *    BEGIN                                                             *
106 *        TEMP := FILEA                                                 *
107 *        FILEA := FILEB;                                               *
108 *        FILEA := TEMP;                                                *
109 *    END;                                                              *
110 ************************************************************************
111 FILEA      . EQU      ITEM1           FIRST PARAMETER
112 FILEB      . EQU      ITEM2           SECOND PARAMETER
113 PTRA       . EQU      REG0            TEMPORARY STORAGE FOR FIRST POINTER
114 PTRB       . EQU      REG1            TEMPORARY STORAGE FOR SECOND POINTER
115 SWAPFILE   MOV       PTRA, (FILEA)    PTRA NOW CONTAINS THE CONTENTS OF FILEA
116            MOV       PTRB, (FILEB)    PTRB NOW CONTAINS THE CONTENTS OF FILEB
117            MOV       (FILEA) , PTRB   UPDATE FILEA WITH PRIOR FILEB
118            MOV       (FILEB) , PTRA   UPDATE FILEB WITH PRIOR FILEA
119            RTS                        RETURN FROM SUBROUTINE
120 ************************************************************************
121 *    PROCEDURE PROCESS_ITEM;                                           *
122 *    BEGIN                                                             *
123 *        FETCH (FILE1) ;                                              *
124 ************************************************************************
125 PROCESS    MOV       ITEM1, FILE1     PASS POINTER TO FILE BLOCK
126            JSR       FETCH              TO THE PROCEDURE "FETCH"
127 ************************************************************************
128 *              IF NOT FILE1@. STATUS = OK                             *
129 ************************************************************************
130            MOV       ITEM1, FILE1     ITEM1 := POINTER TO FILE BLOCK;
131            ADD       ITEM1, #STATUS   (* POINT TO STATUS *)
132            MOV       ITEM1, (ITEM1)   (* FETCH STATUS *)
133            CMP       ITEM1, #OK       IS IT OK?
134 ************************************************************************
135 *              THEN FLUSH (FILE2)                                     *
136 ************************************************************************
137            BEQ       PROCEXIT         ALL OK, SO EXIT
138            MOV       ITEM2, FILE2     PARAMETER FOR "FLUSH"
139            JSR       FLUSH
140 ************************************************************************
141 *        RETURN                                                       *
142 *    END                                                              *
143 ************************************************************************
144 PROCEXIT   RTS                        RETURN FROM "PROCESS_ITEM"
```

In reviewing this tricky address calculation, note that the value of ITEM is treated as a literal constant in the instruction

```
ADD      ITEM1, #ITEM
```

The ADD with a literal can be combined with the prior or succeeding MOV instructions if the machine language permits the index register to be modified by an offset either just before or just after its value is used as an address.

The next phase of the main program is a call to SWAPFILE. This appears in lines 70 through 77. For this call, we pass the addresses of the file pointers and not the pointers themselves. SWAPFILE can then change the contents of the memory locations containing these pointers. If the microprocessor has a rich array of registers, it may be possible to allocate the storage for these pointers in the registers rather than in memory to achieve a slightly faster implementation. SWAPFILE would have to be altered to be consistent with this storage strategy.

After the call to PROCESS_ITEM on line 82, the main program checks the status of the input files in lines 83 through 96, and exits the loop if an end-of-file condition is detected on either file. Note that the access to the status byte of a file block follows the same code template as an access to a record pointer.

Hand-compilation of programs from Pascal or similar high-level language is evidently quite mechanical and can be done virtually error free. Hence, if the original high-level code is correct, the assembly language will be correct. A side benefit of intermixing assembly language and high-level language in the program listing is that it yields excellent documentation for the program.

Hand-translation must still be done carefully, for it can be error-free only if the program author meticulously translates each step into an exactly equivalent code. Our program example shows a subroutine in which the actual implementation differs slightly from the Pascal version of the program. This is the code for procedure SWAPFILE on lines 102 through 120. The original Pascal program is written as if there were no high-speed registers available. Therefore, the program declares a temporary variable, and performs a swap with the aid of this variable. The implementation of the swap in assembly language takes advantage of two machine registers and performs the swap using both of these registers for temporary storage. Hence, the program copies both operands into machine registers in the first step (lines 115 and 116), and then stores back the operands to opposite addresses (lines 117 and 118). The programmer therefore can exert "poetic license" in the translation process, editing the assembly language in order to improve efficiency of the resulting code.

The PROCESS_ITEM subroutine appears on lines 120 through 144. It opens with a subroutine call to FETCH, lines 125 and 126, and uses a machine register, ITEM1, to hold the parameter of the subroutine. On lines 127 through 133, the subroutine checks file status using the now familiar template for access to this variable. Lines 134 through 140 show a conditional call to FLUSH based on the outcome of the status test.

The remainder of the Pascal translation is quite straightforward and is not shown in the example. Now that we have presented a lengthy example of the translation process, we must look more carefully at the purposes of assembly language for program implementation. Because high-level languages are far easier to use and understand than assembly languages, they are always preferred to assembly language for documentation, maintenance, and ease of development. When real-time performance, memory space, or access to specific machine facilities force the designer to seek tools to supplement a high-level language, the next best choice is the use of assembly language in conjunction with the high-level language. The assembly language is used for time-critical portions of the code, and for machine-dependent operations such as I/O. In some applications, particularly where memory space is a critical resource, it may be necessary to abandon high-level languages completely and implement the entire program in assembly language.

The translation example shown in Program 9.4 does not clearly reveal the advantages of assembly language over the compiled code because the hand translation is not terribly different from the code produced by a good compiler. However the example is misleading in this regard. Many compilers generate a code that is much less efficient than even this inefficient assembly-language example. At the low end of efficiency, a purely interpretive language such as BASIC or APL might run several hundred times slower than the code shown. A Pascal compiler can do much better than an interpreter, but the popular UCSD Pascal compilers developed originally at the University of California at San Diego are hybrids of compilers and interpreters. Typical UCSD compiler-generated programs execute 10 to 50 times slower than equivalent assembly language programs. The hybrid scheme compiles Pascal programs into the machine language of a ficticious machine known as the *p-machine*, and then the *p*-machine code is interpreted during program execution. True compilers produce machine-language translations similar to the translation shown in Program 9.4. Many Pascal compilers are of this type, as are most implementations of FORTRAN and COBOL. These compilers can usually produce programs whose efficiency varies from about 5 times slower to about equal to the efficiency of hand translations. The best optimizing compilers produce codes as good or better than code produced by assembly-language programmers that have average ability. Only very skilled programmers can do better.

High-quality optimizing compilers are not yet widely available for most microprocessors. These typically become available anywhere from one to five years after the introduction of a new microprocessor, and for some machines they may never appear. Because new microprocessors with enhanced features are introduced with great regularity, the designer who uses the most innovative new devices will most often have to do so without advanced programming tools.

Therefore the designer frequently is faced with two horns of a dilemma: The designer may prefer high-level languages, but other requirements may force the use of an assembly language. The next section discusses how to achieve the advantages of both languages, and serves as a guide to the designer in deciding where and how to use assembly language.

Pragmatics of Assembly Language

There are three primary factors that force programs to be implemented in assembly language. These are

1. real-time performance constraints,
2. memory-size constraints, and
3. access to machine-dependent facilities.

Of these three points, the last two are gradually becoming unimportant. With dramatic increases in memory size that have occurred in recent years, the memory-size constraint may disappear except possibly at the very low end of the cost spectrum. Machine-dependent facilities can be made accessible to high-level languages by incorporating calls to assembly-language subroutines. For example, many implementations of BASIC provide a USR verb that invokes a user-supplied assembly-language program. (Other facilities for machine-dependent programming in many BASIC interpreters include the PEEK and POKE verbs that, respectively, read from and write to arbitrary locations in memory.) The major unresolved issue appears to be performance related, and this is what we address here.

Real-time deadlines place the greatest constraints on programs. To deal adequately with the problems, the designer must first analyze what portions of the program code are executed while the real-time deadlines are active. Potentially, in the worst case, all of this code may have to be written in assembly language. Typical real-time situations of short duration arise in handling fast I/O devices such as disk interfaces and high-speed serial communications lines. Assembly language may be required for the I/O drivers that perform the block transfers, but may be unnecessary for other codes. Fortunately, the real-time portions of I/O drivers are rather small. (They cannot execute many instructions and still meet the real-time constraint.) A program that calls I/O drivers does not ordinarily run during critical time periods, so that it need not be in assembly language.

When real-time constraints span a relatively long period of time, say tens of milliseconds up to a few seconds, the problems of meeting those constraints are sometimes more difficult than when the constraints are tens of microseconds. In the longer time span, a program executes thousands or millions of instructions, so that is not obvious what code to optimize and how to optimize it. The very short deadlines are associated with a few lines of code, so that the designer can focus attention to a specific region of a program. For longer codes, the most likely places to optimize are the inner loops of iterations. Code in inner loops may be executed tens or hundreds of times more frequently than other code, so that the loops tend to dominate performance even though they represent only a small fraction of the code.

As a guide for the process of program optimization, we list several useful techniques for organizing software and hardware to improve performance to meet real-time constraints.

1. A straightforward hand translation of a high-level language into assembly language may be sufficiently faster than compiler code to meet performance constraints.
2. To achieve higher performance, trace the data flow and sources of overhead during execution. One byte of data, for example, may be accessed by several different subroutines, and could require hundreds or thousands of instructions to process it during

one real-time cycle. If this is the case, then reorganize the computations to avoid the overhead per byte. When data movement is required, try to move pointers to the data instead of moving the data. When processing data, process blocks of data rather than individual bytes to save the overhead of entering and leaving subroutines for each byte processed.

3. Seek ways of overlapping I/O and computation, or of moving some critical operations into specialized hardware. Mathematical processors can perform arithmetic including multiplication and division concurrently with program execution in a main computer. DMA controllers can eliminate the computational burden of block transfers. Extra hardware may increase system cost slightly, but when the hardware is successful, performance improvement may be as high as a factor of two or three.

4. In critical areas of the program code, particularly in the inner loops, make use of machine registers to reduce traffic to and from memory. Use the registers to hold addresses and variables that are accessed in each loop iteration. Reduction in memory traffic can sometimes double or triple the speed of an inner loop. The impact on total system performance depends on the frequency of the loop's execution.

5. Avoid the recalculation of addresses. Compilers often generate extensive code to access an array element such as X(I) or Y(I,J). When array access is made within a loop and the indices are the control variables of the loop, then it is possible to simplify the address calculations. For instance we may calculate the address of the base element [X(1) or Y(1,1)] outside the loop, then calculate the addresses for each successive loop iteration inside the loop by incrementing the address used in the prior iteration. (The address of X(I+1) differs from the address of X(I) by a small constant.)

6. Reduce the overhead of entering and exiting subroutines and of initiating and terminating loops. Loop overhead can be reduced by "unwinding" a loop so that a single loop performs two or three iterations of a calculation. This tends to eliminate some internal branching and testing, and may reduce some register and memory traffic. Subroutine entry and exit overhead can be reduced by saving and restoring only a minimal number of registers. Compilers normally assume the worst case, which forces subroutine calls to save an excessive number of registers. For specific applications the designer knows precisely what must be saved and what does not need to be saved.

7. Turn subroutines into macros, and eliminate the execution time costs for entry and exit. This may greatly increase the size of the code, so this solution is recommended only when memory is sufficently large to accept the increase in program size.

These comments are a general guide for performance optimization. It is best to optimize the gross behavior of the system, particularly the I/O and computer interactions, before attempting to optimize assembly language. The latter optimization may not be necessary if the former is successful. A simple translation to assembly language, such as the one in Program 9.4, when coupled with a reasonable implementation of the I/O system may yield sufficient performance improvement to meet real-time constraints.

The need to incorporate fast and efficient assembly language in some areas of a system is almost universal. However, assembly language has been overused in the past, and is becoming less necessary in the future as other viable languages and hardware alternatives become available. In the next section we treat the implementation of I/O software. For this type of programming, assembly language is still the primary implementation tool and will not easily be displaced.

9.2 SOFTWARE FOR I/O CONTROL

Perhaps the most challenging programming exercise is to write the collection of programs in an I/O system. These programs must work in real time, control several independent devices concurrently, and be insensitive to timing variations that drastically alter the sequence of execution of blocks of code. Moreover, these programs cannot easily be written in high-level languages because of issues related to performance and to machine dependencies. In the following subsections we show how to construct I/O programs by structuring them as coroutines. A coroutine is a generalization of a subroutine that is especially useful for controlling the independent activities, that are characteristic of an I/O system. Unfortunately, few high-level languages support this type of program structure, which is yet one more reason for adopting an assembly language as the implementation language for I/O programs.

In the succeeding subsections we review the concept of coroutines, describe their general applicability to I/O programs, then show this applicability in an extended example of an interrupt-driven program that controls a daisy-wheel printer.

Coroutines: Structure and Implementation

Conway (1963) coined the word "coroutine" to denote a generalization of subroutine. The basic difference between the coroutines and subroutines in program modules is tied to the notion of the "state" of the module: A subroutine does not retain an internal state between calls, whereas a coroutine does. Each entry to a subroutine creates a fresh copy of its internal state variables. But a coroutine entry retrieves the state of the coroutine that existed at its last exit. The state of a subroutine and coroutine both include the variables local to its own routine, but the state also includes the address of the entry point to the routine and the collection of return addresses to the other subroutines whose nested calls first invoked it. Therefore, since a subroutine does not retain state from call to call, each new call to a subroutine enters that routine at a fixed entry point. But coroutines do retain state information, and therefore, each call to a coroutine resumes at the point of the last exit from that coroutine.

Figure 9.2 illustrates the primary differences between subroutines and coroutines. In Fig. 9.2(a) we see a program structured as a collection of subroutines that contain calls from one subroutine to another. The figure shows the run-time stack associated with the nested sequence of calls in which Subroutine A calls Subroutine B, which in turn calls Subroutine C. Each subroutine call creates parameters that are passed to the target subrou-

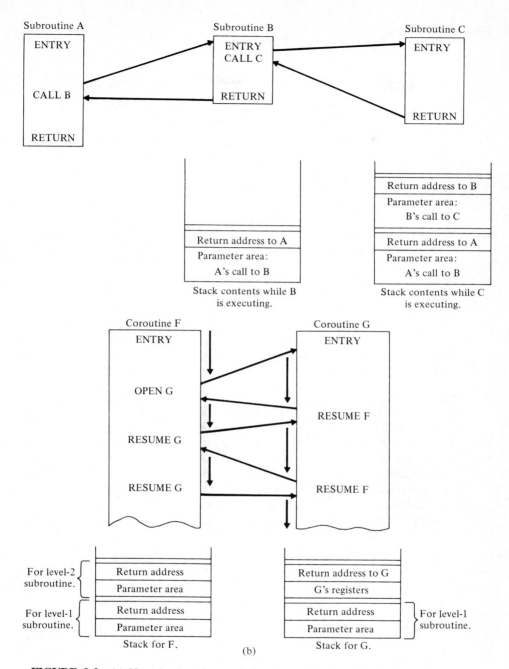

FIGURE 9.2 (a) Nested subroutines and the run-time stack during program execution; (b) coroutines that call each other and their run-time stacks are shown in the state that exists while F is executing. A level-2 subroutine of F resumes G, which has been suspended within a level-1 routine.

tine. Even if the target is declared without parameters, it receives at least one parameter, namely, the return address.

Note that the stack in the figure shows the return addresses to Subroutines A and B, plus other parameter areas created at the calling points of each subroutine. While Subroutine B has control of execution, the stack contains one parameter area. This increases to two areas when Subroutine C is initiated. The stack is an appropriate structure for subroutine calls because parameter areas are allocated and deallocated in a last-in, first-out (LIFO) order, which is precisely how storage is treated in a push-down stack. When a RETURN is executed at the end of a subroutine, the effect is to deallocate an active parameter area, and the area to deallocate is the last one allocated. Thus when Subroutine C reaches the RETURN statement, it deallocates the parameter area created when B called C. The RETURN leaves intact the parameter area created when A called B. Note the relative ordering of the parameter areas on the stack, with the most recent one stored above the older one. Since storage is allocated and deallocated at the top of the stack, the most recently allocated area is in a position to be deallocated next.

The internal state of Subroutine C at any time during its execution consists of the stack contents at that time. When C executes a RETURN, the top parameter area in the stack is popped off the stack, which partially destroys the state of C. Hence, a new call to C cannot recover the parameters of the former call, nor can it recover the address of the exit from the last call to C. Therefore the new call must enter C at a fixed, predetermined entry point.

Contrast this structure with the coroutine structure in Fig. 9.2(b). Here we see two coroutines, Coroutines F and G, that call each other. The calling statement in this case is RESUME. Note that control passes back and forth between F and G with each coroutine continuing where it left off. This is rather different from the control flow noted for subroutines in Fig. 9.2(a).

Figure 9.2(b) shows that each coroutine has an independent stack to hold the internal state of the coroutine. While F has control, F's push-down stack is the active stack. When F calls G with a RESUME, the first part of this process is to store the return address and machine registers on F's stack, and then F's stack is replaced by G's stack as the active stack. At the top of G's stack are G's registers plus the return address to G. In making G's stack active, the registers are restored from the stack, and then the return address is moved to the program counter. Coroutine G restarts with its stack and registers in the state in which they existed at last exit, except possibly for parameters that F passes to G. Parameter passing is done by placing the parameters on G's stack in cells reserved especially for them.

Subroutines lead naturally to a hierarchical control structure in which control passes from a calling program to a subroutine in a master/slave fashion. The subroutine is subordinate to the program that calls it. The control structure for coroutines is not a master/slave structure but rather a peer-to-peer structure. Each type of control structure has specific kinds of algorithms for which it is best suited, and quite often a program must use a combination of both control structures to achieve an efficient implementation.

Consider, for example, a situation in which Coroutine F is sufficiently complex to require a top-down, iterative refinement for its implementation. Then F will almost surely consist of a collection of subroutines. Any of these subroutines can call G, but they do so with a coroutine RESUME statement instead of with a subroutine call. When a deeply nested subroutine of F resumes G, it leaves F's stack intact, including all of the parameter areas and return addresses that are part of that subroutine's state. When G later resumes F, F's state is recovered, and control passes to the deeply nested subroutine at the point immediately after the RESUME that it last issued. Figure 9.2(b) illustrates this point by showing F's stack with two parameter areas and two return addresses active. Hence, the active subroutine of F is nested two levels deep. In G, the active subroutine is nested one level, and the top area of the stack holds the additional state of G that has to be saved while G is suspended.

Several authors such as Knuth (1973), Stone and Siewiorek (1975), and Wakerly (1981) do not explicitly show the separate stack for coroutines that we show here. These authors all treat a special case in which one stack suffices for all coroutines. In this case, all of the state information for Coroutine F and Coroutine G is contained in their return addresses. These are stored at specific addresses in memory to permit control to pass back and forth between the coroutines. Because there is only one stack for both coroutines, it is very difficult for either coroutine to store information safely on that stack because the other coroutine may inadvertently destroy the information by popping the stack. At least one coroutine, and possibly both coroutines, must exit at a RESUME with the stack in exactly the same state as at the last entry. Hence, there are severe restrictions on subroutine calls within the coroutines, because those calls add and delete items at the top of the stack. The more general and useful implementation of coroutines is that shown Fig. 9.2(b) in which each coroutine has an independent stack to hold its current state.

The next section treats the use of coroutines in an application that is not directly concerned with I/O control. Later in the chapter when we treat the problem of controlling several different devices concurrently, we will see that the coroutine structure leads to efficient, modular program implementations.

File Filters: An Application of Coroutines

Perhaps the most visible implementation of coroutines is the *filter*. A *filter* is a program that processes an input file and produces a modified version of that file as an output file. The output file is said to be the *filtered* version of the input file. As an example of a file-filtering operation, consider the preparation of a lengthy text file such as the one used in the production of this textbook. The file is typically subjected to a succession of filtering operations. Some of these might be the following:

1. Look up each word in the dictionary and correct spelling, if necessary.
2. Break strings of words into justified lines. The last word in a line might have to be broken by hyphenation.
3. Break sequences of lines into pages, leaving space for footnotes, figures, and tables on the page of their first references.

While it is possible to perform all the operations in a single program, since each process is relatively complex, the resulting composite program is very difficult to write and main-

FIGURE 9.3   Three file filters that change raw text into composed pages.

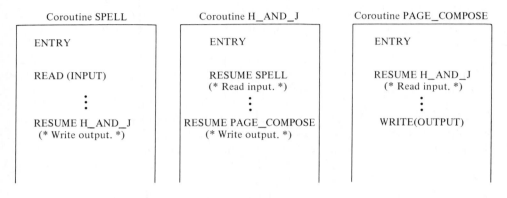

FIGURE 9.4   Filters structured as coroutines.

tain. Moreover, the individual programs can be useful in themselves quite apart from their use in the system of programs. If they are combined together in one program, there is a problem in creating the flexibility to run the programs individually or in any combination. Therefore, a suitable approach is to write these three programs as three individual filters, and to structure them as shown in Fig. 9.3. The SPELL process corrects the spelling of the input file, H_AND_J hyphenates and justifies the file into lines, and PAGE_COMPOSE organizes the lines into pages. Unfortunately, there is considerable overhead in passing the text file through two intermediate files. A more efficient approach is to structure the filters as coroutines and to pass data from one process directly to the next without writing an intermediate file. This type of structure is shown in Fig. 9.4. The idea here is that READ and WRITE operations become coroutine RESUMEs. Program 9.5 makes this point more explicitly. Here we see on lines 14 and 15 a WRITE operation in SPELL programmed in assembly language as if it were a call on a system output routine. The output character is transferred to a register REG1, and a subroutine-jump instruction JSR transfers control to WRITE. Similarly, in the H_AND_J subroutine on lines 43 and 44, a call to the system program READ returns a character in REG1. Immediately after the call, this character is transferred to the variable CHAR. The program fragments on lines 15 and 43 appear to be rather ordinary subroutine calls embedded into the two modules of the text-processing system.

Lines 23 through 28 and 52 through 56 reveal that subroutine calls to READ and WRITE have actually been converted into coroutine calls so that SPELL invokes H_AND_J instead of WRITE, and conversely, H_AND_J invokes SPELL instead of READ. All other aspects of the

PROGRAM 9.5   A Coroutine Example: Text Processing

```
 1  *********************************************************************
 2  *     (* SPELL *)                                                   *
 3  *     BEGIN                                                         *
 4  *        REPEAT                                                     *
 5  *        BEGIN                                                      *
 6  *           (* READ AND PROCESS THE INPUT *)                       *
 7  *           WRITE (CHAR, OUTPUTFILE) ;                             *
 8  *        END UNTIL INPUTFILE. STATUS = EOF                         *
 9  *     END OF SPELL                                                 *
10  *********************************************************************
11  SPELL        ...                       STARTING INSTRUCTION OF "SPELL"
12  LOOP         ...                       FIRST INSTRUCTION OF MAIN LOOP
13               ...
14               MOV      REG1, CHAR       REG1 := CHAR;
15               JSR      WRITE            OUTPUT THE CHARACTER, LINE 23
16               ...
17               BRA      LOOP             LAST INSTRUCTION OF MAIN LOOP
18               ...
19  *********************************************************************
20  *     (* WRITE *)                                                   *
21  *     THIS IS THE COROUTINE LINKAGE TO H_AND_J                     *
22  *********************************************************************
23  WRITE        PUSH     ALL              SAVE THE REGISTERS OF SPELL
24               MOV      SPELLSP, SP      SAVE THE STACK POINTER IN SPELLSP
25               MOV      SP, HJSP         RECOVER THE STACK POINTER FOR H_AND_J
26               MOV      R1 (SP), REG1    PASS A PARAMETER TO H_AND_J
27               PULL     ALL              RESTORE THE REGISTERS FOR H_AND_J
28               RTS                       RETURN TO H_AND_J
29  *********************************************************************
30  *     (* H_AND_J *)                                                 *
31  *     BEGIN                                                         *
32  *        REPEAT                                                    *
33  *        BEGIN                                                     *
34  *           READ (CHAR, INPUT) ;                                   *
35  *           (* PROCESS DATA *)                                     *
36  *           (* WRITE TO OUTPUT FILE *)                             *
37  *        END UNTIL INPUTFILE. STATUS = EOF                         *
38  *     END OF H_AND_J                                               *
39  *********************************************************************
40  H_AND_J      ...                       STARTING INSTRUCTION OF "H_AND_J"
41  LOOP         ...                       FIRST INSTRUCTION OF MAIN LOOP
42               ...
43               JSR      READ             INPUT A CHARACTER TO REG1, LINE 52
44               MOV      CHAR, REG1       CHAR := REG1
45               ...
46               BRA      LOOP             LAST INSTRUCTION OF MAIN LOOP
47               ...
48  *********************************************************************
49  *     (* READ *)                                                    *
50  *     (* COROUTINE LINKAGE TO "SPELL" *)                           *
51  *********************************************************************
52  READ         PUSH     ALL              SAVE THE REGISTERS OF "H_AND_J"
53               MOV      HJSP, SP         SAVE THE STACK POINTER IN HJSP
54               MOV      SP, SPELLSP      RECOVER THE STACK POINTER FOR "SPELL"
55               PULL     ALL              RESTORE THE REGISTERS FOR "SPELL"
56               RTS                       RETURN TO "SPELL"
```

two coroutines can be implemented in standard fashion as though the coroutines were executing in total independence. Each coroutine can be structured as a collection of subroutines, and there are no constraints on the implementation and the utilization of the stack other than the normal constraints for subroutines.

The machine implementation of WRITE appears on lines 23 through 28 of Program 9.5. The first operation is to store the state of the processor in the stack through the use of the PUSH ALL instruction. The intent of this instruction is to push copies of all machine registers onto the stack. (Microprocessors that do not have such an instruction may require several instructions to do the equivalent operation.) Then the stack pointer itself is saved in a storage location reserved for it. At this point, the state of SPELL has been preserved, and the state of H_AND_J can be retrieved.

The first step in restoring state is to reload the stack pointer from the cell reserved for the H_AND_J stack pointer. This occurs on line 25. At the top of the stack are the machine registers, and immediately underneath them is the return address, as shown in Fig. 9.5 where we see the state of both stacks immediately after the PUSH ALL instruction on line 23 has been executed. However, H_AND_J should receive an input character when it is resumed, and this character should be the character produced by the WRITE in SPELL. To obtain this variable, the assembly language program saves the contents of REG1, the register holding the output datum, inserting the contents into the stack at the address that holds the saved value of REG1 for H_AND_J. The instruction that does this operation is MOV R1(SP),REG1, where R1 is the offset in the stack of REG1, and the effective address is the sum of the offset R1 and the current contents of the stack pointer SP.

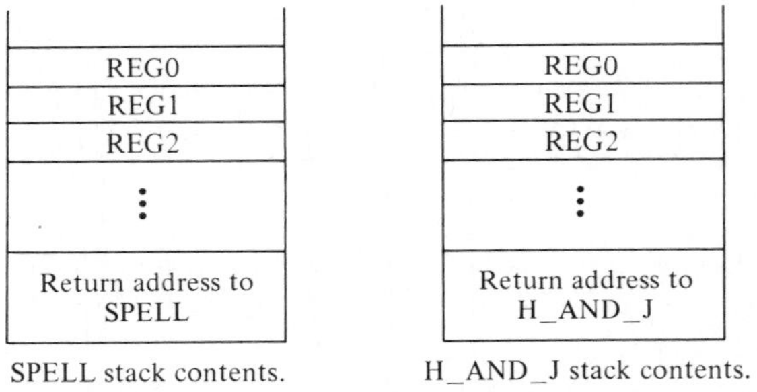

REG0
REG1
REG2
⋮
Return address to SPELL

REG0
REG1
REG2
⋮
Return address to H_AND_J

SPELL stack contents.   H_AND_J stack contents.

FIGURE 9.5   The state of the stacks during the execution of a coroutine call from SPELL to H AND J.

The next instruction, PULL ALL, reverses the action of PUSH ALL and restores the machine registers. The last instruction, RTS, is a subroutine return that pops the program counter from the stack and initiates execution at the return address. The return address will be exposed after the PULL ALL because it is pushed onto the stack by a JSR before the registers are pushed on top of it by a PUSH ALL instruction.

Coroutine linkage for the READ operation in H_AND_J is in lines 52 through 56 of Program 9.5. This is very similar to the WRITE linkage except that it is not necessary to pass a

PROGRAM 9.6   Text Processing with Open and Close Functions

```
 1  ************************************************************************
 2  (* SPELL *)
 3  begin
 4      OPEN (INPUTFILE) ;
 5      OPEN (OUTPUTFILE) ;
 6      repeat
 7      begin
 8          (* Read from an input file. *)
 9          (* Process data. *)
10          WRITE (CHAR, OUTPUTFILE) ;
11      end until INPUTFILE. STATUS = EOF
12      CLOSE (INPUTFILE) ;
13      CLOSE (OUTPUTFILE) ;
14  end
15  ************************************************************************
16  ************************************************************************
17  (* H_AND_J *)
18  begin
19      OPEN (INPUTFILE) ;
20      OPEN (OUTPUTFILE) ;
21      repeat
22      begin
23          READ (CHAR, INPUT) ;
24          (* Process data. *)
25          (* Write data to output file. *)
26      end until INPUTFILE. STATUS = EOF
27      CLOSE (INPUTFILE) ;
28          CLOSE (OUTPUTFILE) ;
29  end
30  ************************************************************************
```

parameter to READ. Therefore, SPELL resumes with its machine state identical to its state just prior to the call to WRITE, with the exception that the program counter has been advanced past the JSR WRITE.

This very simple example illustrates the basic idea of using a coroutine structure to create a filter. The extension to more complex problems is rather straightforward. Consider Program 9.6 where we see the problem somewhat embellished. In this example, the SPELL program is a filter that opens the output file, passes data to the file, then terminates by closing the output file. Correspondingly, the H_AND_J program opens an input file, reads data from that file until it encounters an end-of-file condition, then closes that file. The difficulties in implementing this example in a coroutine pertains to the handling of OPEN and CLOSE, detecting the end-of-file condition, and initializing the programs so that they will work correctly as coroutines. Program 9.7. is an assembly-language implementation of this program.

Before describing Program 9.7 in detail, we list the general guidelines to our solution that are illustrated in the program.

1. OPEN and CLOSE are treated as coroutine calls by inserting a linkage similar to the linkage used to pass control between READ and WRITE.
2. Each coroutine has an initial entry point that creates its stack.
3. Program execution begins at the entry point of the program that reads the intermediate file.
4. When an OPEN is executed on an input file, the effect of that OPEN is to pass control to the initial entry point of the program that writes the intermediate file.
5. When OPEN is executed on an intermediate output file, the effect is that of an ordinary coroutine RESUME, returning to the coroutine that reads the intermediate file.
6. The effect of a CLOSE on an output file is to report an end-of-file status in a RESUME to the corresponding coroutine that reads the file.
7. The effect of a CLOSE on an input file is to invoke the code that terminates the corresponding output coroutine.

If we assume that the program has only the two coroutines shown, then the guidelines we listed indicate that the program should be started at the initialization entry point of H_AND_J, since H_AND_J reads the intermediate file. If PAGE_COMPOSE were included in the example as well, then the program should start at the initialization entry of PAGE_COMPOSE. PAGE_COMPOSE then will invoke the initialization of H_AND_J. The initialization code for H_AND_J appears in lines 45 through 47, where the code sets an initial value into the stack pointer and opens the input file.

The OPEN_IN statement on line 46 is a system call to open an input file; but in the context of the coroutine structure, this statement causes the corresponding output coroutine to initiate. Therefore the call to OPEN_IN invokes a special coroutine interface that passes control to the initialization entry point of SPELL immediately after saving the state of H_AND_J. The SPELL entry, lines 10 through 12, has an initialization code similar to the initialization code in H_AND_J. After executing this code, the flow of control then continues in SPELL until the OPEN_OUT call on line 12. This call passes control back to H_AND_J through the standard coroutine interface on lines 26 through 33.

Now let's examine how READ and WRITE are implemented. We presume that the system routines READ and WRITE return a condition code, say by setting or resetting the condition code for the carry (or C) bit in the processor. We adopt the convention that when the bit is set, the READ or WRITE operation has reached an end of file or has terminated abnormally. When the bit is reset, the operation is completed successfully. The first time this convention is invoked is on line 50, where the JSR READ actually passes control to a coroutine interface shown on lines 68 through 73. Note the instruction CLC for clear carry. This instruction is executed just after the condition codes have been retrieved from the stack. Hence the net effect of the coroutine interface is to return a cleared carry bit to SPELL.

The first execution of READ in H_AND_J returns control to the instruction on line 13 that immediately follows the call to OPEN_OUT. Subsequent READs from H_AND_J return control to code that immediately follows a WRITE in SPELL, such as the example on lines 16 through 18. Note that this code tests the carry bit with the instruction BCS, which branches if the carry bit is set to the termination code for the coroutine. The corresponding actions

PROGRAM 9.7   File Operations for Text Processing in Assembly Language

```
 1  ****************************************************************************
 2  *     (* START HERE *)                                                     *
 3  *     JUMP TO H_AND_J, LINE 45                                             *
 4  ****************************************************************************
 5  START      JMP       H_AND_J           INITIALIZE H_AND_J
 6  ****************************************************************************
 7  *     (* SPELL *)                                                          *
 8  *     INITIALIZATION CODE BEGINS HERE                                      *
 9  ****************************************************************************
10  SPELL      MOV       SP, SPELL_BOT     INITIALIZE STACK FOR "SPELL"
11             ...                         OTHER INITIALIZATION CODE GOES HERE
12             JSR       OPEN_OUT          OPEN THE OUTPUT FILE, LINE 26
13             ...
14  LOOP       ...                         FIRST INSTRUCTION OF MAIN LOOP
15             ...                         READ OR GENERATE THE NEXT CHAR
16             MOV       REG1, CHAR        REG1 := CHAR;
17             JSR       WRITE             OUTPUT THE CHARACTER, LINE 27
18             BCS       EXIT              TAKE EXIT IF CARRY IS SET
19             ...
20             BRA       LOOP              LAST INSTRUCTION OF MAIN LOOP
21  EXIT       JSR       CLOSE             CLOSE THE OUTPUT FILE, LINE 38
22  ****************************************************************************
23  *     (* WRITE AND OPEN_OUT *)                                             *
24  *     THIS IS THE COROUTINE LINKAGE TO H_AND_J                             *
25  ****************************************************************************
26  OPEN_OUT   EQU       *                 ENTRY FOR "OPEN_OUT" AND "WRITE"
27  WRITE      PUSH      ALL               SAVE THE REGISTERS OF "SPELL"
28             MOV       SPELLSP, SP       SAVE THE STACK POINTER IN SPELLSP
29             MOV       SP, HJSP          RECOVER THE STACK POINTER FOR "H_AND_J"
30             MOV       R1 (SP), REG1     PASS A PARAMETER TO "H_AND_J"
31             PULL      ALL               RESTORE THE REGISTERS FOR "H_AND_J"
32             CLEAR     CARRY             REPORT STATUS FOR A NORMAL READ
33             RTS                         RETURN TO "H_AND_J"
34  ****************************************************************************
35  *     (* CLOSE *)                                                          *
36  *     CLOSE THE OUTPUT FILE, AND CALL H_AND_J                              *
37  ****************************************************************************
38  CLOSE      PUSH      ALL               SAVE CURRENT STATE
39             MOV       SPELLSP, SP       SAVE THE STACK POINTER IN SPELLSP
40             MOV       SP, HJSP          RECOVER THE STACK POINTER FOR "H_AND_J"
41             PULL      ALL               RESTORE THE REGISTERS FOR "H_AND_J"
42             SET       CARRY             REPORT STATUS FOR END OF FILE
43             RTS                         RETURN TO "H_AND_J"
44  ****************************************************************************
45  H_AND_J    MOV       SP, HJSP_BOT      INITIALIZE STACK FOR "H_AND_J"
46             JSR       OPEN_IN           OPEN THE INPUT FILE, LINE 62
47             ...                         OTHER INITIALIZATION CODE GOES HERE
48  LOOP       ...                         FIRST INSTRUCTION OF MAIN LOOP
49             ...
50             JSR       READ              INPUT A CHARACTER TO REG1, LINE 69
51             MOV       CHAR, REG1        CHAR := REG1
52             BCS       HJ_EXIT           EXIT ON END OF FILE (CARRY SET)
53             MOV       CHAR, REG1        CHAR := REG1
```

(Continued on next page.)

```
54                    . . .                       SAVE OR PRINT THE CURRENT CHAR
55               BRA       LOOP                   LAST INSTRUCTION OF MAIN LOOP
56  HJ_EXIT     JSR       CLOSE_IN               CLOSE THE INPUT FILE, LINE 80
57                    . . .
58  ************************************************************************
59  *    (* OPEN_IN *)                                                    *
60  *    COROUTINE LINKAGE TO INITIALIZE "SPELL"                          *
61  ************************************************************************
62  OPEN_IN     PUSH      ALL                    SAVE THE REGISTERS OF "H_AND_J"
63               MOV       HJSP, SP               SAVE THE STACK POINTER IN SPELLSP
64               JMP       SPELL                  INITIALIZE THE "SPELL" PROGRAM, LINE 10
65  ************************************************************************
66  *    (* READ *)                                                       *
67  *    THIS IS THE COROUTINE LINKAGE TO "SPELL"                         *
68  ************************************************************************
69  READ         PUSH      ALL                    SAVE THE REGISTERS OF "H_AND_J"
70               MOV       HJSP, SP               SAVE THE STACK POINTER IN HJSP
71               MOV       SP, SPELLSP            RECOVER THE STACK POINTER FOR "SPELL"
72               PULL      ALL                    RESTORE THE REGISTERS FOR "SPELL"
73               CLEAR     CARRY                  REPORT STATUS FOR A NORMAL WRITE
74               RTS                              RETURN TO "SPELL"
75  ************************************************************************
76  *    (* CLOSE_IN *)                                                   *
77  *    CLOSE AN INPUT FILE                                              *
78  *    CLOSE_IN IS A NULL ROUTINE IN THIS CODE.                         *
79  ************************************************************************
80  CLOSE_IN    RTS                               RETURN WITHOUT DOING ANY WORK
```

for a WRITE in SPELL to resume after a READ in H_AND_J are shown in the coroutine interface on lines 50 through 52. In this case, the interface both passes a parameter and sets the condition code in the process of restoring the state of H_AND_J.

Eventually, SPELL exhausts its input file and reaches the CLOSE instruction on line 21. CLOSE invokes a special coroutine interface on lines 38 through 43 that sets the carry bit to indicate an end-of-file condition. The RESUME to H_AND_J results in a branch to the CLOSE in H_AND_J that can terminate SPELL and return its stack and other memory to a pool of available memory. In the program example, this instance of a CLOSE is implemented as a null routine.

This example illustrates how a few interfaces between two independent program modules can couple the modules together, making them coroutines. During program execution, control passes back and forth between the modules in what appears to be a confusing and contorted fashion. Yet the structure of the program is inherently simple because the modules are totally isolated from each other so that each can be written, debugged, and maintained independently. All operations pertinent to a module are encapsulated within it, and there is no interaction among the modules except through the coroutine interfaces. Programs that control I/O devices, particularly interrupt-driven programs, are ideally structured as coroutines, since each coroutine focuses on the control of one device.

Coroutines for I/O Control

Among the most difficult types of programming to implement is I/O control. The primary difficulty lies in the real-time nature of the control problem. The computer must adapt to the timing of the device. Instructions cannot be executed at arbitrary times. They have to be synchronized to external events. The control of just one device can be a difficult problem. But just imagine the problems of juggling control among five to ten devices, all operating in real time. Techniques based on coroutine structures can greatly simplify the development of this kind of the program.

Synchronization to external signals is the key requirement for I/O programs. A typical I/O driver has to perform operations equivalent to those shown in Program 9.8. Note that the program issues a command to a device, then has to wait for a ready signal. Program 9.8 shows that there is, in general, some internal state in the I/O driver in that the commands may be issued in a particular sequence. For example, a floppy-disk controller can successively load the head, seek a new track, then read from a particular sector on the track. If there were no other processing to be done, then the controller program might well be implemented as shown in Program 9.8 with busy loops, testing and waiting for a READY status. However, in many cases the processor cannot afford to spend the time in the busy loop. Therefore, we have to consider other mechanisms that can improve program efficiency.

PROGRAM 9.8   The Structure of a Typical I/O Driver

```
procedure DRIVER;
begin
    (* Prepare to initiate I/O. *)
    WAIT (DEVICE_STATUS) ;
    (* Issue the first command. *)
    COMMAND := FIRST_OPERATION;
    START_IO (DEVICE,COMMAND) ;
    (* Wait for completion. *)
    WAIT (DEVICE_STATUS) ;
    (* Issue the next command. *)
    COMMAND := SECOND_OPERATION;
    START_IO (DEVICE,COMMAND) ;
    (* Accept a block of data from the device. *)
    for I := 1 to BLOCKLENGTH do
    begin
        (* Wait for completion. *)
        WAIT (DEVICE_STATUS) ;
        BLOCK (I) := READ_IO (DEVICE.DATA) ;
    end;
end;
```

There are at least two widely used methods for controlling multiple devices. We show the polling method in Program 9.9 and the interrupt-driven method in Program 9.10. For polling, the individual device drivers issue a RESUME instead of a WAIT. The resume returns to a polling program that continuously loops through a cycle of coroutine calls to the

PROGRAM 9.9   The Structure of a Polled I/O Driver

```
procedure DRIVER1;
begin
    (* Prepare to initiate I/O. *)
    while not (DEVICE_STATUS = READY) do RESUME MAIN;
    (* Issue the first command. *)
    COMMAND := FIRST_OPERATION;
    START_IO (DEVICE,COMMAND) ;
    (* Wait for completion. *)
    while not (DEVICE_STATUS = READY) do RESUME MAIN;
    (* Issue the next command. *)
    COMMAND := SECOND_OPERATION;
    START_IO (DEVICE,COMMAND) ;
    (* Accept a block of data from the device. *)
    for I := 1 to BLOCKLENGTH do
    begin
        (* Wait for completion. *)
        while not (DEVICE_STATUS = READY) do RESUME MAIN;
        BLOCK (I) := READ_IO (DEVICE_DATA) ;
    end;
end;
    (* This is the structure of the main program. *)
    program MAIN;
    repeat forever
    begin
        RESUME DRIVER1;
        RESUME DRIVER2;
        RESUME DRIVER3;
        . . .
    end;
```

device drivers. This method is both the simplest and preferred method for implementing I/O drivers. It has drawbacks, however, and cannot be used for all cases. One problem is that there is an unpredictable delay between the time a device reaches the READY condition and the time that the I/O program services it. Some devices must be serviced within a fixed time after becoming READY, and therefore are not easily controlled through polling. The second problem also relates to performance. Polling expends a considerable number of machine cycles that might otherwise be available for other purposes. Performance degradation due to polling is usually unimportant in dedicated controllers because cycles wasted in polling cannot otherwise be captured for useful work. For general-purpose applications, however, I/O is performed concurrently with many other tasks. Cycles lost to I/O in these applications may severely handicap the ability of the system to do the other non-I/O tasks at a reasonable pace.

Program 9.10 illustrates how interrupts are used in place of polling. In this case, the interrupt-driven program alters the interrupt vector entry address prior to resuming an interrupted program. The new address in the interrupt vector is the entry point of the next phase of the interrupt handler. When an interrupt occurs, the effect of the interrupt is identical to a coroutine RESUME to the interrupt handler. The state of the interrupted pro-

PROGRAM 9.10   The Structure of an Interrupt-Controlled I/O Driver

```
procedure DRIVER;
(* This program is started through a conventional procedure call.
      The device it controls is assumed to be ready when the program
      is first entered. *)
begin
      (* Prepare for the reentry after an interrupt. *)
      DEVICE_VECTOR := ADDRESS_OF(CMD2);
      (* Issue the first command. *)
      COMMAND := FIRST_OPERATION;
      START_IO(DEVICE,COMMAND);
      (* Return to calling program. *)
      return;
CMD2: (* Reenter here after an interrupt. *)
      (* Prepare for the reentry after an interrupt. *)
      DEVICE_VECTOR := ADDRESS_OF(ACCEPT_DATA);
      (* Issue the next command. *)
      COMMAND := SECOND_OPERATION;
      START_IO(DEVICE, COMMAND);
      (* Accept a block of data from the device. *)
      for I := 1 to BLOCKLENGTH do
      begin
            RETURN FROM INTERRUPT;
ACCEPT_DATA: (* Reenter here after interrupt. *)
            BLOCK(I) := READ_IO(DEVICE.DATA);
      end;
RETURN FROM INTERRUPT;
end;
```

gram is preserved and then recovered later when the handler resumes an interrupted program. The interrupt method reduces latency because the interrupt program can be invoked almost immediately after the interrupt request. Additional latency may occur if an interrupt request is locked out by the processing of a higher priority or noninterruptible task. The designer can easily calculate the worst-case delay for any interrupt, and thereby bound the latency of a response to an interrupt request. The interrupt program suffers no loss of efficiency because of repeated status tests as does the polling program, but there is some inefficiency in the process of leaving and entering the interrupt handler. Interrupt overhead becomes excessive at very high transfer rates if interrupts are used to process each datum. In this case, DMA control is preferred; and in lieu of DMA, it may be necessary to transfer data with programmed busy loops without interrupts in order to meet the real-time constraints on data transfer.

Therefore, we have at our disposal three generic ways of doing I/O:

1. For a dedicated device, we can use programmed busy loops.
2. To control several devices, we can poll and test the device status registers in either a cyclic fashion or according to some priority scheme.
3. To reduce overhead and worst-case latency, we can use interrupt-driven device handlers.

We now examine the design issues in putting these techniques together to create an efficient I/O-control system.

Since interrupt programming is substantially more difficult to create correctly and to debug, the preferred solution is polling. However, devices that operate under real-time deadlines may have to be controlled by the interrupt method. Therefore the first step of a design process is to organize the I/O handlers into two groups according to whether they do or do not use the interrupt system. (A controller dedicated to one device can use simple busy loops.) Programs controlled through polling use standard mechanisms for calling subroutines, resuming coroutines, and passing and receiving parameters. Programs controlled through the interrupt system cannot interface directly to the remainder of the programming system because an interrupt program is initiated at unpredictable times and, therefore, is not synchronized to the activity in the remainder of the programming system. Therefore, in general, each interrupt handler requires a small data region for buffering data. External data received by an I/O handler are held in this region until they can be passed to an independent part of the program. Similarly, as data are produced for output by the programming system at large, they are stored in the buffer until the I/O handler can transfer them to an I/O device. Since buffer storage is first-in, last-out, the appropriate data structure for the buffer is a queue. Consequently, the usual communication of an interrupt program with a programming system is through a queue. The actual implementation of queueing is more complex than our description here because of the special handling of empty queues, full queues, and interrupts that occur while one program or another is manipulating the queues. A detailed example later in Section 9.2 illustrates precisely how to implement the queueing structure in assembly language for a real system.

At this stage of the design process, each I/O handler has been classified as interrupt driven or driven through polling. For each interrupt-driven program, we construct a queue to receive data from or to transmit data to that program. All programs that interface to interrupt handlers do so through queues. All other I/O is treated through conventional subroutine or coroutine calls. Now when we have treated each independent handler as a coroutine, we treat the main program, if there is one, as another independent coroutine. Then each coroutine is implemented as an independent, isolated program. As coroutines are completed, they can be tested in isolation, then tested together as a working system. When this procedure is followed, creating a complex I/O system with interrupt-driven devices becomes a much simpler task, because the programmer can focus on small self-contained modules. Moreover, by using techniques outlined later, the programmer can eliminate most of the difficulties caused by the random timing of interrupts.

A Detailed Example of an I/O Controller

The best way to describe how to create a complex I/O control program is to show a detailed example. Our choice of example is the printer controller illustrated in Fig. 9.6. This controller has an RS-232-C input port through which it receives printable data as well as commands that control the format of the printing. The physical printer is a so-called

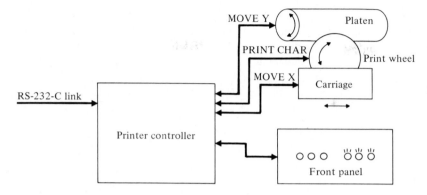

FIGURE 9.6   Diagram of interfaces to the printer controller.

"daisy-wheel" printer, the Diablo Hytype I printer, which has an interface similar to most other daisy-wheel printers. The figure shows that the printer has three degrees of mechanical freedom. The computer can spin the wheel to align any character with the print hammer, can move the carriage to position the character horizontally, and can rotate the platen to position the character vertically.

The printer interface is quite straightforward. A data bus carries 11 bits of information. These 11 bits encode either a distance increment or the ASCII code for a printable character. Three different command lines — one each for printwheel, carriage, and platen — can be exercised by the computer to control each possible movement of the three devices. Each command line has an accompanying status line to indicate when the printer has completed the corresponding command. The printer can actually move in all three directions simultaneously. Logic within the printer guarantees that all movement has ceased when the hammer strikes the print wheel, and the printer controller need not be concerned with this problem. The printer guarantees, as well, that overlapped commands will be executed as if they had occurred sequentially. Hence, if the computer issues a command to move the print wheel to the character "a" position, and then commands a carriage move, the printer will spin the print wheel and strike the letter "a" before the carriage moves. On the other hand, if the computer reverses the sequence and issues the carriage move first, the printer will move the carriage and spin the print wheel simultaneously, and will strike the letter "a" after both movements have ceased.

A control line to the printer can lift or drop the ribbon. The ribbon has to be in a lifted position during printing. When the printer is placed in a NOT READY (off-line) condition, the computer should drop the ribbon to facilitate paper positioning and ribbon changing.

For local control of the printer, there are various buttons and lights on the printer console. (One of these buttons is an OFF-LINE button that signals the controller to stop the printer and drop the ribbon as mentioned above.) Other controls and indicators permit an operator at the printer to skip a line or to skip to a heading or to observe the status of the printer.

The function of the controller program is to operate the RS-232-C interface, the printer mechanism, and the buttons and lights. A hardware diagram of the I/O interface is shown in Fig. 9.7. The RS-232-C connection is implemented by a serial I/O port; and in this case the signal line RTS (Request to Send) is manipulated by the program to control the rate of characters coming across the link. When the program makes RTS inactive, the transmitter end of the link should stop transmitting. Transmission restarts when the program reasserts RTS. This connection (or a functionally equivalent one) is required to stop and start the flow of data, for otherwise the transmitter will send data much faster than the data can be printed. Without flow control, the data will pile up at the printer controller and overflow the buffers there.

The interface between the controller and the printer mechanism is made through parallel ports. The control panel's push buttons and lights are also interfaced through the same type of port. Open-collector drivers and Schmitt trigger receivers form the electrical interface. Signals to the printer mechanism are active low pulses of very short duty cycle. Therefore, the open-collector drivers terminated with matched load impedances dissipate very little power. Because the transmission distance is short, and because the interface lines are properly terminated with adequate ground lines for return currents, the electrical interface is quite satisfactory at normal TTL voltage levels.

The design decisions that were made in developing the interface program are the following:

1. The printer mechanism, buttons, and lights have no critical real-time constraints. Therefore these devices will be controlled through polling.

2. The RS-232-C link has a real-time constraint. Even after deasserting RTS, the link will deliver up to two characters because of the effect of double buffering in the transmitter. The processor must respond to a received character and remove it from the buffer register of the serial port within one character time after the character is transferred to the buffer register. If the computer fails to respond within the time constraint, the transmitted character will be lost. Therefore, the serial link will be run under interrupt control, and the characters received on the serial link will be buffered in an input queue.

3. To improve the efficiency of the printer, movements in the X and Y (carriage and platen) directions will be accumulated and issued only when necessary to place characters at a specific point on the page. Hence, a series of spaces will give rise to a single printer command to move the carriage the accumulated movement of those spaces.

4. If the input queue is empty, then all commands are issued immediately to the printer, and no accumulation occurs. This permits the printer to follow the exact movements of a slow typist. If accumulation were not turned off, the printer would tend to lag behind the typist during sequences of spaces and line feeds, and that would be rather disconcerting.

5. The interface should accept certain specified sequences of characters beginning with the ASCII code ESC to set margins and for other control purposes.

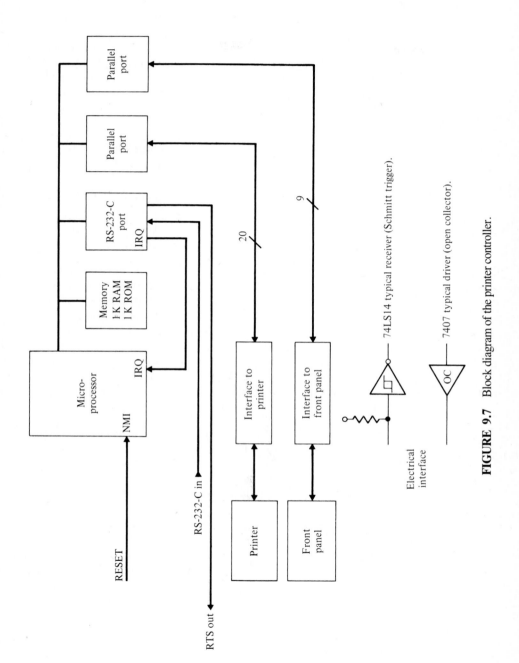

FIGURE 9.7 Block diagram of the printer controller.

6. Each visible character printed causes two distinct control actions. The first is a print-wheel movement, and the second is a carriage advance by an amount DELTA_X, where DELTA_X is a variable that determines the width of the characters. The horizontal resolution of the printer is 60 steps per inch (120 per inch for later models). Standard pica fonts have 10 characters per inch, and thus require a DELTA_X value of 6. Elite fonts have 12 characters per inch, and require a DELTA_X value of 5. The DELTA_X value can be modified by an ESC sequence or by depressing a font-change push button on the console.

Although this description is not complete in all of the details required for a printer interface, it contains a sufficient number of interesting constraints to make the programming example nontrivial and informative.

We choose to implement coroutines for each of the following programs:

1. The RS-232-C link.
2. The front panel monitor.
3. The program that extracts a character from the input queue and prints it.

It is not necessary to implement these particular programs with separate stacks as indicated in the prior section, so that in this example we use a simpler coroutine linkage. The state of each coroutine in this example is contained solely in the return address.

Because our intent is to show the program in assembly language and because the problem is rather complex, we choose to show the implementation routine by routine, and we leave out details unrelated to the constraints listed. Again we use a top-down approach to reveal the program implementation from the highest level first. Program 9.11 is the main program-initialization section and polling loop. A Pascal-like description of the main program appears in the opening comment. The initialization consists of calls on procedures that do the following operations:

1. IRUPT_VECTOR.   This creates the interrupt vectors for the RS-232-C port and for a RESET push button. The RS-232-C link must be a maskable interrupt, but RESET can be maskable or nonmaskable. The software is made somewhat simpler if the two interrupts vector to different locations without needing software intervention. The RS-232-C interrupt vector is initialized to the first entry point of the serial-link coroutine.
2. HEAD_POS.   This routine clears variables that indicate the current position of the print head and the X and Y movements remaining to be issued.
3. SERIAL_INIT.   This routine configures the serial port. But the RTS signal remains off, and no characters should be transmitted across the link as a result of this call.
4. BUTTONS_N_LIGHTS.   This routine configures the parallel port for the control console. It also turns on indicator lamps that are to be on initially.
5. PRINT_INIT.   This routine configures the parallel port to the printer mechanism, and issues a command to position the carriage at the left margin.
6. RTS_ON.   This routine asserts RTS to start the transmitter at the other end of the link. Characters received in the future will post interrupts that vector the computer to the interrupt handler for the link.

7. RIB_DOWN. This routine places the ribbon in the down (nonprinting) position. (When the power is turned on, the printer should initialize itself in the off-line state with the ribbon down.)

The main polling loop is very simple. The first step in each pass through the loop is to read the front panel. If any button is depressed, the PANEL program reacts by commanding a corresponding action. For example, depressing the OFF-LINE push button causes an internal variable RDY to be toggled. Immediately after polling the front-panel, the main

PROGRAM 9.11   The Main Program of the I/O Controller

```
 1  ******************************************************************************
 2  *   MAIN PROGRAM                                                            *
 3  *   BEGIN                                                                   *
 4  *       INITIALIZE;                                                         *
 5  *       RIBBON DOWN;                                                        *
 6  *       REPEAT FOREVER                                                      *
 7  *       BEGIN                                                               *
 8  *           READ PANEL;                                                     *
 9  *           IF NOT READY THEN RIBBON DOWN                                   *
10  *           ELSE                                                            *
11  *           BEGIN                                                           *
12  *               RESUME OUTPUT;                                              *
13  *               IF EMPTY (QUEUE) THEN FORCE_IO;                             *
14  *           END;                                                            *
15  *       END;                                                               *
16  ******************************************************************************
17  MAIN       JSR    IRUPT_VECTOR        SET THE INTERRUPT VECTOR
18             JSR    HEAD_POS            INITIALIZE PRINTER VARIABLES THAT
19  *                                        GIVE THE CURRENT HEAD POSITION
20             JSR    SERIAL_INIT         INITIALIZE THE SERIAL PORT
21             JSR    BUTTONS_N_LIGHTS    INITIALIZE FRONT PANEL CONTROL
22             JSR    PRINT_INIT          INITIALIZE PRINTER PORT AND RESTORE
23  *                                        PRINTER HEAD TO HOME POSITION
24             JSR    RTS_ON              TURN ON REQ-TO-SEND, START XMITTER
25             JSR    RIB_DOWN            DROP THE RIBBON (NONPRINTING POSITION)
26  MAINLOOP   JSR    PANEL               READ THE FRONT PANEL
27             MOV    REG1, RDY           TEST "RDY"
28             CMP    REG1, #0
29             BEQ    MAIN1               PRINTER IS READY IF RDY = 0
30             JSR    RIB_DOWN            NOT READY SO DROP THE RIBBON
31             BRA    MAINLOOP            REPEAT UNTIL PRINTER IS READY
32  MAIN1      JSR    RIB_UP              READY TO PRINT, SO LIFT RIBBON
33             MOV    REG1, OUTCHAR       FIND LAST RETURN ADDRESS TO THE
34  *                                        OUTPUT COROUTINE
35             JSR    (REG1)              JUMP THERE WITH A SUBROUTINE CALL
36             MOV    REG1, TOTAL         IS THE QUEUE EMPTY?
37             CMP    REG1, #0
38             BNE    MAINLOOP            NOT EMPTY, SO REPEAT THE LOOP
39             JSR    FORCIO              EMPTY, SO FORCE OUTPUT OF
40  *                                        ACCUMULATED MOVEMENT
41             BRA    MAINLOOP            REPEAT THE LOOP
```

program examines the variable RDY. If RDY is not zero, the printer is in an off-line state, and the main program continues to loop through the routines that drop the ribbon and read the front panel until the OFF-LINE button is pushed.

If the main program finds RDY equal to 0 on line 29, then the computer is ON-LINE. In response to RDY, the program lifts the ribbon on line 32. (No harm is done if the ribbon is already lifted.) The next step is to output a character from the input queue to the printer mechanism. Since this is a coroutine call, the method used in lines 33 through 35 of the example is to copy the latest return address of the output routine into a machine register, and then to perform a subroutine jump to that address with an indexed effective address. (Other address modes can be used here if the microprocessor does not have indexing mode available for subroutine calls.)

After calling the output routine, the main program could in theory return to the top of the loop. However, since the output coroutine is supposed to accumulate carriage and platen movement, it is necessary to determine if the printer can keep up with a slow input stream by outputting the accumulated movement immediately. Therefore the main program tests the variable TOTAL, which keeps track of the number of characters in the input queue that are awaiting printing. If this number is nonzero, then the main program can poll again from the beginning of the loop. Otherwise the main program calls FORCIO to dump the accumulated movement immediately.

Having dispensed with the main program, we move to the interrupt handler for the serial link shown in Program 9.12. This program does nothing except to queue the input character. Consequently, as it has a very simple structure and does not need to retain state between calls, it is written as a subroutine rather than as a coroutine. It makes no use at all of the stack other than as a temporary storage area for registers of the interrupted program. The program opens with an instruction that turns off the interrupt system. Next it executes a PUSH ALL instruction on line 2, followed by an access to the serial port for the character just received. Now the program is ready to queue a character. If the program were to permit link interrupts to occur before the PUSH ALL or during the queueing operation while the queue status variables are changing, the later interrupt could interfere with the earlier one and leave the queue or the stored machine registers in an inconsistent state. Therefore interrupts are not permitted during the execution of this program. Interrupt requests are held pending by the serial port until the end of the operation.

The queueing operation performs the following processes:

1. Lines 4 through 9. Updates the input pointer to the queue to point to the next available space. Lines 6 and 8 make the queue a circular structure by forcing the successor of the last element in the storage block to be the first element of the block.
2. Line 10. Stores the character at the next position in the queue.
3. Lines 11 through 13. Increments TOTAL, the number of items in the queue.
4. Lines 14 through 18. Checks to see that there are at least ten vacant places in the queue; if not, calls RTS_OFF to deassert RTS and thereby to shutdown the transmitter.
5. Lines 19 through 20. Restores prior state, turns on interrupts and exits.

PROGRAM 9.12   Interrupt-Handler for the Serial Link

```
 1  OUTPUT    CLR    I_MASK              DISABLE INTERRUPTS
 2            PUSH   ALL                 SAVE THE STATE OF THE INTERRUPTED PROGRAM
 3            MOV    REG1, LINKDATA      RETRIEVE THE BYTE RECEIVED
 4            MOV    REG2, Q_IN          OBTAIN QUEUE INPUT-POINTER
 5            INC    REG2                POINT TO NEXT SPACE
 6            CMP    REG2, #Q_END        AT END OF STORAGE?
 7            BLE    IRUPT1              BRANCH IF POINTER IS STILL VALID
 8            MOV    REG2, #Q_START      OTHERWISE, RESET POINTER
 9  IRUPT1    MOV    Q_IN, REG2          UPDATE THE QUEUE POINTER
10            MOV    (REG2), REG1        STORE INPUT BYTE INTO QUEUE
11            MOV    REG2, TOTAL         TOTAL = NUMBER OF ITEMS IN QUEUE
12            INC    REG2
13            MOV    TOTAL, REG2         INCREASE THE COUNT
14            CMP    REG2, #Q_LNG-10     IS TOTAL WITHIN 10 OF FILLING QUEUE?
15            BGE    IRUPT2              BRANCH IF AT LEAST 10 EMPTY SLOTS
16  *                                       ARE LEFT IN THE QUEUE
17            JSR    RTS_OFF             SHUT DOWN THE TRANSMITTER
18  *                                       QUEUE NEARLY FULL
19  IRUPT2    PULL   ALL                 RESTORE PRIOR
20            SET    I_MASK              INTERRUPTS ON
21            RTI                        RETURN FROM INTERRUPT
```

Note how simple this program is as a result of choosing a queue as the interface between the interrupt-driven part of the program and the polling part of the program. The reason for choosing to have ten cells vacant in the queue instead of a smaller number like 0, 1, or 2, is to provide a little protection from buffering at the transmitter. The transmitter, in general, sends up to two characters after RTS is deasserted. But each time a character is removed from the queue, RTS is reasserted, which could bring more than one character across the link. By choosing ten as the limit, we have established a comfortable margin at the very small cost of wasting up to ten bytes of a queue.

The program may be somewhat simpler for microprocessors that store all registers on the stack whenever an interrupt occurs. The 68XX family generally passes control to the interrupt handler, with the interrupts turned off and all registers pushed into the stack. For this processor family, the instructions on lines 1, 2, 19, and 20 are unnecessary.

This brings us to the OUTPUT coroutine, Program 9.13, which is indeed a coroutine. The coroutine can exit back to the main program at any one of several points. The most frequently used exits are at points where the coroutine is awaiting the completion of a carriage movement, platen movement, or print-wheel action. In these cases, the coroutine exits to the main program and returns during each polling loop to test the status of the printer mechanism. The coroutine may also be waiting because the input queue is empty. In this case, each pass through the main program returns to the output coroutine to make another attempt to extract a character from the queue. Another entry point is associated with sequences of nonprinting control characters. After receiving the ESC character that opens such a sequence, the coroutine reenters at a series of instructions that interpret the next few characters.

Here is a brief analysis of the actions of the OUTPUT coroutine.

1. Lines 1 through 4. OUTPUT is the very first entry point. At this point the coroutine calls GET_CHAR to remove a character from the queue. If none exists, GET_CHAR returns with the carry bit of the condition code set, and control passes to CALL_MAIN to RESUME the main program.

2. Lines 48 through 56. We skip forward to show the code for CALL_MAIN to illustrate how the coroutine linkage is implemented in this program. Since CALL_MAIN performs a subroutine jump, the return address for reentry to OUTPUT is at the top of the stack when CALL-MAIN takes control. CALL_MAIN moves the return address to its reserved location in OUT_CHAR, and then pops the stack. The stack should now be in a state identical to its state at the point of entry to the output coroutine. At the top of the stack is the return address to the main program. Therefore, the RTS instruction executed next on line 56 of CALL_MAIN returns control back to the main program. Note that no status of the output program can be held in the stack from call to call. This is the case in any coroutine implementation that uses a single stack.

3. Lines 5 and 6. These lines test to see if the character obtained (now in the register REG1) is printable. The least printable character has the ASCII code 21_{16}. Other ASCII characters to which the printer responds are space, line feed, carriage return, and escape, none of which result in a hammer strike on the print wheel.

4. Lines 7 through 47. Printable characters are processed as a series of distinct operations. First, on lines 7 though 21, the carriage is moved by the amount accumulated to this point. If the carriage is busy then the coroutine exits to the main program and returns to retest the carriage. The test of carriage status is made on lines 15 through 17 by comparing the status word with 0. In this example we presume that a ready status is indicated by a 0, but more generally that the status will be the value of a single bit rather than of the entire word. In this case the status test requires that the program isolate the bit through a shift or mask operation.

5. Lines 22 through 35. After moving the carriage, the program moves the platen using the same methodology as before.

6. Lines 36 through 47. When platen movement has been completed, the program prints the character. This, too, follows the same methodology as for carriage and platen movement.

7. Line 46. Ordinary typewriters advance the carriage after striking a character. The daisy-wheel printer need not advance immediately. The output program simulates an ordinary typewriter by scheduling the advance with the call to STEP_X. STEP_X merely accumulates an additional DELTA_X of X-movement, and does not move the carriage at this time. This accumulated X-movement, plus any other subsequent movement from multiple spaces and carriage returns, will be done in a single carriage-movement operation just before printing the next visible character. It is also possible for STEP_X to keep track of a right-hand margin, and to advance to a new line if the next printing character moves too far to the right. This code is not shown in the listing

of STEP_X on lines 90 through 93. After the call to STEP_X the coroutine exits in a state in which it is ready to retrieve another character from the input queue.

8. Lines 57 through 79. These lines show the handling of space, carriage return, and line feed. For space and carriage return, the accumulated amount of carriage movement is altered. For line feed, the accumulated platen movement is altered. Since none of these three special characters depends on the mechanical state of the printer mechanism, they can be removed from the queue at a rate much faster than the transmitter can transmit; and therefore, processing them in this fashion tends to speed up the printer relative to the speed of the serial link.

9. Lines 80 through 86. These lines process sequences that begin with the ESC code. After receiving an ESC, the coroutine resumes the main program, and reenters at an instruction that extracts another character from the queue. Strictly speaking, it is unnecessary to resume the main program immediately after the ESC, but this call gives the main program a polling opportunity between characters. The handling of specific escape sequences is not shown in the program example.

PROGRAM 9.13   The Output Coroutine for the Printer Controller

```
1  OUTPUT     JSR    GET_CHAR        OBTAIN CHARACTER FROM QUEUE
2             BCC    OUT_CHK         BRANCH IF QUEUE NOT EMPTY (CARRY CLEAR)
3  OUTEXIT    JSR    CALL_MAIN       OTHERWISE, RESUME MAIN PROGRAM, LINE 54
4             JMP    OUTPUT          RECHECK THE QUEUE
5  OUT_CHK    CMP    REG1,#21H       VISIBLE CHARACTER?
6             BLO    SPECIAL         BRANCH IF LOW (NOT VISIBLE), LINE 60
7  *****************************************************************************
8  *    THE CHARACTER IN REG1 IS A VISIBLE CHARACTER                         *
9  *****************************************************************************
10            MOV    T1,REG1         SAVE THE CHARACTER TEMPORARILY IN T1
11            JSR    CALC_X          FIND ACCUMULATED X MOVEMENT, LINE 94
12            MOV    T2,REG2         SAVE X MOVEMENT TEMPORARILY
13            CMP    REG2,#0         IS THE X MOVEMENT (IN REG2) = 0?
14            BEQ    OUT2            BRANCH IF MOVE IS NOT PENDING
15 OUT1       MOV    REG3,CR_STATE   IS THE CARRIAGE BUSY?
16            CMP    REG3,#0         0 SIGNIFIES READY
17            BEQ    OUTX            BRANCH TO MOVE CARRIAGE
18            JSR    CALL_MAIN       COROUTINE CALL BACK TO MAIN PROGRAM
19            JMP    OUT1            TEST AGAIN WHEN PROGRAM RESUMES HERE
20 OUTX       MOV    REG2,T2         RESTORE X MOVEMENT IN REG2
21            JSR    X_MOVE          OUTPUT THE X MOVEMENT
22 *****************************************************************************
23 *    THE FOLLOWING CODE MOVES THE PLATEN.                                 *
24 *****************************************************************************
25 OUT2       JSR    CALC_Y          MOVE ACCUMULATED Y MOVEMENT TO REG2
26            MOV    T2,REG2         SAVE Y MOVEMENT TEMPORARILY
27            CMP    REG2,#0         IS THE Y MOVEMENT (IN REG2) = 0?
28            BEQ    OUT4            BRANCH IF MOVE IS NOT PENDING
29 OUT3       MOV    REG3,PL_STATE   IS THE PLATEN BUSY?
```

(Continued on next page.)

```
30              CMP      REG3,#0           0 SIGNIFIES READY
31              BEQ      OUTY              BRANCH TO MOVE PLATEN
32              JSR      CALL_MAIN         COROUTINE CALL BACK TO MAIN PROGRAM
33              JMP      OUT3              TEST AGAIN WHEN PROGRAM RESUMES HERE
34 OUTY         MOV      REG2,T2           RESTORE Y MOVEMENT IN REG2
35              JSR      Y_MOVE            OUTPUT THE Y MOVEMENT
36 **************************************************************************
37 *     THE FOLLOWING CODE PRINTS THE CHARACTER.                          *
38 **************************************************************************
39 OUT4         MOV      REG3,PW_STATE     IS THE PRINT WHEEL BUSY?
40              CMP      REG3,#0           0 SIGNIFIES READY
41              BEQ      OUTPW             BRANCH TO SPIN THE PRINT WHEEL
42              JSR      CALL_MAIN         COROUTINE CALL BACK TO MAIN PROGRAM
43              JMP      OUT4              TEST AGAIN WHEN PROGRAM RESUMES HERE
44 OUTPW        MOV      REG1,T1           RECOVER PRINTABLE CHARACTER
45              JSR      PRINT             OUTPUT THE CHARACTER IN REG1
46              JSR      STEP_X            ACCUMULATE DELTA_X, LINE 90
47              JMP      OUTEXIT           RETURN TO START OF COROUTINE, LINE 3
48 **************************************************************************
49 *     THIS CODE RESUMES THE MAIN PROGRAM.                               *
50 *     THE TOP TWO BYTES IN THE STACK CONTAIN THE REENTRY                *
51 *     ADDRESS TO OUTPUT.  BENEATH THOSE BYTES LIES THE                  *
52 *     RETURN ADDRESS TO THE MAIN PROGRAM.                               *
53 **************************************************************************
54 CALL_MAIN    MOV      OUTCHR,(SP)       POP THE RETURN ADDRESS TO OUTCHR
55              INC      SP,2              SP := SP + 2 (* ADDRESS HAS TWO BYTES *)
56              RTS                        RETURN TO MAIN PROGRAM
57 **************************************************************************
58 *     THIS CODE HANDLES NONPRINTING CHARACTERS                          *
59 **************************************************************************
60 SPECIAL      CMP      REG1,#SPACE       IS IT A SPACE?
61              BEQ      DOSPACE           BRANCH TO DO SPACE
62              CMP      REG1,#CR          IS IT A CARRIAGE RETURN?
63              BEQ      DOCR              BRANCH TO DO CARRIAGE RETURN
64              CMP      REG1,#LF          IS IT A LINE FEED?
65              BEQ      DOLF              BRANCH TO DO LINE FEED
66              CMP      REG1,#ESC         IS IT AN ESCAPE SEQUENCE?
67              BEQ      DOESC             BRANCH TO ESCAPE CODE
68 OUTEX        JSR      CALL_MAIN         OTHERWISE, IGNORE IT
69              JMP      OUTPUT            RETURN TO START
70 DOSPACE      JSR      STEP_X            ACCUMULATE DELTA_X, LINE 90
71              JMP      OUTEX             RESUME MAIN, LINE 68
72 DOCR         MOV      REG1,LEFT_MARG    FIND X POSITION OF LEFT MARGIN
73              SUB      REG1,CURR_X       DECREASE BY CURRENT X POSITION
74              MOV      ACCUM_X,REG1      ACCUMULATE THIS AMOUNT OF X MOVEMENT
75              JMP      OUTEX             RESUME MAIN, LINE 68
76 DOLF         MOV      REG1,ACCUM_Y      FIND PRESENT Y POSITION
77              ADD      REG1,DELTA_Y      INCREASE ACCUMULATION
78              MOV      ACCUM_Y,REG1      UPDATE ACCUM_Y
79              JMP      OUTEX             RESUME MAIN, LINE 68
80 **************************************************************************
81 *     THIS CODE HANDLES ESCAPE SEQUENCES                                *
82 **************************************************************************
```

```
83 DOESC      JSR      CALL_MAIN       RESUME MAIN PROGRAM
84            JSR      GET_CHAR        OBTAIN CHARACTER FROM QUEUE
85            BCS      DOESC           BRANCH IF QUEUE EMPTY (CARRY SET)
86 ESC1       . . .                    PROCESS NEXT CHARACTER IN SEQUENCE
87 *******************************************************************************
88 *   AUXILIARY ROUTINES                                                       *
89 *******************************************************************************
90 STEP_X     MOV      REG1, ACCUM_X   ACCUM_X := ACCUM_X + DELTA_X
91            ADD      REG1, DELTA_X
92            MOV      ACCUM_X, REG1
93            RTS
94 CALC_X     MOV      REG1, ACCUM_X   CURR_X := CURR_X + ACCUM_X
95            ADD      REG1, CURR_X
96            MOV      CURR_X, REG1
97            MOV      REG1, ACCUM_X   REPORT THE ACCUMULATED X MOVEMENT
98            CLR      ACCUM_X         CLEAR THE ACCUMULATED AMOUNT
99            RTS
```

At this point, we examine the subroutine GET_CHAR in Program 9.14 to illustrate how it works in conjunction with the interrupt handler. Since GET_CHAR manipulates the queue variables, it too must run with interrupts off. Otherwise, if an interrupt were to occur while these variables were being updated, the result would be an inconsistent set of variables, and the queueing programs would fail. Immediately after shutting off the interrupts on line 1, GET_CHAR turns on RTS to restart the transmitter. This is permissible because GET_CHAR extracts one character from the queue, leaving a space for a new character. However, there is a possible problem if the transmitter sends a minimum of two characters in response to this action. The code shown works correctly with a specific collection

PROGRAM 9.14   The Get Character (Queue Output) Subroutine

```
 1 GET_CHAR   CLR      I_MASK          DISABLE INTERRUPTS
 2            JSR      RTS_ON          TURN ON THE TRANSMITTER
 3            MOV      REG1, TOTAL     HOW MANY BYTES IN THE QUEUE?
 4            CMP      REG1, #0
 5            BEQ      GETNONE         EXIT WITH NO CHARACTER
 6            MOV      REG1, Q_OUT     POINTER TO HEAD OF QUEUE
 7            INC      REG1            ADVANCE THE POINTER
 8            CMP      REG1, #Q_END    AT END OF STORAGE?
 9            BLE      GET1            BRANCH IF POINTER STILL VALID
10            MOV      REG1, #Q_START  OTHERWISE, RESET THE POINTER
11 GET1       MOV      Q_OUT, REG1     UPDATE THE POINTER
12            MOV      REG1, (REG1)    RETRIEVE THE NEXT CHARACTER
13            MOV      REG2, TOTAL     DECREASE THE QUEUE COUNT
14            DEC      REG2
15            MOV      TOTAL, REG2
16            CLEAR    CARRY           NOTIFY THAT A CHARACTER WAS FOUND
17            JMP      GETEXIT
18 GETNONE    SET      CARRY           NOTIFY THAT NO CHARACTER WAS FOUND
19 GETEXIT    SET      I_MASK          ENABLE INTERRUPTS
20            RTS
```

of software and hardware at both ends of the link. To be absolutely sure that the code is correct, the call of RTS_ON should occur only if there is sufficient space to receive the minimum number of characters that can be transmitted.

After turning on the transmitter, GET_CHAR proceeds to extract a character from the queue if there is one. The carry bit is set or cleared depending on whether the queue is empty or nonempty, and then GET_CHAR exits with interrupts turned on.

There are many other supporting routines that are not described in this example. These other routines implement the remaining functions in a standard way, and do not illustrate the specific problems related to I/O, interrupts, and coroutines.

In this detailed discussion of the example, we touched on the important ideas contained in the design process. The coroutine structure greatly simplifies the program by breaking the program into small, self-contained modules. Synchronization with the external link is handled through a very small interrupt routine; and the queue, in essence, decouples the behavior of the interrupt handler from the rest of the program. As testimony to the power of the implementation technique, a 500-byte version of the program described on these pages was written and tested over a two-day period. Testing was done by simulating the actions of the printer, and the simulation turned up about three or four transcription errors. When the simulated system worked properly, the program was transferred to EPROM and installed in the printer. It worked the first time and has never failed in 18 months of operation.

OTHER SOURCE MATERIAL

Among the many texts available for instruction in assembly-language programming, Knuth, vol. 1 (1973) is perhaps the most comprehensive in techniques and the implementation of data structures. Wakerly (1981) is especially recommended for the breadth of coverage and for the melding together of assembly language with a high-level language.

The term ''coroutines'' was coined by Conway (1963) in a paper that showed several interesting techniques for the implementation of a compiler. Knuth (1973) reports that the idea had been used in programs much earlier than Conway's article, but Conway's paper brought the idea before the public and spread its use. Dahl, Dijkstra, and Hoare (1972) is a very interesting treatment of structured programming, with a good of deal of information on coroutine structures.

The merge algorithm described in the text is one of the more popular algorithms for merging data files. Knuth, vol. 3, (1973) is the definitive source for algorithms and background information for sorting and merging.

Bibliography

Altnether, J. "High Speed Memory System Design Using 2147H," AP-74, Intel Corporation, Santa Clara, CA, March 1980.

Artwick, B. A. *Microcomputer Interfacing.* Englewood Cliffs, NJ: Prentice-Hall, 1980.

Barna, A., and D. I. Porat. *Introduction to Microcomputers and Microprocessors.* New York: Wiley-Interscience, 1976.

Blakeslee, T. R. *Digital Design with Standard MSI and LSI.* 2d ed. New York: Wiley-Interscience, 1979.

Borrill, P. L. "Microprocessor Bus Structures and Standards." *IEEE Micro,* vol. 1, no. 1 (February 1981): 84−95.

Chaney, T. J., and C. E. Molnar. "Anomalous Behavior of Synchronizer and Arbiter Circuits." *IEEE Trans. on Computers,* vol. C-22, No. 4 (April 1973): 421−422.

Close, C. M., and D. K. Frederick. *Modeling and Analysis of Dynamic Systems.* Boston: Houghton-Mifflin, 1978.

Coates, T. "Interfacing to the Interface: Practical Considerations beyond the Scope of the IEEE Standard 488." *1975 Wescon Professional Program,* San Francisco, Session 3, 3/3-1 through 3/3-6.

Cohen, D. "On Holy Wars and a Plea for Peace." *Computer,* vol. 14, no. 10 (October 1981): 48–54.

Conway, M. E. "Design of a Separable Transition-Diagram Compiler." *CACM,* vol. 6, no. 7 (July 1963): 396−408.

Dahl, O.-J.; E. W. Dijkstra; and C. A. R. Hoare. *Structured Programming.* New York: Academic Press, 1972.

Digital Equipment Corporation. *PDP-11 Bus Handbook.* Maynard, MA: Digital Press, 1979.

Dorf, R. C. *Modern Control Systems.* 3d ed. Reading, MA: Addison-Wesley, 1980.

Doty, K. *Fundamentals of Microcomputer Architecture.* Portland, OR: Matrix, 1979.

Eckhouse. R. H., Jr. *Minicomputer Systems: Organization and Programming (PDP-11).* Englewood Cliffs, NJ: Prentice-Hall, 1975.

Electronic Industries Association. "Interface between Data Terminal Equipment and Data Communication Equipment Employing Serial Binary Data Interchange," EIA Standard RS-232-C. Washington, DC: EIA, August 1969.

363

Farmer, W. W., and E. E. Newhall. "An Experimental Distributed Switching System To Handle Bursty Computer Traffic." *Proceedings ACM Problems in the Optimization of Data Communications Systems*, Pine Mountain, GA. New York: ACM, October 1969, 1−33.

Fletcher, W. I. *An Engineering Approach to Digital Design*. Englewood Cliffs, NJ: Prentice-Hall, 1980.

Forbes, B. "Using the 8292 GPIB Controller," AP-66, Intel Corp., Santa Clara, CA, 1980.

Gardner, F. M. *Phaselock Techniques*. New York: Wiley, 1977.

Fisher, E., and C. Jensen. *PET and the IEEE- 488 Bus (GPIB)*. Berkeley, CA: Osborne, 1980.

Fluke, J. M. "System Considerations in Using the IEEE Digital Instrument Bus." *1975 Wescon Professional Program*, San Francisco, Session 3, 3/4-1 through 3/4-6.

Gill, A. *Machine and Assembly Language Programming of the PDP-11*. Englewood Cliffs, NJ: Prentice-Hall, 1978.

Givone, D. D., and R. P. Roesser. *Microprocessors/Microcomputers: An Introduction*. New York: McGraw-Hill, 1980.

Harman, J. "IBM-Compatible Disk Drives." *Byte*, vol. 4, no. 10 (October 1979): 100−113.

Hilburn, J. L., and P. N. Julich. *Microcomputers/Microprocessors: Hardware, Software, and Applications*. Englewood Cliffs, NJ: Prentice-Hall, 1976.

Hoeppner, J. F., and L. H. Wall. "Encoding/Decoding Techniques for Double Floppy Disk Capacity." *Computer Design*, vol. 19, no. 2 (February 1980): 127−135.

IEEE. "IEEE Standard Digital Interface for Programmable Instrumentation," IEEE Std. 488−1975 (April 1975).

_____. "IEEE Standard Digital Interface for Programmable Instrumentation," IEEE Std. 488−1978 (1978).

IEEE 796 Bus Working Group. "Proposed Microcomputer System 796 Bus Standard." *Computer*, vol. 13, no. 10 (October 1980): 89−105.

IEEE Task 696.1/D2. "Standard Specification for the S-100 Bus Interface Devices." *Computer*, vol. 12, no. 6 (July 1979): 28−52.

Intel Corporation. "Memory Design Handbook." Santa Clara, CA: Intel Corp., 1977.

_____. "Component Data Catalog 1982." Santa Clara, CA: Intel Corp., 1982.

Johnson, D.; J. L. Hilburn; and P. M. Julich. *Digital Circuits and Microcomputers*. Englewood Cliffs, NJ: Prentice-Hall, 1979.

Kane, G. *CRT Controller Handbook*. Berkeley, CA: Osborne, 1980.

Klingman, E. E. *Microprocessor Systems Design*. Englewood Cliffs, NJ: Prentice-Hall, 1977.

Knoblock, D. E. "Identifying, Understanding, and Selecting among the Capabilities Provided by the IEEE Standard 488." *1975 Wescon Professional Program*, San Francisco, Session 3, 3/1-1 through 3/1-5.

Knoblock, D. E.; D. C. Loughry; and C. A. Vissers. "Insight into Interfacing." *IEEE Spectrum*, vol. 12, no. 5 (May 1975): 50–57.

Knuth, D. E. *Fundamental Algorithms*. 2d. ed. The Art of Computer Programming, vol. 1. Reading, MA: Addison-Wesley, 1973.

––––––. *Sorting and Searching*. The Art of Computer Programming, vol. 3. Reading, MA: Addison-Wesley, 1973.

Kraft, G. D., and W. N. Toy. *Mini/Microcomputer Hardware Design*. Englewood Cliffs, NJ: Prentice-Hall, 1979.

Krutz, R. L. *Microprocessors and Logic Design*. New York: Wiley, 1980.

Kryka, T. "An MC68488 GPIA and MC6821 PIA Team Up as a GPIB Controller," AN-800, Motorola, Phoenix, AZ, 1979.

Lee, R. C. "Microprocessor Implementation of a Measurement Instrument and Its Interface." *1975 Wescon Professional Program*, San Francisco, Session 3, 3/2-1 through 3/2-8.

Leventhal, Lance A. *Introduction to Microprocessors: Software, Hardware, and Programming*. Englewood Cliffs, NJ: Prentice-Hall, 1978.

Levy, J. "Buses, the Skeleton of Computer Structures." In *Computer Engineering: A DEC View of Hardware Systems Design* by C. G. Bell; J. C. Mudge; and J. E. McNamara. Bedford, MA: Digital Press, 1978.

Lipovski, G. J. *Microcomputer Interfacing*. Lexington, MA: D. C. Heath, 1980.

McNamara, J. E. *Technical Aspects of Data Communication*. 2d. ed. Bedford, MA: Digital Press, 1981.

Mead, C., and L. Conway. *Introduction to VLSI Systems*. Reading, MA: Addison-Wesley, 1980.

Metzler, E., and J. Oliphant. "Single-Supply, 16-K Dynamic RAM Is Ready for Denser Systems." *Electronic Design*, vol. 19 (13 September 1978): 64–69.

Metcalfe, R. M., and D. R. Boggs. "Ethernet: Distributed Packet Switching for Local Computer Networks." *CACM*, vol. 19, no. 7 (July 1976): 395–404.

Morrison, R. *Grounding and Shielding Techniques in Instrumentation*. 2d ed. New York: Wiley-Interscience, 1977.

Moschytz, G. S. "Miniaturized RC Filters Using Phased-Locked Loop. *Bell Systems Technical Journal*, vol. 44, no. 5 (May-June 1965), 823–870.

Motorola Corporation. "M6800 Microcomputer System Design Data." Phoenix, AZ: Motorola, 1976.

_____. "Getting Aboard the 488-1975 Bus." Phoenix, AZ: Motorola (undated).

Murray, J., and G. Alexy. "CRT Terminal Design Using the Intel 8275 and 8279," AP-32, Intel Corporation, Santa Clara, CA, November 1977.

NEC Microcomputers. "Floppy Disk Controller Users' Manual." Lexington, MA: NEC, 1977.

Noyce, R. N., and M. E. Hoff, Jr. "A History of Microprocessor Development at Intel." *IEEE Micro*, vol. 1, no. 1 (February 1981): 8–21.

Ogdin, C. A. *Microcomputer Management and Programming*. Englewood Cliffs, NJ: Prentice-Hall, 1980.

Osborne, A., and J. Kane. *Some Real Microprocessors*. Introduction to Microcomputers, vol. 2. Berkeley, CA: Osborne, 1978.

_____. *Some Real Support Devices*. Introduction to Microcomputers, vol. 3. Berkeley, CA: Osborne, 1978.

Ott, H. W. *Noise Reduction Techniques in Electronic Systems*. New York: Wiley, 1976.

Peatman, J. B. *Microcomputer-Based Design*. New York: McGraw-Hill, 1977.

Pierce, J. R.; C. H. Coker; and W. J. Krophl. "An Experiment in Addressed Block Data Transmission around a Loop." *IEEE Int. Conv. Rec.*, March 1971: IEEE, 222–223.

Pierce, J. "How Far Can Data Loops Go?" *IEEE Trans. Commun.*, vol. COM-20 (June 1972): 527–530.

Rolander, T. "MULTIBUS Interfacing," AP-28, Intel Corp., Santa Clara, CA, 1977.

Stone, H. S. and D. P. Siewiorek. *Computer Organization and Data Structures: PDP-11 Edition*. New York: McGraw-Hill, 1975.

Soucek, B. *Microprocessors and Microcomputers*. New York: Wiley-Interscience, 1976.

Summers, J. "Microprocessor-GPIB Interfacing with the 96LS488," APP-351, Fairchild, Mt. View, CA, May 1980.

Tanenbaum, A. S. *Computer Networks*. Englewood Cliffs, NJ: Prentice-Hall, 1981.

Thurber, K. J.; E. D. Jensen; *et al.* "A Systematic Approach to the Design of Digital Busing Structures." *AFIPS, Proceedings of the 1972 FJCC*, vol. 41, part II. Montvale, NJ: AFIPS Press, 719–740.

Wakerly, J. "Intel MCS-48 Microprocessor Family, A Critique." *Computer*, vol. 12, no. 2 (February 1979): 22–31.

——. *Microcomputer Architecture and Programming.* New York: Wiley, 1981.

Western Digital. "FD 179X-01 Floppy Disk Formatter/Controller Family." Newport Beach, CA: Western Digital (undated).

Wharton, J. "Using the Intel 8085 Serial I/O Lines," AP-29, Intel Corp., Santa Clara, CA, 1977.

White, D. J. *Electromagnetic Interference and Compatibility*, vols. 1–5. Germantown, MD: White Consultants, 1971.

Wiatrowksi, C. A., and C. H. House. *Logic Circuits and Microcomputer Systems.* New York: McGraw-Hill, 1980.

APPENDIX A / THE ASCII CODE

Second Hex Digit	First Hex Digit							
	0	1	2	3	4	5	6	7
0	NUL	DLE	SP	0	@	P	` or '	p
1	SOH	DC1	!	1	A	Q	a	q
2	STX	DC2	' '	2	B	R	b	r
3	ETX	DC3	#	3	C	S	c	s
4	EOT	DC4	$	4	D	T	d	t
5	ENQ	NAK	%	5	E	U	e	u
6	ACK	SYN	&	6	F	V	f	v
7	BEL	ETB	' or '	7	G	W	g	w
8	BS	CAN	(	8	H	X	h	x
9	HT	EM	)	9	I	Y	i	y
A	LF	SUB	*	:	J	Z	j	z
B	VT	ESC	+	;	K	[	k	{
C	FF	FS	,	<	L	\	l	|
D	CR	GS	−	=	M	]	m	}
E	SO	RS	.	>	N	^	n	~
F	SI	US	/	?	O	_	o	DEL

Definitions of Control Symbols

NUL	Null	DLE	Data link escape
SOH	Start of heading	DC1	Device control 1
STX	Start of text	DC2	Device control 2
ETX	End of text	DC3	Device control 3
EOT	End of tape	DC4	Device control 4
ENQ	Enquiry	NAK	Negative acknowledge
ACK	Acknowledge	SYN	Synchronize
BEL	Bell	ETB	End of transmitted block
BS	Backspace	CAN	Cancel
HT	Horizontal tab	EM	End of medium
LF	Line feed	SUB	Substitute
VT	Vertical tab	ESC	Escape
FF	Form feed	FS	File separator
CR	Carriage return	GS	Group separator
SO	Shift out	RS	Record separator
SI	Shift in	US	Unit separator
SP	Space	DEL	Delete

APPENDIX B / THE RS-232-C
CONNECTOR STANDARD

Pin Number	Circuit	CCIT ID	Direction	Description
1	AA	101	—	Protective ground (shield).
2	BA	103	Terminal to modem	Transmitted data.
3	BB	104	Modem to terminal	Received data.
4	CA	105	Terminal to modem	Request to send.
5	CB	106	Modem to terminal	Clear to send.
6	CC	107	Modem to terminal	Data set ready.
7	AB	102	—	Signal ground (common return).
8	CF	109	Modem to terminal	Received line signal detector (carrier detected).
9	—	—	—	Reserved for testing.
10	—	—	—	Reserved for testing.
11	—	—	—	Unassigned.
12	SCF	122	Modem to terminal	Secondary received line signal detector.
13	SCB	121	Modem to terminal	Secondary clear to send.
14	SBA	118	Terminal to modem	Secondary transmitted data.
15	DB	114	Modem to terminal	Transmitter signal element timing (terminal transmitter clock).
16	SBB	119	Modem to terminal	Secondary received data.
17	DD	115	Modem to terminal	Receiver signal element timing (modem receiver clock).
18	—	—	—	Unassigned.
19	SCA	120	Terminal to modem	Secondary request to send.
20	CD	108.2	Terminal to modem	Data terminal ready.
21	CG	110	Modem to terminal	Signal quality detector.
23	CH	111	Terminal to modem	Data signal rate selector, or
	CI	112	Modem to terminal	Data signal rate selector.
24	DA	113	Terminal to modem	Transmitter signal element timing (terminal transmitter clock).
25	—	—	—	Unassigned.

APPENDIX C / THE RS-449
CONNECTOR STANDARD

Pin Assignments for the 37-Pin Connector

Pin Number	Circuit	Direction	Type	Description
1	Shield	—	Ground	Protective shield.
2	SI	From modem	A–A′	Signaling-rate indicator.
3	Spare	—	—	—
4	SD	To modem	A–A′	SEND data.
5	ST	From modem	A–A′	SEND timing.
6	RD	From modem	A–A′	RECEIVE data.
7	RS	To modem	A–A′	Request to send.
8	RT	From modem	A–A′	RECEIVE timing.
9	CS	From modem	A–A′	Clear to send.
10	LL	To modem	A–A′	Local loopback.
11	DM	From modem	A–A′	Data mode.
12	TR	To modem	A–A′	Terminal ready.
13	RR	From modem	A–A′	Receiver ready.
14	RL	To modem	A–A′	Remote loopback.
15	IC	From modem	A–A′	Incoming call.
16	SF	To modem	A–A′	Select frequency, or
	SR	To modem	A–A′	Signaling rate selector.
17	TT	To modem	A–A′	Terminal timing.
18	TM	From modem	A–A′	Test mode.
19	SG	—	C–C′	Signal ground.
20	RC	From modem	C–B′	RECEIVE common.
21	Spare	—	—	—
22	SD	To modem	B/C–B′	SEND data.
23	ST	From modem	B/C–B′	SEND timing.
24	RD	From modem	B/C–B′	RECEIVE data.
25	RS	To modem	B/C–B′	Request to send.
26	RT	From modem	B/C–B′	RECEIVE timing.
27	CS	From modem	B/C–B′	Clear to send.
28	IS	To modem	A–A′	Terminal in service.
29	DM	From modem	B/C–B′	Data mode.
30	TR	To modem	B/C–B′	Terminal ready.
31	RR	From modem	B/C–B′	Receiver ready.
32	SS	To modem	A–A′	Select standby.
33	SQ	From modem	A–A′	Signal quality.
34	NS	To modem	A–A′	New signal.
35	TT	To modem	B/C–B′	Terminal timing.
36	SB	From modem	A–A′	Stand-by indicator.
37	SC	To modem	C–B′	SEND common.

Pin Assignments for the 9-Pin Connector

Pin Number	Circuit	Direction	Type	Description
1	Shield	—	Ground	Protective shield.
2	SRR	From modem	A–A'	Secondary receiver ready.
3	SSD	To modem	A–A'	Secondary SEND data.
4	SRD	To modem	A–A'	Secondary RECEIVE data.
5	SG	—	C–C'	Signal ground.
6	RC	From modem	C–B'	RECEIVE common.
7	SRS	To modem	A–A'	Secondary request to send.
8	SCS	From modem	A–A'	Secondary clear to send.
9	SC	To modem	C–B'	SEND common.

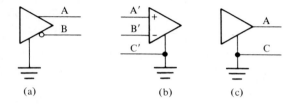

(a)   (b)   (c)

FIGURE C.1 Type codes for connections for RS-449 links: (a) Balanced transmitter; (b) differential receiver; (c) single-ended transmitter.

APPENDIX D / IEEE-488 BUS MULTILINE INTERFACE MESSAGES

	High Hex Digit							
Low Hex Digit	0 (ACG)	1 (UCG)	2 (LAG)	3 (LAG)	4 (TAG)	5 (TAG)	6 (SCG)	7 (SCG)
0	—	—	L00	L16	T00	T16	S00	S16
1	GTL	LLO	L01	L17	T01	T17	S01	S17
2	—	—	L02	L18	T02	T18	S02	S18
3	—	—	L03	L19	T03	T19	S03	S19
4	SDC	DCL	L04	L20	T04	T20	S04	S20
5	PPC	PPU	L05	L21	T05	T21	S05	S21
6	—	—	L06	L22	T06	T22	S06	S22
7	—	—	L07	L23	T07	T23	S07	S23
8	GET	SPE	L08	L24	T08	T24	S08	S24
9	TCT	SPD	L09	L25	T09	T25	S09	S25
A	—	—	L10	L26	T10	T26	S10	S26
B	—	—	L11	L27	T11	T27	S11	S27
C	—	—	L12	L28	T12	T28	S12	S28
D	—	—	L13	L29	T13	T29	S13	S29
E	—	—	L14	L30	T14	T30	S14	S30
F	—	—	L15	UNL	T15	UNT	S15	—

COMMAND LEGEND		COLUMN HEADING LEGEND	
GTL	Go To Local	ACG	Addressed Command Group
SDC	Selected Device Clear	UCG	Universal Command Group
PPC	Parallel Poll Configure	LAG	Listen Address Group
GET	Group Execute Trigger	TAG	Talk Address Group
TCT	Take Control	SCG	Secondary Command Group
LLO	Local Lock Out		
DCL	Device Clear		
PPU	Parallel Poll Unconfigure		
SPE	Serial Poll Enable		
SPD	Serial Poll Disable		
Li	Listen Address i		
UNL	Unlisten		
Ti	Talk Address i		
UNT	Untalk		
Si	Secondary Address i		

Notes:
1. The high hex byte is encoded on DIO7, DIO6, and DIO5. The low hex byte is encoded on DIO4 through DIO1.
2. All multiline messages are sent and received with ATN asserted.

INDEX/GLOSSARY

---

†Numerical index of devices cited is at end of this section.

Eckhouse, R. H., Jr., 30
ECL (emitter-coupled logic), 55
Edge-triggered   Sensitive to a change in voltage
rather than to a voltage level; 227–8
Effective-address calculation   The process of
computing the address of an operand by
means of calculations that may involve
index registers and indirect addresses; 324
Electrical isolation   The state of having no direct
low-impedance electrical connection; 52,
172–4, 176–7, 188–90, 205
Emitter-coupled logic; *see* ECL
ETB (end of transmitted block), 81
Ethernet   A coaxial-cable interconnection scheme
used for data communication among
computers; 201
ETX (end of text), 181–2

Farmer, W. W., 185
Feedback-control system   A system in which an
output signal is combined with an input signal to produce a new output signal; 255–60
Fiber optics   An interconnection system that uses
very fine strands of transparent material to
carry information encoded in the form of
modulated light; 51
FIFO (first in, first out); *see* Queue
File   A data structure composed of a collection of
records that is usually stored in auxiliary
memory; 322–33, 339–46
File block   A structure that contains all information pertinent to the control of a file; 328–9
Filter (in the context of programs)   A program
that processes a sequential input file and
produces a modified version of the file as a
sequential output file; 339–46
Flag (in SDLC protocol)   A sync pattern that
establishes the start of a block; 182–3, 198
Flat cable; *see* Ribbon cable
Fletcher, W. I., 40
Flip-flop   A one-bit memory; 107
Floppy disk   A flexible, jacketed magnetic disk
used for the storage of digital data; 216,
265–89
controller design, 271–90
Flow control (in data communications)   Control
applied to data transmitters to prevent buffer overflow at receivers, 190–2
Flux transition   A reversal of a magnetic field in a
local region of a recording surface; 266–7,
272
FM (frequency modulation); *see* single-density
recording
FORTH   A computer language; 320
FORTRAN   A computer language oriented for
scientific calculations; 33
Frame counter   A counter in a video display that
counts the number of scan lines in a frame,

then generates control information when a
frame has been completed; 305–7
Front porch   The leading portion of a horizontal
sync pulse for a video signal; 301–2
Full duplex   A bidirectional communications link
that can be used in both directions concurrently; 297
See also Half duplex
Fully interlocked asynchronous protocol   A bus
protocol in which all transitions of MAS-
TER and SLAVE signals are interlocked to
occur in a fixed order; 95–8, 206, 215,
219–20, 228–33, 239, 241–2
Function (in programming languages)   A subroutine that returns a value, 324

Gap   (1) the region between a sector identifier and
a data block on a floppy disk; (2) a physical
break in read/write or erase head; 270–1
Gardner, F. M., 261
GCR (group code recording)   A recording technique in which a group of four-bits is
encoded by a group of five bits, and no
other bits are used to record clocking information; 267–8
Gill, A., 30
Givone, D. D., 40
Graphic mode, 316–17
Ground loop   A low-impedance closed loop composed primarily of ground conductors or an
earth connection; 44–5, 172
Grounding techniques, 43–5
for board-to-board connections, 78–82
for RS–232–C, 168
for shields, 48–50

Half-duplex   A bidirectional communications
link capable of being using in only one
direction at a time; 297
See also Full duplex
Halfword   A datum whose length in bits is half
that of a word (used in the context of
machines with 32-bit words, a halfword
denotes a 16-bit datum); 8
Handshake; *see* Fully interlocked asynchronous
handshake
Hard sectoring   The method of identifying sector
boundaries on a magnetic disk by means of
physical marks such as holes in the disk; 268
Harman, J., 289
HDLC (High-level Data Link Control), 179,
181–5, 197–201, 245
Head-loading (of a floppy disk)   The action of
bringing the read/write head in contact
with the magnetic disk; 275, 281–2
High-level Data Link Control; *See* HDLC
Hilburn, J. L., 41
Hoare, C. A. R., 362

techniques for using, 54–70
termination of, 56–60
Transistor-transistor logic; *see* TTL
Tri-state logic, 68, 74, 78, 131–3, 207, 212–15, 227
TTL (transistor-transistor logic), 61, 74–7, 86, 170, 174, 352
Tunnel erase (in magnetic recording), 270–271
Twisted pair   An interconnection consisting of a pair of conductors twisted together; 52–3, 78–80

UART (universal asynchronous receiver/transmitter); *see* Serial interface
UCSD Pascal (University of California at San Diego Pascal system); 333
Unbalanced interconnection   An electrical interconnection in which a signal is encoded as a voltage with respect to a fixed ground reference that is common to all signals on the same interface; 54, 80, 175
Unibus; *see* DEC, Unibus
USR   A command in BASIC that invokes a user-supplied subroutine; 334

Vectored interrupt   A device-identification technique in which the highest priority device with a pending interrupt request forces program execution to branch to an interrupt program for that device; 21–3, 354
Vertical retrace   The period during which the beam of a video display returns to the top of the display in preparation for the sweep of the next frame; 300–3, 316, 319
Vertical sync   A signal that generates the vertical displacement of a video beam; 300–3, 305–7, 312, 316, 319

Video shift-register, 293–5, 309, 315
VLSI (very large-scale integration), 107, 121, 216
Voltage-controlled oscillator, 252–3, 255

Wakerly, J., 41, 339, 362
Wall, L. H., 289
Wave impedance   The impedance of a transmission line with respect to waves that propagate along the line; 55, 65, 71
Wharton, J., 289
White, D. J., 82–3
Wiatrowski, C. A., 40
Word (in memory systems)   A collection of bits that can be transferred simultaneously to or from memory by executing one instruction; 6
Word boundary   The boundary between two adjacent words, usually in the context of byte-addressable machines in which words must begin at addresses that are a multiple of the number of bytes per word; 8–11
Word length   The number of bits per word; 7
Word-organized memory   A memory partitioned into individual words, each identified by a unique address; 7–11
Write   The act of transferring information to a memory or I/O subsystem from a central processor; 3
bus transaction, 92–4, 96
memory, 10–11, 127–32
I/O, 12–15

Zero-reference point   A point on a chassis whose potential is a zero-voltage reference for signals in the chassis; 49–50

NUMERICAL INDEX OF DEVICES CITED†

LSI-11, 8–9, 110, 112–13, 291
Z80, 36–7, 39, 115, 122–3, 284–5, 320, 327
iAPX86, 7–8
LM339, 290
NEC372, 280
iAPX432, 7–8, 100, 320
LM741, 84–5
NEC765, 280
8T38, 76
8T95, 75–6
8T96, 75–6
8T97, 75–6
8T98, 75–6
MC1372, 319
MC1488, 170–1, 186–8

MC1489, 170–1
WD1691, 288
WD1771, 275–80
WD1791, 275–6, 280
LM1889, 319
2114, 158, 160, 319
i2117, 129–40, 157
i2118, 157
WD2143, 287
2147, 127, 157
2316, 135
2332, 135
2364, 135
2532, 135
2564, 135
Am26LS31, 79

Am26LS32, 79
2670, 313–14
2671, 313–15
2672, 313–15
2673, 313–15
2704, 135
2708, 135
2716, 135, 242
2732, 135, 242
2764, 135
i3242, 137
MC3438, 76
MC3480, 137
MC3486, 79
MC3487, 79
i4004, 7, 39–40

†In numerical order, disregarding letters and closing up numbers.